International Law in World Politics

SECOND EDITION

International Law

in World Politics

An Introduction

Shirley V. Scott

LYNNE
RIENNER
PUBLISHERS

BOULDER
LONDON

Published in the United States of America in 2010 by
Lynne Rienner Publishers, Inc.
1800 30th Street, Boulder, Colorado 80301
www.rienner.com

and in the United Kingdom by
Lynne Rienner Publishers, Inc.
3 Henrietta Street, Covent Garden, London WC2E 8LU

Library of Congress Cataloging-in-Publication Data
Scott, Shirley V.
International law in world politics : an introduction / Shirley V. Scott.
 — 2nd ed.
  p. cm.
Includes bibliographical references and index.
ISBN 978-1-58826-745-0 (pbk. : alk. paper)
1. International law. I. Title.
KZ3410.S38 2010
341—dc22

2010018939

British Cataloguing in Publication Data
A Cataloguing in Publication record for this book
is available from the British Library.

Printed and bound in the United States of America

 The paper used in this publication meets the requirements
of the American National Standard for Permanence of
Paper for Printed Library Materials Z39.48-1992.

5 4 3 2

Contents

Figures

Preface

IN THE YEARS SINCE THE FIRST EDITION OF THIS BOOK WAS PUB-lished, international law has greatly increased in public prominence. Debate regarding the legality of the 2003 invasion of Iraq continued well after the overthrow of Saddam Hussein and became integral to public discussion regarding the ethics and purpose of the war. Deadlock within the World Trade Organization has highlighted the increased negotiating strength of the developing world, and climate change has shone a spotlight on questions regarding the efficacy of processes of international law creation and enforcement. The questions of the likely impact of the rise of China on US foreign policy and engagement with international law and the extent to which China will during this century be in a position to shape international norms in its own image are, similarly, of topical importance to an audience far broader than the community of international lawyers.

It has therefore never been more important for all those with an interest in world affairs to come to grips with the workings of the system of international law, its core concepts, principles, rules, methods of law creation, and enforcement. It is no exaggeration to say that without such a foundation, students of international relations, world history, or diplomacy are unable to make full sense of their subject matter. Men and women in a range of professions, including journalism, government service, and international business, are now at a disadvantage if they lack literacy in international law.

The primary purpose of *International Law in World Politics* is to introduce international law to those who have no prior training in law. The book is intended to be readable without being simplistic and to provide the reader with a framework within which to understand international legal developments in their political context. It has at the same time proven valuable for law students who are seeking a political perspective on "black letter" international law. Although context is important to an understanding of any legal system, it is arguably essential to a full appreciation of the workings of international law.

This second edition updates and extends the first edition and includes a chapter dedicated to international law concerning the use of force. I have endeavored to impress on readers the value of reference to international law documents themselves as opposed to reliance on paraphrased accounts of those documents. To that end, I have compiled a volume of documents that can serve as an accompanying text. Essential treaties and primary sources discussed in this edition are referenced to their location in *International Law and Politics: Key Documents*.

Whether you are reading this book as a member of the global community seeking to educate yourself in world affairs or as required reading for a formal course of study, I wish you well in your quest for knowledge and understanding of the system of international law and its functioning in world politics.

International Law and World Politics Entwined

INTERNATIONAL LAW IS A SYSTEM OF RULES, PRINCIPLES, AND concepts governing relations among states and, increasingly, intergovernmental and nongovernmental organizations, individuals, and other actors in world politics. Features of the modern system of international law appeared in the late nineteenth century; since World War II international law has expanded at a rapid rate such that there is now virtually no aspect of world politics that can be fully understood without some knowledge of international law. International law is also impacting national legal systems to an unprecedented extent. National court cases may turn on a point of international, rather than municipal, law and national decisionmakers must now consider a constantly increasing number of international law obligations in the policymaking process.

International law addresses the environment, trade, arms control, human rights, use of the oceans, terrorism, refugees, and much more, and within each of these fields of international law the number of rules, principles, and concepts continues to increase. This book does not, however, aim to turn readers into experts in any specific field of international law, but to equip them with a mental map of what international law is and how it works as an integral component of world politics. Whether or not they have studied law previously, readers will then be in a position to make sense of specific developments as they occur and to develop a greater depth of knowledge of any particular branches of international law as future needs and interests arise.

If we are to understand how the system operates within world politics, we need to appreciate that although international law is an integral part of politics, it is also to a large extent autonomous. International law has considerable cohesion as a system of interrelated rules, principles, and concepts that operate within the political milieu and yet are to some extent distinct from it. Political terms such as *sovereignty, state,* and *genocide* may also be used within the system of international law but with different meanings. Chapters 1 to 4 will consider further the entwining of international law with politics before we go on to focus in Chapter 5 on the autonomy of the system of international law.

■ How Does International Law Compare with Law in the Domestic Context?

Whether we are aware of it or not, most of us approaching international law for the first time intuitively bring certain assumptions about law in a domestic situation and expect international law to be the equivalent at an international level. This can be an asset where there are similarities between the two, but there are some aspects of the system of law in most liberal democracies that do not have an obvious parallel at the international level. We will begin by making some comparisons between domestic law—often called *municipal law*—and international law. To those whose main interest is world politics, it may at first seem strange to realize that an understanding of international law is essential to understanding political dynamics. Let us then begin our brief comparison by considering how it is that law— whether domestic or international—can be considered integral to political processes.

A political system can be defined as "any persistent pattern of human relationships that involves, to a significant extent, control, influence, power, or authority."[1] We often think first of national political systems, such as those of the United States or of India, but we can also talk about the politics internal to a school, or even to a family. When we analyze the operation of a political system we find that not everyone has equivalent power. In other words, control over political resources—the means by which one person can influence the behavior of other persons—is not distributed evenly.[2] The study of politics is in large part the study of the process that determines who gets what and who can do what in a particular political unit. At a national level in a democracy, the legislature makes and implements political decisions by passing legislation. Legislation is law, and so we can see that law is one mechanism through which politics may be conducted. Another domestic arena in which decisions are made that impact the distribution of the benefits of society is the courtroom. A legal judgment can have an immediate impact, for example, on who receives a family's inheritance or on whether indigenous people have the same rights to land as other members of society. Politics and law are thus intimately related.

In the same way that domestic politics is entwined with law, international law is integral to world politics and may affect the global distribution of power. A free trade agreement may be to the benefit of exporting countries more than importing countries. The International Court of Justice (ICJ) may delimit a maritime boundary between two states that then determines which country is able to exploit valuable oil resources. International law is integral to international structures of power, but the place of international law in world politics cannot be appreciated unless one has a basic understanding as to how the system of international law functions. As a first step toward this goal it may be useful to draw some more comparisons and contrasts between the legal and political systems of modern liberal democracies and those in the international arena.

A Legislature to Make the Law?

One of the most important distinctions between the domestic legal system of liberal democratic societies and the system of international law is that there is no international legislature to pass legislation and "make law." Although this difference is sometimes lamented, it is worth pondering the question that, if there were to be a world government, of whom would we want it to be made up? The closest equivalent in world politics to a domestic legislature is the United Nations (UN) General Assembly. Every state represented in the General Assembly gets one vote, but the resulting decision is not law in the same way that an act of parliament or congress is a law. A General Assembly resolution is a political decision that may indicate the direction law is likely to take but which most lawyers do not recognize as "law."

If international law is not created by legislation, from where, then, does international law come? To put it differently, if we wanted to find what the rules, principles, and concepts of international law had to say on a subject—for example, hijacking or maritime safety—where would we go to find out?

Treaties. The main source of international law today is treaties, also known as conventions. Treaties are agreements between states, between states and international organizations, or between international organizations. A bilateral treaty is an agreement between two parties. International organizations commonly make agreements with their host state or with a state in which they are conducting a conference. An example of one type of bilateral treaty between states is the extradition treaty, which governs the surrender of fugitives from justice by the fugitive's state of residence to another state claiming criminal jurisdiction. Another example of a bilateral treaty is a status of forces agreement (SOFA), which provides for the legal status of military forces and the conditions under which one state can station them in another state. A SOFA includes, for example, which state has the primary duty to investigate and prosecute members of the armed forces suspected of committing crimes in the receiving state. The United States has concluded status of forces agreements with over fifty countries in which its troops are stationed or operating.[3] These have often been controversial in the domestic politics of the host countries. In the 1960s, the proposed US-Iran SOFA and the exemption it would grant US military personnel from the jurisdiction of Iranian courts was held up by Ayatollah Ruhollah Khomeini as distastefully reminiscent of the colonial domination of Iran.[4] More recently, the North Atlantic Treaty Organization's Status of Forces Agreement of 1951[5] became a subject of controversy following an incident in which a US Marine EA-6B Prowler on a low-level training flight in the Italian Alps severed a cable-car line, killing twenty people.[6] The US-Japan SOFA came to the fore as an issue in 2001–2002 in relation to rape and arson attacks by US servicemen in Okinawa.[7] The revision of the US-South Korea SOFA became an issue in June 2002 after two United States soldiers driving an armored mine-clearing vehicle in South Korea crushed two school girls to death; the United States had army court-martialed the two service personnel but they were acquitted and rapidly transferred out of the country. Following the terrorist attacks of September 11, 2001, the United States quickly concluded a SOFA with the Kyrgyz Republic in Central Asia, prior to basing combat and combat support units at Manas as part of Operation Enduring Freedom. The US in November 2008 signed a SOFA agreement with Iraq providing for the continued presence of US and multinational forces in Iraq and providing a timetable for their withdrawal by the end of 2011.[8]

In the context of antiballistic missile systems, the 1972 Treaty on the Limitation of Anti-Ballistic Missile Systems (ABM Treaty) between the United States and the Soviet Union, another bilateral treaty, was designed to prevent either state from deploying a nationwide antiballistic missile system for defending its territory. The treaty was premised on the idea of "mutually assured destruction" (MAD) as a deterrent to the use of nuclear weapons. In the 1990s the Clinton administration sought unsuccessfully to modify the treaty to permit the deployment of a limited national missile defense system but failed to win the agreement of Russia. Although the treaty is of unlimited duration, its terms provide that each party has the right to withdraw from it, with six months' notification, if it decides that extraordinary events related to the subject matter of the treaty have "jeopardized its supreme interests." In 2001, President George W. Bush decided to abandon the ABM Treaty. The 2002 Treaty Between the United States of America and the Russian Federation on Strategic Offensive Reductions, providing for the reduction and limitation of strategic nuclear warheads by Russia and the United States, is another example of a bilateral treaty relating to arms control.[9]

Multilateral treaties are agreements between three or more states. Those states may belong to one geographical region—it may be an African regional treaty on human rights, for example; or the treaty may aim at global participation in order, for example, to protect the world from catastrophic climate change. The term *plurilateral* is sometimes used to refer to treaties in which participation is limited by purpose, geography, or both.[10] Some one hundred multilateral treaties have been negotiated per year since 1945.[11] The entwining of international law with world politics is evident in the realm of treaties insofar as treaties are the product of negotiations between states and states can be expected to approach those negotiations—whether on trade or marine pollution—as a political exercise. Each state will bring its own political objectives and strategies to the negotiating table and, as the product of those negotiations, the resultant treaty text is likely to reflect the political compromises that were required to reach agreement.

A treaty is usually dated from the year of agreement on the text. This may differ significantly from the date on which the treaty becomes law and the parties are bound by its terms. The text of the Third United Nations Convention on the Law of the Sea, for example, was agreed in 1982, but the convention did not receive the necessary support to enter into force (become law) until 1994. The UN Charter requires members to register all new treaties with the UN Secretariat, which publishes them in the *United Nations Treaty Series* (*UNTS*), available in hard copy and by Internet.[12] Other places in which to locate treaties are *International Legal Materials* (*ILM*), the *League of Nations Treaty Series* (*LNTS*), the *United Kingdom Treaty Series* (*UKTS*), and Internet collections including the Multilaterals Project at the Fletcher School of Law and Diplomacy at Tufts University, Massachusetts.[13]

A treaty is divided into articles and, within an article, into paragraphs and subparagraphs. "Article 48(4)(a)" refers to article 48, paragraph 4, subparagraph (a). In a long treaty, articles may be grouped into chapters, sections, and parts. The treaty may include annexes, and there may be subsequent treaties that build on it, usually entitled "protocols."

The earliest known treaty dates from around 3000 B.C., preserved on a border stone between Lagash and Umma in Mesopotamia.[14] The important contemporary principle of *pacta sunt servanda*—that states are bound to carry out in good faith the obligations they have assumed by treaty—is thought to derive from the fact that early treaties were often considered sacred.[15] And although states are expected to carry out their treaty obligations in good faith, a state is not bound by treaties to which it is not a party. This is because a state is, by definition, *constitutionally independent,* which means that a state must consent to be bound by a treaty before it becomes bound, consent being another basic concept in the system of international law.

We will look at the concept of consent more fully in Chapter 5 and at multilateral treaties in more detail in Chapters 8 and 9.

Custom. The second most important source of international law today is custom. Custom is created by what states do, where that action is carried out with a view to the rules and principles of international law. Customary international law was at one time the most important source of international law. As an example, the rules on the treatment of diplomats evolved through custom. The treatment by one state of the representative of another may have been accepted as valid, or it may have been the subject of protest and discussion. Rules gradually evolved as to how states would treat diplomats, and those rules are termed *customary international law.* Custom is in many cases codified into a treaty; when formulated into a written document, the rules, principles, and concepts naturally appear more precise and are less subject to change. The customary international law relating to the treatment of diplomats was to a large extent codified in the 1961 Vienna Convention on Diplomatic Relations.

Not everything that a state does or does not do contributes to customary international law. Certain habitual practices may emerge; all diplomatic stationery may be of a certain color, for example, for purely pragmatic or practical reasons. The practice of a state can only be used as evidence of custom if the *opinio juris* component is present (i.e., that the state has been choosing to act in that way for reasons of law). Custom can be quite a slow way of creating law, although that is not always the case. The law defining that the airspace superjacent to land territory, internal waters, and the territorial sea is a part of state territory, and as a consequence other states may only use such airspace for navigation or other purposes with the agreement of the territorial sovereign, developed in a relatively short period concurrent with the development of aviation and the impact of World War I.[16]

The entwining of international law with world politics is evident in relation to custom in that it may well have been specific political goals that prompted the state in question to engage in a particular practice (or not to act). The US response to the terrorist attacks of September 11, 2001, and the attitude of other states to that response appears to have confirmed an evolution of customary international law to include a right to use force in self-defense against a terrorist attack (see Figure 1.1).

There is usually some room for maneuver in arguing whether or not a particular rule of customary international law exists. Here we get another glimpse of where politics enters the equation. If one is representing a state before the International Court of Justice, one is likely to argue for or against the emergence of a particular principle or rule of customary international law on the basis of one's overall case and strategic goals. We will be looking at international customary law in more detail in Chapters 3 and 5.

A Police Force to Enforce the Law?

Apart from there not being an international legislature, another difference between most domestic legal systems and the system of international law is that there is no international police force to enforce compliance. For many,

Figure 1.1 Customary International Law and the Right to Use Force in Response to a Terrorist Attack

The right of a state to defend itself is well established in customary international law. It was also incorporated into treaty law, as article 51 of the United Nations Charter. The type of attack on a state envisaged by the drafters of the Charter was, understandably, that of one state against another. Debate began in the 1980s as to the right of a state to respond with force to terrorism under article 51. When in 1986 the United States claimed that its bombing of military targets in Libya in response to an explosion at the LaBelle disco in Berlin, which killed two US servicemen and wounded seventy-eight Americans, was an act of self-defense, international reaction was largely negative;[1] a draft Security Council resolution condemning the strike was supported by a majority of members of the Security Council but vetoed by the United States and the United Kingdom.[2] A US missile attack of June 26, 1993, which destroyed the Iraqi intelligence headquarters in Baghdad in response to an alleged Iraqi plan to kill President George H. W. Bush, was again justified as self-defense. This time the majority of Security Council members accepted the US position that the attack was a justified act of self-defense, although China and some Islamic states voiced criticism.[3]

On August 20, 1998, the United States launched seventy-nine Tomahawk cruise missiles at targets associated with Osama bin Laden's terrorist network, including paramilitary training camps in Afghanistan and a pharmaceutical factory in Sudan that the United States claimed had been making chemical weapons.[4] Bin Laden had been linked to the bombing on August 7, 1998, of US embassies in Nairobi, Kenya, and Dar es Salaam, Tanzania. The United States argued that the strikes were in self-defense consistent with article 51 of the UN Charter. Russia condemned the attacks, as did Pakistan and several Arab countries. The Non-Aligned Movement condemned the US attack as "unilateral and unwarranted," and that September, UN Secretary-General Kofi Annan criticized "individual actions" against terrorism, implying disapproval of the US strikes.[5] Most US allies supported the attacks, although France and Italy issued only tepid statements of support.

Following the terrorist attacks of September 11, 2001, the United States constructed an extensive coalition. NATO and parties to the Inter-American Treaty of Reciprocal Assistance identified the terrorist attacks as "armed attacks," as referred to in article 51, and the United States drew a strong link between the Taliban and Al-Qaida, thus implicating a state

(continues)

Figure 1.1 continued

---

in the "armed attack" as would traditionally have been expected under article 51. In a letter to the Security Council of October 7, the United States stated that it had initiated actions "in the exercise of its inherent right of individual and collective self-defense."[6] Following Operation Enduring Freedom and the wide support given to the US-led coalition bombing in response to September 11, it could be said that customary international law had evolved such that the right of self-defense now included military responses against states that actively support or willingly harbor terrorist groups that have already attacked the responding state.[7]

Five years later, the international community "gingerly accepted" Israel's claim that its use of force in southern Lebanon was a valid act of self-defense against Hezbollah attacks.[8]

Notes

1. Alan D. Surchin, "Terror and the Law: The Unilateral Use of Force and the June 1993 Bombing of Baghdad," *Duke Journal of Comparative and International Law* 5 (1995), 457–497.

2. Draft text no. S/18016/Feb.1, S/PV.2682, April 21, 1986, p. 43.

3. Surchin, "Terror and the Law," 467–468.

4. Sean D. Murphy, "Contemporary Practice of the United States Relating to International Law," *American Journal of International Law* 93, no. 1 (1999): 161–194, esp. 161.

5. Jules Lobel, "The Use of Force to Respond to Terrorist Attacks: The Bombing of Sudan and Afghanistan," *Yale Journal of International Law* 24 (1999), 537–557, esp. 538.

6. Letter to Security Council from the Permanent Representative of the United States of America to the United Nations, addressed to the President of the Security Council, dated October 7, 2001. UN Document S/2001/946 (October 7, 2001).

7. Michael Byers, "Terrorism, the Use of Force, and International Law After 11 September," *International and Comparative Law Quarterly* 51, no. 2 (2002), 401–414, esp. 410.

8. Michael N. Schmitt, "'Change Direction' 2006: Israeli Operations in Lebanon and the International Law of Self-Defense," *Michigan Journal of International Law* 29 (2007–2008), 127–164, esp. 139.

---

this is a great deficiency of international law and the reason why international law is not more politically effective.[17] It might seem that if states were compelled to respect international law on, say, the use of force, we would live in a much more peaceful and ordered world. The great hiccup here is the concept of "sovereignty" and the related concept of consent. International law operates in a states system that is anarchical, meaning that there is no over-arching government, and international law is, at least theoretically, a horizontal system made up of sovereign equals. The same question that was posed in the context of a world government can be posed here: if there were a country or body tasked with enforcing international law, which would we want it to be?

We must also be careful not to push too far our domestic analogy of law enforcement by the police. The police forces in a domestic system primarily enforce criminal law. The bulk of the international law governing relations among states does not address the criminal behavior of states but is better compared with the civil law of rights and wrongs, claims and defenses, and in a municipal system the outcomes of these matters are usually negotiated or settled through courts, much as they are in international law.

There are some methods of enforcement of international law, although when viewed as a whole, the picture may still look patchy. Individual states can attempt to ensure that other states respect the rules of international law in their mutual relations by measures of *retorsion,* unfriendly but legal acts, such as the severance of diplomatic relations, a practice that is used to indicate displeasure with the policies or actions of another state. A second form of enforcement of international law by an individual state is that of *countermeasures.* Countermeasures are acts that would be illegal had they not been carried out in response to an illegal act of the other party. Countermeasures must be proportional to the breach to which they were a response and may not include the use of force.[18] One of the most important ways of ensuring compliance with multilateral treaties is to write into the treaty verification measures—ways of checking that the other states party to that treaty are complying. Verification measures may include a system of inspections or of reporting. If the UN Security Council believes that there is a threat to international peace, breach of the peace, or an act of aggression, it can impose sanctions of an economic, diplomatic, or military nature.[19] The Security Council also has the power to enforce a decision of the ICJ. Article 94(2) of the UN Charter provides that if any party to a case "fails to perform the obligations incumbent upon it under a judgment rendered by the Court, the other party may have recourse to the Security Council, which may, if it deems necessary, make recommendations or decide upon measures to be taken to give effect to the judgment."

Compliance with international law is sometimes promoted through the provision of assistance via an intergovernmental organization (IGO). The United Nations Environment Programme (UNEP), for example, provides technical assistance to help developing countries implement environmental treaty obligations. The United Nations Programme of Technical Cooperation assists with human rights–related activities such as training law enforcement personnel and members of national judiciaries.[20]

National courts sometimes enforce international law. The Alien Tort Claims Act of 1789[21] grants jurisdiction to US federal courts over "any civil action by an alien [someone who is not a US citizen] for a tort only, committed in violation of the law of nations or a treaty of the United States." The reason for the act is not certain, but it was likely intended either to secure the prosecution of pirates or to protect diplomats. The act rose to prominence and became a source of controversy in the early 1980s, since when it has been used to bring cases against both individuals and companies for claimed breaches of international human rights law committed outside the United States. The Torture Victim Protection Act of 1991[22] creates a right for victims, including aliens, of state-sponsored torture and summary execution in other countries to sue in federal courts.

A judiciary? Although there is no international legislature, there is a world court, situated in The Hague in the Netherlands. The Permanent Court of International Justice operated from 1922 to 1946, then was replaced by the International Court of Justice, one of the six principal organs of the United Nations. The operation of the ICJ is underpinned by the principle of consent: the ICJ can hear a contentious case between states only if those states have consented to the Court doing so. This may sound extraordinary on first hearing, but there is a fascinating entwining of law with politics evident in a state deciding whether to consent to the jurisdiction of the Court. The decision as to whether to be involved in a case before the Court may well be a political decision, but it will be made on the basis of the rules, principles, and concepts of international law and, no doubt, on the prospects of a successful outcome. In some cases, like that relating to Iran's holding of US hostages in Tehran from 1979 to 1981, a state may decide that it is not in its interests to have the case heard by the Court, but the Court will find that the state concerned has, in fact, given its consent. To understand how this could come about requires understanding of the relevant law and the political context in which it was functioning. We will be looking at this in more detail in Chapters 5 and 7.

Article 38(1) of the Statute of the International Court of Justice sets out the basis on which the Court is to reach a decision:

1. The Court, whose function is to decide in accordance with international law such disputes as are submitted to it, shall apply:

   a. International conventions, whether general or particular, establishing rules expressly recognized by the contesting States;
   b. international custom, as evidence of a general practice accepted as law;
   c. the general principles of law recognized by civilized nations;
   d. subject to the provisions of Article 59, judicial decisions and the teachings of the most highly qualified publicists of the various nations, as subsidiary means for the determination of rules of law.

We have already considered the first two of these: conventions (more usually referred to as treaties) and customary international law. Although treaties and custom are the two most common sources of international law, it is important to consider also the rest of article 38(1) because, although in the narrow sense the article refers only to the sources of international law to be drawn on by the ICJ, it is widely held to be a statement of all of the current sources of international law.

The reference to "civilized nations" in 38(1)(c) refers to the fact that being "civilized" used to be a criterion for participation in the system of international law. This is no longer the case, and it is widely accepted that "civilized nations" now means "states." The term "general principles" refers to general principles of law common to a representative majority of domestic legal orders, which includes "the main forms of civilization and the principle legal systems of the world."[23] "General principles of law" was included in the Statute of the Court in case gaps remained after the consideration of treaties and custom.[24] The ICJ has also drawn on general principles originating in international relations and general principles applicable to all kinds of legal relations.[25] The principle of good faith, for example, requires parties to deal honestly and fairly with each other.[26] Applied to treaties, it means that a treaty should be interpreted "in accordance with the ordinary meaning to be given to the terms of the treaty in their context and in the light of its object and purpose."[27] A state should not attempt to find unintended meanings in a treaty that would result in it gaining an unfair advantage over the other party.

Article 38(1)(d) refers to judgments of tribunals and courts as well as to the writings of distinguished international lawyers as "subsidiary means for the determination of rules of law." This means that "judicial decisions," such as the judgments of the International Court of Justice and learned texts by famous international lawyers, can also be looked at to enhance understanding of what international law may have to say on a particular issue. The phrase "subsidiary means for the determination of rules of law" means that judges and the most highly qualified publicists of the various nations do not create law as such but clarify what that law has to say on a particular issue; judicial decisions and learned writings are subordinate to the first three sources.[28]

Although the ICJ is the only international court or tribunal with general jurisdiction, there has in recent years been a proliferation of judicial and quasi-judicial bodies with subject-specific jurisdiction.[29] Notable examples include the Law of the Sea Tribunal, established in Hamburg, Germany, under the provisions of the 1982 Law of the Sea Convention, and the Appellate Body of the World Trade Organization. There have been calls for an international environment court.[30] There are also regional courts and tribunals. The oldest court operating in Europe is the European Court of Justice of the

European Communities, which began its work in 1952 as the Court of Justice of the European Coal and Steel Community. The past two decades have seen the establishment of ad hoc war crimes tribunals, such as the International Criminal Tribunals for the Former Yugoslavia (ICTY) and for Rwanda (ICTR), as well as hybrid courts in Timor-Leste, Kosovo, Sierra Leone, and Cambodia. Internationalized or hybrid, criminal courts apply a mixture of international and national law.

The Rule of Law

If we accept that law is a part of politics and that politics is about who gets what and how in a particular political order, the most important principle could be said to be that of the *rule of law*.[31] The essence of this principle is that everyone is equal before the law. It does not matter whether one is a wealthy professional, unemployed, or a member of the political bureaucracy; one is subject to the same laws on theft or on murder. Of course, there may well be cases in which individuals do not appear to be treated equally by the law—for example, white-collar crime is less likely to lead to a jail sentence than breaking and entering. Although such examples seem at first glance to undercut the principle of the rule of law, that principle serves as a normative basis for law: it establishes what the law *should* do, even though it does not always do so.

Critics of a law or its implementation often seek to demonstrate its inadequacy by showing that the law is not commensurate with the principle of the rule of law, and they use this as a basis for demanding change to the law or its improved implementation. Mandatory sentencing, which removes the discretion of a judge to vary punishments has, for example, been criticized by those who believe that despite purportedly treating all offenders equally, it tends to have the greatest impact on those segments of the community who are most likely to commit the type of crime in question. In the Northern Territory of Australia the crimes covered by a scheme of mandatory sentencing that operated between 1996 and 2001 were "crimes of poverty" most likely to have been committed by Indigenous offenders.[32] In 2002 some commentators claimed that the intervention of the Queen of England in the criminal trial of Princess Diana's former butler, which led to the prosecution withdrawing the charge and the butler being declared not guilty, "vividly demonstrated that not everyone is equal before British law";[33] the episode led to calls from inside the Labour Party to reform the queen's immunity from giving evidence in civil and criminal proceedings.[34]

The principle of the "rule of law" also exists in the system of international law, where it gives rise to the principle of the *sovereign equality of states*.[35] States are the main actors in international law, and according to this fundamental principle, all states are legally equal. Of course, just as the principle of the rule of law does not always match reality in a domestic legal system, so it does not do so in the system of international law. In the same way that members of society enjoy different levels of wealth and opportunity, states differ drastically in terms of history, income, resources, and political systems. There is therefore little prospect of all states carrying equivalent weight in international law. The perceived importance of the United States, as the world's greatest military power, signing the treaty to establish the International Criminal Court (ICC) meant that the United States would be more influential than a weak state in the negotiations.

Sometimes small states carry less weight at treaty negotiations simply because they do not have the staff, expertise, or knowledge to contribute; a small state that has only a handful of trained international lawyers cannot hope to match the input of a major power. At the ICC several sets of negotiations were held simultaneously on different issues, making it impossible for any one delegate to attend more than a small percentage of the sessions.[36] It was also notable that the text was drafted only in English; it was several months after the finalization of the treaty that it was available in the other five languages that, according to the treaty itself, are "equally authentic."[37] The principle of the sovereign equality of states nevertheless plays a normative role within the system of international law and gives rise to specific rules regarding the operation of the system. Some states may carry more negotiating weight than others, but a state is not bound by a treaty if its consent to be bound by a treaty was procured by the coercion of its representative, and a treaty is void if it has been procured by the threat or use of force.

■ International Law and Power

It is readily apparent that international law is closely related to the political context in which it operates. What is fascinating, however, is to try to discern the exact nature of the relationship between the two. It has been a mainstream assumption in the study of international relations since 1945 that international law has little impact on the "real world" of politics—at least when it comes to the core issues of war and peace. It is a perspective closely related to the realist school of international relations theory, which focuses on states as the principal actors in world politics and sees them as being in a constant struggle to compete for greater power (and thereby security). Realists have tended to conceptualize power as emanating from tangible factors such as military and economic might. This leaves no room for an independent role for international law. Realism has a long tradition in the study of international relations; in fact, it was in existence long before international relations emerged as a discipline. Whereas the discipline of international relations is usually dated from the years just after World War I,

The History of the Peloponnesian Wars, written by Thucydides in about 400 B.C., is often considered an early realist work. Realist thinking continues to dominate government thinking, and its influence extends to most of those working for international organizations such as the United Nations.[38]

The empirical literature inspired by realist thought generally adopts a simplistic attitude to international law, and assuming that the law has no important role to play, often leaves it out of the story altogether. Hence, the bulk of writing on what is generally regarded as having been the most serious crisis in the Cold War—the Cuban Missile Crisis—makes no mention of international law. The US decision to impose a "quarantine" around Cuba to prevent Soviet ships carrying nuclear missiles capable of targeting the United States from reaching Cuba, is often discussed with no reference to the legality of such a quarantine. This makes for a rather skewed historical account of the episode because the historical evidence points to international law as having featured strongly in the US decisionmaking process. The United States was not prepared to take any action that was categorically illegal and settled for a way of proceeding that was at least of possible legality. Moreover, the United States went to great length to justify the actions it took in terms of international law.

Some realist writers acknowledge the existence of international law but do so in order to dismiss its impact on real world events. Dean Acheson, former US secretary of state, commented in regard to the Cuban Missile Crisis that "the power, prestige, and position of the US had been challenged. . . . [L]aw simply does not deal with such questions of ultimate power. . . . The survival of states is not a matter of law."[39] Hans Morgenthau, the most famous realist thinker of the post–World War II years and a lawyer by training, was disappointed by the inadequacies of international law. He portrayed international law as a system seeking to constrain powerful states, and he found it lacking. Morgenthau was highly critical of what he perceived to be the absence of an effective international judicial system and of serious weaknesses in the system of enforcement. He considered that its primitive system of law enforcement made it easy for strong states both to violate international law and to enforce it, thereby putting the rights of weaker states in jeopardy.[40]

There would appear to be a considerable element of truth in what Morgenthau thought. Contrary to the ideal of the rule of law, international law has generally supported the powerful. This is perhaps most clearly evidenced in relation to the general prohibition on the use of force in international law; maintenance of peace supports the status quo. Powerful states usually play a greater role than others do in creating the law, and they have a greater capacity to see that the law is enforced against other states. But if this were the whole story, it would be a sad—and dull—one, and one would wonder why the decisionmakers in less powerful states were so gullible as to continue to support a system designed solely for their exploitation.

International law may be generally supportive of those with power, but it does on occasion also help the less powerful, whether individually or collectively. Nauru, one of the smallest countries in the world, was able to bring Australia—which had administered Nauru under the League of Nations Mandate System and the UN Trusteeship System—to the negotiating table in respect of the rehabilitation of its mined-out phosphate lands, when the proceedings Nauru had initiated against Australia in the ICJ appeared likely to result in an outcome favorable to Nauru.[41] Consider another example: after World War II a number of smaller states made what at the time seemed to be extraordinary claims to fisheries zones that gradually came to be regarded as part of international law, albeit only when accepted by the powerful states.[42] International law was, similarly, the mechanism by which many new states of the third world emerged as independent entities during the process of decolonization.

International law not only helps weaker states survive in the maelstrom of world politics but also serves to constrain, at least to a certain extent and on certain occasions, the actions of the powerful. In his analysis of the functions that international law had fulfilled during the Cuban Missile Crisis, Abram Chayes found that international law had both been a basis of justification or legitimation for action and provided organizational structures, procedures, and forums—in addition to being a factor in constraining US policy choices.[43] Other writers have identified functions fulfilled by international law in world politics, including those of "providing rules of the game, fostering stable expectations, positing criteria by which national governments and others can act reasonably and justify their action, and providing a process of communication in a crisis."[44] It has been the concern of many international lawyers that in the post–Cold War international order in which there is only one superpower, international law does not exert as powerful a constraining influence on the United States as it did in the days when the Soviet Union could more readily check any US breaches of international law. This was particularly the case during the administration of George W. Bush and the "war on terror."

The complexity of the relationship between international law and world politics is fascinating. We will be better equipped to consider this complexity once we have a better understanding of the system of international law. We will now go on to look at the main actors in international law.

■ Notes

1. Robert A. Dahl, *Modern Political Analysis,* 4th ed. (Englewood Cliffs, NJ: Prentice-Hall, 1984), p. 10.
2. Ibid., p. 31.

3. *Treaties and Other International Acts Series (TIAS)* of the Department of State includes, for example, those with Antigua and Barbuda (*TIAS* number 9054), Ascension Island (3603), Australia (5349), Bahamas (11058), Bahrain (7263, 8208, 8632), Canada (2846, 3074), Denmark (2846, 4002), Diego Garcia (6196, 7481, 8230), Egypt (10238), France (2846), Germany (2846, 5351, 5352, 7759, 10367), Greece (2846, 3649), Honduras (10890, 11256), Iceland (2295), Italy (2846), Jamaica (2105), Japan (4510), Korea (6127), Luxembourg (2846), Marshall Islands (11671), Netherlands (3174), New Zealand (4151), Norway (2846, 2950), Panama (10032), Papua New Guinea (11612), Portugal (2846), St. Lucia (2105), Saudi Arabia (2812, 5830, 7425), Spain (2846), Sudan (10322), Trinidad and Tobago (2105), Turkey (2846, 3020, 3337, 6582, 9901), Turks and Caicos Islands (9710, 9711), and United Kingdom (2846, 11537).

4. Gary Sick, *All Fall Down: America's Fateful Encounter with Iran* (London: I. B. Tauris, 1985), p. 10.

5. Agreement Between the Parties to the North Atlantic Treaty Organization Regarding the Status of Their Forces, June 19, 1951, 199 United Nations Treaty Series (UNTS) 67. For commentary, see Dieter Fleck, ed., *The Handbook of the Law of Visiting Forces* (Oxford: Oxford University Press, 2001).

6. W. Michael Reisman and Robert D. Sloane, "The Incident at Cavalese and Strategic Compensation," *American Journal of International Law* 94, no. 3 (July 2000): 505–515.

7. B. Norman, "The Rape Controversy: Is a Revision of the Status of Forces Agreement with Japan Necessary?" *Indiana International and Comparative Law Review* 6, no. 3 (1996): 717–740, esp. 731.

8. John R. Crook, ed., "Contemporary Practice of the United States Relating to International Law," *American Journal of International Law* 103 (2009): 132.

9. 41 *International Legal Materials (ILM)* 799 (2002).

10. John Gamble, Ryan Watson, and Lauren Piera, "Ocean Regimes as Reflected in 500 Years of Multilateral Treaty-Making," in Aldo Chircop, Ted L. McDorman, and Susan J. Rolston, eds., *The Future of Ocean Regime-Building* (Leiden, the Netherlands: Martinus Nijhoff, 2009), pp. 87–104, esp. 98.

11. This figure is estimated from the information provided in Christian L. Wiktor, *Multilateral Treaty Calendar 1648–1995* (The Hague: Martinus Nijhoff, 1998).

12. Available at http://treaties.un.org.

13. Available at http://fletcher.tufts.edu/multilaterals.

14. Treaty relations were more elaborate in ancient China and India. Wiktor, *Multilateral Treaty Calendar 1648–1995*, p. ix.

15. Ibid., pp. ix–x.

16. Ian Brownlie, *Principles of Public International Law*, 4th ed. (Oxford: Clarendon, 1990), p. 119.

17. For a defense of international law against this charge, see Mary Ellen O'Connell, *The Power and Purpose of International Law* (Oxford: Oxford University Press, 2008).

18. C. Tomuschat, "General Course on Public International Law," *Recueil des Cours* 281 (1999): 376.

19. See articles 39 to 42 of the UN Charter.

20. Ian Martin, "The High Commissioner's Field Operations," in Gudmundur Alfredsson, Jonas Grimheden, Bertram G. Ramcharan, and Alfred de Zayas, eds., *International Human Rights Monitoring Mechanisms: Essays in Honour of Jakob Th. Möller* (The Hague: Martinus Nijhoff, 2001), pp. 403–414.

21. United States Code section 1350. See Ralph G. Steinhardt and Anthony D'Amato, eds., *The Alien Tort Claims Act: An Analytical Anthology* (Ardsley, NY: Transnational, 1999).

22. United States Code section 1359. See Craig Scott, ed., *Torture as Tort: Comparative Perspectives on the Development of Transnational Human Rights Litigation* (Oxford: Hart, 2001).

23. Hermann Mosler, "General Principles of Law," *Encyclopedia of Public International Law* 2 (1995): 511–527, esp. 516–517. On "general principles" see also L. G. Lammers, "General Principles of Law Recognized by Civilized Nations," in Fritz Kalxhoven, Pieter Jan Kuyper, and Jahan G. Lammers, *Essays on the Development of the International Legal Order in Memory of H. F. van Panhuys* (The Netherlands: Alphen aan den Rijn, 1980), 53–75; H. Mosler, "To What Extent Does the Variety of Legal Systems of the World Influence the Application of the General Principles of Law Within the Meaning of Article 38(1)(c) of the Statute of the International Court of Justice," in Hugo Grotius, *International Law and the Grotian Heritage* (The Hague: T. M. C. Asser Institut, 1985), pp. 173–185; and M. C. Bassiouni, "A Functional Approach to General Principles of International Law," *Michigan Journal of International Law* 11 (1990): 768–818.

24. Mosler, "General Principles of Law," p. 516.

25. Ibid., 511–527.

26. Anthony D'Amato, "Good Faith," *Encyclopedia of Public International Law* 2 (1995): 599–601, esp. 599.

27. *Vienna Convention on the Law of Treaties,* article 31(1).

28. Peter Malanczuk, *Akehurst's Modern Introduction to International Law,* 7th rev. ed. (London: Routledge, 1997), pp. 56–57.

29. For a table of international judicial bodies, quasi-judicial, implementation control, and other dispute settlement bodies, see the Project on International Courts and Tribunals, Supplement to the *New York University Journal of International Law and Politics* 31, no. 4, available at http://www.pict-pcti.org.

30. This is, for example, one of the goals of the International Court of the Environment Foundation. See its website at http://www.icef-court.org.

31. Hayek explained that the rule of law means that "government is bound in all its actions by rules fixed and announced beforehand so that it is possible to foresee with fair certainty how authority will use its coercive powers in given circumstances and to plan one's individual affairs on the basis of this knowledge." F. A. Hayek, *The Road to Serfdom* (London: G. Routledge, 1944), p. 39.

32. Berit Winge, "Mandatory Sentencing Laws and Their Effect on Australia's Indigenous Population," *Columbia Human Rights Law Review* 33 (2002): 693–732.

33. Peter Wilson, "Queen Tilts Crown, Puts Royals Before Court of Public Opinion," *Australian,* November 4, 2002, p. 13.

34. See Peter Gould, "The Queen and the Law," *BBC News Online,* November 4, 2002, http://news.bbc.co.uk; and Patrick Wintour and Clare Dyer, "Queen Did Nothing Wrong, Says Blair," *Guardian,* November 5, 2002, available at http://www.guardian.co.uk.

35. See R. P. Anand, "Sovereign Equality of States in International Law," *Recueil des Courses* 197 (1986/III): 1–228; R. A. Klein, *Sovereign Equality Among States: The History of an Idea* (Toronto: University of Toronto Press, 1974); and P. H. Koojimas, *The Doctrine of the Legal Equality of States: An Enquiry into the Foundations of International Law* (Leyden, the Netherlands: Sijthoff, 1964).

36. Bartram S. Brown, "The Statute of the ICC: Past, Present, and Future," in Sarah B. Sewall and Carl Kaysen, eds., *The United States and the International Criminal Court: National Security and International Law* (Lanham, MD: Rowman and Littlefield, 2000), pp. 61–84, esp. 62.

37. Antonio Cassese, "The Statute of the International Criminal Court: Some Preliminary Reflections," *European Journal of International Law* 10 (1999): 144–171, esp. 145.

38. Richard Falk, *Human Rights Horizons: The Pursuit of Justice in a Globalizing World* (New York: Routledge, 2000), p. 22.

39. Dean Acheson, "Remarks by the Honorable Dean Acheson, Former Secretary of State," *Proceedings of the American Society of International Law* (April 25–27, 1963), p. 17.

40. Hans J. Morgenthau, *Politics Among Nations: The Struggle for Power and Peace,* 5th ed. (New York: Alfred A. Knopf, 1973), p. 27.

41. V. S. Mani, "International Litigation and Peaceful Settlement of Disputes: A Case Study of *Certain Phosphate Lands in Nauru,*" in UN Office of Legal Affairs, *Collection of Essays by Legal Advisers of States, Legal Advisers of International Organizations, and Practitioners in the Field of International Law* (New York: United Nations, 1999), pp. 415–433. See also Antony Anghie, "'The Heart of My Home': Colonialism, Environmental Damage, and the Nauru Case," *Harvard International Law Journal* 34 (1993): 445–506.

42. This point was made by Oscar Schachter, "The Role of Power in International Law, *American Society of International Law Proceedings* 93 (2000): 203.

43. A. Chayes, *The Cuban Missile Crisis* (New York: Oxford University Press, 1974), pp. 41–42.

44. For the full list, see Anne-Marie Slaughter Burley, "International Law and International Relations Theory: A Dual Agenda," *American Journal of International Law* 87 (1993): 205–239, esp. 205.

2

States in International Law

THERE IS A CONSIDERABLE OVERLAP BETWEEN THE ACTORS IN world politics and those in international law. States, intergovernmental organizations (IGOs), nongovernmental organizations (NGOs), and individuals are key players in both, although the influence of each actor may be greater in one system than in the other. We can designate as actors important to the system of international law those that help make, implement, monitor, and/or enforce international law, as well as those that make judicial decisions on the basis of international law. In this chapter we will look at states as participants in both international law and world politics.

States are the most important actors in the system of international law. As we have already seen, state practice gives rise to custom, and interstate negotiations produce treaties. When states negotiate treaties it is to them that the responsibilities, as well as the rights, primarily fall. Only states can take part in contentious proceedings before the International Court of Justice. And though states are not permitted to request an advisory opinion of the ICJ, they are permitted to make written and/or oral statements to the Court in such cases.

The state is also the principal actor in world politics. A state is defined according to the territory it encompasses; it is delineated by sharp frontiers.[1] The geopolitical principle of territorial exclusivity means that once a portion of territory is designated a state, that territory and its inhabitants are to be governed independently of the populations of other portions of territory. It is easy to take for granted that the world be divided on a territorial basis into political-legal units, but this is not the only possible arrangement; we could, for example, be governed by the heads of our respective religions, no matter where on earth we each live.[2]

It is easy to see how international politics and international law are interrelated when we consider that a test of a state's domestic legal system is the basis for membership of the international political system. To belong to the international (i.e., political) system of states, a state must be sovereign—that is, it must have constitutional independence.[3] The question as to whether a state is or is not sovereign is determined by constitutional, rather than international, law.[4]

The fundamental importance of sovereignty to the system of international law was explained in a classic statement by Max Huber in the Island of Palmas case: "Sovereignty in the relations between states signifies independence. Independence in regard to a portion of the globe is the right to exercise therein, to the exclusion of any other state, the functions of a state."[5] It is because sovereignty signifies independence that some states, in their diplomacy with other states, have emphasized the importance of the sovereignty concept. Chinese diplomats have argued strongly that sovereignty must remain an inviolable principle to protect the weak.[6]

Because a state has constitutional independence, its domestic legal system has traditionally not been subject to scrutiny by international law but is what is referred to as the "reserved domain." As Huber explains, "The development of the national organization of States during the last few centuries and, as a corollary, the development of international law, have established this principle of the exclusive competence of the State in regard to its own territory in such a way as to make it the point of departure in settling most questions that concern international relations."[7]

The sovereign independence of a state gives it the capacity to enter into relations with other states. This capacity is considered to be a key criterion of statehood. Other criteria include a permanent population, a defined territory, and a government.[8] Although international lawyers continue to debate the precise definition of statehood, the reality in an anarchic state-based system is that a state is a political entity that other states accept as being a state. Thus, when it is said that there are now "about" 190 states, this is not just due to a lack of research precision. Different states may actually believe there to be different numbers of states, depending on which other political entities they have accepted as being states.

The distinction between a formal definition of statehood and what happens in practice has been debated in international law in terms of, on the one hand, *constitutive theory,* which holds that an entity becomes a state through recognition by other states—whether or not it meets suggested international standards for statehood—and the *declaratory theory,* which holds that an entity can become a state even if not recognized by other states if it meets the criteria for statehood required by international law.[9] The first example of the recognition of a new state was the recognition by Spain of the United Netherlands in 1648.[10]

■ The Spread of the States System

The territorially defined state is generally regarded as having originated in Europe. Statelike entities, at least in the sense of political units, have existed in a number of parts of the world, including precolonial Africa, but the identification of a state primarily on the basis of exact geographical boundaries has been rare.[11] Precolonial Africa, for example, did not consist of states existing within a fixed border. Although the form of political organization varied between parts of Africa and over time, it is safe to generalize that the notion of a boundary was unknown. Various types of frontier existed, as did mutual separation zones such as deserts. Most African political-social units were identifiable according to their king or chief. These communities were regarded as having rights over the land they inhabited and utilized, but this was not the factor by which the political unit was defined.[12]

There is some difference of opinion as to the exact date at which the modern state came into being, but confirmation of the territorially defined state as the basic unit at the international level is usually dated from the Treaty of Westphalia of 1648.[13] That treaty ended the Thirty Years' War and the political dominance of the Roman Catholic Church. It established a territorial baseline that was repeatedly referred to in treaties until 1789.[14] Even before the state system was firmly established in Europe it was spreading through European states, thereby increasing their wealth, power, and prestige. The first round of empire building—in the sixteenth, seventeenth, and eighteenth centuries—established empires in North America and South America. A second round of empire building occurred in the nineteenth century, when European states divided up Africa and much of the Middle East and Asia, and the United States and Japan acquired overseas colonial holdings. This second round of empire coincided with the first proliferation of states; between 1870 and 1930 the number of states in Europe expanded from about 15 to 35. The second proliferation of states took place between 1945 and 1990 as old colonial empires fell; the number of states increased from about 54 in 1945 to about 170 in 1990. A third proliferation of states has taken place since the end of the Cold War, as established states including Czechoslovakia, the USSR, and Yugoslavia have dissolved.[15]

Much of the expansion of the states system over the past two centuries has come about because of the ideal of the nation-state. Although as in, for example, the Latin term *jus gentium,* or "law of nations," international lawyers sometimes use the term *nation* synonymously with that of *state,* most political scientists now distinguish among a nation, a state, and a nation-state. A *state* is a technical term for "country," but a *nation* is a group of people of the same nationality who speak the same language and share a culture. It is possible to have a nation without a state, as was the case with the Jews before 1947. But from the time of the revolutions in France and America in the late eighteenth century we have had the ideal that states should be nation-states (i.e., that each nation should have its own state). Japan is one of the purest examples of a nation-state; most states contain people of a number of nationalities. The tension between the ideal of every nation having its own state and the reality of the geographical intermixing of peoples has underlain much bloodshed over the past two centuries.

The legal principle that has supported the twentieth-century growth in the number of states has been that of *self-determination:* the principle that those people living within a particular territory have the right to choose their own political system. The term gained prominence with its use by President Woodrow Wilson during and after World War I. Wilson announced that the new international order to be established after the war was to be based "upon justice and upon the rights of all people to determine for themselves their own governments."[16] This self-rule theoretically "would minimize the thrust for territorial expansion and make war less likely."[17] Self-determination of peoples is listed in the UN Charter as a general purpose of the United Nations [article 1(2)] and as a specific purpose of the United Nations in the promotion of economic and social cooperation (article 55).

The International Covenant on Civil and Political Rights (ICCPR) and the International Covenant on Economic, Social and Cultural Rights (ICESCR) share a common article 1(1), which proclaims that "[a]ll peoples have the right of self-determination. By virtue of that right, they freely determine their political status and freely pursue their economic, social, and cultural development." *Peoples* is thus sometimes used in international law in a sense similar to that of *nation,* to refer to an "ethnic group linked by common history" that also "must itself delineate the purview of its common existence and settle criteria for belonging to the group."[18] Self-determination may, as in the union of East and West Germany, lead to integration with an independent state[19] or to free association with an independent state; in the case of Puerto Rico the people opted for a special legal status within a state. More commonly it means that "a people under colonial domination is entitled to create a new state where none existed before" and that "people living within the framework of an extant state secede from it and establish [their] own independent country."[20] The right of a people to self-determination is thus "loaded with political and psychological gun-powder,"[21] because the principle does not prohibit civil war as a means of attaining a favored political status, nor does it specify a means by which to resolve a conflict between overlapping rights to self-determination—as witnessed by Palestine, the Indian subcontinent, and Cyprus.[22]

■ State Succession

How one state replaces another and with what legal and political consequences were important questions during the process of decolonization in the 1950s and 1960s. Their importance was renewed in the last decade of the twentieth century with the reunification of Germany and the breakup of the Soviet Union and the Socialist Federal Republic of Yugoslavia. There are two multilateral treaties on the subject—the Vienna Convention on the Succession of States in Respect of Treaties of 1978, and the Vienna Convention on State Succession in Respect of State Property, Archives, and Debts of April 8, 1983; the latter has not yet entered into force. Despite these treaties, there is much uncertainty in this area of international law.

The dissolution of the USSR gave rise to three categories of states. The Baltic states have claimed to be identical to the three states that had existed on their territory until 1940 and hence are not successor states to the USSR; the Russian Federation has claimed to be the continuing state of the USSR and hence took the seat of the former USSR in the Security Council and declared that it would continue to honor treaties entered into by the USSR; and the former republics of the USSR other than the Baltic republics have been treated as successor states.[23]

The situation was different as regards Yugoslavia. Initially, lawyers disagreed as to whether the state had dissolved, producing several successor states, or whether there was one continuator state from which the other four had succeeded. The United States refused to accept that Serbia and Montenegro were a continuation of Yugoslavia. The Republic of Bosnia and Herzegovina, the Republic of Croatia, the Republic of Slovenia, the former Yugoslav Republic of Macedonia, the Republic of Serbia, and Montenegro are now all members of the United Nations.

■ Recognition of States

One of the first problems faced by a state is that of its recognition. The act of *recognition,* by which one state recognizes that another exists, may be either *express*—via a formal statement recognizing the new state—or *implied* through actions such as, for example, the making of a bilateral treaty arranging for commercial relations.[24] The law regarding recognition has been one of the most controversial areas of international law.[25] This is, in part, because decisions as to whether to recognize a state do not always hinge on whether the state meets the broad criteria of statehood but may turn on foreign policy objectives. States have sometimes used nonrecognition as a way of signifying disapproval or have granted recognition almost in anticipation of statehood, as a means of helping establish the independence of the new state. In 1903 the United States recognized Panama only three days after its revolt from Colombia.

Having been under UN administration since 1999, Kosovo in February 2008 declared its independence from Serbia. The United States, United Kingdom, and certain European Union (EU) states recognized the independence of the Republic of Kosovo, whereas Russia and some other states have argued that Kosovo's secession and/or the recognition of that secession would be a breach of international law.[26] By resolution 63/3, the UN General Assembly on October 8, 2008, requested an advisory opinion of the International Court of Justice on the legality of Kosovo's unilateral declaration of independence.

Questions of recognition have traditionally arisen not only when a new state seeks to establish its independence but also when a new government assumes control, usually by force, and wants to engage in relations with other governments. This practice had its origins in the competing claims to succession of European monarchs.[27] In 1977 the US State Department announced that, because twentieth-century policy had created the international impression that US recognition or nonrecognition signified approval or disapproval of governments, the State Department would henceforth focus not on recognition but on whether the United States wished to establish or maintain diplomatic relations with new governments.[28] The US government has continued to recognize new states as they become independent, but the question of recognition no longer arises for the United States when a new government comes to power through a means other than independence.[29] In 1977 the United Kingdom announced that it too had decided that it would no longer accord recognition to governments,[30] as did Australia in 1988.[31] The tendency to "exploit recognition [of states] for political purposes" means that it may "eventually suffer the same fate as that of recognition of governments."[32]

One act is an unequivocal statement of the full recognition of a state: the establishment of diplomatic relations.[33] Diplomatic relations are established by mutual consent. The 1961 Vienna Convention on Diplomatic Relations listed the functions of a diplomatic mission as consisting, inter alia, of representing the sending state in the receiving state; protecting in the receiving state the interests of the sending state and of its nationals, within the limits permitted by international law; negotiating with the government of the receiving state; ascertaining by all lawful means conditions and developments in the receiving state, and reporting thereon to the government of the sending state; promoting friendly relations between the sending state and the receiving state, and developing their economic, cultural, and scientific relations.[34] The ambassador to a state may be "recalled" as a mark of displeasure with another state. In May 1998 the United States recalled its ambassador to India in response to the Indian nuclear tests of May 11 and 13. A stronger political weapon is the severance of diplomatic relations. This is a unilateral act, although international organizations may, as a measure of collective sanction, resolve that their members sever diplomatic relations with a state.

■ The Jurisdiction of the State

Jurisdiction is legal authority and can relate to legislative, executive, and judicial action. A state has jurisdiction over all persons, property, and activities in its territory and its airspace and in the waters subject to its sovereignty. According to the *active personality principle* a state may prosecute its nationals for crimes committed anywhere in the world. A state has jurisdiction over a ship, aircraft, or spacecraft registered in its state, as well as over all persons and property on board that ship, aircraft, or spacecraft. According to the *objective territorial principle* or the *effects doctrine,* a state also has jurisdiction over a person whose behavior outside its territory causes injury within its territory; and by the *protective principle* a state may punish acts that threaten its security even if committed by nonnationals outside of the territory of the state. Although this much is uncontroversial, other aspects of international law relating to the jurisdiction of the state are not as clear-cut. It is not completely clear, for example, as to whether a state may exercise jurisdiction only where there is a recognized basis for its exercise or in the absence of any prohibition on its exercise.

The so-called *passive personality* principle, by which some states assert the right to try a foreigner for injuring its nationals outside its territory, is not so widely accepted as a basis of state jurisdiction. The principle is invoked in some national legislation pertaining to terrorism. There are also some internationally defined criminal offenses for which a state has jurisdiction to arrest and try a person no matter where the offense occurred. Exactly which offenses are subject to such universal jurisdiction is not agreed, but most states would agree that such obligations *erga omnes* include slavery, piracy, genocide, certain war crimes and crimes against humanity, and offenses covered by the various multilateral treaties on terrorism.[35] Human rights litigation based on universal jurisdiction has in recent years been brought in Austria, France, the Netherlands, Senegal, Spain, and the United Kingdom with respect to crimes committed in Chad, Chile, Mauritania, Rwanda, Sudan, and Yugoslavia.[36]

The most fundamental prohibition on the jurisdiction of the state is that over another state. Because states enjoy sovereign equality at least theoretically, no state has the legal right to exercise its jurisdiction over another state. A state may not perform any governmental act or send its agents to arrest or restrain any person or property in the territory of another state without the latter's consent. State immunity comes into play particularly in relation to the exercising of judicial jurisdiction. Under the doctrine of *absolute state immunity* the courts in one state cannot hear any case brought against a foreign state—in relation, for example, to human rights violations or environmental damages—unless that state has waived its immunity and consented to the proceedings.[37] By the middle of the twentieth century the doctrine of absolute immunity was giving way to that of *restrictive immunity,* which imposes some limits on the immunity of the state.[38] The change to restrictive immunity came about, at least in part, because national courts did not agree that a state, when acting in a commercial capacity, should enjoy a privileged position as compared to private traders.[39] Although more states now appear to accept the doctrine of restrictive immunity rather than absolute immunity,[40] the exact nature of the limits is not yet fully agreed; in particular, the question has been raised as to whether immunity from jurisdiction should be denied to states that violate fundamental human rights.[41]

Closely related to state immunity is *head-of-state immunity,* by which a head of state enjoys immunity from the jurisdiction of a foreign court. In October 1998 Spain issued an international warrant for the arrest of Senator Augusto Pinochet, who was at that time receiving medical treatment in the United Kingdom. Pinochet was arrested on October 17, 1998. A second provisional warrant stated, inter alia, that Pinochet between January 1, 1988, and December 1992 "intentionally inflicted severe pain or suffering on another in the performance or purported performance of his official duties." On March 24, 1999, the House of Lords ruled that Senator Pinochet was not entitled to immunity in relation to acts of torture.[42] The House of Lords was the most prominent court to date to hold that heads of state can under certain circumstances be held responsible for gross violations of human rights.[43] The decision was hailed as a great victory by the human rights movement.

Such excitement was tempered by subsequent events. Home Secretary Jack Straw ruled on March 2, 2000, that Pinochet would not be extradited because of his frail medical condition, and so Pinochet was able to leave the United Kingdom for Chile. Three years later, in a case involving questions of universal jurisdiction as well as immunity, the ICJ decided that a serving minister for foreign affairs enjoys full immunity from criminal jurisdiction and inviolability.[44] In April 2000 a Belgian investigating magistrate had issued an arrest warrant against the foreign minister of the Democratic Republic of Congo, Abdulaye Yerodia Ndombasi, pending a request for extradition to Belgium for alleged crimes constituting serious violations of international humanitarian law relating to his allegedly having provoked the continuation of massacres of Tutsi people in 1998.[45] The Congo responded to the issuing of the arrest warrant by bringing proceedings against Belgium before the International Court of Justice. The judgment in the *Case Concerning the Arrest Warrant of 11 April 2000 (Democratic Republic of the Congo v. Belgium)* disappointed the human rights community. More recently, the International Criminal Court on March 4, 2009, issued an arrest warrant for President al-Bashir of Sudan, on two counts of war crimes and five counts of crimes against humanity in Darfur. This was the first time that the Court had indicted a sitting head of state.

Just as one state is immune from the jurisdiction of another state, and heads of state enjoy immunity because of their functional relationship to the state, so is a state not able to exercise its criminal and administrative jurisdiction in relation to accredited diplomats, as the representatives of other states.[46] Although required to respect the laws and regulations of the receiving state and not to interfere in the internal affairs of that state,[47] diplomatic agents are not liable to any form of arrest or detention.[48] Diplomatic immunity is sometimes controversial when it has been abused, in which instance the receiving state must receive an express waiver of immunity by the sending state before proceeding to prosecution. The receiving state can, at any time, declare a diplomatic agent *persona non grata* (an unwelcome person) and expel him or her from the state; it has become standard in such circumstances for the sending state to then make a similar declaration regarding an equal number of the other state's envoys.

With the growth of environmental, human rights, and humanitarian law the principle of noninterference in the internal matters of a state is no longer absolute. The extent to which this is the case and to which the concept of sovereignty should or may change further is not clear-cut. There is ongoing debate regarding relations between individual states and the United Nations. In the same way that a state is not meant to exercise its jurisdiction in relation to another state, so is the United Nations not, at least theoretically, to intervene in the internal affairs of states. Article 2(7) of the UN Charter states:

> Nothing contained in the present Charter shall authorise the United Nations to intervene in matters which are essentially within the domestic jurisdiction of any State or shall require the Members to submit such matters to settlement under the present Charter; but this principle shall not prejudice the application of enforcement measures under Chapter VII.

Chapter 3 will consider in more detail the operation of the United Nations and the role of intergovernmental organizations in general in the system of international law.

▉ Notes

1. See K. Boulding, "National Images and International Systems," in R. E. Kasperson and J. V. Minghi, eds., *The Structure of Political Geography* (Chicago: Aldine, 1969), pp. 341–349, esp. 344. Compare the conceptualization of variable space that existed in Southeast Asian thought. See S. J. Tambiah, *Culture, Thought, and Social Action: An Anthropological Perspective* (Cambridge, MA: Harvard University Press, 1985), p. 260.

2. "A society is not inconceivable . . . and might even be desirable, in which nations governed people but not territories and claimed jurisdiction over a defined set of citizens, no matter where on the earth's surface they happened to live." Boulding, "National Images and International Systems," p. 344.

3. Alan James, *Sovereign Statehood: The Basis of International Society* (London: Allen and Unwin, 1986), p. 30.

4. Ibid., p. 40.

5. *Island of Palmas Case* (Netherlands/USA) (1928), *Reports of International Arbitral Awards,* 2:829, 838.

6. Evan A. Feigenbaum, "China's Challenge to *Pax Americana,*" *Washington Quarterly* (Summer 2001): 31–43, esp. 33.

7. *Island of Palmas Case,* p. 838.

8. Convention on the Rights and Duties of States, article 1, December 26, 1933, known as the Montevideo Convention 165 League of Nations Treaty Series 19, reprinted in 28 *American Journal of International Law Supplement* 75 (1934).

9. For summaries of the debate see Ian Brownlie, *Principles of Public International Laws,* 4th ed. (Oxford: Clarendon Press, 1979), pp. 16–23; James R. Crawford, *The Creation of States in International Law* (Oxford: Clarendon, 1979), pp. 16–23; John Dugard, *Recognition and the United Nations* (Cambridge: Grotius, 1989), pp. 7–9; and Hersch Lauterpacht, *Recognition in International Law* (Cambridge: University Press, 1948), pp. 38–66. Such a debate is now likely to be "beside the point." Thomas D. Grant, *The Recognition of States: Law and Practice in Debate and Evolution* (London: Praeger, 1999), p. 123.

10. Jochen Abr. Frowein, "Recognition," *Encyclopedia of Public International Law* 9 (1986): 341. The US declaration of independence gave rise to a dispute between France and Britain as to the possibility of recognizing the new state as a subject of international law.

11. For discussion on defining the state, see J. Genet, "Introduction: Which State Rises?" *Historical Research* 65, no. 157 (June 1992): 119–133.

12. M. Shaw, *Title to Territory in Africa* (Oxford: Clarendon, 1986), pp. 27–29.

13. See discussion in Kenneth Dyson, *The State Tradition in Western Europe: A Study of an Idea and Institution* (New York: M. Robertson, 1980), p. 28. See also G. R. Potter, "The Beginnings of the Modern State," *History* 31 (1946): 73–84. The treaty can be found at http://www.yale.edu/lawweb/avalon/westphal.htm.

14. Gottman has traced the evolution of the relationship between people and their space prior to the modern state. He distinguished three turning points: that reported by Homer and Aristotle when people gathered into communities constituted by several villages, the notion of the vast Hellenistic world that was then assimilated into the Roman Empire, and that change, around 1500 A.D., by which personal allegiance came to be replaced by the national allegiance of the people to the sovereign. J. Gottman, *The Significance of Territory* (Charlottesville: University Press of Virginia, 1973), pp. 123–127. Modelski believes the evidence supports 1500 A.D. as a suitable cut-off point. G. Modelski, "The Long Cycle of Global Politics and the Nation-State," *Comparative Studies in Society and History* 20 (1978): 214–235.

15. The information in this paragraph derives from Daniel S. Papp, *Contemporary International Relations: Frameworks for Understanding,* 5th ed. (Boston: Allyn and Bacon, 1997), pp. 33–43.

16. Charles L. Mee Jr., *The End of Order: Versailles 1919* (London: Secker and Warburg, 1981), p. 11.

17. Papp, *Contemporary International Relations,* p. 38.

18. Yoram Dinstein, "Collective Human Rights of Peoples and Minorities," *International and Comparative Law Quarterly* 25 (January 1976): 102–120, esp. 105.

19. Shelley Wright, "The Individual in International Human Rights: Québec, Canada, and the Nation-State," *Saskatchewan Law Review* 59, no. 2 (1995): 437–469, esp. 459.

20. Dinstein, "Collective Human Rights of Peoples and Minorities," p. 108. Principle VI of General Assembly Resolution 1541(XV) states that a non-self-governing territory can be said to have reached a full measure of self-government by: (a) emergence as a sovereign independent state; (b) free association with an independent state; or (c) integration with an independent state.

21. Ibid.

22. See also M. Koskenniemi, "National Self-Determination Today: Problems of Legal Theory and Practice," *International and Comparative Law Quarterly* 43 (1994): 241; and R. McCorquodale, "Self-Determination: A Human Rights Approach," *International and Comparative Law Quarterly* 43 (1994): 857–885.

23. Jan Klabbers, Martti Koskenniemi, Olivier Ribbelinhk, and Andreas Zimmermann, eds., *State Practice Regarding State Succession and Issues of Recognition: The Pilot Project of the Council of Europe* (The Hague: Kluwer Law International, 1999), pp. 92ff.

24. D. J. Harris, *Cases and Materials on International Law,* 5th ed. (London: Sweet and Maxwell, 1998), p. 147.

25. Hans Kelsen, "Recognition in International Law: Theoretical Observations," *American Journal of International Law* 35 (1941): 605–617, esp. 605.

26. Christopher J. Borgen, "Introductory Note to Kosovo's Declaration of Independence," 47 *International Legal Materials (ILM)* 461 (2008). See also Jure Vidmar, "International Legal Responses to Kosovo's Declaration of Independence," *Vanderbilt Journal of Transnational Law* 42 (2009): 779–851.

27. Frowein, "Recognition," p. 341.

28. "Diplomatic recognition," *Department State Bulletin* 77 (1977): 462, cited in D. J. Harris, *Cases and Materials on International Law,* 5th ed. (London: Sweet and Maxwell, 1998), p. 159. This approach had its roots in the Estrada Doctrine employed by Mexico in the 1930s. See *American Journal of International Law* 25 (1931), Supplement No. 203.

29. Mary Beth West and Sean D. Murphy, "The Impact on US Litigation of Non-Recognition of Foreign Governments," *Stanford Journal of International Law* 26 (1990): 435–478, esp. 456.

30. "Statement by the Foreign Secretary (Lord Carrington), Hansard, H. L., vol. 408, cols. 1121–1122, April 28, 1980," in Harris, *Cases and Materials on International Law,* pp. 155–156.

31. Minister for Foreign Affairs and Trade, Press Release, January 19, 1988, reprinted in *Australian International Law News* (1988): 49. Although Australia's change in recognition policy had been contemplated for some time, the immediate impetus seemed to be Australia's relations with Fiji following the coups of May and September 1987. Hilary Charlesworth, "The New Australian Recognition Policy in Comparative Perspective," *Melbourne University Law Review* 18 (June 1991): 1–25, esp. 1–2.

32. Matthew C. R. Craven, "What's in a Name? The Former Yugoslav Republic of Macedonia and Issues of Statehood," *Australian Year Book of International Law* 16 (1995): 199–239, esp. 217–218.

33. Frowein, "Recognition," p. 342. See, generally, P. K. Menon, *The Law of Recognition in International Law: Basic Principles* (Lewiston, NY: Edwin Mellen, 1994).

34. Vienna Convention on Diplomatic Relations, article 3 (April 18, 1961), United Nations Treaty Series (UNTS) 500, pp. 95–221. The text is also in Shirley

V. Scott, ed., *International Law and Politics: Key Documents* (Boulder, CO: Lynne Rienner, 2006), 44–57.

35. See the discussion in M. Cherif Bassiouni, "Universal Jurisdiction for International Crimes: Historical Perspectives and Contemporary Practice," *Virginia Journal of International Law* 42, no. 1 (2001): 81–156.

36. For details and discussion, see Menno T. Kamminga, "Lessons Learned from the Exercise of Universal Jurisdiction in Respect of Gross Human Rights Offenses," *Human Rights Quarterly* 23, no. 4 (2001): 940–974.

37. See Jürgen Bröhmer, *State Immunity and the Violation of Human Rights* (The Hague: Martinus Nijhoff, 1997); and Hazel Fox QC, *The Law of State Immunity,* 2nd ed. (Oxford: Oxford University Press, 2008).

38. See Lakshman Marasinghe, "The Modern Law of Sovereign Immunity," *Modern Law Review* 54, no. 5 (1991): 664–684.

39. Magdalini Karagiannakis, "State Immunity and Fundamental Human Rights," *Leiden Journal of International Law* 11 (1998): 9–43, esp. 12; and Michael Singer, "Abandoning Restrictive Sovereign Immunity: An Analysis in Terms of Jurisdiction to Prescribe," *Harvard International Law Journal* 26, no. 1 (1985): 1–61.

40. Karagiannakis, "State Immunity and Fundamental Human Rights," p. 12.

41. Ibid., pp. 9–43.

42. "United Kingdom House of Lords: Regina v. Bartle and the Commissioner of Police for the Metropolis and Others Ex Parte Pinochet" [March 24, 1999], 38 ILM 581 (1999).

43. Jürgen Bröhmer, "Immunity of a Former Head of State General Pinochet and the House of Lords: Part Three," *Leiden Journal of International Law* 13 (2000): 207–216, esp. 236. See also Andrea Bianchi, "Immunity Versus Human Rights: The Pinochet Case," European Journal of International Law 10, no. 2 (1999): 237–277; C. H. Powell and A. Pillay, "Revisiting Pinochet: The Development of Customary International Criminal Law," *South African Journal on Human Rights* 17, no. 4 (2001): 477–502; Rosanne Van-Alebeek, "The Pinochet Case: International Human Rights Law on Trial," *British Yearbook of International Law* 71 (2000): 29–70; and Diana Woodhouse, ed., *The Pinochet Case: A Legal and Constitutional Analysis* (Oxford: Hart, 2000).

44. *"Pinochet* Revisited," *International and Comparative Law Quarterly* 51 (2002): 959–966.

45. "Application Instituting Proceedings Filed in the Registry of the Court on 17 October 2000," in the *Case Concerning the Arrest Warrant of 11 April 2000 (Democratic Republic of the Congo v. Belgium),* p. 5.

46. "Except in the case of (a) a real action relating to private immovable property situated in the territory of the receiving State, unless he holds it on behalf of the sending State for the purposes of the mission; (b) an action relating to succession in which the diplomatic agent is involved as executor, administrator, heir or legatee as a private person and not on behalf of the sending State; (c) an action relating to any professional or commercial activity exercised by the diplomatic agent in the receiving State outside his official functions." Vienna Convention on Diplomatic Relations, article 31.

47. Ibid., article 41(1).

48. Ibid., article 29.

3

Intergovernmental Organizations in International Law

AN INTERGOVERNMENTAL ORGANIZATION (IGO) IS AN INTERNA-
tional organization made up of states. IGOs play an important role in both
world politics and international law, although political scientists have long
debated the extent to which IGOs have an independent influence on world
politics as opposed to functioning as a conduit for the foreign policy of powerful states. The United Nations (UN) is the best-known IGO (actually it is
a family of IGOs), but it is by no means the most typical. The typical IGO
is regional and deals with a single issue. The Northwest Atlantic Fisheries
Organization, for example, aims for the optimum utilization, rational management, and conservation of fishery resources in the Northwest Atlantic;
the Intergovernmental Authority on Development aims to achieve economic
integration and sustainable development in Eastern Africa. The UN, by contrast, is a multi-issue, global IGO. It is made up of six principal organs: the
Security Council, the General Assembly, the Economic and Social Council,
the Trusteeship Council, the Secretariat, and the International Court of Justice. It also includes many other bodies in a complex institutional network.
Major regional, multi-issue IGOs include the League of Arab States (Arab
League), the Organization of American States (OAS), and the African Union.

International law is important to IGOs as political actors, most fundamentally because an IGO is established by a multilateral treaty setting out
the goals, structure, and methods of operation of the IGO.[1] The Northwest
Atlantic Fisheries Organization was established by the Convention on Future Multilateral Cooperation in the Northwest Atlantic Fisheries; the United
Nations was established by the UN Charter. IGOs have the capacity to enter
into treaty relations. International organizations have mostly entered into
bilateral treaty relationships, often of an institutional purpose. There are,

for example, numerous treaties between international organizations and states setting out details of headquarters arrangements. Other bilateral treaties concluded between states and IGOs are of a functional purpose intended, for example, to give aid to developing countries. The rules for such treaties can be found in the Convention on the Law of Treaties Between States and International Organizations 1986. Although this has not yet entered into force, it is widely considered to reflect customary international law on the subject. International organizations cannot be a party to contentious proceedings before the ICJ, but the General Assembly, the Security Council, and certain other UN organs and agencies can request advisory opinions of the International Court of Justice.

The European Union (EU) is the most advanced example of regional economic and political integration. The European Union can be understood as a supranational organization insofar as EU law has direct effect in member states and in some areas EU law overrides national law. The EU has long had a common trade policy. The Treaty of Lisbon, which entered into force on December 1, 2009, represents a significant evolutionary step for the EU. The EU now has a single legal personality as is required to conclude treaties. The EU had already concluded some treaties, which were often "mixed agreements," with both the European Community and its member states as contracting parties. The EU can now be expected to more frequently act alone in concluding treaties in those areas in which the EU is competent to legislate.

IGOs play a major role in the system of international law. This is true of the creation of international law, because IGOs sponsor new multilateral treaties and contribute to the development of customary international law through their institutional practices. It is also true of the enforcement of international law. Intergovernmental organizations across a whole range of subject areas devise ways of enforcing relevant treaties and monitor the effectiveness of the treaties with which they are associated.

The United Nations is ultimately inseparable from the contemporary system of international law. Though, as we have seen, virtually all IGOs are created by international treaty and may enter into treaty relationships, the influence on the system of international law of the United Nations is far more than that of other IGOs. The UN is so integral to the current system of international law that we would not recognize international law if we extricated the United Nations from it. There are several reasons for this. First, we have the broad reach of the United Nations and the breadth of the subjects it addresses. The United Nations has almost universal membership, and the UN Charter addresses some of the most basic issues in world politics, such as the use of force. Second, article 103 of the UN Charter states that "[i]n the event of a conflict between the obligations of the Members of the United

Nations under the present Charter and their obligations under any other international agreement, their obligations under the present Charter shall prevail." The UN Charter thus "trumps" other treaties. Third, hundreds of treaties have been concluded by United Nations organs or by diplomatic conferences convened by the UN. These treaties relate not only to a wide range of substantive issue areas but also to the operation of the system of international law itself, such as the laws relating to the negotiation of treaties. And fourth, the United Nations plays a key role not only in the creation of international law but in its enforcement and in the judicial settlement of disputes at a global level and in a multi-issue capacity.

This chapter will focus on the United Nations because of its enormous importance to the current system of international law. We will look at the principal organs, specialized agencies, and other UN bodies that are of most significance to the system of international law because of the roles they play in creating, implementing, enforcing, and/or undertaking judicial decision-making on the basis of the rules, principles, and concepts of international law. Some, such as the General Assembly, deal with a broad range of subject matter; others, as we shall see, specialize in one field. We turn first to the principal organs and to the other United Nations programs and organs whose governing bodies report directly to the principal organs.

■ The Security Council

The United Nations took its name from the wartime coalition of Allies that was formed to defeat the Berlin-Rome-Tokyo Axis in World War II. There were fifty founding members.[2] Membership of the United Nations is now virtually universal. Although states obviously value UN membership, any member of the UN accepts a major limitation on its sovereign independence. By article 25 of the UN Charter, member states agree to carry out the decisions of the Security Council; this means that the Security Council has legal power over states. Article 24(1) of the Charter confers on the Security Council primary responsibility for the maintenance of international peace and security. The key function of the Security Council in world politics is thus a political one, but it is one closely related to international law. Although it is not a judicial body, the Security Council does have authority to make some quasi-judicial determinations, as for example, to determine an aggressor state, and it has on a number of occasions made determinations regarding particular points of law. These have generally been uncontroversial, such as stating that genocide is a flagrant violation of international law, but they have not always been so clear-cut.[3] The Security Council also has a role to play in backing up the International Court of Justice. By article 94(2) of the UN Charter, the Security Council may "make recommendations or decide upon measures to be taken to give effect to an ICJ judgment." It has not, to date, explicitly taken such action.[4]

Chapter VI of the UN Charter is entitled "Pacific Settlement of Disputes." According to article 33(1), "The parties to any dispute, the continuance of which is likely to endanger the maintenance of international peace and security, shall, first of all, seek a solution by negotiation, enquiry, mediation, conciliation, arbitration, judicial settlement, resort to regional agencies or arrangements, or other peaceful means of their own choice."

The Security Council may, at any stage, recommend appropriate procedures or methods of adjustment in a dispute. Should the parties to a dispute not have settled it by one of the above means, they are to refer it to the Security Council.[5]

Chapter VII of the UN Charter provides for the Security Council to decide what measures are to be taken to maintain or restore international peace and security, including the imposition of sanctions and/or the use of military force. The Security Council must first make an affirmative finding of a "threat to the peace, breach of the peace, or act of aggression." Of these, the Security Council has most often identified a "threat to the peace." Having identified a threat to the peace, breach of the peace, or act of aggression, the Council may call upon the parties concerned to comply "with such provisional measures as it deems necessary or desirable," and/or it may call upon member states to apply nonmilitary or military means of restoring peace. Nonmilitary means are listed in article 41 as the complete or partial "interruption of economic relations and of all rail, sea, air, postal, telegraphic, radio, and other means of communication, and the severance of diplomatic relations." They are what are commonly referred to as *sanctions*,[6] although that term does not appear in the Charter.

The Security Council used sanctions only twice during the Cold War: on Rhodesia in 1966 and on South Africa in 1977. Sanctions were used much more frequently in the first post–Cold War decade; indeed, the 1990s has been referred to as the "sanctions decade,"[7] with sanctions having been authorized against Iraq, Haiti, Libya, the former Yugoslavia, and Rwanda, among others. The Security Council has more recently imposed sanctions on Iran as part of its efforts to ensure that Iran does not acquire a nuclear weapons capability.[8] We will consider further the authorization of military force by the Security Council in Chapter 6.

The Security Council is the UN body that authorizes peacekeeping missions. Since the first UN peacekeeping mission in 1948, there have been more than sixty operations around the world (see Figure 3.1, p. 36). Since the end of the Cold War the Security Council has on the basis of its Chapter VII powers taken a number of types of actions other than imposing economic sanctions or authorizing use of force. In May 1993 the Security Council established the

International Tribunal for the Prosecution of Persons Responsible for Serious Violations of International Humanitarian Law Committed in the Territory of the Former Yugoslavia Since 1991, and in May 1994 it went on to establish the International Tribunal for Rwanda, in both cases mandating the co-operation of all states with the tribunal.[9] Other subsidiary bodies created by the Security Council have included the UN Compensation Commission for the payment of damages arising out of Iraq's invasion of Kuwait and the United Nations Monitoring, Verification, and Inspection Commission.

Since 2001 the Security Council has used its Chapter VII powers to require all states to take or not take specific actions not limited to disciplining a particular country.[10] The Security Council passed a series of resolutions in 2008 in response to the alarming increase in attacks upon, and hijacking of, vessels off Somalia. Resolution 1816 (2008), for example, essentially decided that states cooperating with the Transitional Federal Government of Somalia to repress the piracy could treat the territorial waters of Somalia as if they were the high seas.[11] Several resolutions have required states to adopt legislation and administrative acts in their internal legal systems. Resolution 1373 (2001) contained a "detailed and seemingly exhaustive list of obligations that states should undertake in the collective struggle against terrorism"[12] and established the Counter-Terrorism Committee to monitor the resolution's implementation. The Council decided in resolution 1540 (2004) that states were not to support efforts of nonstate actors to access nuclear, chemical, or biological weapons and their means of delivery; that states were to legislate at a national level to prohibit nonstate access to these weapons; and that states were to adopt and enforce effective domestic controls to, inter alia, develop and maintain appropriate border controls and law enforcement efforts to prevent illicit trafficking in such items. Resolution 1540 also established a committee to receive reports from states, and states were "called" to report on measures taken to implement the resolution.

Such decisions have been criticized as the Council inappropriately "legislating" for the international community, raising the question as to whether there are any legal limits on what the Security Council may identify as a threat to the peace under article 39.[13] The clear majority of writers take the view that the Council's determination under article 39 is essentially political and that the principal limitation on the powers of the Council is the voting procedure of the Security Council.[14] The Council has five permanent members—China, France, the Russian Federation, the United Kingdom, and the United States of America. The other ten members are elected by the General Assembly for two-year terms. The Security Council makes some decisions of a procedural nature; these require an affirmative vote of any nine members. In the case of all other decisions, there must be an affirmative vote of nine members, which includes the concurring votes of the permanent members.

Figure 3.1 United Nations Peace Operations

None of the terms "peacekeeping," "peace enforcement," or "peace-building" are found in the UN Charter. The primary types of peace operations that have nevertheless been conducted by the United Nations are:

Peace Enforcement Operations
These are authorized under Chapter VII of the UN Charter. These are designed to restore international peace and security. The UN inevitably becomes a party to conflict, and these actions may involve massive use of force.

Peacekeeping Operations
Dag Hammarskjöld, former UN Secretary-General, referred to peacekeeping as belonging to Chapter "Six and a half," meaning that it fits somewhere between traditional methods of peaceful dispute resolution and the more forceful actions provided for in Chapter VII. Although there are debates as to the exact constitutional basis of peacekeeping, its constitutionality has not really been in doubt since the decision of the ICJ in the *Expenses* case in the early 1960s.[1] In the case of peacekeeping, the international presence is there with the consent of the state in whose territory it is operating, in a situation in which peace has already been established. Peacekeeping may involve UN military and/or police personnel and may include civilians. The UN presence may implement or monitor the implementation of arrangements relating to the control of conflicts (cease-fires, separation of forces, etc.) and their resolution or undertake a variety of other tasks, such as ensuring the safe delivery of humanitarian relief. Troops are authorized to use force in self-defense only. The UN Truce Supervision Organization (UNTSO), established in 1948 to report on Arab-Israeli cease-fire and armistice violations, is often regarded as having been the first peacekeeping operation. The first UN mission explicitly referred to as a "peacekeeping" operation was the first UN Emergency Force (UNEF I) deployed in response to the 1956 Suez Crisis; this was actually authorized by the General Assembly on the basis of the Uniting for Peace Resolution and article 22 of the Charter. There has been an evolution in peacekeeping since then. More recent examples include those deployed to Somalia in 1992–1993 (UNOSOM I), 1993–1995 (UNOSOM II); and East Timor since May 2002 (UNMISET).[2] From 1948 to June 2002 the UN spent an estimated U.S.$26.1 billion on peacekeeping operations, but funding UN peacekeeping has been problematic since the 1960s.

(continues)

Figure 3.1 continued

Chapter VII and Peacekeeping
Although there is a clear conceptual difference between peacekeeping and peace enforcement, in practice the difference has become difficult to discern. The use of peacekeeping forces to enforce provisional measures (cease-fires, withdrawals) began with the Congo in 1960.[3] The first UN operation in Somalia (UNOSOM I) was established in April 1992 to monitor the cease-fire in Mogadishu and escort deliveries of humanitarian supplies.[4] Resolution 775 (1992) authorized an increase in the strength of UNOSOM. When the situation deteriorated further, the Security Council established the Unified Task Force (UNITAF) to secure a safe environment for the delivery of humanitarian aid. By Resolution 794 of December 3, 1992, the Security Council, "acting under Chapter VII of the Charter of the United Nations, [authorized] the Secretary-General and Member States . . . to use all necessary means to establish as soon as possible a secure environment for humanitarian relief operations in Somalia." UNITAF was replaced by UNOSOM II, which was to complete the task begun by UNITAF for the restoration of peace, stability, and law and order. The size and mandate of the UN Operation was further expanded by Resolution 814 (1993).[5]

Multidimensional Peacekeeping Operations
These are the operations, more common since the end of the Cold War, that are designed to carry out a range of tasks, including peacemaking, peace-building, and/or preventive diplomacy (see below). The first multifunctional operation established at the end of the Cold War was the UN Transitional Assistance Group (UNTAG) deployed to Namibia in February 1989.

Preventive Diplomacy
Diplomatic activity designed to prevent or limit potential or actual conflict. This action is carried out under Chapter VI and may involve the preventive deployment of military forces to deter violence.

Peacemaking
In his 1999 annual report on the work of the UN, Secretary-General Kofi Annan defined "peacemaking" as the "use of diplomatic means to persuade parties in a conflict to cease hostilities and to negotiate a peaceful settlement of their dispute." These are actions under Chapter VI of the UN Charter, which may include any of the methods listed in article 33(1)—in particular negotiation or mediation.

(continues)

Figure 3.1 continued

Peacebuilding
Operations carried out under Chapter VII in postconflict situations. This action involves the identification and support of measures and structures that will promote peace and build trust and interactions among former enemies in an endeavor to prevent a return to conflict. It often involves strengthening and rebuilding civil infrastructure and institutions to help solidify peace. The practice of peacebuilding predates the term. Examples include El Salvador, Nicaragua, Haiti, Cambodia, Namibia, Mozambique, Angola, Liberia, Guinea-Bissau, and the Central African Republic.

Notes
    1. Hilaire McCoubrey and Nigel D. White, *The Blue Helmets: Legal Regulation of United Nations Military Operations* (Aldershot: Dartmouth, 1996), p. 39.
    2. Information on individual peacekeeping missions can be found on the UN Peacekeeping website at www.un.org.
    3. See McCoubrey and White, *Blue Helmets,* pp. 51ff.
    4. See, inter alia, E. Clemons, "No Peace to Keep: Six and Three Quarters Peacekeepers," *New York University Journal of International Law and Politics* 26 (1993): 107–141, esp. 134ff; and Samuel M. Makinda, "Somalia: Lessons from the United Nations Experience," in Tom Woodhouse, Robert Bruce, and Malcolm Dando, eds., *Peacekeeping and Peacemaking: Towards Effective Intervention in Post–Cold War Conflicts* (London: Macmillan, 1998), pp. 166–178.
    5. The authorization resolutions of all peacekeeping operations up to the time of publication can be found in Michael Bothe and Thomas Dörschel, eds., *UN Peacekeeping: A Documentary Introduction* (The Hague: Kluwer Law International, 1999).

It has become accepted practice that this vote may include abstentions by permanent members. If there is doubt as to whether an issue is substantive or procedural, there is a procedural vote to decide the matter. Article 27(3) requires that a state that is a party to a dispute must abstain. Council members have treated the word *dispute* quite literally and not abstained in matters that might, for example, lead to a dispute.

Given the sweeping powers of the Security Council, it is not surprising that there are periodic calls for the Council to be more democratic and to contain broader geographic representation. This was particularly true during the lead-up to the 2005 World Summit. Several proposals for enlarging the Council were debated, some involving an expansion of the veto, others not. No such radical reform eventuated. By article 108, the UN Charter can be amended only with the consent of all the permanent members of the Security Council—something not easily achieved.

■ The General Assembly

The General Assembly[15] is also essentially a political organ of the United Nations, although by article 13(1)(a) one of its functions is "encouraging the progressive development of international law and its codification." The General Assembly makes several types of decisions. A General Assembly resolution is a document recommending a particular course of action to member states. It is a political document, although it may contribute to the emergence of new customary international law.[16] Having greater influence on international law than a General Assembly resolution, although still not legally binding, is the General Assembly declaration, such as the Universal Declaration of Human Rights or the Declaration on Principles of International Law Concerning Friendly Relations and Cooperation among states in accordance with the Charter of the UN.[17] A declaration may contain a codification of customary law or of general principles of law.[18] The General Assembly may use a resolution to adopt a convention or treaty that has been drafted elsewhere, and to recommend that states sign and ratify the treaty. Treaties adopted in this way include the Genocide Convention, the International Covenant on Civil and Political Rights and the International Covenant on Economic, Social and Cultural Rights, the Convention on the Rights of the Child, the Treaty on Principles Governing the Activities of States in the Exploration and Use of Outer Space Including the Moon and Other Celestial Bodies, and the Treaty on the Non-Proliferation of Nuclear Weapons. The General Assembly also on occasion convenes an international conference to which is submitted a draft treaty prepared by, for example, the International Law Commission. Examples of treaties concluded at such international conferences include the Vienna Convention on Diplomatic Relations and the Vienna Convention on the Law of Treaties.

Unless it is specially convened, the General Assembly meets once a year, from September to December. Time constraints mean that only the most politically explosive issues are explored thoroughly by the Assembly when meeting in plenary session. Agenda items are usually considered first in committee. Of the six main committees, those most important to international law are the Third Committee—the Social, Humanitarian, and Cultural Committee; and the Sixth—the Legal Committee. The Sixth Committee offers comments on draft treaties, including those prepared by the International Law Commission. Human rights treaties, including the Genocide Convention and the International Covenants, have usually been concluded within the Third Committee or the Commission on Human Rights, with input from the Sixth Committee.[19]

The International Law Commission

The International Law Commission (ILC)[20] was set up by the General Assembly in 1947.[21] It is made up of thirty-four international lawyers, each of whom is elected for a five-year term by the General Assembly to serve in their personal capacity rather than as government representatives. The *progressive development* of international law refers to "the preparation of draft conventions on subjects which have not yet been sufficiently developed in the practice of states,"[22] and *codification* refers to "the more precise formulation and systematization of rules of international law in fields where there already has been extensive state practice, precedent, and doctrine."[23] Codification and progressive development are interrelated.

The first session of the ILC was held in 1949, at which time custom was still the primary source of international law. The ILC usually works by one member being appointed special rapporteur; he or she will provide reports on a particular issue area. The ILC uses those reports to prepare a first provisional draft of its articles on a particular topic. This is submitted to the General Assembly, which deals with the matter through its Sixth (Legal) Committee. The draft articles may be submitted to member states for comments. When the ILC has completed its final set of draft articles, it is submitted to states for a decision as to what is to be done with them. Although a treaty need not be the end product of the Commission's work, it has been common for the General Assembly to convene an international conference at which the draft articles are incorporated into a convention. The ILC prepared, for example, a draft of the 1961 Vienna Convention on Diplomatic Relations and the 1963 Vienna Convention on Consular Relations, as well as the 1969 Vienna Convention on the Law of Treaties and the 1997 Convention on the Non-Navigable Uses of International Watercourses. It also prepared a draft statute for an international criminal court.

Committee on the Peaceful Uses of Outer Space

The Committee on the Peaceful Uses of Outer Space (COPUOS)[24] was set up by General Assembly Resolution 1472 (XIV) in 1959. It has played a major role in the development of international space law.[25] Treaties drafted by COPUOS include the 1967 Treaty on Principles Governing the Activities of States in the Exploration and Use of Outer Space, including the Moon and Other Celestial Bodies; and the Agreement Governing the Activities of States on the Moon and Other Celestial Bodies of 1979. Typically, the treaty has been drafted in a working group or in the Legal Sub-Committee before being considered by COPUOS as a whole and passed on to a main committee of the General Assembly; finally, the General Assembly adopts a resolution containing the agreed text and recommends it for the approval of states.[26] COPUOS has adopted most of the various conventions by consensus, the idea being that although this may slow down the work of the Committee, the resulting agreements will have the full support of all states.

The United Nations Environment Programme

The United Nations Environment Programme (UNEP)[27] was established following the 1972 United Nations Conference on the Human Environment in Stockholm, Sweden. Its headquarters are in Nairobi, Kenya. UNEP's Governing Council reports to the General Assembly through the Economic and Social Council (ECOSOC). A number of the major global environmental treaties have been negotiated under its auspices, including the Vienna Convention for the Protection of the Ozone Layer and the Montreal Protocol on Substances that Deplete the Ozone Layer, the Basel Convention on the Control of Transboundary Movements of Hazardous Wastes and Their Disposal, and the Convention on Biological Diversity.

UNEP serves as the secretariat for a number of environmental agreements and has also been active in the development of nonbinding instruments such as the London Guidelines for the Exchange of Information on Chemicals in International Trade. Through its regional offices for Asia and the Pacific, Europe, Latin America and the Caribbean, and West Asia, UNEP also provides, at the request of states, legal and technical assistance to enhance their environmental legislation and institutions, including those involved in implementing international environmental conventions. There have been proposals for replacing UNEP or linking it to a world environment organization, which would be institutionally independent and better-funded than UNEP. One of the tasks generally proposed for such an organization would be that of initiating and preparing new treaties.[28]

The UNEP, the United Nations Development Programme, and the World Bank were partners in establishing the Global Environment Facility (GEF) in 1991. Originally part of the World Bank, the GEF is now a separate institution. It plays an important role in helping with the financial implementation of global environmental treaties, particularly on the part of developing countries and those with economies in transition. Treaties in relation to which it plays a key role include the Convention on Biological Diversity, the United Nations Framework Convention on Climate Change, the Stockholm Convention on Persistent Organic Pollutants, and the UN Convention to Combat Desertification.

The Conference on Disarmament

The Conference on Disarmament (CD) was established by the UN General Assembly's first Special Session on Disarmament in 1978 as a forum for the negotiation of multilateral disarmament treaties. It is the successor to other Geneva-based negotiating fora: the Ten-Nation Committee on Disarmament

(1960), the Eighteen-Nation Committee on Disarmament (1962–1968), and the Conference of the Committee on Disarmament (1969–1978). The Conference on Disarmament has a special relationship with the United Nations. It adopts its own rules of procedure by which it conducts its work by consensus and decides its own agenda. It does, however, take into account the recommendations made by the General Assembly, and it reports to the General Assembly annually or more frequently. Treaties negotiated by the CD and its predecessors include the Treaty on the Non-Proliferation of Nuclear Weapons (NPT); the Convention on the Prohibition of Military or Any Other Hostile Use of Environmental Modification Techniques; the Convention on the Prohibition of the Development, Production, and Stockpiling of Bacteriological (Biological) and Toxin Weapons and on their Destruction; the Convention on the Prohibition of the Development, Production, Stockpiling, and Use of Chemical Weapons and on Their Destruction; and the Comprehensive Nuclear Test-Ban Treaty. In the years following its 1996 completion of the Comprehensive Nuclear Test-Ban Treaty, the CD was unable to agree on which issues to negotiate. With the conclusion of the Ottawa Landmines Convention outside of the Conference on Disarmament, commentators warned of a loss of status if disarmament negotiations shifted elsewhere.[29] A breakthrough to the twelve-year deadlock came in 2009 with agreement to establish four working groups. These would work toward a verifiable treaty banning the production of fissile material for use in nuclear weapons, nuclear disarmament, the prevention of an arms race in outer space, and assurances that non-nuclear weapon states will not be attacked with nuclear weapons.

■ Economic and Social Council

The UN Economic and Social Council (ECOSOC)[30] was established by Chapter X of the UN Charter as the principal organ to coordinate the economic and social work of the United Nations and its specialized agencies and institutions. ECOSOC does, however, work "under the authority" of the General Assembly (article 60), and, in practice, its status hardly differs from that of the subsidiary and special organs created by the General Assembly under article 22.[31] ECOSOC makes recommendations on human rights, convenes international human rights conferences, and prepares draft conventions for submission to the General Assembly on matters falling within its competence. Article 68 of the Charter provides that ECOSOC may create commissions as required; much of the work of ECOSOC is carried out in one of its subsidiary and related bodies.

Several of the multilateral treaties initiated by ECOSOC provide for the establishment of committees to receive reports from states on the implementation of the treaty in question and, in some, to deal with individual petitions or communications. The principal committees are shown in Figure 3.2. These committees have played a significant part in the ongoing development and implementation of international human rights law.

The Human Rights Council

The United Nations Human Rights Council (HRC)[32] was established in 2006 to replace the UN Commission on Human Rights. The Commission on Human Rights had been set up by ECOSOC in 1946 as the principal UN body concerned with the promotion and protection of human rights. The Commission on Human Rights was responsible for submitting proposals, recommendations, and investigative reports on human rights issues through ECOSOC to the General Assembly. It undertook the initial drafting of the Universal Declaration of Human Rights in 1947–1948 and drafted the International Covenant on Civil and Political Rights and the International Covenant on Economic, Social, and Cultural Rights as well as the Convention on the Elimination of Racial Discrimination, and the Convention on the Rights of the Child. From the 1970s on, the Commission on Human

Figure 3.2 The Principal UN Human Rights Treaty–Monitoring Bodies

Monitoring Body	International Human Rights Instrument
Committee on the Elimination of Racial Discrimination	International Convention on the Elimination of All Forms of Racial Discrimination (CERD)
Committee on Economic, Social, and Cultural Rights	International Covenant on Economic, Social, and Cultural Rights (ICESCR)
Human Rights Committee	International Covenant on Civil and Political Rights (ICCPR)
Committee on the Elimination of Discrimination Against Women	Convention on the Elimination of All Forms of Discrimination Against Women (CEDAW)
Committee Against Torture	Convention Against Torture and Other Cruel, Inhuman, or Degrading Treatment or Punishment (CAT)
Committee on the Rights of the Child	Convention on the Rights of the Child (CROC)
Committee on the Protection of the Rights of all Migrant Workers and Members of Their Families	International Convention on the Protection of the Rights of All Migrant Workers and Members of Their Families
Committee on the Rights of Persons with Disabilities	Convention on the Rights of Persons with Disabilities

Rights took an active role in collecting information regarding violations of human rights.[33] In 1993 the Office of the UN High Commissioner for Human Rights was created to supervise the implementation of all human rights.[34]

The Commission on Human Rights was replaced in large measure because of dissatisfaction that states with extensive histories of human rights abuses had been able to gain membership and play prominent roles in the commission, presumably with the intention of deflecting attention from their own records. Structural innovations in the Human Rights Council include that members are elected by secret ballot in the General Assembly rather than by ECOSOC and that they can be removed from the HRC by a two-thirds majority vote if their state commits "gross and systematic violations of human rights." The HRC meets more often than did the commission, and the much-criticized selective review has been replaced by a new universal periodic review mechanism, by which all states are to be subject to regular review. The council has a complaint procedure to address consistent patterns of gross and reliably attested violations of all human rights and fundamental freedoms occurring in any part of the world. The Human Rights Council receives advice from an eighteen-member Advisory Committee, intended to function as a think-tank for the HRC,[35] and has established a five-member subsidiary Expert Mechanism on the Rights of Indigenous Peoples.[36] Although the HRC is widely considered an improvement on the commission, politics may still enter its deliberations to a greater extent than is desirable for furthering the cause of human rights. Dissatisfied with the "reforms," the United States in 2006 voted against the creation of the Human Rights Council, but in 2009 under the Obama administration it stood for election to the council.[37]

Commission on the Status of Women

The Commission on the Status of Women[38] was established by ECOSOC in 1946 as a subcommission but by ECOSOC Resolution 11(II) of June 21, 1946, was changed into an independent commission. This commission has undertaken the preparatory work for a number of treaties on women's rights. Early efforts included the 1953 Convention on the Political Rights of Women[39] and the 1957 Convention on the Nationality of Married Women. In 1975 the General Assembly called on the commission to prepare a draft for the Convention on the Elimination of All Forms of Discrimination Against Women (CEDAW). The commission began with fifteen members but now consists of forty-five members elected by ECOSOC for four years.

Commission on Sustainable Development

The Commission on Sustainable Development[40] was created in December 1992 as a functional commission of the ECOSOC. Its role is to monitor and report on the implementation of Agenda 21 and the Rio Declaration on Environment and Development, products of the 1992 Earth Summit, as well as on the subsequent Johannesburg Plan of Implementation.

UN Permanent Forum on Indigenous Issues

The UN Permanent Forum on Indigenous Issues[41] was created by ECOSOC in 2000 with a mandate to discuss indigenous issues relating to economic and social development, culture, the environment, education, health, and human rights. The Permanent Forum is made up of sixteen independent experts functioning in their personal capacity for three-year terms. Article 42 of the UN Declaration on the Rights of Indigenous Persons provides that the Permanent Forum shall promote respect for and full application of the provisions of the Declaration and follow up its effectiveness.

The International Court of Justice

The International Court of Justice (ICJ), one of the principal organs of the UN, plays three important roles in the system of international law. First, and perhaps most obviously, it makes decisions between disputing parties on the basis of the rules, principles, and concepts of international law. Article 2(3) of the UN Charter imposes a basic obligation on states to settle their disputes by peaceful means. There is a range of ways by which states can do so; a judicial decision by the International Court is the most formal. The International Court of Justice also offers advisory opinions—that is, clarifying specific points of law. And third, the ICJ contributes to the ongoing creation and clarification of the rules, principles, and concepts of international law. This is an indirect process, because it may relate to a point of law other than that most obviously the subject of a request for an advisory opinion or judgment in a contentious case. Much of the detail regarding customary international law, for example, has been developed by the ICJ (see Figure 3.3).

During the nineteenth century there was no world court, but there was a considerable amount of international arbitration by ad hoc tribunals. Public international arbitration in its modern form dates from the Jay Treaty of 1794. This agreement between Britain and the United States to address the many disputes still existing after Britain's formal acknowledgment of US independence in 1783[42] generated 536 arbitral awards between 1799 and 1804. More than 200 other international arbitral tribunals were established between 1795 and 1914.[43]

The 1899 Convention for the Pacific Settlement of International Disputes established the Permanent Court of Arbitration, which was somewhat modified by the second Hague Conference in 1907. States could designate

Figure 3.3 Customary International Law and the International Court of Justice

Article 38 of the Statute of the International Court of Justice defines custom as "evidence of a general practice accepted as law." Although this definition is provided in the context of the sources of law to be applied by the ICJ, it is widely accepted as a general definition of custom. The definition indicates the two essential elements of custom: state practice, and *opinio juris*. *State practice* is what states do as well as what they do not do. How far from the coast, for example, does a state enforce its customs laws? *Opinio juris* is the "psychological" component of the act: the belief that the state was acting out of due regard for the law on the subject in question. The necessity to customary international law of those two factors was confirmed by the ICJ in its 1996 Advisory Opinion on the Legality of the Threat or Use of Nuclear Weapons.[1]

A definition of "custom" does not, though, go far in helping an international lawyer—or judge—determine whether or not a particular rule of international custom exists. There needs to be more detailed rules and principles regarding the nature and extent of the necessary state practice. A lot of this detail has been provided in judgments of the ICJ. Publicists have also contributed to the ongoing process of its refinement. Bin Cheng, for example, proposed in 1965 that United Nations resolutions on outer space constituted "instant" international customary law, thereby suggesting that only *opinio juris* is essential to the formation of custom.[2] This was a quite extreme view that has not been generally accepted. Let's take some of the other questions that might be asked in determining whether or not a particular rule of customary international law has yet crystallized and see what the ICJ has said as regards each.

How Will We Know *Opinio Juris* When We See It?

In the *North Sea Continental Shelf Cases* of 1969 the ICJ stated:

> Not only must the acts concerned amount to a settled practice, but they must also be such, or be carried out in such a way, as to be evidence of a belief that this practice is rendered obligatory by the existence of a rule of law requiring it. . . . The States concerned must therefore feel that they are conforming to what amounts to a legal obligation. The frequency, or even habitual character of the acts is not in itself enough. There are many international acts, e.g. in the field of ceremonial and protocol, which are performed almost invariably, but which are motivated only by considerations of courtesy, convenience or tradition, and not by any sense of legal duty.[3]

(continues)

Figure 3.3 continued

How Much State Practice Is Required for the Formation of Customary International Law?

It is possible for only two states to create a bilateral custom, but the bulk of customary international law is "general." A rule of general customary law binds all states other than "persistent objectors," even those states that had not participated in the formation of that rule.[4] In its 1950 Asylum judgment, the ICJ said that a customary rule must be "in accordance with constant and uniform usage."[5] The ICJ has stated that general customary international law requires there to have been "extensive" state practice involving those states that are "specially affected":

> Although the passage of only a short period of time is not necessarily, or of itself, a bar to the formation of a new rule of customary international law on the basis of what was originally a purely conventional rule, an indispensable requirement would be that within the period in question, short though it might be, State practice, including that of States whose interests are specially affected, should have been both extensive and virtually uniform in the sense of the provision invoked.[6]

What Degree of Uniformity Must There Be in State Practice?

In its 1986 Nicaragua judgment the Court stated:

> The Court does not consider that, for a rule to be established as customary, the corresponding practice must be in absolutely rigorous conformity with the rule. In order to deduce the existence of customary rules, the Court deems it sufficient that the conduct of States should, in general, be consistent with such rules, and that instances of State conduct inconsistent with a given rule should generally have been treated as breaches of that rule, not as indications of the recognition of a new rule.[7]

With What Implications for Those Not Engaging in the Practice?

By the "persistent objector principle," a state that is aware of a practice with which it does not agree and protests consistently against the emergence of a rule from the very beginning will not be bound by the rule, although the objecting state cannot necessarily prevent the creation of that rule. There have not been many examples of the application of the principle. It is very difficult for a state to establish that it has been a persistent objector. The process by which custom evolves is often clear only in

(continues)

Figure 3.3 continued

retrospect, and a state will tend to deny that a custom has emerged at all rather than to acknowledge the custom but claim to be a persistent objector.[8] There has been considerable debate as to whether it is really possible for a state—particularly a relatively weak one—to remain indefinitely outside of law recognized by the vast majority of states.[9] The ICJ nevertheless appeared to recognize the persistent objector principle in the 1951 *Fisheries* case (*United Kingdom v. Norway*) when it stated that the rule in question "would appear to be inapplicable as against Norway, inasmuch as [Norway] has always opposed any attempt to apply it to the Norwegian coast."[10]

Notes

1. *Legality of the Threat or Use of Nuclear Weapons, Advisory Opinion, I.C.J. Reports* 1996, p. 226, 253, para. 64.

2. Bin Cheng, "United Nations Resolutions on Outer Space: 'Instant' International Customary Law?," *Indian Journal of International Law* 5 (1965): 23–48.

3. *North Sea Continental Shelf, Judgment, I.C.J. Reports 1969*, pp. 3, 45, para. 77.

4. See, generally, M. H. Mendelson, "The Formation of Customary International Law," *Recueil des Courses 1998* (The Hague: Martinus Nijhoff, 1999), pp. 214ff.

5. *Asylum, Judgment, I.C.J. Reports* 1950, pp. 266, 276.

6. *North Sea Continental Shelf, Judgment, I.C.J. Reports* 1969, pp. 3, 43, para. 74.

7. *Military and Paramilitary Activities in and Against Nicaragua (Nicaragua v. United States of America), Merits, Judgment, I.C.J. Reports* 1986, pp. 14, 98, para. 186.

8. Maurizio Ragazzi, *The Concept of International Obligations Erga Omnes* (Oxford: Clarendon, 1997), p. 65.

9. See, inter alia, Jonathan Charney, "The Persistent Objector Rule and the Development of Customary International Law," *British Yearbook of International Law* 56 (1985): 1–24; T. L. Stein, "The Approach of the Different Drummer: The Principle of the Persistent Objector in International Law," *Harvard International Law Journal* 26 (1985) 457–482; and Stephen J. Toope, "Powerful but Unpersuasive? The Role of the United States of America in the Evolution of Customary International Law," in M. Byers and G. Nolte, eds., *United States Hegemony and the Foundations of International Law* (Cambridge: Cambridge University Press, 2003), 287–316.

10. *Fisheries, Judgment, I.C.J. Reports 1951*, pp. 116, 131.

specific arbitrators to sit on ad hoc tribunals that would hear cases voluntarily submitted and give legally binding awards.[44] The Permanent Court of Arbitration still exists and has become more active over the past two decades.[45] Hopes that arbitration would become the normal way of dealing with interstate disputes died with World War I and were largely replaced by hopes for international judicial proceedings. The Permanent Court of International Justice (PCIJ) was established in 1922 based on article 14 of the Covenant of the League of Nations. Although the PCIJ was used quite frequently in the 1920s and operated until 1940, it was, of course, unable to prevent World War II and was dissolved in April 1946 when the ICJ was established to replace it.

Contentious Cases

The International Court of Justice is the prime judicial body in the UN system, although it does not have the power to review decisions of the Security Council in the same way that the highest court is, in some countries, vested with the review or appellate jurisdiction. The ICJ is best known for its work to settle disputes between states (see Figure 3.4). The Court only has jurisdiction over a case if the states involved have given their consent to the jurisdiction of the Court, although this can be a more complex proviso than it might seem at first glance.

Procedure in contentious cases begins with the institution of proceedings and appointment of agents, then moves to written proceedings, followed by oral proceedings, deliberations, and judgment. If there is no judge of the nationality of a party, that party may choose a person to sit as a judge ad hoc for that case. The written proceedings involve the parties filing pleadings—usually a memorial and a countermemorial—within the time-limits fixed by the Court. If the Court thinks it appropriate, there may also be a reply and a rejoinder. A state making an application to have a case heard by the ICJ may request that the Court issue *provisional measures* to protect the interests of the parties pending judgment on the merits (see Figure 3.5). A request for provisional measures is treated by the Court as a matter of urgency, and the Court's decision is given as an order of the Court. Article 41 of the statute refers to the Court as having the power to "indicate" provisional measures. Until 2001 there was some debate as to whether this meant that it was compulsory to comply with provisional measures. In its LaGrand judgment of June 27, 2001, the Court clarified that "orders on provisional measures . . . have binding effect."[46]

Preliminary objections must be filed within the time limit set for the filing of the countermemorial. They may involve a respondent state arguing that the Court does not have jurisdiction to hear the case, or that the case is inadmissible. In seeking to argue against admissibility it may be claimed, for

Figure 3.4 Some Contentious Cases Heard by the ICJ
(by date case was finalized)

1949	Corfu Channel (*UK v. Albania*)
1950	Asylum (Colombia/Peru)
1951	Fisheries (*UK v. Norway*)
1952	Anglo-Iranian Oil Co. (*UK v. Iran*)
1953	Minquiers and Ecrehos (France/UK)
1955	Nottebohm (*Liechtenstein v. Guatemala*)
1956	Antarctica (*UK v. Chile*)
1957	Certain Norwegian Loans (*France v. Norway*)
1960	Right of Passage over Indian Territory (*Portugal v. India*)
1961	Barcelona Traction, Light and Power Company, Limited (*Belgium v. Spain*)
1962	Temple of Preah Vihear (*Cambodia v. Thailand*)
1966	South West Africa (*Ethiopia v. South Africa*)
1969	North Sea Continental Shelf (Federal Republic of Germany/Netherlands)
1974	Nuclear Tests (*New Zealand v. France*)
1978	Aegean Sea Continental Shelf (*Greece v. Turkey*)
1981	United States Diplomatic and Consular Staff in Tehran (*United States of America v. Iran*)
1986	Frontier Dispute (Burkino Faso/Republic of Mali)
1991	Military and Paramilitary Activities in and Against Nicaragua (*Nicaragua v. United States of America*)
1993	Certain Phosphate Lands in Nauru (*Nauru v. Australia*)
1994	Territorial Dispute (Libyan Arab Jamahiriya/Chad)
1995	East Timor (*Portugal v. Australia*)
1995	Maritime Delimitation Between Guinea-Bissau and Senegal (*Guinea-Bissau v. Senegal*)
1998	Vienna Convention on Consular Relations (*Paraguay v. United States of America*)
1998	Fisheries Jurisdiction (*Spain v. Canada*)
1999	Legality of Use of Force (*Yugoslavia v. Spain*)
1999	Legality of Use of Force (*Yugoslavia v. United States of America*)
2000	Aerial Incident of August 10, 1999 (*Pakistan v. India*)
2001	Armed Activities on the Territory of the Congo (*Democratic Republic of the Congo v. Burundi*)
2001	LaGrand (*Germany v. United States of America*)
2002	Arrest Warrant of April 11, 2000 (*Democratic Republic of the Congo v. Belgium*)
2002	Sovereignty over Pulau Ligitan and Pulau Sipadan (Indonesia/Malaysia)
2003	Questions of Interpretation and Application of the 1971 Montreal Convention Arising from the Aerial Incident at Lockerbie (*Libyan Arab Jamahiriya v. United Kingdom*)
2003	Oil Platforms (*Islamic Republic of Iran v. United States of America*)
2004	Avena and Other Mexican Nationals (*Mexico v. United States of America*)
2004	Legality of Use of Force (*Serbia and Montenegro v. Belgium*)
2005	Certain Property (*Liechtenstein v. Germany*)
2007	Application of the Convention on the Prevention and Punishment of the Crime of Genocide (*Bosnia and Herzegovina v. Serbia and Montenegro*)
2008	Sovereignty over Pedra Branca/Pulau Batu Puteh, Middle Rocks and South Ledge (Malaysia/Singapore)

(continues)

Figure 3.4 continued

2008	Certain Questions of Mutual Assistance in Criminal Matters (*Djibouti v. France*)
2009	Request for Interpretation of the Judgment of March 31, 2004, in the Case Concerning Avena and Other Mexican Nationals (*Mexico v. United States of America*)

Figure 3.5 Examples of Cases in Which the ICJ Has Indicated Provisional Measures (by year of the order)

1979	United States Diplomatic and Consular Staff in Tehran (*United States of America v. Iran*)
1984	Military and Paramilitary Activities in and Against Nicaragua (*Nicaragua v. United States of America*)
1986	Frontier Dispute (Burkina Faso/Republic of Mali)
1996	Land and Maritime Boundary Between Cameroon and Nigeria (*Cameroon v. Nigeria*)
2003	Avena and Other Mexican Nationals (*Mexico v. United States of America*)
2008	Application of the International Convention on the Elimination of All Forms of Racial Discrimination (*Georgia v. Russian Federation*)

example, that essential provisions of the ICJ Statute have not been complied with or that the dispute no longer exists. Where preliminary objections are raised it is usual for the Court to suspend the proceedings on the merits. The opposing party may make a written submission, followed by oral proceedings. The Court will provide a judgment on the preliminary objections, or, if they are found not to be of an exclusively preliminary character, the preliminary objections may be considered at the same time as the merits. This was done, for example, in the East Timor *(Portugal v. Australia)* case. A third-party state, if it considers that it has a legal interest that may be affected by a decision, may request permission to intervene; it is then up to the Court to decide on the request. Intergovernmental organizations may also provide the Court with information relevant to the cases before it and will be asked by the Court to do so if its constituent instrument or "an international convention adopted thereunder" is being examined by the Court.

The ICJ does not operate according to the rule of stare decisis (that it must follow the precedent of previous decisions) but, primarily for the sake of consistency and predictability, the Court takes its past decisions carefully into account in each new judgment it delivers. The judgment of the Court is compulsory for states party to the case in question, and compliance has generally been good, though far from perfect.[47] A judgment has no binding force except for the parties and in respect of that particular case. There is no right of appeal, although article 60 of the statute provides that the Court can provide an interpretation of a judgment at the request of any party. By article 61 of the statute, an application for a revision of a judgment can be made only if the application is based on the "discovery" of a "fact" of a decisive nature that was unknown to the Court and to the party claiming revision when the judgment was given. Ignorance of the fact cannot have been due to negligence, and the application for revision must be made within six months of the discovery of the new fact and within ten years of the judgment. On February 3, 2003, the ICJ found that an application by the Federal Republic of Yugoslavia for revision of the 1996 judgment in the *Genocide* case (Preliminary Objections) was inadmissible because not all of the aforementioned conditions had been met. Proceedings had been instituted by Bosnia and Herzegovina on March 20, 1993, against Yugoslavia (Serbia and Montenegro) concerning a series of alleged violations of the 1948 Genocide Convention. Yugoslavia had unsuccessfully challenged the jurisdiction of the Court and the admissibility of the case and in 2001 had requested a revision of the judgment.

Advisory Opinions

The ICJ is authorized to answer any "legal question" asked it by the General Assembly or the Security Council.[48] The General Assembly may authorize other UN organs and specialized agencies to request advisory opinions "on legal questions arising within the scope of their activities."[49] Those international organizations currently so nominated include ECOSOC, the International Labour Organization (ILO), the World Health Organization, World Bank, International Monetary Fund, International Maritime Organ ization, and International Atomic Energy Agency. The UN Secretary-General does not currently enjoy that power, although there have been suggestions that this be changed as well as that national courts be able to request advisory opinions.[50]

As with contentious cases, written proceedings are usually followed by oral proceedings. The registrar will give notice of the request to all states entitled to appear before the Court. Article 66 of the Statute of the International Court of Justice provides that once the Court has received a request for an advisory opinion, it will give states and international organizations considered likely to be able to provide information on the question at hand an opportunity to submit their views in writing or orally. Time limits are given within which the Court will receive written statements or hear oral statements relating to the question. In the course of presenting its opinion, the Court may make reference to arguments that were put to it in these statements. Advisory opinions are not legally binding on the requesting party but have generally been accepted—at least in a formal sense.

Although the International Court of Justice does not have a strongly developed role as an organ of judicial review—that is, examining whether United Nations bodies have operated within their powers—several advisory opinions have responded to "constitutional" questions pertaining to the operation of the United Nations. One such issue that gave rise to a request for an advisory opinion is that of the financing of UN operations.

1962 Advisory Opinion on UN Expenses

By article 17(2) of the UN Charter, the General Assembly approves the budget of the United Nations and apportions the expenses among UN members. The unwillingness of states to contribute in full and on time has been a perennial issue for the world body. States that have refused to pay have rarely done so because they were unable to, but rather, out of political opposition to the use to which the finances were to be put.[51]

The ICJ's 1962 advisory opinion on UN expenses[52] addressed the financing of UN peacekeeping operations. The General Assembly had decided that the United Nations Emergency Force in the Middle East (UNEF I) and the UN Operations in the Congo (ONUC) constituted expenses of the UN organization and that this money could therefore be apportioned in accordance with the power granted to the General Assembly by article 17(2) of the UN Charter.[53] But France, Eastern Bloc states, and the Soviet Union were not happy with the operations and refused to contribute to their financing.[54] On December 20, 1961, the General Assembly adopted Resolution 1731 (XVI) requesting an advisory opinion on the question of whether such peacekeeping expenses "constitute 'expenses of the Organization' within the meaning of Article 17, paragraph 2, of the Charter of the United Nations."

The opinion of the Court, handed down on July 20, 1962, was that peacekeeping costs should be considered "expenses" of the UN organization to be borne by all member states, as provided for in article 17. The Soviet Union had adopted the position that the financial obligations of the UN member states concerning actions for upholding universal peace and security could be determined only on the basis of agreements between the Security Council and member states.[55] The Charter confers "primary" responsibility for the maintenance of international peace and security on the Security Council. The Court pointed out that primary responsibility is not exclusive responsibility;[56] the Charter is clear that the General Assembly is also to be concerned with international peace and security.[57]

Although by General Assembly Resolution 1854 (XVII) of December 18, 1962, the Assembly accepted the Court's opinion, France and the USSR still refused to pay their contributions. By article 19 of the UN Charter, a member state that is behind in its payments to the equivalent of two years' contributions cannot vote in the General Assembly unless the Assembly is satisfied "that the failure to pay is due to conditions beyond the control of the Member." During the nineteenth session of the General Assembly when there were in fact sixty-two member states in arrears on one or both of the special peacekeeping accounts,[58] the issue was avoided by conducting all business without a vote being taken; decisions were either postponed or taken by acclamation. After that, the General Assembly reverted to its normal procedures, but without applying article 19 to the states in question. It was decided that peacekeeping operations would be paid from voluntary contributions to a special fund, which meant that no member state was in arrears in the payment of its contributions under article 19. The United States, which had been adamant that article 19 be applied, acquiesced but made clear that it "reserved the same option to make exceptions if, in its view, there were strong and compelling reasons to do so."[59]

The question put to the Court for an advisory opinion must be a legal one, but there is likely to be a clear political motive behind it. Because international organizations are made up of states, questions that prompt a request for an advisory opinion are likely to relate to matters of contention among states. Underlying the differences of opinion in regard to the financing of peacekeeping were political differences over the role being played by what were essentially Western peacekeeping operations. The financing of peacekeeping operations has continued to be a problem for the United Nations, with many members not paying in full and on time.[60]

2004 Advisory Opinion on Construction of a Wall in the Occupied Palestinian Territory

In 2002 Israel began constructing a barrier hundreds of kilometers long on Israeli-occupied territories on the West Bank and partly on the Green Line, the armistice lines established between Israel and its neighbors in 1949. Supporters of the wall consider it necessary to protect Israeli civilians from Palestinian suicide bombers, and it would appear to have been successful in that regard. Opponents point out that the route taken by the wall deviates from the Green Line into territory captured by Israel in 1967 and so represents an illegal attempt to annex territory, and that it has had a negative impact on the lives of Palestinians. A UN Security Council resolution to declare the barrier illegal where it deviated from the Green Line was in October 2003 vetoed by the United States.

On December 8, 2003, the UN General Assembly asked the ICJ for an advisory opinion on the following question:

> What are the legal consequences arising from the construction of the wall being built by Israel, the occupying Power, in the Occupied Palestinian

Territory, including in and around East Jerusalem, as described in the report of the Secretary-General, considering the rules and principles of international law, including the Fourth Geneva Convention of 1949, and relevant Security Council and General Assembly resolutions?[61]

The Court is not required to answer every request for an advisory opinion, and the US government and many commentators took the view that the Court should decline this request rather than allow itself to be used as a back-door route to deciding a contentious case to which the state in question would not have given its consent. [62] The Court does not reject an advisory opinion because the legal question asked is closely surrounded by politics.

The Court elected to proceed, and in its opinion explored questions of international humanitarian law, human rights law, self-determination, and the law of the use of force. The Court found by 14–1 that the construction of the wall was contrary to international law and that Israel was under an obligation to cease and reverse its construction of the wall in the Occupied Palestinian Territory. Israel was under an obligation to make reparation for all damage caused by the construction of the wall in the Occupied Palestinian Territory, and other states were to take steps to avoid supporting continued construction of the wall.

This opinion highlights the fact that the difference between contentious proceedings and advisory opinions may not in practice be very great. In this situation, the matter could not have been brought as a contentious case most basically because Palestine is not a state. Advisory cases offer greater opportunity for participation by a number of states as well as intergovernmental organizations and "nascent State entities" such as Palestine.[63]

■ Specialized Agencies and Other Autonomous Organizations in the UN System

The International Labour Organization

The International Labour Organization (ILO)[64] was founded in 1919 and became the first specialized agency of the UN in 1946. It formulates international labor standards in the form of recommendations or guidelines for national action, and conventions, which are open to ratification as treaties; it was the first permanent organization to draft treaties on a regular basis.[65] The ILO has adopted more than 180 conventions and 190 recommendations, of which eight conventions are considered fundamental to the rights of human beings at work.[66] The ILO has a tripartite structure unique in the

UN system, by which workers and employers participate as equal partners with governments in the work of its governing organs. A system of supervision provides for regular reporting on measures taken to give effect to the provisions of an instrument. There is a complaint procedure by which a ratifying member state, an International Labour Conference delegate, or the governing body can bring a complaint against another member state believed to be not satisfactorily implementing an ILO convention it has ratified.

The International Maritime Organization

The International Maritime Organization (IMO)[67] is a specialized agency of the UN. It was founded by the 1948 Convention of the Intergovernmental Maritime Consultative Organization (IMCO). This treaty did not enter into force until 1958, and the IMCO met for the first time in 1959. The name was changed to the International Maritime Organization in 1982. By article 3 of the 1948 convention, the IMO was "to provide for the drafting of conventions, agreements, or other suitable instruments, and to recommend these to governments and to intergovernmental organizations, and to convene such conferences as may be necessary." The IMO has been responsible for a number of important treaties relating to maritime safety, marine environmental protection, and maritime security. These include the International Convention for the Safety of Life at Sea (SOLAS) in 1974,[68] the International Convention for the Prevention of Pollution from Ships, as Modified by the Protocol of 1978 Relating Thereto (MARPOL 73/78), and the Hong Kong International Convention for the Safe and Environmentally Sound Recycling of Ships in 2009.[69]

The International Atomic Energy Agency

The International Atomic Energy Agency (IAEA)[70] is an autonomous agency that plays an essential role in the implementation of several disarmament and nonproliferation treaties, including the NPT. The IAEA was established in 1957[71] to "accelerate and enlarge the contribution of atomic energy to peace, health, and prosperity throughout the world" while ensuring, as far as it is able, that assistance provided by the IAEA, at its request or under its supervision or control would not be used in such a way as to further any military purpose. In 1961 the IAEA established an international safeguards system to ensure that material was not diverted from peaceful uses to build nuclear weapons or nuclear explosive devices. Under article 3 of the NPT, each non-nuclear-weapon state party to the treaty undertakes to accept safeguards, as set forth in an agreement to be negotiated with the IAEA, to verify the fulfillment of obligations assumed under the treaty and to prevent diversion of nuclear energy from peaceful uses to nuclear weapons or other nuclear explosive devices.

■ The UN and Other IGOs

The United Nations is integrally related to the contemporary global system of international law to an extent not true of any other IGO. It is in the ICJ Statute, annexed to the UN Charter, that we find the most widely accepted statement of the sources of international law; and the UN Charter contains rules, principles, and concepts fundamental to the contemporary system of international law including the sovereign equality of states and the peaceful settlement of disputes. Indeed, the UN Charter plays a role akin to the constitution of the international community.[72] Many treaties, on a range of subject matter, have come about via the work of the United Nations, and UN bodies play a key role in monitoring the implementation of many of those treaties. The International Court of Justice, the most important of the international courts and tribunals, is a UN organ.

Although this chapter has focused on the UN as the IGO most important to the system of international law, virtually all IGOs have been founded by a multilateral treaty. We will consider a number of those other IGOs in the context of treaty regimes.

■ Notes

1. Exceptions include the Inter-American Defense Board and the International Wool Study Group. Henry G. Schermers and Niels M. Blokker, *International Institutional Law: Unity Within Diversity,* 3rd rev. ed. (The Hague: Martinus Nijhoff, 1995), p. 23.

2. These were Argentina, Australia, Belarus, Belgium, Bolivia, Brazil, Canada, Chile, China, Colombia, Costa Rica, Cuba, Denmark, Dominican Republic, Ecuador, Egypt, El Salvador, Ethiopia, France, Greece, Guatemala, Haiti, Honduras, India, Iran, Iraq, Lebanon, Liberia, Luxembourg, Mexico, Netherlands, New Zealand, Nicaragua, Norway, Panama, Peru, Philippines, Poland, Russian Federation, Saudi Arabia, South Africa, Syria, Turkey, Ukraine, United Kingdom, United States, Uruguay, Venezuela, and Yugoslavia. Lawrence Ziring, Robert Riggs, and Jack Plano, *The United Nations: International Organization and World Politics,* 3rd ed. (Fort Worth, TX: Harcourt College Publishers, 2000), p. 68.

3. See discussion in Frederic L. Kirgis Jr., "The Security Council's First Fifty Years," *American Journal of International Law* 89 (1995): 527–532.

4. Although it has assisted in the enforcement of decisions under authority derived from other sources. Karin Oellers-Frahm, "Article 94 UN Charter," in Andreas Zimmermann, C. Tomuschat, and Karin Oellers-Frahm, eds., *The Statute of the International Court of Justice: A Commentary* (Oxford: Oxford University Press, 2006), pp. 174–175.

5. Charter of the United Nations, article 37(1).

6. See, inter alia, Lori Buck, et al., "Sanctions as a Gendered Instrument of Statecraft: The Case of Iraq," *Review of International Studies* 24 (1998): 69–84; Paul Conlon, *United Nations Sanctions Management: A Case Study of the Iraq Sanctions Committee, 1990–1994* (New York: Transnational, 2000); Christopher C. Joyner, "Collective Sanctions as Peaceful Coercion: Lessons from the United Nations Experience," *Australian Yearbook of International Law* 16 (1995): 241–270;

Peggy Kozal, "Is the Continued Use of Sanctions as Implemented Against Iraq a Violation of International Human Rights?" *Denver Journal of International Law and Policy* 28, no. 4 (Fall 2000): 383–400; John Mueller and Karl Muller, "Sanctions of Mass Destruction," *Foreign Affairs* 78 (May/June 1999): 43–53; Chantal de Jonge Oudraat, "Making Economic Sanctions Work," *Survival* 42, no. 3 (2000): 105–127; and Thomas G. Weiss, David Cortright, George A. Lopez, and Larry Minear, *Political Gain and Civilian Pain: Humanitarian Impacts of Economic Sanctions* (Lanham, MD: Rowman and Littlefield, 1997).

7. David Cortright and George A. Lopez, eds., *The Sanctions Decade: Assessing UN Strategies in the 1990s* (Boulder, CO: Lynne Rienner, 2000).

8. See Jeremy Matam Farrall, *United Nations Sanctions and the Rule of Law* (Cambridge: Cambridge University Press, 2007).

9. Security Council Resolution 827 para. 4 and Security Council Resolution 955, para. 2.

10. Paul C. Szasz, "The Security Council Starts Legislating," *AJIL* 96, no. 4 (2002): 901–905, esp. 901.

11. See "Introductory Note to United Nations Security Council: Piracy and Armed Robbery at Sea—Resolutions 1816, 1846 & 1851" for background to, and explanation of, the resolutions. 48 *International Legal Materials (ILM)* 129 (2009). See also Tullio Treves, "Piracy, Law of the Sea, and Use of Force: Developments off the Coast of Somalia," *European Journal of International Law* 20 (2009): 399–414.

12. Edward C. Luck, *UN Security Council. Practice and Promise* (London: Routledge, 2006), p. 103.

13. One of the few who believe that there are any such limits is Erika de Wet, *The Chapter VII Powers of the United Nations Security Council* (Oxford: Hart, 2004), p. 176.

14. Sir Michael Wood, "The UN Security Council and International Law," lecture delivered at Hersch Lauterpacht Memorial Lectures, Cambridge, UK, November 8, 2006, available at www.lcil.cam.ac.uk.

15. See www.un.org/ga/.

16. For consideration of the question as to whether unanimously adopted resolutions of the General Assembly may create "instant" customary international law, see Bin Cheng, "United Nations Resolutions on Outer Space: 'Instant' International Customary Law?" *Indian Journal of International Law* 5 (1965): 23–48. See also R. A. Falk, "On the Quasi-legislative Competence of the General Assembly," *American Journal of International Law* 60 (1966): 782–791; N. G. Onuf, "Professor Falk on the Quasi-legislative Competence of the General Assembly," *American Journal of International Law* 64 (1970): 349–355; and Blaine Sloan, *UN General Assembly Resolutions in Our Changing World* (Ardsley-on-Hudson, NY: Transnational, 1991).

17. General Assembly Resolution 2625 (XXV).

18. Henry G. Schermers and Niels M. Blokker, *International Institutional Law: Unity Within Diversity*, 3rd rev. ed. (The Hague: Martinus Nijhoff, 1995), pp. 772–773. See also O. Y. Asamoah, *The Legal Significance of the Declarations of the General Assembly of the United Nations* (The Hague: Martinus Nijhoff, 1966).

19. See Mohammed Ahsen Chaudhri, "Origin, Composition, and Functions of the Sixth Committee," *Revue Egyptienne de droit international* 29 (1973): 211–232.

20. See www.un.org/law/ilc/.

21. General Assembly Resolution 174 (II), November 21, 1947.

22. Statute of the International Law Commission, article 15.

23. Ibid.

24. See http://www.oosa.unvienna.org/oosa/COPUOS.

25. See, inter alia, N. Jasentuliyana, "Treaty Law and Outer Space: Can the United Nations Play an Effective Role?" *Annals of Air and Space Law* 11 (1986): 219–226; and N. Hosenball, "The United Nations Committee on the Peaceful Uses of Outer Space: Past Accomplishments and Future Challenges," *Journal of Space Law* 7 (1979): 95–113.

26. Ralph G. Steinhardt, "Outer Space," in Christopher C. Joyner, ed., *The United Nations and International Law* (Washington, DC: ASIL; Cambridge: CUP, 1997), pp. 336–361 and 339–340.

27. See http://www.unep.org.

28. Frank Biermann, "The Case for a World Environment Organization," *Environment* 42, no. 9 (2000): 23–31. For a dissenting opinion on the establishment of a world environment organization, see the commentary on p. 44.

29. See, inter alia, Wade Boese, "CD Negotiating Session Concludes Without Progress," *Arms Control Today,* October 2001, available at http://www.armscontrol.org.

30. See www.un.org/ecosoc.

31. Christian Tomuschat, "General Assembly," in Christiane Philipp and Rüdiger Wolfrum, eds., *United Nations: Law, Policies, and Practice,* vol. 1 (Dordrecht, the Netherlands: Martinus Nijhoff, 1995), pp. 548–557, esp. p. 555.

32. See www2.ohchr.org/english/bodies/hrcouncil/.

33. Schermers and Blokker, *International Institutional Law,* p. 876.

34. See, inter alia, Bhaswati Mukherjee, "United Nations High Commissioner for Human Rights: Challenges and Opportunities," in Gudmundur Alfredsson, Jonas Grimheden, Bertram G. Ramcharan, and Alfred de Zayas, eds., *International Human Rights Monitoring Mechanisms: Essays in Honour of Jakob Th. Möller* (The Hague: Martinus Nijhoff, 2001), pp. 403–414.

35. See http://www2.ohchr.org.

36. Ibid.

37. John R. Crook, ed., "Contemporary Practice of the United States Relating to International Law," *American Journal of International Law* 103 (2009): 325–367, esp. 357.

38. See http://www.un.org/womenwatch.

39. 193 United Nations Treaty Series (UNTS) 2613.

40. See http://www.un.org.

41. See http://www.unhchr.ch/indigenous.

42. Mark Janis, "The International Court," in Mark W. Janis, ed., *International Courts for the Twenty-First Century* (The Hague: Kluwer, 1992), p. 14.

43. Ibid.

44. Ibid.

45. See http://www.pca-cpa.org.

46. LaGrand *(Germany v. United States of America),* June 27, 2001, at para. 109.

47. Constanze Schulte, *Compliance with Decisions of the International Court of Justice* (New York: Oxford University Press, 2004).

48. Charter of the United Nations, article 96(1).

49. Ibid., article 96(2).

50. Taslim O. Elias, "How the International Court of Justice Deals with Requests for Advisory Opinions," in Jerzy Makarczyk, ed., *Essays in International Law in Honour of Judge Manfred Lachs* (The Hague: Martinus Nijhoff, 1984), p. 357, fn 4. See also Hersch Lauterpacht, "Decisions of Municipal Courts as a Source of International Law," *British Yearbook of International Law* 10 (1929): 65–95; and Stephen M. Schwebel, "Preliminary Rulings by the International Court of Justice at the Instance of National Courts,' *Virginia Journal of International Law* 28 (1988): 495–496.

51. See Robert F. Gorman, *Great Debates at the United Nations: An Encyclopedia of Fifty Key Issues, 1945–2000* (Westport, CT: Greenwood, 2001), pp. 162–168.

52. *Certain Expenses of the United Nations (Article 17, Paragraph 2, of the Charter), Advisory Opinion, ICJ Reports 1962*, p. 151.

53. Ibid., p. 178.

54. For a detailed account of the politics behind the Certain Expenses Advisory Opinion, see David Wilkinson, "The Article 17 Crisis: The Dispute over Financing the United Nations," in Lawrence Scheinman and David Wilkinson, *International Law and Political Crisis: An Analytic Casebook* (Boston: Little, Brown, 1968), pp. 211–249; and Stanley Hoffmann, "A World Divided and a World Court Confused: The World Court's Advisory Opinion on UN Financing," in Scheinman and Wilkinson, *International Law and Political Crisis,* pp. 251–273.

55. The views of the USSR were presented to the ICJ in "Memorandum of the USSR Government on the Procedure of Financing the Operations of the United Nations Emergency Force in the Middle East and the United Nations Operations in the Congo," *ICJ Pleadings: Certain Expenses of the United Nations (Article 17, Paragraph 2, of the Charter),* pp. 270–274.

56. *Certain Expenses of the United Nations (Article 17, Paragraph 2, of the Charter), Advisory Opinion, ICJ Reports 1962,* pp. 151, 163.

57. Ibid.

58. Norman J. Padelford, "Financing Peacekeeping: Politics and Crisis," *International Organization* 19 (1963): 444–462, esp. 445.

59. UN General Assembly Official Record, 19th Session, Annexes, Annex No. 21, A/5916/Add.1, pp. 86–87, cited in Marjorie M. Whiteman, *Digest of International Law* 13 (1968): 331–332. See also Wilfried Koschorreck, "Financial Crisis," in Philipp and Wolfrum, *United Nations: Law, Policies and Practice,* pp. 523–531.

60. Andrzej Abraszewski, "Financing of the Peace-keeping Operations of the United Nations," *International Geneva Yearbook* 7 (1993): 79–95, esp. 84–85. On UN financing, see Jose E. Alvarez, "Financial Responsibility," in O. Schachter and C. C. Joyner, eds., *United Nations Legal Order,* vol. 2 (Cambridge: Cambridge University Press, 1995): 1091–1119; M. J. Peterson, *The General Assembly in World Politics* (Boston: Allen and Unwin, 1986), pp. 123–135; Anthony McDermott, *The New Politics of Financing the UN* (New York: St. Martin's, 1999); and Henry G. Schermers and Niels M. Blokker, *International Institutional Law: Unity Within Diversity,* 3rd rev. ed. (The Hague: Martinus Nijhoff, 1995), pp. 598–599.

61. Legal Consequences of the Construction of a Wall in the Occupied Palestinian Territory, Advisory Opinion, *ICJ Reports 2004,* July 9, 2004, para. 1, available at http://www.icj-cij.org.

62. Michla Pomerance, "The ICJ's Advisory Jurisdiction and the Crumbling Wall Between the Political and the Judicial," *American Journal of International Law* 99 (2005): 26–42.

63. Michelle Burgis, "Discourses of Division: Law, Politics, and the ICJ Advisory Opinion on the Legal Consequences of the Construction of a Wall in the Occupied Palestinian Territory,' *Chinese Journal of International Law* 7 (2008): 33–63, esp. 47.

64. See www.ilo.org.

65. Steve Charnovitz, "The International Labour Organization in Its Second Century," *Max Planck Yearbook of United Nations Law* 4 (2000): 147–184, esp. 148. See also Héctor Bartolomei de la Cruz, Geraldo von Potobsky, and Lee Swepston, *The International Labor Organization: The International Standards System and Basic Human Rights* (Boulder, CO: Westview, 1996).

66. These are the Freedom of Association and Protection of the Right to Organize Convention of 1948, the Right to Organize and Collective Bargaining Convention of 1949, the Forced Labour Convention of 1930, the Abolition of Forced Labour Convention of 1957, the Discrimination (Employment and Occupation) Convention of 1958, the Equal Remuneration Convention of 1951, Minimum Age Convention of 1973, and the Worst Forms of Child Labour Convention of 1999.

67. See http://www.imo.org.

68. The first version of SOLAS was adopted in 1914, the second in 1929, the third in 1948, and the fourth in 1960. The 1960 convention was the first major task of the IMO. A completely new version was adopted in 1974, which made it easier to amend the treaty rather than to have to replace it.

69. Texts are available on the IMO website.

70. See http://www.iaea.org.

71. The Statute of the International Atomic Energy Agency was approved on October 23, 1956, and entered into force on July 29, 1957. The text is available at the IAEA website. See B. G. Bechoefer, "Negotiating the Statute of the International Atomic Energy Agency," *International Organization* 13, no. 1 (1959): 38–59; and Lawrence Scheinman, *The International Atomic Energy Agency and World Nuclear Order* (Washington, DC: Resources for the Future, 1987).

72. Cf. Pierre-Marie Dupuy, "The Constitutional Dimension of the Charter of the United Nations Revisited," *Max Planck Yearbook of United Nations Law* 1 (1997): 1–33; B. Fassbender, "The United Nations Charter as Constitution of the International Community," *Columbia Journal of Transnational Law* 36 (1998): 529–619; and R. Macdonald, "The Charter of the United Nations in Constitutional Perspective," *Australian Year Book of International Law* 20 (1999): 205–231.

4

Nonstate Actors
in International Law

STATES AND INTERGOVERNMENTAL ORGANIZATIONS MADE UP OF states may be the dominant actors in international law, but they are not the only actors. In this chapter we consider the role in international law of non-state actors: multinational corporations, public-interest nongovernmental organizations (NGOs), and individuals. Nonstate actors have not been given a very large formal role in making, implementing, and/or enforcing international law, or in making judicial decisions on the basis of international law. In this chapter we will examine the ways in which nonstate actors nevertheless exert considerable influence on the rules, principles, and concepts of international law.[1]

■ Nongovernmental Organizations

Strictly speaking, the acronym NGO encompasses all "nongovernmental organizations," including public-interest organizations—the vast majority of which are not-for-profit organizations—and multinational corporations (MNCs), or multinational enterprises (MNEs) as they are often termed. MNEs wield political power primarily through sheer economic muscle. Examples include large oil companies such as Exxon Mobil and retailer Wal-Mart, which have annual incomes well above the gross domestic product of most states. Examples of public-interest NGOs include humanitarian NGOs such as CARE and Community Aid Abroad; human rights organizations such as Amnesty International; and environmental organizations such as Greenpeace. The International Chamber of Commerce is an NGO, as is the International Olympic Committee. Like intergovernmental organizations, the International Olympic Committee has a general assembly consisting of its members, a more limited governing body, and a permanent secretariat.

63

However, its membership is not made up of representatives of states, or of the national Olympic committees, but of leading personalities from national and international sports.[2]

Just as there are enormous differences among states and among IGOs, so is there a huge variety of public-interest NGOs. Public-interest NGOs differ, for example, in the distribution of their membership, the way they operate, the ratio of paid staff to volunteers, and in whether or not they receive funding from governments. NGOs in the developed North tend to be wealthier and to have greater access to information than NGOs in the less developed South.[3] International NGOs (INGOs) are sometimes distinguished from national NGOs; some believe that the term *NGO* should be reserved exclusively for those with members in at least three countries.[4] Not-for-profit NGOs are sometimes now encompassed under the term *civil society organization*. In recognition of the fundamental differences between MNCs and other types of NGOs and of the widespread usage of *NGO* to refer only to public-interest NGOs, the term *NGO* will be used here to refer only to nonprofit organizations.

Public-interest NGOs can to some extent be perceived as the political counterweight to giant corporations. Although both are generally "single-issue" actors in contrast to states (which must deal with a multitude of issues), the ultimate objectives of each are in contrast. Corporations must necessarily focus on their profit or "bottom-line"; public-interest NGOs work for their perception of the common good. And whereas public-interest NGOs are generally comparatively rich in legitimacy but capital-poor, profit-oriented organizations are generally capital-rich but lack legitimacy.[5] Transnational networking of NGOs has in recent years been greatly facilitated by the Internet; approximately a thousand NGOs worked under the umbrella organization called the International Campaign to Ban Landmines to bring about a multilateral treaty on landmines.

Formal vs. Informal Influence on International Law

There is a considerable discrepancy between the political influence wielded by both multinational enterprises and public-interest NGOs and their formal roles in the system of public international law. We have seen that treaties are negotiated by states and by IGOs, that the rights and obligations specified in multilateral treaties fall overwhelmingly on states, and that the existence or not of a rule of customary international law is determined on the basis of state practice. NGOs and MNCs nevertheless often have a significant indirect influence on multilateral treaty making. Knowledge is a source of power for many NGOs; some environmental NGOs, for example, possess greater scientific, technical, and statistical expertise than many governments. The vigorous opposition of Exxon to scientific evidence of human-induced climate change and to the Kyoto Protocol based on that evidence is likely to have influenced the decision of the US government not to ratify the Kyoto

Protocol; the Republican administration of George W. Bush was elected with the help of US$1.2 million from Exxon Mobil, and key individuals within his administration had formerly worked in the oil industry.[6] NGOs are sometimes accredited as observers at intergovernmental meetings at which treaties are negotiated and monitored. A notable example was the 1992 UN Conference on Environment and Development (UNCED) at which some 1,500 NGOs were formally recognized.[7]

Sometimes the influence of NGOs on treaty making is direct. NGO and corporate interests sometimes fund a delegation to, say, an international environmental conference; they may even write speeches and contribute directly to the formulation of national policy.[8] The International Campaign to Ban Landmines was given a formal seat at the table during the negotiations, and its contribution was recognized in the treaty itself.[9] There may be more than one corporate interest on any specific issue. At the climate change negotiations, oil and gas interests were pitted against the insurance industry.[10]

Corporations sometimes play crucial roles in the implementation of international law, despite their not having an international legal obligation to do so. The World Heritage Committee, for example, has recognized that some states are unable or unwilling to prevent mining and oil and gas companies from engaging in exploitative activities that threaten listed sites and so have sought to engage directly with the companies.[11] Better known is the role of NGOs in helping to implement and monitor compliance with international environmental and human rights law. NGOs channel independent information to the UN human rights committees, promote knowledge and understanding of the committees' work, and monitor the implementation by governments of the recommendations of the treaty bodies.[12] Indeed, the human rights treaties bodies could not operate effectively without NGO participation.[13] Under article 8 of the Convention on Wetlands of International Importance, the International Union for the Conservation of Nature and Natural Resources was given the function of performing the Secretariat's duties until the appointment of another organization or government.[14]

Neither a public-interest NGO nor an MNC can request an advisory opinion of the International Court of Justice or be a party to contentious proceedings before the ICJ. Although the ICJ has permitted an NGO to file an amicus curiae brief in an advisory case,[15] the Court's rules would need to be amended to permit it to accept directly amicus filings from NGOs in contentious cases.[16] A state may nevertheless take up the claim of a corporation that has been created and is regulated by its laws. A state may include an amicus brief prepared by an NGO in its own submission in a contentious case, and NGOs have sometimes worked behind the scenes to help bring about an advisory opinion.

The 1996 Advisory Opinion on the Legality of the Threat of Use of Nuclear Weapons had its origins in the work of a small group of international jurists, who, in March 1987, had written an open letter to the prime ministers of New Zealand and Australia.[17] The document "Case for the World Court" had then been circulated to all UN members having accredited representatives in New Zealand and Australia.[18] The World Court Project, an umbrella grouping of NGOs, was launched in May 1992, sponsored by the International Association of Lawyers Against Nuclear Arms (IALANA), the International Peace Bureau, and the International Physicians for the Prevention of Nuclear War.[19] Intensive lobbying by a network of antinuclear activists and NGOs and support from the Non-Aligned Movement[20] resulted in requests for an advisory opinion being produced by both the World Health Organization and the General Assembly.[21]

Some international courts and tribunals, particularly regional human rights courts, are more open than the ICJ to the involvement of MNCs and NGOs. Those that give legal standing to NGOs to participate directly in proceedings include the European Court of Human Rights, the Inter-American Commission of Human Rights, the African Commission for Human and Peoples' Rights, the African Court, and, to some extent, the European Court of Justice.[22] Indirect participation by NGOs, through the provision of amicus curiae submissions, has expanded rapidly in recent years, particularly to international criminal courts and to panels and the appellate body of the World Trade Organization. NGOs are also officially mentioned in the statutes of the ICC, ICTY, and ICTR as important sources of information on which the prosecutor may draw.[23]

Two NGOs that have had a particular impact on the body of rules, principles, and concepts that constitute international law are the International Commission of Jurists and the International Committee of the Red Cross. We will look at each in turn.

International Commission of Jurists. The International Commission of Jurists[24] is an international NGO whose global goal is to support and advance the international rule of law. The commission achieves its mission through a variety of activities, including the promotion and monitoring of human rights mechanisms and the preparation of amicus curiae and legal opinions to build and strengthen human rights jurisprudence and influence policymakers. The International Commission of Jurists was, for example, influential in ensuring the timely entry into force of the African Charter of Human and Peoples' Rights. Members of the International Commission of Jurists engaged in a series of visits to the heads of state of African countries to help overcome doubts and fears regarding the charter.[25]

International Committee of the Red Cross. The International Committee of the Red Cross (ICRC) has played a major role in the development and implementation of international humanitarian law, having a more direct impact on both than any other NGO. ICRC fact-finding has paved the way for new treaty initiatives in the field of international humanitarian law. At the diplomatic conference at which a treaty text is to be finalized, the ICRC has been granted official access to plenary sessions and working groups as well as permission to speak directly to delegations, to issue official statements at meetings, and to submit draft articles; indeed, it has on occasion functioned as a legal expert and unofficial cohost of conferences.[26] The ICRC concludes agreements with states concerning, for example, the visitation of political detainees or the exchange of prisoners of war. The role of the ICRC in the implementation of that law is explicitly provided for in several of the treaties of international humanitarian law, including the Geneva Conventions.

The ICRC was founded on the initiative of a Genevese merchant, Henri Dunant, who in 1859 witnessed the Battle of Solferino in the Italian War of Unification. He was shocked at the lack of systematic care for the wounded, who were simply left to die on the battlefields, often robbed and murdered by locals. Dunant organized volunteers to care for the wounded and in 1862 published *A Memory of Solferino*.[27] The next year a small group of Genevese established a committee to propagate Dunant's ideal of an impartial corps of civilian volunteers to care for the wounded in wartime; this was the beginning of the International Committee of the Red Cross.[28] The International Red Cross movement consists of three interrelated components: the set of National Red Cross Societies, the League of Red Cross Societies, and the ICRC.

Although the ICRC has been included here among NGOs that have been important to international law, it is unlike any other NGO; aspects of its functioning are more akin to those of an IGO. The ICRC budget is covered mostly by contributions from states, it has signed headquarters agreements with more than fifty states, and ICRC delegates enjoy a status similar to that of officials from IGOs. But the ICRC is definitely not an IGO; it is established under Swiss private law, and no government has control over its composition or activity.[29]

NGOs at the UN

Public-interest NGOs work closely with the United Nations. In the relief and refugee sector, for example, member governments may provide financial support and aid packages, but much of the work on the ground is subcontracted to NGOs.[30] The UN Charter, however, makes only one reference to NGOs. Article 71 provides that ECOSOC may make "suitable arrangements for consultation with non-governmental organizations which are concerned with matters within its competence." Arrangements were made in the late 1940s to bring article 71 into effect, and these have been reviewed in 1950, 1968, and 1996.

There are three categories of NGO status at the United Nations. *General consultative status* is for large international NGOs whose area of work covers most of the issues on the Council's agenda. *Special consultative status* is for NGOs that have special competence in a few fields of the Council's activity. *Inclusion on the roster* is for NGOs whose competence enables them to make occasional and useful contributions to the work of the United Nations and that are available for consultation upon request. NGOs with general status have the right to place items on the provisional agenda of the Council; NGOs of general and special status may submit brief written statements that can be published as UN documents and be circulated to members of the Council or subsidiary bodies.[31] Since 1996, NGOs that are based in a single country—known as national NGOs—have been encouraged to apply for consultative status.[32]

■ The Individual as a Participant in International Law

Even though the state is by far the most important actor in international law, individuals have some measure of what international lawyers refer to as *legal personality;* that is, of being capable of exercising certain rights and being subject to certain duties on their own account.[33] One field of international law in which this has for centuries been the case is that relating to diplomats. The field remained largely part of customary international law for many years, until the 1961 Vienna Convention on Diplomatic Relations provided a "comprehensive formulation of the rules of modern diplomatic law."[34] The oldest established rule of diplomatic law is that the person of a diplomatic agent is inviolable.[35] This was codified in article 29 as having two components. First, the individual is not liable to any form of arrest or detention; and second, the individual is to be treated with respect by the receiving state—the latter is to "take all appropriate steps to prevent any attack on [this individual's] person, freedom, or dignity." Article 31 provides that a diplomatic agent has immunity from the criminal jurisdiction of the receiving state and its civil and administrative jurisdiction. It is intended to ensure that diplomats can play the role accorded to them. But diplomatic staff and other persons enjoying privileges and immunities do have some corresponding obligations toward the receiving state. Article 41 specifies the duty to respect laws and regulations of the receiving state, not to interfere in the internal affairs of the receiving state, to communicate with the government of the receiving state through the ministry of foreign affairs, and not to use the mission premises in any manner incompatible with the functions of the mission.

There is always a danger that diplomatic privileges and immunities may be abused. But the receiving state does have some comeback. By article 32 of the Vienna Convention, the sending state may expressly waive the immunity of a diplomatic agent. It is also open to the receiving state under article 9 at any time to declare a member of the diplomatic staff of a mission persona non grata or that any other member of the staff of the mission is not acceptable. One celebrated case involved the shooting of a London police officer from the Libyan diplomatic mission in 1984. All the occupants of the Libyan People's Bureau were declared persona non grata and ordered to leave the country. [36] Concerned by the high level of illegal parking of diplomatic vehicles and the failure to pay resultant fines, the United Kingdom decided in the mid 1980s that continued failure to respect parking regulations or to pay fines would result in individuals being declared persona non grata. Although the decision of the UK government was without precedent, the number of parking tickets cancelled on grounds of diplomatic immunity fell from 108,845 in 1984 to 2,328 in 1993.[37]

In international law as a whole, it is the fields of international human rights and international humanitarian law that deal most with individuals.[38] The Nuremberg Tribunal established unequivocally that individuals receive obligations under international law and that international law must be enforced against individuals. Article 4 of the 1948 Convention on the Prevention and Punishment of the Crime of Genocide stipulates that "persons committing genocide . . . shall be punished, whether they are constitutionally responsible rulers, public officials, or private individuals." Crimes against humanity and war crimes also incur individual criminal responsibility under international law.

Article 25 of the Rome Statute of the International Criminal Court gives the Court jurisdiction over not only those individuals who have, individually or jointly, committed a crime; but those who have ordered or induced such a crime, who have facilitated or contributed to the commission of a crime or attempted to commit a crime (unless the person gave up the criminal purpose without the crime having been committed); or who have directly and publicly incited others to commit genocide.[39] Well established in international law is the principle of *command responsibility,* by which a superior—whether military or civilian—is criminally responsible for the acts committed by subordinates if he or she knew or had reason to know that the subordinate was about to commit such acts or had done so and the superior failed to take necessary and reasonable measures to prevent such acts or to punish the perpetrators thereof.[40]

Although international human rights law does concern individuals, the obligations of states toward individuals under international human rights law is, strictly speaking, vis-à-vis other parties to the treaty in question, rather than vis-à-vis its citizens. Individuals gain their rights when the states concerned implement the relevant legal instrument through legislation and acts of execution at the national level. A number of human rights instruments provide for individuals to petition human rights monitoring bodies, but this is generally only the case where the state in question has accepted the treaty provision. An exception to this is the Eleventh Protocol to the European Convention on

Human Rights, which entered into force on November 1, 1998, and by which citizens of states that became parties to this convention can automatically take a case to the European Court of Human Rights. Even though several human rights treaties provide for one state to act against another accused of committing human rights violations, in practice states have been very reluctant to do so.

Individuals are in their own right important to the creation of international law because the writings of publicists are a secondary source of international law. The first "comprehensive and systematic" treatise in modern international law is considered to be *De Jure Belli ac Pacis,* written by Hugo Grotius in 1625. Individuals serve on some international bodies, such as the International Law Commission and the Sub-Commission on the Promotion and Protection of Human Rights, in their own private capacity on the basis of their individual expertise rather than as representatives of states. Judges on the International Court of Justice are "independent"; article 2 of the ICJ Statute provides that the judges be elected "regardless of their nationality from among persons of high moral character, who possess the qualifications required in their respective countries for appointment to the highest judicial offices, or are jurisconsults of recognized competence in international law."

Individuals are not able to be a party to a case before the ICJ or to ask an advisory opinion of the Court, but a state can bring a claim on behalf of one of its nationals. The Ambatielos case of 1953,[41] for example, involved the government of Greece taking up the claim of one of its nationals against the UK government. The involvement of individuals in international adjudication has more typically taken the form of special arbitration schemes to deal with claims from private parties against a specific country arising out of a specific event.[42] The US-Iran Claims Tribunal was established following the Tehran hostage crisis and the restructuring of the Iranian economy. Although nationals of either party were entitled to access the tribunal, there is no doubt that the tribunal was primarily established for the settlement of the claims of US nationals against Iran.[43]

It is worth remembering that even though states retain a much more important formal role in the creation and operation of international law than individuals, they are inanimate entities; it is in each case individuals of the decisionmaking elite who make decisions on behalf of the state.

■ The Significance of a State-Centric System of International Law in a Globalized World

Political scientists have for many decades debated whether the state is "withering away" at the hands of other international actors, in particular the multinational corporation. Despite the apparent increase in political, and legal, importance of other international actors vis-à-vis states, the formal workings of the system of international law retains a preeminent role for states. As we have seen, states play a leading role as the primary creators and subjects of international law. Other actors—such as the media—may often be very influential in world politics without having a legal personality in international law. It is important to note, however, that while most writing on NGOs asserts their increasing political significance,[44] some writers have pointed out that the political influence of public-interest NGOs is often assumed rather than established by empirical evidence.[45]

The discrepancy between the real world influence of some nonstate actors and the formal supremacy of states is a challenge to the effectiveness of international law. Most wars, for example, are now civil wars rather than interstate wars. How, then, can state-based international humanitarian law that addresses human rights during times of conflict hope to regulate effectively the actions of players who are in many cases at war with the state?[46] A comparable challenge is faced by nonstate actors who are seeking to influence the evolution of international law. An NGO—or even the UN Secretary-General, who wants to ask an advisory opinion of the ICJ, must at this stage work indirectly, through an IGO. Although often required to wield their influence through indirect mechanisms, we have seen that the influence of NGOs on international law may be considerable. This is prompting increasing debate on the subject of NGO accountability.[47]

Perhaps the most obvious implication of the dominant formal role of states in international law is that all issues to be addressed by international law have to be transformed into issues between states, whether or not states are the key political player in the issue area under consideration. International law has thus responded to the acts of nonstate terrorist groups in terms of issues of the legality of forceful responses by states to terrorist acts and the responsibility of a state to arrest and prosecute or extradite those who commit terrorist acts. Similarly, in the case of marine pollution, corporations are the main polluters of the world's oceans, but the current regulatory regime, negotiated by states, relies primarily on states taking measures to reduce and monitor oil pollution.[48] The use of private military and security companies in armed conflict and occupation has raised issues regarding the degree to which the state that has engaged the services of those companies is responsible for the conduct of the contractors.[49]

In Chapter 5 we will explore in more detail how international law functions to address issues that arise in relationships among states and, to a lesser extent, the relationships among states and other international actors in world politics.

■ Notes

1. See, inter alia, Andrea Bianchi, ed., *Non-State Actors and International Law* (Aldershot, UK: Ashgate, 2009); Pierre-Marie Dupuy and Luisa Vierucci, eds., *NGOs in International Law: Efficiency in Flexibility?* (Cheltenham, UK: Edward

Elgar, 2008); and Stephen Tully, *Corporations and International Lawmaking* (Leiden, the Netherlands: Martinus Nijhoff, 2007).

2. Christoph Vedder, "The International Olympic Committee: An Advanced Non-Governmental Organization and the International Law," *German Yearbook of International Law* 27 (1984): 233–258.

3. A. Doherty, "The Role of Nongovernmental Organizations in UNCED," in B. I. Spector, G. Sjostedt, and I.W. Zartman, eds., *Negotiating International Regimes: Lessons Learned from the United Nations Conference on Environment and Development (UNCED)* (London: Graham and Trotman, 1994), pp. 199–218, esp. 211–212.

4. Martin A. Olz, "Non-Governmental Organizations in Regional Human Rights Systems," *Columbia Human Rights Law Review* 28 (1997): 307–374, esp. 314, fn 16.

5. Russel Lawrence Barsh and Nadia Khattak, "Non-Governmental Organizations in Global Governance: Great Expectations, Inconclusive Results," in G. Alfredsson and M. Stavropoulou, eds., *Justice Pending: Indigenous Peoples and Other Good Causes* (The Hague: Martinus Nijhoff, 2002), pp. 15–31, esp. 30.

6. Julian Borger and Terry Macalister, "The Good Oil for Exxon Is Having a Buddy in the White House," *Sydney Morning Herald,* April 18, 2001, p. 10.

7. Dianne Otto, "Nongovernmental Organizations in the United Nations System: The Emerging Role of International Civil Society," *Human Rights Quarterly* 18 (1996): 107–141, esp. 118.

8. Comments of Prof. Philippe Sands, in panel session on "The Challenge of Non-State Actors," chaired by Anne-Marie Slaughter, 92 *American Society of International Law Procedures* 29 (1998).

9. International Campaign to Ban Landmines, "Ban History," http://www.icbl.org.

10. Comments of Prof. Philippe Sands, in panel session on "The Challenge of Non-State Actors."

11. Natasha A. Affolder, "The Private Life of Environmental Treaties," *American Journal of International Law* 103 (2009): 510–525.

12. See Michael O'Flaherty, *Human Rights and the UN: Practice Before the Treaty Bodies* (London: Sweet and Maxwell, 1996), pp. 1–15. NGOs also play an important role in regional human rights systems. See Olz, "Non-Governmental Organizations in Regional Human Rights Systems," 307–374.

13. See Anne F. Bayefsky, ed., *The UN Human Rights Treaty System in the 21st Century* (The Hague: Kluwer, 2000), chapters 13–17.

14. Convention on Wetlands of International Importance, October 12, 1972, 11 *International Legal Materials (ILM)* 963 (1972).

15. *Amicus curiae* means literally "friend of the court." An amicus curiae brief is one filed to a court by a person or organization who is not a party to the case, but who has an interest in the outcome.

16. Ruth Wedgwood, "Legal Personality and the Role of Non-Governmental Organizations and Non-State Political Entities in the United Nations System," in Rainer Hofmann, ed., *Non-State Actors as New Subjects of International Law: International Law—From the Traditional State Order Towards the Law of the Global Community,* Proceedings of an International Symposium of the Kiel Walther-Schücking Institute of International Law, March 25–28, 1998 (Berlin: Ducker and Humblot, 1999), pp. 21–36, esp. 25; and Anna-Karin Lindblom, *Non-Governmental*

Organizations in International Law (Cambridge: Cambridge University Press, 2005), p. 304.

17. The origins of the process by which the ICJ came to address the question of the legality of nuclear weapons, between 1945 and 1987, are traced in Kate Dewes and Commander Robert Green (Retired), "The World Court Project: How a Citizen Network Can Influence the United Nations," *Pacifica Review* 7, no. 2 (1995): 17–37, esp. 18–20.

18. H. J. Evans, "The World Court Project on Nuclear Weapons and International Law," *New Zealand Law Journal* (July 1993): 249–252.

19. Ibid. For the story of how the questions came to be asked of the Court, see Ved P. Nanda and David Krieger, *Nuclear Weapons and the World Court* (New York: Transnational, 1998), pp. 69–86.

20. Edda Kristjansdottir, "The Legality of the Threat or Use of Nuclear Weapons Under Current International Law: The Arguments Behind the World Court's Advisory Opinion," *International Law and Politics* 30 (1997–98): 291–368, esp. 298–299.

21. Ibid., p. 291.

22. Pierre-Marie Dupuy and Luisa Vierucci, eds., *NGOs in International Law: Efficiency in Flexibility* (Cheltenham, UK: Edward Elgar, 2008), pp. 157–158.

23. Lindblom, *Non-Governmental Organizations in International Law*, p. 304.

24. See Howard B. Tolley Jr., *The International Commission of Jurists: Global Advocates for Human Rights* (Philadelphia: University of Pennsylvania Press, 1994).

25. C. Tomuschat, "General Course on Public International Law," *Recueil des Cours* 281 (1999): 312.

26. Louise Doswald-Beck, "Non-Governmental Entities in Treaty-Making," in V. Gowlland-Debbas, ed., *Multilateral Treaty-Making* (The Hague: Kluwer, 2000), pp. 41–44, esp. 43; and David P. Forsythe, *The Humanitarians: The International Committee of the Red Cross* (Cambridge: Cambridge University Press, 2005), p. 30.

27. H. Dunant, *A Memory of Solferino* (Washington, DC: American Red Cross, 1959).

28. See Michael Ignatieff, "Unarmed Warriors," *New Yorker*, March 24, 1997, pp. 54–71.

29. For discussion of the legal status of the ICRC, see Anton Schlögel, "IRC—International Red Cross," in Rüdiger Wolfrum and Christiane Philipp, eds. *United Nations: Law, Policies, and Practice*, vol. 2 (Dordrecht, the Netherlands: Martinus Nijhoff, 1995), pp. 814–819. See also David P. Forsythe and Barbara Ann J. Rieffer-Flanagan, *The International Committee of the Red Cross: A Neutral Humanitarian Actor* (London: Routledge, 2007).

30. Ruth Wedgwood, "Legal Personality and the Role of Non-Governmental Organizations and Non-State Political Entities in the United Nations System," in Hofmann, *Non-State Actors as New Subjects of International Law* p. 23.

31. "Arrangements and Practices for the Interaction of Nongovernmental Organizations in All Activities of the United Nations System," Report of the Secretary-General, UN Document A/53/170, July 10, 1998.

32. Peter Willetts, "From 'Consultative Arrangements' to 'Partnership': The Changing Status of NGOs in Diplomacy at the UN," *Global Governance* 6 (2000): 191–212, esp. 192.

33. P. K. Menon, "The International Personality of Individuals in International Law: A Broadening of the Traditional Doctrine," *Journal of Transnational Law and Policy* 1 (1992): 151–182, esp. 152.

34. Eileen Denza, *Diplomatic Law: A Commentary on the Vienna Convention on Diplomatic Relations,* 2nd ed. (Oxford: Clarendon, 1998), p. 2.

35. Ibid., p. 210.

36. See J. Craig Barker, *The Abuse of Diplomatic Privileges and Immunities: A Necessary Evil?* (Aldershot, UK: Dartmouth, 1996).

37. Denza, *Diplomatic Law,* pp. 70–71.

38. See, inter alia, Thomas Graditzky, "Individual Criminal Responsibility for Violations of International Humanitarian Law Committed in Non-international Armed Conflicts," *International Review of the Red Cross* 322 (1998): 29–56; Edoardo Greppi, "The Evolution of Individual Criminal Responsibility Under International Law," *International Review of the Red Cross* 81 (1999): 531–552; Steven R. Ratner and Jason S. Abrams, *Accountability for Human Rights Atrocities in International Law,* 2nd ed. (Oxford: Oxford University Press, 2001); and Louis B. Sohn, "The New International Law: Protection of the Rights of Individuals Rather Than States," *American University Law Review* 32 (1982): 1–64.

39. For discussion, see K. Kittichaisaree, *International Criminal Law* (Oxford: Oxford University Press, 2001), pp. 233–250.

40. Ibid., p. 251. This is found in article 28 of the ICC Statute.

41. *Ambatielos Case (Merits), Judgment, ICJ Reports 1953,* p. 10.

42. Neville March Hunnings, *The European Courts* (London: Cartermill, 1996), p. 6.

43. Wayne Mapp, *The Iran-United States Claims Tribunal: The First Ten years, 1981–1991—An Assessment of the Tribunal's Jurisprudence and Its Contribution to International Arbitration* (Manchester: Manchester University Press, 1993), p. 21.

44. See, for example, Kal Raustiala, "States, NGOs, and International Environmental Institutions," *International Studies Quarterly* 41 (1997): 719–740.

45. Russel Lawrence Barsh and Nadia Khattak, "Non-Governmental Organisations in Global Governance: Great Expectations, Inconclusive Results," in G. Alfredsson and M. Stavropoulou, eds., *Justice Pending: Indigenous Peoples and Other Good Causes* (The Hague: Martinus Nijhoff, 2002), pp. 15–31.

46. See Lindsay Moir, *The Law of Internal Armed Conflict* (Cambridge: Cambridge University Press, 2002).

47. See Lisa Jordan and Peter van Tuijl, eds., *NGO Accountability: Politics, Principles, and Innovations* (London: Earthscan, 2006).

48. See, inter alia, David S. Ardia, "Does the Emperor Have No Clothes? Enforcement of International Laws Protecting the Marine Environment," *Michigan Journal of International Law* 19 (1998): 497–567; and Emeka Duruigbo, "Reforming the International Law and Policy on Marine Oil Pollution," *Journal of Maritime Law and Commerce* 31, no. 1 (2000): 65–87, esp. 85.

49. Carsten Hoppe, "Passing the Buck: State Responsibility for Private Military Companies," *European Journal of International Law* 19 (2008): 989–1014.

5

The Logical Structure
of International Law

ALTHOUGH IT IS IMPORTANT TO NOTE THE EXTENT TO WHICH IN-ternational law can be understood only in relation to the political context within which it operates, it is just as vital to recognize the degree to which international law is a discrete entity distinguishable, even if with somewhat blurred boundaries, from that political milieu in which it operates. International law may be entwined with world politics, but it is not enmeshed. International law has considerable autonomy as a system of interrelated rules, principles, and concepts. The rules, principles, and concepts of international law can be found within the sources of international law that we considered in Chapter 1. They function as a medium of communication and interaction in world politics.

The constituent rules, principles, and concepts of international law can be divided into three groups on the basis of the subject matter with which they deal. Because there is a logical interrelatedness between the ideas at the three levels, they can be depicted in a pyramid shape (see Figure 5.1). At the base is a theory or philosophy of international law that justifies and unifies the system of international law. Level 2 consists of a body of principles and rules that relate to the operation of the system of international law itself. And at Level 3 is the mass of rules, principles, and concepts concerning all the substantive issues that arise in relations between states (and, to a lesser extent, between other international actors).

The pyramid has been depicted as wider at the bottom to represent the foundational role played by the underlying philosophy of international law and the way in which each level builds logically on that below it. But in terms of quantity, the pyramid would be more accurate if drawn upside-down, because the bulk of the content of the rules, principles, and concepts

**Figure 5.1 International Law as a System of
Interrelated Rules, Principles, and Concepts**

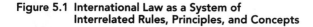

Level Three
Rules, principles,
and concepts per-
taining to the operation of
the system of world politics
(e.g., law relating to the use of
force; international aviation law)

Level Two
Rules, principles, and concepts
pertaining to the operation of the system
of international law (e.g., sources of international
law; law relating to the operation of the ICJ)

Level One
The underlying philosophy/theory
of the system of international law (e.g., natural law; positivism)

of international law pertains to world politics, as depicted at Level 3. The interrelationship of the ideas at the three levels of the system lends the system strength and cohesion and facilitates distinguishing ideas that are part of the pyramid from those that belong to other realms.

Chapters 5 and 6 aim to introduce some of the substantive content of international law by looking at examples of the content of each of these three levels and at the interrelationship between the three levels. Chapter 7 will show how elements from all three levels are combined in the construction of a legal argument.

◼ Level One: The Underlying Philosophy/ Theory of the System of International Law

If international law is to have cohesion as a set of interrelated ideas, there must be an underlying theory or philosophy of the system that answers such fundamental questions as, Where does international law come from? and Why should a state comply with a rule of international law? International lawyers have formulated two main answers to such questions: natural law and legal positivism. Positivism is currently the dominant philosophy, but elements of natural-law thinking remain detectable in the system.

Natural Law

Advocates of a naturalist theory of law believe that there are principles of natural law that exist independently of people; the task for people is to find what the law is. Aristotle and the ancient Greeks are generally regarded as having first developed the concept of natural law, although it gained far greater prominence under the Romans.[1] The heyday of a naturalist theory of law occurred during the sixteenth and seventeenth centuries. The Spaniards Vitoria (1486–1546) and Suarez (1548–1617) expounded a theological version of natural law by which law was merged with theology and God was the source of legal authority. But the best known of the naturalist writers was the Dutchman Hugo Grotius (1583–1645), often regarded as the founder of modern international law. Grotius enunciated a secular theory of natural law in his work *De Jure Belli ac Pacis* (1625), by which "the source of all law is mankind's native sense of justice, which corresponds with the needs of society since without a bond of mutual trust no association of any kind can exist."[2] According to Grotius:

> This maintenance of the social order . . . is the source of law properly so-called. To this sphere of law belong the abstaining from that which is another's, the restoration to another of anything of his which we may have, together with any gain which we may have received from it; the obligation to fulfil promises, the making good of a loss incurred through our fault, and the inflicting of penalties upon men according to their deserts.[3]

Customary international law is subordinate to natural law; "the binding force even of that part of [international law] that originates in consent is based on the law of nature as expressive of the social nature of man."[4] As for God:

> Natural law is the rule of right reason which teaches us that an act is just in so far as it conforms to natural reason, and morally just or unjust and consequently forbidden or commended by God himself as the Author of nature. This natural law does not change. God Himself cannot change the scheme of things so that two and two do not make four.[5]

Despite his emphasis on natural law, Grotius also drew on the "voluntary" law of nations, as evidenced in the practice of states, when it came to the detail of matters such as diplomatic immunities or the law of war. "The significance of the law of nature in [*De Jure Belli ac Pacis*] is that it is the ever-present source for supplementing the voluntary law of nations, for judging its adequacy in the light of ethics and reason, and for making the reader aware of the fact that the will of states cannot be the exclusive or even, in the last resort, the decisive source of the law of nations."[6]

Samuel Pufendorf (1632–1694), in contrast, denied that any international law could arise from custom or from treaties; the only international law there could be was that which was part of natural law.[7] In expounding his purely natural-law conception of the law of nations, Pufendorf did not go into as much detail as Grotius as to just what the content of international law should be.[8] Indeed, it may well have been difficult to do so within a purely natural-law framework. A naturalist philosophy of law works well to justify some legal rules but has a harder time with others. An adherent of a naturalist philosophy of law would likely claim, for example, that there is a universal prohibition on murder. But a prohibition on murder is one of the least contentious of all rules. And even here, it is difficult to determine if there should be any exceptions to the basic rule, and what, if any, they should be.[9] As a theory that might be called on to justify one interpretation of the law over another or to settle a fine point of law, a naturalist theory of law is inadequate. It could not, for example, readily settle a dispute as to whether a fishing zone extends five or seven kilometers from the shore. By 1700 the natural-law theory of international law was beginning to lose favor. Several late-eighteenth-century jurists such as Moser and Martens attempted to reconcile natural law with the emergent positivism, but by the late nineteenth century, key jurists such as Westlake and Hall were exclusively positivist.[10]

Positivism

Positivism is the belief that law is made by people. Positivists claim that rather than deduce the law that derives from some higher source, people make rules. In a domestic situation the rules are likely to be made by either a legislative authority or a sovereign. In the international legal system it is states that make the law. "International law is a law between states, which concerns states only and exclusively," wrote Lasso Oppenheim in 1908.[11] Positivists believe that because states make the law, law derives from the will of states; it is the fact that states have consented to international law that makes it obligatory. The importance to the modern system of international law of consent was explained by the Permanent Court of International Justice in the 1927 Lotus Case: "International law governs relations between independent states. The rules of law binding upon states therefore emanate from their own free will as expressed in conventions or by usages generally accepted as expressing principles of law."[12]

In the early years of the twentieth century, American international lawyers set out to develop a "science of international law," to be contrasted with natural law.[13] Writing in the second volume of the *American Journal of International Law,* Oppenheim sought to distinguish positivism from the natural law of Grotius:

The fact that Grotius and many of his followers did start from the law of nature can not be authoritative for the method to be applied now-a-days when there are enough customary and conventional rules in existence for the construction of a fairly complete system of international law, and when we know that any rule of the so-called law of nature lacks all legal force and authority.

Now, how are the existing recognized rules of international law to be ascertained?

In so far as conventional rules are concerned, it is to a certain extent easy to find them. They are written rules. . . . However great the authority of a writer may be who asserts the existence of a rule, and be it Grotius himself, the science of international law has no right to lay down the rule concerned as really existent and universally or generally recognized unless it can be ascertained that the members of the family of nations have customarily or by a law-making treaty accepted the rule.[14]

Although positivists have sought to distance themselves from natural theory and the two are often contrasted, in practice the two traditions have not been diametrically opposed. Closely associated with the natural-law tradition, Grotius has, for example, been subject to a wide variety of interpretations, not all of which portray his views as diametrically contrastable with positivism.[15] Despite the prominence today of positivism, there has been something of a scholarly revival of natural-law thinking under the banner of "new natural law theory."[16]

Positivism arguably provides a better philosophical basis for a sophisticated system of international law as we have it today because it is much easier to identify what the law is: the law is what states have constructed the law to be. But there is an obvious problem in practice, and it is the perennial problem for lawyers during the era of positivism. The positivist challenge has been how to distinguish *international law* from *policy*. If international law is what states construct international law to be, presumably because those involved perceive it as suiting them to have law of that nature, then how is it possible to make international law something more than a mere excuse for state behavior? Legal positivism must constantly work to establish a clear divide between what is in the realm of international law and what is politics if it is to be able to justify why states should comply with international law.

In their efforts to develop a system of international law that can readily be identified and justified as such, international lawyers have sought to exclude all "nonlegal" considerations. The set of interrelated ideas that we call "international law" is kept distinct from moral and religious ideas or ideas of natural justice. The key questions asked about a (political) action by a legal positivist are, Is the action in question legal? and/or Is this state or intergovernmental organization in compliance with international law? The answers provided are reasoned on the basis of the rules, principles, and concepts found within the sources of international law. You will remember from Chapter 1 that these sources are treaties, custom, general principles of law, judicial decisions, and the teachings of the most highly qualified publicists.

Refer to Figure 5.2 as an example of positivism in practice. Its subject is the question of a sanctuary for whales in the Southern Ocean. The International Whaling Commission (IWC) was established by the 1946 International Convention on the Regulation of Whaling. In 1982 the IWC instituted what was effectively a moratorium on commercial whaling, to be renewed on a yearly basis. In a further move to protect depleting whale stocks, the International Whaling Commission established a Southern Ocean Whale Sanctuary in 1994 to protect Antarctic whale stocks from exploitation.[17] Although welcomed by many as a step forward in the protection of whales, the creation of the sanctuary was firmly opposed by Japan.

Japan claimed that the establishment of the sanctuary was illegal. In support of its position Japan drew on a legal analysis prepared by William Burke of the University of Washington (see Figure 5.2). As you read the extract from the analysis by Burke, do not necessarily try to understand it but view it solely as an example of a legal argument premised on positivism. First, note that it is providing an answer as to whether a certain action—in this case the designation of a Southern Ocean Sanctuary—is or is not legal, and whether a particular actor—in this case the International Whaling Commission—is or is not in compliance with the treaty by which it was founded. Underpinning this piece of writing is an assumption that action in world politics is capable of being categorized as either legal or illegal; the commission is either in compliance or not in compliance with the treaty by which it was established. Second, consider the way in which the writing develops an answer to the question of legality: it does so by drawing on the rules, principles, and concepts found within the sources of international law. The legal instrument in question in the example is the International Convention for the Regulation of Whaling.

We will look at a longer example of positivism-in-practice when we consider the legality of the use of force against Yugoslavia, Afghanistan, and Iraq in Chapter 6. Here we will examine some of the content of the other two levels of the pyramid of ideas that constitute international law.

■ Level Two: International Law Pertaining to the Operation of the System of International Law

Any system of law must include rules about the operation of the legal system itself. International law must, for example, include rules regarding who

Figure 5.2 Memorandum of Opinion on the Legality of the Designation of the Southern Ocean Sanctuary by the International Whaling Commission

by Professor William T. Burke,
School of Law, University of Washington

This is a memorandum of opinion on the legality of the action taken by the International Whaling Commission (IWC) in adoption [of] the Southern Ocean Sanctuary. The specific legal issue is whether the IWC complied with its basic charter, the International Convention for the Regulation of Whaling (ICRW). The conclusion is that it did not, considering the actions of the IWC and subsidiary bodies and the requirements spelled out in Articles I and V. . . .

**Applicable Law in the
Light of the ICRW**

The IWC has clear authority under its basic charter to establish a sanctuary area. Article V(1) provides for adoption of amendments to the Schedule "fixing (c) open and closed areas, including the designation of marine sanctuaries." Under Article 1, the Schedule is agreed to be a part of the Convention which the Commission is authorized to amend from time to time "in accordance with the provisions of Article V." This provision of Article 1 raises the fundamental question involved in the sanctuary, whether the Commission acted "in accordance with Article V."

To comply with Article V(2), amendments to the Schedule (designation of a Sanctuary for present purposes) shall (a) "be such as are necessary to carry out the objectives and purposes of the Convention and to provide for the conservation, development, and optimum utilization of the whale resources"; (b) "be based on scientific findings"; and (d) "take into consideration the interests of the consumers of whale products and the whaling industry." In the actual text, the term "shall" is appended to each one of these requirements, suggesting that each is to be met when an amendment is adopted. It is apparent, however, that the third listed requirement is not a significant condition; "shall take into consideration" is a formula that serves mainly as a reminder of relevant interests rather than mandating satisfaction of such interests. . . .

Source: Presented to the 1995 Annual Meeting of the International Whaling Commission by Japan as paper IWC/47/38 under agenda item 13, and is available at http://www.highnorth.no/. It was published in *Ocean Development and International Law* 27 (1996): 315–326.

can participate in the negotiation of a treaty, who can initiate proceedings before the International Court of Justice, for how long a treaty will last, and so on. The answers given to such questions must be commensurate with the underlying philosophy of international law. Thus, for example, because positivism assumes states to be the principal actors in international law, so is it likely to be states that are accorded the most important role in the formulation of a treaty text. Questions pertaining to the sources of international law are themselves answered on the basis of the rules, principles, and concepts found in the sources of international law. Details of the international law on custom, for example, have been clarified in judgments of the International Court of Justice, as was shown in Figure 3.3. We will look at the law on ICJ jurisdiction as an example of the content of Level 2.

Jurisdiction of the ICJ

Because positivism is the philosophy underpinning the contemporary system of international law, the assumptions of positivism underpin law relating to the operation of the International Court of Justice. Positivism regards states as sovereign, and the related principle of consent stipulates that international law only exists because states have agreed to it. Applied to the jurisdiction of the ICJ, this means that the Court only has jurisdiction where states have given their consent to its jurisdiction. It is not, however, always as clear-cut as one might presume as to whether or not a state has given its consent. When considering whether to bring a case before the Court, states may be in disagreement not only over the substance of the dispute itself but also over the question of whether the Court has jurisdiction to hear the case. Article 36(6) of the statute provides that in the event of a dispute as to whether the Court has jurisdiction, the matter is settled by a decision of the Court. A state against which proceedings have been initiated may well raise preliminary objections to the admissibility of a case (whether the case is one appropriate for the Court to hear) and to the jurisdiction of the Court (whether the Court has the authority to hear this particular case). Although the possibility of raising preliminary objections is a necessary safeguard in the process, it also offers a useful tactic for a state that does not want the issue heard by the Court at all, or that hopes to slow down the process. About half the cases brought before the Court never reach the merits stage at which is addressed the substance of the dispute.

Let us therefore go on to look at the rules, principles, and concepts pertaining to the jurisdiction of the ICJ. The two key documents relating to the operation of the ICJ are the Statute of the ICJ and the Rules of Court.[18] The ICJ Statute, an annex to the UN Charter, provides the broad framework within which the Court is to operate. The details of its procedure are found in the Rules of Court. Article 30 of the UN Charter provides that "the Court shall frame rules for carrying out its functions. In particular, it shall lay down rules of procedure." The Rules of Court currently in force were adopted in 1978 and have subsequently been amended.

Under article 93(1) of the Charter, "[a]ll members of the UN are *ipso facto* parties to the Statute of the ICJ." The ICJ does not have jurisdiction over a state that is not a party to the ICJ Statute. A state that is not a member of the UN may become a party to the ICJ Statute on conditions to be determined in each case by the General Assembly upon the recommendation of the Security Council or to become a party to the statute without being a member of the UN by accepting the conditions set out in article 93(2). Nauru and Switzerland became parties to the ICJ Statute without becoming members of the United Nations.[19]

Being a party to the ICJ Statute is not, though, enough to give the Court jurisdiction over a case. A state must also have given its consent to the jurisdiction of the Court. A state may give the Court an "open slate" to decide any case brought against it, give its consent to decide only the particular case in question, or adopt a position somewhere in between these two positions. There are four ways in which a state party to the ICJ Statute may indicate its consent to the jurisdiction of the ICJ: special agreement, compromissory clause, article 36(2) of the ICJ Statute, and *forum prorogatum*.

Special agreement. States in a dispute with each other may agree to take that dispute to the ICJ. They will then negotiate a treaty, called a "compromis," containing the wording of the dispute as it is to be presented to the Court for a decision. This is a minimalist approach to consenting to the jurisdiction of the Court because that consent relates only to the immediate dispute. The issues brought to Court by this means tend not to have been the most highly charged politically;[20] but they also tend to be ones regarding which the Court's decision is respected, leading to the peaceful resolution of the dispute.[21] Cases initiated by agreement between the parties are indicated in the title of a case by a slash (/). They include the *Asylum* case (Colombia/Peru), the *Minquiers and Ecrehos* case (France/UK), and the *Continental Shelf Case* (Tunisia/Libyan Arab Jamahiriya).

States do not always want a particular issue heard by the ICJ. This means that it is not always possible to negotiate a compromis. Instead, one state may elect to bring a case before the Court unilaterally. In its application instituting proceedings it must then demonstrate to the Court that the other party or parties have given their consent to its jurisdiction elsewhere. These cases are indicated in the title of a case by "v." (e.g. *Cambodia v. Thailand*).

Compromissory clause. Over 270 bilateral and multilateral treaties contain a clause providing that in the event of a dispute concerning the interpretation or operation of that treaty, the parties will take the matter to the ICJ. Such a clause is called a *compromissory clause*. Treaties containing a compromissory clause include the Convention Relating to the Status of Refugees (1951), the Treaty of Peace with Japan (1951), the Convention on the Elimination of All Forms of Racial Discrimination (1966), and the United Nations Framework Convention on Climate Change (1992). The UN Charter does not contain such a clause.

A good example of a compromissory clause in a multilateral treaty is found in article 9 of the Genocide Convention: "Disputes between the Contracting Parties relating to the interpretation, application, or fulfilment of the present Convention, including those relating to the responsibility of a State for genocide or any of the other acts enumerated in Article 3, shall be submitted to the International Court of Justice at the request of any of the parties to the dispute."

Sometimes when a state agrees to be bound by a treaty, it enters a reservation to the compromissory clause, which means that that clause is an exception to which the state has not consented. This makes it possible for a state to be a party to a treaty with a compromissory clause but still not to have given its consent to the jurisdiction of the Court to decide matters arising from the implementation of that treaty.

Article 36(2) of the Statute of the ICJ. Article 36(2) is the so-called optional clause. When the ICJ was being planned, some wanted it to have compulsory jurisdiction and some did not. Article 36(2) was the agreed compromise by which a state can choose to give its consent to ICJ jurisdiction ahead of any dispute.[22]

Article 36(2) states:

> The States parties to the present Statute may at any time declare that they recognize as compulsory *ipso facto* and without special agreement, in relation to any other States accepting the same obligation, the jurisdiction of the Court in all legal disputes concerning:
>
> a. the interpretation of a treaty;
> b. any question of international law;
> c. the existence of any facts which, if established, would constitute a breach of an international obligation;
> d. the nature or extent of the reparation to be made for the breach of an international obligation.

Declarations of the acceptance of the compulsory jurisdiction of the Court under Article 36(2) can be found on the website of the Court (see Figure 5.3).

It is rare for a state not to include in its declaration some limits on the sorts of cases it is prepared to have the Court hear. Specified exceptions are referred to as "reservations." Some of the most common types of reservations that states have included in their declarations under article 36(2) are:

Figure 5.3 Example of a Declaration Made Under Article 36(2) of the Statute of the ICJ

I have the honour on behalf of the Republic of Georgia to declare that, in accordance with paragraph 2 of Article 36 of the Statute of the International Court of Justice, the Republic of Georgia recognizes as compulsory *ipso facto* and without special agreement, in relation to any other State accepting the same obligation, the jurisdiction of the Court in all legal disputes referred to in paragraph 2 of Article 36 of the Statute of the International Court of Justice.

Tbilisi, 16 June 1995

(Signed) Alexander CHIKVAIDZE, Minister of Foreign Affairs of the Republic of Georgia

---

• *Temporal*. If a state does not place some time limits on its acceptance of the Court's jurisdiction, that acceptance will apply to all cases, whether or not the dispute began before the declaration was made. A state may stipulate, for example, that its declaration will not enter into force immediately; or that the declaration may cover only a limited time—say, the next five years. Alternatively, the declaration may only include disputes arising after a certain date or those in which the "situations or facts giving rise to a dispute" are subsequent to a particular date.

• *Subject matter*. A declaration sometimes includes a reservation to particular topics about which the state does not want the Court to hear a dispute, or occasionally, it will refer to those topics which are the only ones on which the state is prepared to have the Court hear a case. Reservations as to subject matter often relate to territorial issues. Egypt's 1957 declaration only accepts the jurisdiction of the ICJ should a dispute arise involving the Egyptian control and management of the Suez Canal.

• *Multilateral treaty reservation or Vandenburg reservation*. This was first used by the United States in 1946. It excludes "disputes arising under a multilateral treaty unless (1) all Parties to the treaty affected by the decision are also parties to the case before the Court, or (2) the USA specifically agrees to jurisdiction."

• *Regarding particular states*. A state may include a reservation to disputes with particular states. The UK declaration has included a reservation to "disputes with the Government of any other country which is a Member of the Commonwealth."[23]

• *Domestic jurisdiction reservation*. This was first used in the UK's 1929 declaration of jurisdiction of the Permanent Court of International Justice

(PCIJ), which excluded "disputes with regard to questions which by international law fall exclusively within the jurisdiction of the UK." Many scholars regard this reservation as redundant. It is a general principle of international law that an international court has no jurisdiction over domestic issues.

• Another type of domestic jurisdiction reservation is *the "self-judging" or Connally reservation.* This was first used by the United States, which in 1946 exempted from the Court's compulsory jurisdiction "disputes with regard to matters which are essentially within the domestic jurisdiction of the USA as determined by the USA." There has been widespread debate regarding the validity of this type of domestic jurisdiction reservation. Many scholars agree with Sir Hersch Lauterpacht in his minority opinion in the *Norwegian Loans* case that the reservation is contrary to article 36(6); in the event of a dispute regarding jurisdiction, the Court will determine. Judge Lauterpacht elaborated on that view in the 1959 *Interhandel* case. But the Court accepted this reservation in *Certain Norwegian Loans* (1957). In the 1986 *Nicaragua* case, Judge Schwebel said that while continuing to see "great force" in the position of Lauterpacht, he appreciated the argument that "since declarations incorporating self-judging provisions apparently have been treated as valid, certainly by the declarants, for many years, the passage of time may have rendered Judge Lauterpacht's analysis less compelling today than when it was made."[24]

• *On condition of reciprocity.* Many states include a condition of reciprocity in their declaration. Article 36(3) allows a state a choice as to whether its declaration is to be on condition of reciprocity, although some international lawyers consider this reservation unnecessary because article 36(2) provides that the optional clause applies only "in relation to any other State accepting the same obligation."[25]

In the *Norwegian Loans* case (1957) the ICJ allowed Norway to draw on the reservations in the declaration of France and hence deny the jurisdiction of the Court. The case arose from a dispute regarding a French loan to Norway. It had been agreed that France could ask to be repaid in gold; later, concerned at its gold supplies, Norway passed legislation withdrawing the convertibility of the krone; France wanted the matter settled by the ICJ whereas Norway argued that it could be settled by municipal courts. The French declaration included a reservation to "all matters within its domestic jurisdiction as it understood that phrase." Norway was able to rely on the French declaration to avoid the jurisdiction of the Court. In the *Interhandel* case (1959) the Court explicitly recognized that a state may invoke a reservation contained in the declaration of the other party to the dispute.[26]

There has been an increase in the number of states accepting the compulsory jurisdiction of the ICJ, from twenty-three in 1945 to forty-five in

1975, to sixty-six in 2010, although this is not an increase as a proportion of the total number of states. States that had accepted the optional clause (with or without reservations) as of 2010 are Australia, Austria, Barbados, Belgium, Botswana, Bulgaria, Cambodia, Cameroon, Canada, Costa Rica, Côte d'Ivoire, Cyprus, Democratic Republic of Congo, Denmark, Djibouti, Commonwealth of Dominica, Dominican Republic, Egypt, Estonia, Finland, Gambia, Georgia, Germany, Greece, Republic of Guinea, Guinea-Bissau, Haiti, Honduras, Hungary, India, Japan, Kenya, Lesotho, Liberia, Liechtenstein, Luxembourg, Madagascar, Malawi, Malta, Mauritius, Mexico, Netherlands, New Zealand, Nicaragua, Nigeria, Norway, Pakistan, Panama, Paraguay, Peru, Philippines, Poland, Portugal, Senegal, Slovakia, Somalia, Spain, Sudan, Suriname, Swaziland, Sweden, Switzerland, Togo, Uganda, United Kingdom of Great Britain and Northern Ireland, and Uruguay.

Why would a state choose to agree ahead of time to have a case against it heard by the Court? Perhaps, most importantly, because a state cannot take another state to Court on the basis of article 36(2) unless it has itself accepted the clause. In addition, states are sometimes keen to demonstrate their faith in the system and preparedness to have their own actions held up to judicial scrutiny.

States have sometimes withdrawn their acceptance but, within a short space of time, replaced it with a new one, usually with an additional or modified reservation. Canada used such a tactic in relation to its concerns regarding marine pollution in waters off its Arctic coast. Canada's 1970 Arctic Waters Pollution Prevention Act gave the Canadian government wide powers to regulate shipping within 100 nautical miles of Canada's Arctic coast. No doubt concerned that another state would claim that this was not consistent with existing international law, Canada added a reservation to its declaration under article 36(2) so as to exclude from the Court's compulsory jurisdiction "disputes arising out of or concerning jurisdiction or rights claimed or exercised by Canada in respect of the conservation, management, or exploitation of the living resources of the sea, or in respect of the prevention or control of pollution or contamination of the marine environment in marine areas adjacent to the coast of Canada." Prime Minister Pierre Trudeau explained that there was a "very grave risk that the World Court would find itself obliged to find that coastal States cannot take steps to prevent pollution. Such a legalistic decision would set back immeasurably the development of law in this critical area."[27] Canada's unilateral move appears to have been an important factor in changing customary international law in respect of the rights of coastal states to introduce and enforce pollution prevention measures beyond the territorial sea.[28] In 1994 Canada again amended its declaration when it passed An Act to Amend the Coastal Fisheries Protection Act.[29]

Since 1951 a number of declarations have expired, been withdrawn, or terminated without being replaced. These have included the declarations of Bolivia, Brazil, China, El Salvador, France, Guatemala, Iran, Israel, South Africa, Thailand, Turkey, and the United States. The withdrawal of the United States from the compulsory jurisdiction of the Court came in 1985, as a reaction of the United States to the 1984 decision of the Court in the Nicaragua case jurisdiction and admissibility). This case concerned a dispute between the government of the Republic of Nicaragua and the government of the United States arising out of military and paramilitary activities in Nicaragua and in the waters off its coasts, responsibility for which was attributed by Nicaragua to the United States. In its application instituting proceedings, Nicaragua relied on article 36 of the ICJ Statute and the declarations accepting the compulsory jurisdiction of the Court of itself and the United States to demonstrate that the Court had jurisdiction to hear the case. The United States argued against the Court having jurisdiction but, much to the anger of the United States, the ICJ found that it did indeed have jurisdiction to hear the case. The United States did not participate further in the proceedings and in 1985 terminated its optional clause declaration. This left the UK as the only remaining permanent member of the Security Council to have accepted the optional clause. In a press statement announcing the action, the United States cited as one of its reasons for this action the fact that so few states, including the USSR, had accepted the Court's compulsory jurisdiction. "The essential underpinning of the UN system, of which the World Court is a part, is the principle of universality."[30]

The US secretary of state, George Shultz, in a letter to the UN Secretary-General, stated:

> I have the honor on behalf of the Government of the United States of America to refer to the declaration of my Government of 26 August 1984, concerning the acceptance by the United States of America of the compulsory jurisdiction of the International Court of Justice, and to State that the aforesaid declaration is hereby terminated, with effect six months from the date hereof.[31]

Forum prorogatum. The final way in which a state might indicate its consent to the jurisdiction of the ICJ is through the doctrine of *forum prorogatum.* According to this doctrine the Court has jurisdiction where the parties have given their consent by separate acts expressly or impliedly accepting it, one of those acts being the making of a unilateral application under article 40(1) of the Court's Statute.[32] This means that a state may submit a dispute to the Court under article 40(1) of the ICJ Statute on the basis of *forum prorogatum* even if the other state has not yet validly recognized the jurisdiction of the ICJ. The other state may then give its consent even if implicitly by, for example, making a submission to the Court on the merits of the case.

An example of an attempt to bring a case to the ICJ on the basis of *forum prorogatum* is the *Antarctica* cases of 1955–1956. After World War II, the United Kingdom, Chile, and Argentina claimed title to overlapping pieces of territory in Antarctica. Attempts to resolve the dispute by diplomatic means having been unsuccessful, the UK proposed on a number of occasions that the ICJ be asked to rule on the matter. On May 4, 1955, the United Kingdom instituted proceedings before the Court against Argentina and Chile although in its application to the Court the UK recognized that, as far as it was aware, Argentina and Chile had not yet accepted the Court's jurisdiction. Neither Argentina nor Chile was prepared to have the matter heard by the Court; they did not regard the question as one amenable to compromise. In a note of August 1, 1955, Argentina informed the Court of its refusal to accept the Court's jurisdiction to deal with the case. In these circumstances, the Court found that neither Chile nor Argentina had accepted its jurisdiction to deal with the cases. The Court removed the cases from its list on March 16, 1956. The issue of overlapping asserted sovereignties in the area of Antarctica opposite South America remains unresolved to this day, the 1959 Antarctic Treaty providing for the parties to agree to disagree on the question of Antarctic sovereignty.

The Rules of Court now provide in article 38(5) that an application based on *forum prorogatum* will be transmitted to the state against which the application is made, but not entered onto the general list of the Court, nor any action be taken in the proceedings, unless and until the state against which such an application is made consents to the jurisdiction of the Court for the purposes of the case.

We will look at an example of the law of ICJ jurisdiction in practice in Chapter 7.

■ Level Three: International Law Pertaining to Substantive Issues in World Politics

Level 3 of the system of rules, principles, and concepts that constitute international law pertains to substantive issues in relations between states—and, to a lesser extent, other international actors. There is thus international law dealing with the regulation of international trade, telecommunications, climate change, use of space, and so on. Perhaps the central substantive issue addressed by contemporary international law is that of the use of force. The United Nations Charter aimed "to save succeeding generations from the scourge of war" and provided rules as to when force is and is not permissible. The prevention of the use of force by aggressor states is a goal shared by international law and the United Nations. Both seek to do a lot more than prevent the use of force—the UN deals with education, poverty alleviation, and other pressing issues; and international law covers technical fields such as postal arrangements and deals with virtually every issue in relations between states—but international law and the United Nations are commonly judged to a very considerable extent on their capacity to keep world peace. Philip Alston has referred to a right to peace as the "raison d'être" of modern international law;[33] J. L. Brierly referred to establishing and maintaining a distinction between the legal and the illegal use of force as the "primary task of all legal systems."[34] We will examine the body of international law concerned with whether it is permissible for a state to use force against another state in Chapter 6. The term used to refer to all the law on a particular topic is *regime,* and in Chapters 9–12 we will be looking at the international law regimes on arms control, human rights, international humanitarian law, and the environment.

■ The Autonomy of International Law vs. Its Entwining with World Politics

In this chapter we have stepped inside the pyramid of rules, principles, and concepts that constitute international law. We have seen that legal positivism has as its most basic premise that law is made by people and that, as the underlying philosophy of the system of international law, positivism assumes that international law derives from the will of sovereign states. In seeking to exclude all "nonlegal" factors from legal analysis, positivism assumes that an answer to any question as to the legality of an action or the compliance of a state (if at Level 3) or a question pertaining to the operation of an aspect of the system of international law (if at Level 2) can be answered on the basis of the rules, principles, and concepts found within the sources of international law.

The exclusion of nonlegal factors from positivist legal argument lends considerable autonomy to the system of interrelated ideas that constitutes international law. Although they may not think of their task in these terms, a considerable amount of work by international lawyers goes into retaining the relative autonomy and cohesion of the system of ideas that constitutes international law. In recent years, for example, there have been efforts to develop a clear-cut definition of terrorism;[35] the truism bears out that what to one person is a terrorist may to another be a freedom fighter. Instead of one comprehensive convention, a patchwork of treaties has appeared over the years, most of which address specific types of terrorist actions (see Figure 5.4); following the 1988 bombing of Pan Am Flight 103, for example, states negotiated a Convention on the Marking of Plastic Explosives for the Purpose of Identification. Although it was thought that a definition and comprehensive convention on terrorism might be achievable in the wake of the September 11, 2001, terrorist attacks, this goal proved elusive, primarily

Figure 5.4 Global Multilateral Treaties on Terrorism

1963	Convention on Offences and Certain Other Acts Committed on Board Aircraft
1970	Convention for the Suppression of Unlawful Seizure of Aircraft
1971	Convention for the Suppression of Unlawful Acts Against the Safety of Civil Aviation
1973	Convention on the Prevention and Punishment of Crimes Against Internationally Protected Persons, Including Diplomatic Agents
1979	International Convention Against the Taking of Hostages
1980	Convention on the Physical Protection of Nuclear Material
1988	Protocol for the Suppression of Unlawful Acts of Violence at Airports Serving International Civil Aviation, Supplementary to the Convention for the Suppression of Unlawful Acts Against the Safety of Civil Aviation
1988	Convention for the Suppression of Unlawful Acts Against the Safety of Maritime Navigation
1988	Protocol for the Suppression of Unlawful Acts Against the Safety of Fixed Platforms Located on the Continental Shelf
1991	Convention on the Marking of Plastic Explosives for the Purpose of Identification
1997	International Convention for the Suppression of Terrorist Bombings
1999	International Convention for the Suppression of the Financing of Terrorism
2005	International Convention for the Suppression of Acts of Nuclear Terrorism

because of the problem of definition. Agreement on a definition of *aggression* in international law has proven equally problematic.

Aspects of international law where the boundary is not clear-cut tend to come in for considerable criticism and elicit proposals for change. Customary international law, for example, is sometimes criticized for not being sufficiently distinguishable from policy.[36] The lack of precision in the international law on humanitarian intervention, as highlighted by events during the Kosovo crisis, prompted debate regarding the merits of codifying the law of humanitarian intervention and what suitable criteria for its legality might be.[37]

Although there is an ongoing process by which the boundary between the rules, principles, and concepts of international law are distinguished from those of politics, there may be some blurring of that boundary. The term *soft law* is sometimes used to designate an ambiguous zone at the boundary of international law and politics. It is used to refer both to political norms that may nevertheless appear to function as "quasi" law or as law-in-the-making as well as to the contents of a treaty or other clearly legal source where those provisions are vague or weak.[38] "Nonlegal soft law"[39] is found primarily in the economic and environmental branches of international law. It includes industry codes of conduct, declarations, resolutions of international organizations, and agreements between states that are not legally binding.[40] The final act of the 1975 Conference on Security and Co-operation in Europe (the Helsinki Final Act),[41] for example, declared the determination of the parties to "act in accordance with the provisions contained in the above texts" but also stipulated that the document "is not eligible for registration under Article 102 of the Charter of the United Nations" as it would be if it had been a treaty. Of course, from a positivist perspective "it remains essential to maintain the distinction between the law *de lege lata* and the law *de lege ferenda,* between the codification of existing law and the progressive development of law, between legal norms and non-legal norms as regards their binding effect, and ultimately between the legal system and the political system."[42]

The relative autonomy of the system of international law depends not only on the retention of a sharp delineation between what is "law" and what is "politics" or "morality" but also on the continued cohesiveness of the contents of the system of international law. This cohesion derives from the logical interrelationship between ideas at the three levels of international law. One of the key concepts in legal positivism is *consent.* Its influence on law at other levels can most readily be seen in debates relating to the operation of the system of international law—that is, at the second level. A fundamental principle of the law of treaties, for example, is that treaties are binding only on those states that are parties to that treaty. This could not be otherwise if the law of treaties is to be consistent with the principle of consent, which is integral to legal positivism.

The interrelatedness of the ideas at all three levels of international law means that international law cannot change fundamentally on any one level without implications for international law at other levels. We have seen how the principle of consent pervades not only the law of treaties but that of the International Court of Justice. Proposals to improve international law commonly contain the proposition that the ICJ should have *compulsory jurisdiction*—that states accused of breaching international law be compelled to appear before the Court. This chapter has endeavored to demonstrate that unless the system is to be left with internal inconsistencies, which would likely weaken its normative force,[43] such a change could not be implemented without corresponding change in the philosophy underpinning the system of international law as a whole.

▧ Notes

1. Robert J. Beck, Anthony Clark Arend, and Robert D. Vander Lugt, eds., *International Rules: Approaches from International Law and International Relations* (Oxford: Oxford University Press, 1996), p. 34.

2. C. G. Roelofsen, "Grotius and International Law: An Introduction to Some Themes in the Field of the Grotian Studies," in L. E. Van Holk and C. G. Roelofsen,

eds., *Grotius Reader: A Reader for Students of International Law and Legal History* (The Hague: T. M. C. Asser Institut, 1983), p. 17.

3. Cited in James Brown Scott, "Introduction," in Hugo Grotius, *The Law of War and Peace,* translated by Francis W. Kelsey (Indianapolis: Bobbs-Merrill, 1925), p. xxxv.

4. H. Lauterpacht, "The Grotian Tradition in International Law," *British Year Book of International Law 1946,* pp. 1–53, esp. 21.

5. Scott, "Introduction," p. xxxiii.

6. Lauterpacht, "The Grotian Tradition in International Law," pp. 21–22.

7. Hans Wehberg, "Introduction," in Samuel Pufendorf, *Elementorum Jurisprudentiae Universalis Libri Duo,* vol. 2, translated by William Abbott Oldfather (Buffalo, NY: William S. Hein, 1995), p. xv.

8. Ibid., pp. xiv–xv.

9. Cf. the discussion in P. Malanczuk, *Akehurst's Modern Introduction to International Law,* 7th rev. ed. (London: Routledge, 1997), p. 16.

10. Antony Anghie, "Finding the Peripheries: Sovereignty and Colonialism in Nineteenth-Century International Law," *Harvard International Law Journal* 40, no. 1 (1999): 1–80, 12–13.

11. Lassa Oppenheim, "The Science of International Law: Its Task and Method," *American Journal of International Law* 2 (1908): 313–356, esp. 340.

12. Permanent Court of International Justice, series A, no. 10, p. 18.

13. Francis Boyle, *World Politics and International Law* (Durham, NC: Duke University Press, 1985), pp. 17–27.

14. Oppenheim, "The Science of International Law," pp. 333–334.

15. See discussions by Benedict Kingsbury and Adam Roberts, "Introduction: Grotian Thought in International Relations," in Hedley Bull, Benedict Kingsbury, and Adam Roberts, eds., *Hugo Grotius and International Relations* (Oxford: Clarendon, 1992), pp. 1–64, esp. 30–38; and Roelofsen, "Grotius and International Law," pp. 16–17.

16. See, for example, John Finnis, *Natural Law and Natural Rights* (Oxford: Clarendon, 1980); and Robert P. George, *In Defense of Natural Law* (Oxford: Clarendon, 1999).

17. See, inter alia, Maria Clara Maffei, "The International Convention for the Regulation of Whaling," *International Journal of Marine and Coastal Law* 12, no. 3 (1997): 287–305.

18. The Statute of the ICJ and Rule of Court can be found on the ICJ website, http://www.icj-cij.org; and Shirley V. Scott, ed., *International Law and Politics: Key Documents* (Boulder, CO: Lynne Rienner, 2006), pp. 30–43.

19. In March 2002 a Swiss referendum supported Switzerland joining the United Nations.

20. Mark W. Janis, *An Introduction to International Law,* 3rd ed. (Gaithersburg, NY: Aspen, 1999), pp. 128–129.

21. Ibid., p. 128.

22. Malanczuk, *Akehurst's Modern Introduction to International Law,* p. 284.

23. United Kingdom Declaration Accepting the Compulsory Jurisdiction of the Court, reprinted in International Court of Justice, *Yearbook 1998–1999,* pp. 129–130.

24. *Military and Paramilitary Activities In and Against Nicaragua (Nicaragua v. United States of America), Jurisdiction and Admissibility, Judgment, ICJ Reports 1984,* p. 392 at 601–602.

25. See discussion in Stanimir A. Alexandrov, *Reservations in Unilateral Declarations Accepting the Compulsory Jurisdiction of the International Court of Justice* (Dordrecht, the Netherlands: Martinus Nijhoff, 1995), pp. 17–32.

26. *Interhandel Case, Judgment of March 21, 1959: ICJ Reports 1959,* p. 6 at 23.

27. Cited in Michael Byers, *Custom, Power, and the Power of Rules: International Relations and Customary International Law* (Cambridge: Cambridge University Press, 1999), p. 93.

28. Ibid., p. 94.

29. See discussion in ibid., pp. 97–98.

30. The press statement was reproduced in 24 *International Legal Materials (ILM)* 1744 (1985).

31. 24 *ILM* 1743 (1985).

32. D. J. Harris, *Cases and Materials on International Law,* 5th ed. (London: Sweet and Maxwell, 1998), p. 999.

33. P. Alston, "Peace as a Human Right," *Bulletin of Peace Proposals* 11 (1980): 319.

34. J. L. Brierly, "International Law and Resort to Armed Force," *Cambridge Law Journal* 4 (1932): 308–319, esp. 308.

35. See Ben Saul, *Defining Terrorism in International Law* (Oxford: Oxford University Press, 2006).

36. On this theme and related challenges of customary international law more generally, see Hilary Charlesworth, "The Unbearable Lightness of Customary International Law," *Proceedings of the Ninety-Second Annual Meeting of the American Society of International Law: The Challenge of Non-State Actors* 92 (1998): 44–47; Major Ian G. Corey, "The Fine Line Between Policy and Custom: *Prosecutor v. Tadic* and the Customary International Law of Internal Armed Conflict," *Military Law Review* 166 (2000): 145–157; and M. Koskenniemi, "The Normative Force of Habit: International Custom and Social Theory," *Finnish Yearbook of International Law 1990* 1 (1990): 77–89.

37. See, inter alia, Peter Hilpold, "Humanitarian Intervention: Is There a Need for a Legal Reappraisal?" *European Journal of International Law* 12, no. 3 (2001): 437–467; Nicholas J. Wheeler, "Legitimating Humanitarian Intervention: Principles and Procedures," *Melbourne Journal of International Law* 2, no. 2 (2001): 550–567; and the UK House of Commons, Foreign Affairs Committee Fourth Report, Session 1999–2000, available at http://www.parliament.the-stationery-office .co.uk.

38. See Tadeusz Gruchalla-Wesierski, "A Framework for Understanding Soft Law," *McGill Law Journal* 30 (1984): 37–88, esp. 44.

39. C. M. Chinkin, "The Challenge of Soft Law: Development and Change in International Law," *International and Comparative Law Quarterly* 38 (October 1989): 850–866.

40. See, inter alia, R. R. Baxter, "International Law in 'Her Infinite Variety,'" *International and Comparative Law Quarterly* 29 (1980): 549–566; A. E. Boyle, "Some Reflections on the Relationship of Treaties and Soft Law," *International and Comparative Law Quarterly* 48, no. 4 (October 1999): 901–913; Chinkin, "The Challenge of Soft Law"; Ulrich Fastenrath, "Relative Normativity in International Law," *European Journal of International Law* 4 (1993): 305–340; and Prosper Weil, "Towards Relative Normativity in International Law?" *American Journal of International Law* 77 (1983): 413–442.

41. 14 *ILM* 1293 (1975). See Oscar Schachter, "The Twilight Existence of Nonbinding International Agreements," *American Journal of International Law* 71 (1977): 296–304, esp. 296.

42. Malanczuk, *Akehurst's Modern Introduction to International Law,* p. 54.

43. See, generally, Thomas M. Franck, *The Power of Legitimacy Among Nations* (Oxford: Oxford University Press, 1990), p. 150ff.

6

International Law
and the Use of Force

INTERNATIONAL LAW ADDRESSES A WIDE RANGE OF SUBJECTS
that may arise in relations among states, including the environment, refugees, genocide, and the use of force. The body of law that seeks to limit recourse to force is of special importance to the system of international law because law represents an attempt to replace anarchy with order. To the degree that the most powerful states seem able to get away with behaving as bullies, international law will appear inconsequential. Force can also be a means of ensuring respect for law; indeed, the fact that the League of Nations did not provide for adequate enforcement of its rules was assumed a factor contributing to World War II. One of the innovations introduced by the planners of the United Nations was that the Security Council could resort to using force if necessary to restore international peace and security.

This chapter will outline the basic principles and rules concerning the use of force that were incorporated in the Charter of the United Nations, before applying those to examine the legality of three recent uses of force: that against Yugoslavia during the Kosovo crisis, that against Afghanistan following the attacks of September 11, 2001, and the 2003 invasion of Iraq. It is highly recommended that this chapter be read in conjunction with the entire United Nations Charter, which can be found on the Internet or in a book of international law documents.[1]

■ Historical Background
International law has not always opposed the initiation of war. In fact, rules outlawing the use of war as a means of settling disputes are relatively new in the evolution of international law. During the era of colonization from the seventeenth to the nineteenth century, for example, international law

regulated the acquisition of territory by European states. Where the Europeans encountered a political unit interacting with other political units in a manner to which the European state could relate—in the East Indies, for example—international law required that the unit be respected as a like form of legal entity and relations conducted with it on the basis that it was an international political-legal unit in its own right. But international law did not forbid war. It was acceptable, where necessary, to utilize force against foreign political units, so long as that war was conducted in accordance with contemporary legal standards.

Older than the international law pertaining to whether or not force can be used (*jus ad bellum*) is a body of law imposing limitations on the conduct of hostilities (*jus in bello*).[2] Prior to the twentieth century it had for several hundred years been accepted that states could go to war to redress grievances. Naturalist lawyers such as Aquinas and Augustine argued for a distinction between just and unjust wars, maintaining that in the natural sphere of things, it was sometimes moral to go to war. But this distinction did not become a part of modern international law.[3] In the years after the Peace of Westphalia, war was accepted as part of political reality; indeed, the right to resort to arms was considered an important attribute of state sovereignty.[4]

The horrors of World War I prompted attempts to have international law reduce the instances in which states resort to force. In article 12(1) of the Covenant of the League of Nations, members agreed that "if there should arise between them any dispute likely to lead to a rupture, they will submit the matter either to arbitration or to inquiry by the Council, and they agree in no case to resort to war until three months after the award by the arbitrators or the report by the Council." By article 13(4) members agreed to "not resort to war against a Member of the League which complies" with the award rendered. The fact that states were required to submit to certain procedures of peaceful dispute settlement did not, however, displace the assumption that war was a right of a sovereign state.[5] The trouble with the phrase *resort to war* was that in the conflict between China and Japan between 1937 and 1941, for example, all involved parties were able to maintain the fiction that, despite the hostilities, the fact that there had been no declaration of war[6] meant that actual war did not exist.[7]

The General Treaty for the Renunciation of War,[8] also known as the Kellogg-Briand Pact and the Pact of Paris (1928), marked another major milestone in the evolution of *jus ad bellum*.[9] This was the first time that states recognized a comprehensive prohibition of war as an instrument of national policy. Article I of the General Treaty for the Renunciation of War stated: "The High Contracting Parties solemnly declare in the names of their respective peoples that they condemn recourse to war for the solution of international controversies, and renounce it as an instrument of national policy in their relations with one another." This meant that states could still distinguish between use of force and an actual declaration of war; it was not clear as to whether the treaty prohibited armed force short of war.[10] Sixty-three states, virtually the whole of the international community at that time, were parties to the treaty when World War II started in 1939.[11]

Following World War II, international law took another major step in the direction of forbidding armed conflict. This time it was not war but the use of force that was outlawed.[12] The Charter of the United Nations provides that states may use force only in self-defense or when authorized by the Security Council. The Charter provides the basis of the contemporary international legal framework addressing the use of force.

■ The Contemporary International Legal Framework

The essentials of the body of international law addressing whether and under what circumstances a state may use force against another state are relatively clear cut. Most fundamental is article 2(4) of the UN Charter: "All members shall refrain in their international relations from the threat or use of force against the territorial integrity or political independence of any State, or in any other manner inconsistent with the Purposes of the United Nations."

Note the reference to the threat, as well as to the use, of force.[13] It is perhaps unfortunate that the second half of this article can be read so to qualify the first half—suggesting that the use of force is prohibited only where the objective is to overthrow the government or seize the territory of another state or if inconsistent with the purposes of the UN.[14] Those drafting the Charter did not intend article 2(4) to be interpreted in this narrow fashion,[15] and article 2(4) can best be understood as a general prohibition on the use of force. The prohibition on the use of force is such a fundamental component of international law and so widely accepted that it is often considered *jus cogens,* meaning that it is a peremptory norm of international law from which no derogation can be permitted.

Self-Defense

Article 2(4) remains the general rule, to which there are two exceptions. First is self-defense. The right to defend oneself if attacked is a part of customary international law and could be said to be a part of natural law. Article 51 of the UN Charter provides:

> Nothing in the present Charter shall impair the inherent right of individual or collective self-defence if an armed attack occurs against a Member of the United Nations, until the Security Council has taken measures necessary to maintain international peace and security. Measures taken by

> Members in the exercise of this right of self-defence shall be immediately
> reported to the Security Council and shall not in any way affect the au-
> thority and responsibility of the Security Council under the present Char-
> ter to take at any time such actions as it deems necessary in order to
> maintain or restore international peace and security.

This implies a three-step response to an armed attack: first, that the state under attack will act as necessary to defend itself; second, that the state will report those actions to the Security Council; and third, that the Security Council will take charge of the situation and act to restore international peace and security.

Customary international law fills in much of the detail regarding the law of self-defense—in particular, that the key requirements of an act of self-defense are immediacy, necessity, and proportionality. These were part of pre-Charter customary international law and date from correspondence between Great Britain and the United States in 1841–1842, in what is known as the *Caroline* case. Daniel Webster of the United States wrote to Henry Fox: "It will be for . . . [Her Majesty's] Government to show a necessity of self-defence, instant, overwhelming, leaving no choice of means, and no moment for deliberation."[16] The UK acquiesced in that test for the legality of an act of self-defense.

The International Court of Justice has also contributed to confirming and clarifying the meaning and scope of the right to self-defense. The ICJ has on more than one occasion confirmed the customary law requirements of necessity and proportionality,[17] and in the 1986 *Nicaragua* case it clari-fied the fact that the right to collective self-defense, which allows a nonat-tacked state to assist an attacked state, must involve the state in question believing that it is the victim of an armed attack and requesting such assis-tance.[18] The Court has also explained that not submitting a report to the Se-curity Council does not of itself invalidate a claim to self-defense but may be one of the factors indicating whether the state in question was convinced that its actions were in self-defense.[19]

Security Council Authorization

Security Council authorization for the use of force constitutes the second ex-ception to the prohibition on the use of force in the UN Charter. The key pro-visions of the Charter are found in chapter VII, which opens with article 39, setting out the jurisdictional basis for the Security Council to make deci-sions with which states are compelled to comply: "The Security Council shall determine the existence of any threat to the peace, breach of the peace, or act of aggression and shall make recommendations, or decide what meas-ures shall be taken in accordance with Articles 41 and 42, to maintain or re-store international peace and security."

It is therefore a precondition for the Security Council using its powers under chapter VII that it has deemed there to be either "a threat to the peace, breach of the peace, or act of aggression." Use of this language in one of its resolutions can be interpreted as the Security Council signaling that it deems an issue of sufficient potential seriousness to warrant the Council using its chapter VII powers at some future point. Hence the significance, for example, of the Security Council adopting Resolution 1368 on September 12, 2001, the day after the terrorist attacks on New York and Washington, condemning the acts "as a threat to international peace and security" (see Figure 6.1).

Figure 6.1 Reading a Resolution of the Security Council

The Security Council publishes its decisions, or resolutions, which are referred to by number and year. The resolutions can be found at www.un .org/documents/scres.htm.

A resolution is written as one long sentence, divided into clauses. A resolution can be understood as consisting of three sections: the resolution "head," preamble, and operative section:

• The head, for example, "The Security Council."
• Preambular paragraphs give the background, including previous Security Council resolutions on the subject. They often begin with the phrases "takes note," "referring," or "reaffirming." They often end in a comma.
• Operative paragraphs include the actions to be taken to address the issue. They may begin with, "calls upon," or "accepts." They usually finish with a semi-colon; the last ends with a full stop.

When reading a Security Council resolution, look out for "codes," such as:

• "threat to the peace, breach of the peace, or act of aggression," which refers to article 39 of the Charter, thereby paving the way for possible Council decisions under chapter VII;
• "such action as may be necessary," which refers to article 42 of the Charter, in which the Council is empowered to authorize use of force;
• "chapter VII": A decision taken under chapter VII is one with which all states are compelled to comply, and may include sanctions and/or use of force;
• "decides to remain seized of the matter": The Council is going to monitor the issue. The implication may be that the Council is reserving the right to be the body that follows up the issue (as opposed to the general assembly, for example).

Article 41 provides that the Council may decide to employ sanctions. If those efforts have failed or if the Security Council deems them likely to fail, it can respond as it considers appropriate, including with the use of force. Article 42 stipulates:

> Should the Security Council consider that measures provided for in Article 41 [complete or partial interruption of economic relations and of rail, sea, air, postal, telegraphic, radio, and other means of communication, and the severance of diplomatic relations] would be inadequate or have proved to be inadequate, it may take such action by air, sea, or land forces as may be necessary to maintain or restore international peace and security. Such action may include demonstrations, blockade, and other operations by air, sea, or land forces of Members of the United Nations.

Article 43(1) provided for states to enter into "special agreements" with the UN to make available "armed forces, assistance, and facilities . . . necessary for the purpose of maintaining peace and security." A Military Staff Committee was to be established (article 47) to advise the Security Council on its military requirements for maintaining peace and security. This committee was, in fact, established, but the agreements envisaged in article 43 never became a reality in the Cold War environment.

The Security Council has nevertheless recommended or requested the use of military action on the part of states.[20] By Resolution 83 (1950) the Security Council determined that an "armed attack upon the Republic of Korea by forces from North Korea constitutes a breach of the peace," and by Resolution 84 (1950) it recommended "that all Members providing military forces and other assistance . . . make such forces available to a unified command under the United States of America." By Resolution 678 of November 29, 1990, the Security Council authorized member states to "use all necessary means . . . to restore international peace and security in the area" if Iraq failed to meet a deadline for the fulfilment of previous resolutions requiring its forces to leave Kuwait.[21] Figure 6.2 gives examples of Security Council authorizations to use force.

Although the basic framework regarding the use of force in international law is clear, a number of issues provoke controversy. Naturally, those issues addressed in the scholarly literature at any point of time tend to reflect recent events and rhetoric. We will now assess the legality of three uses of force and the questions they have raised within the body of international law.

■ 1999 Operation Allied Force and the Legality of Humanitarian Intervention

The 1999 NATO bombing of the Federal Republic of Yugoslavia during the Kosovo crisis gave rise to emotions of outrage against both those committing

Figure 6.2 Examples of Security Council Authorizations to Use Force

Place	Who Was Authorized	Purpose of the Use of Force	Resolution	Year
Korea	Members of the United Nations under US command and the UN flag	"to repel the armed attack upon the Republic of Korea by forces from North Korea"	83 and 84	1950
Kuwait	Member states in cooperation with Kuwait	"to uphold and implement resolution 660 (1990) [concerning Iraq's invasion of Kuwait on August 2, 1990] and all subsequent relevant resolutions and to restore international peace and security in the area"	678	1990
Somalia	The Secretary-General and member states	"to establish as soon as possible a secure environment for humanitarian relief operations"	794	1992
East Timor	A multinational force under a unified command structure	"to restore peace and security in East Timor, to protect and support UNAMET [United Nations Mission in East Timor] in carrying out its tasks and, within force capabilities, to facilitate humanitarian assistance operations"	1264	1999
Sudan (Darfur)	UNMIS (United Nations Mission in Sudan)	"to protect United Nations personnel, facilities, installations and equipment, to ensure the security and freedom of movement of United Nations personnel, humanitarian workers, assessment and evaluation commission personnel, to prevent disruption of the implementation of the Darfur Peace Agreement by armed groups, without prejudice to the responsibility of the Government of the Sudan, to protect civilians under threat of physical violence, in order to support early and effective implementation of the Darfur Peace Agreement, to prevent attacks and threats against civilians, to seize or collect, as appropriate, arms or related material whose presence in Darfur is in violation of the Agreements and the measures imposed by paragraphs 7 and 8 of resolution 1556, and to dispose of such arms and related material as appropriate"	1706	2006
Within the territorial waters of Somalia	States and regional organizations cooperating with the Transitional Federal Government (TFG) in the fight against piracy and armed robbery at sea off the coast of Somalia, for which advance notification has been provided by the TFG to the Secretary-General	To repress acts of piracy and armed robbery at sea	1846	2008

atrocities and those inflicting suffering by their bombing.[22] Analysis of the legality of the NATO use of force within the framework of legal positivism requires us to put aside all emotional responses to focus on the rules, principles, and concepts found within the sources of international law. Our consideration should involve both treaty and customary international law.

For the majority of international lawyers the case is clear that the NATO bombing was illegal. The source most important to reaching that conclusion is the UN Charter. Article 103 provides that "in the event of a conflict between the obligations of the Members of the UN under the present Charter and their obligations under any other international agreement, their obligations under the present Charter shall prevail." This means that the Charter trumps other treaties. Consistent with article 103 of the UN Charter, article 7 of the 1949 North Atlantic Treaty reads: "The Treaty does not affect, and shall not be interpreted as affecting, in any way the rights and obligations under the Charter of the Parties which are Members of the United Nations, or the primary responsibility of the Security Council for the maintenance of international peace and security." Article 2(4) of the UN Charter categorically prohibits the use of force. The collective self-defense exception is not applicable in this case because article 51 refers to attacks against members of the United Nations; it has to be a state claiming a right of self-defense. Kosovo was part of a sovereign state; Yugoslavia was not attacking another state. The second exception to the prohibition on the use of force is on the authorization of the Security Council. Although there were three relevant Security Council resolutions,[23] none explicitly authorized the use of force. Under article 53(1) authorization can be given to a regional organization, but a regional organization must not take action without that authorization.

Just as there does not appear to be a basis in treaty law for the NATO bombing, so would most international lawyers consider there not to have crystallized a customary international rule of humanitarian intervention.

Humanitarian Intervention

There is some discussion among international lawyers regarding whether there is a customary rule permitting the use of force without a Security Council resolution in the event of gross violations of human rights. The appropriateness of there being a right of "humanitarian intervention"[24] finds support in scholarly writings from as early as the seventeenth century, when Hugo Grotius wrote that "where [rulers] provoke their people to despair and resistance by unheard of cruelties, having themselves abandoned all the laws of nature, they lose the rights of independent sovereigns, and can no longer claim the privilege of the law of nations."[25]

In terms of positivist international law, the crystallization of a customary law of humanitarian intervention would require there to have been sufficient instances of states intervening in areas of humanitarian crisis but also that those interventions had been accompanied by the necessary *opinio juris*. Some international lawyers believe that customary international law predating the Charter permitted humanitarian intervention;[26] Simon Chesterman, in contrast, considers that pre-Charter state practice illustrates a paucity of evidence of a general right of humanitarian intervention in customary international law. The three main examples of allegedly humanitarian intervention in the nineteenth century are the joint intervention of Great Britain, France, and Russia in aid of Greek insurgents in 1827; the French occupation of Syria in 1860–1861; and the US intervention in Cuba during its war with Spain in 1898.[27]

The majority of international lawyers do not consider that the right, if it existed, survived the Charter's general prohibition on the use of force.[28] Article 2(4) makes no explicit reference to humanitarian intervention. The two most discussed cases of humanitarian intervention between the UN Charter of 1945 and the NATO intervention during the Kosovo crisis are those of the Indian intervention in East Pakistan leading to the secession of East Pakistan from West Pakistan in 1971, and Tanzania's intervention in Uganda in 1979 to overthrow Idi Amin's regime. It is unlikely that the requisite *opinio juris* was present in either case; indeed, both India and Tanzania quoted the right to self-defense under article 51 rather than a right or obligation of humanitarian intervention.[29] Examples of humanitarian intervention by the United Nations since the end of the Cold War—Bosnia-Herzegovina, Somalia, and Rwanda—were UN actions authorized by the Security Council. Also countering the idea of an existing customary international law of humanitarian intervention is the fact that there have been numerous examples of human rights atrocities since World War II that did not meet with an international response.

Some lawyers have adopted the position that, even if there were a recognized international rule of humanitarian intervention, the nature of the NATO use of force disqualified it as an example of humanitarian intervention. Bombing from a height of 15,000 feet inevitably endangers civilians and would not seem to be compatible with the concept of humanitarian intervention.

Although a mainstream legal analysis would most readily lead to the conclusion that the use of force by NATO states during the Kosovo crisis was not legal, some scholars have constructed legal arguments for its having been legal. The argument is sometimes made that article 2(4) does not rule out a "lawful" use of force and that a lawful humanitarian intervention will not undermine the "territorial integrity or political independence of any State or be inconsistent with the purposes of the UN."[30] Julie Mertus argued, for example, that a close reading of the UN Charter supports humanitarian intervention in Kosovo-like situations—that is, in cases in which an outside alliance acts unilaterally to redress human rights violations committed by the regime of a third state.[31] By article 55 of the Charter, the UN is to promote, inter alia, "universal respect for, and observance of, human rights and fundamental freedoms for all without distinction as to race, sex, language, or religion." By article 56, members "pledge themselves to take joint and separate action in co-operation with the Organisation for the achievement of the purposes set forth in Article 55." Some lawyers maintain that these provisions temper the prohibition on the use of force in article 2(4). As we saw above, however, this view does not reflect the intentions of those crafting the Charter, nor is it the predominant interpretation of article 2(4).

A second way of arguing within a legal positivist framework that the bombing was legal is to justify it in terms of customary international law as a case of humanitarian intervention. Both lines of argument are made more difficult by the fact that NATO did not argue them; indeed, NATO provided no single coherent legal justification for its actions but emphasized its legitimacy as a response to the humanitarian "catastrophe" in Kosovo.[32] In the joint hearings before the ICJ on Yugoslavia's requests for interim measures during the NATO bombing campaign, only Belgium justified its actions on the basis of a right of humanitarian intervention.[33]

Morality vs. Legality

Many international lawyers found that, on a personal level, it was difficult to reach the conclusion that the NATO bombing was contrary to international law because it appeared to them to have been the morally correct thing to do. This led to considerable debate regarding the relationship between international law and morality and between *de lege lata* (international law as it currently stands) and *de lege ferenda* (law as it should be). Bruno Simma concluded that only a thin red line separated NATO's action from international legality but that NATO's use of force without Security Council authorization should remain an exception lest NATO undermine the universal system of collective security.[34] Michael Glennon argued that the discrepancy between international law and morality in this scenario meant that the law should be changed and brought into line with contemporary standards of morality and justice.[35]

Some scholars have considered that the morality of the bombing campaign was even more dubious than its legality. Key considerations raised here are, first, that from relatively few refugees prior to the air strikes, up to 800,000 fled their homes after the strikes had begun;[36] and second, that if NATO's motivation was really humanitarian, why did it conduct a high-altitude bombing campaign in which civilians were bound to suffer casualties? The campaign resulted in some 500 civilian deaths.[37]

The Uniting for Peace Resolution

Is there any other action that the NATO states could have taken to make their campaign legal? One possibility, although it may not have been successful, is by way of the Uniting for Peace resolution. In 1950 the Security Council was only able to take action in relation to North Korea because the Soviet Union was boycotting the Council in protest at the membership of Taiwan. Once the Soviet representative returned to the Council it became very hard to pass subsequent resolutions on Korea. The United States then introduced a discussion paper into the General Assembly, which became the basis for the Uniting for Peace resolution. The resolution provided, inter alia, that

> if the Security Council, because of lack of unanimity of the permanent members, fails to exercise its primary responsibility for the maintenance of international peace and security in any case where there appears to be a threat to the peace, breach of the peace, or act of aggression, the General Assembly shall consider the matter immediately with a view to making appropriate recommendations to members for collective measures, including in the case of breach of the peace or act of aggression the use of armed force when necessary, to maintain or restore international peace and security.

The resolution also provided that an emergency special session of the General Assembly may be convened outside of the session period if there is a breach of or a threat to peace or an act of aggression. The session may be summoned either by the Security Council—the veto does not apply on a procedural resolution—or by a simple majority of members of the General Assembly.

The Uniting for Peace resolution was of particular value to the United States and the West during the years of their domination of the General Assembly but of less relevance as the North-South dynamic grew in importance. It was used on a number of occasions (in relation to Hungary in 1956; the Middle East in 1956, 1958, 1967, and 1980; the Congo in 1960; Bangladesh in 1971; Afghanistan in 1980; and Namibia in 1981) to bring about emergency special sessions though not as a basis for recommending collective military measures.

Codifying Humanitarian Intervention and the Responsibility to Protect

A UK Select Committee on Foreign Affairs found in 2000 that the NATO bombing of Serbia during the Kosovo crisis had been of dubious legality and supported moves to establish in the United Nations new principles governing humanitarian intervention.[38] The UK submitted to the UN Secretary-General a framework for intervention based on six principles: that there should be more concentration on conflict prevention; that the use of armed force should only be a last resort; that immediate responsibility for halting violence lies with the state in which it occurs; that when a government has shown that it is unwilling or unable to cope with a humanitarian catastrophe the international community has a duty to intervene; that any use of force should be proportionate to achieving the humanitarian purposes of the mission and carried out in accordance with international law; and that the use of force must be collective and only in exceptional circumstances should it be undertaken without the express authority of the Security Council in the UN.[39] Debate in the General Assembly has not demonstrated a consensus view that a right to humanitarian intervention should be codified. Whereas publics in the West may believe that their governments should not stand idly by while atrocities occur within other states, China, Russia, and many other states in the developing world are naturally wary of international law legitimizing forcible intervention. Such concerns were subsequently exacerbated by the invasion of Iraq.[40]

The International Commission on Intervention and State Sovereignty, a body set up by the government of Canada with funding from several US foundations and the UK and Swiss governments, in 2001 promoted the notion of a "responsibility to protect," which is said to include three separate responsibilities: the responsibility to prevent, the responsibility to react, and the responsibility to rebuild. The use of coercive force is to be the last resort in meeting the second of these responsibilities.[41] The notion of a responsibility to protect can therefore be understood as an attempt to move beyond the legal and political difficulties surrounding the concept of humanitarian intervention, not least of which is the term itself. The concept of humanitarian intervention juxtaposes humanitarian concerns with a term closely associated with coercive military action.[42]

The responsibility to protect is a political rather than legal concept, although some commentators point to it building on already existing principles of international law.[43] It cannot be said, however, that humanitarian intervention—other than on the authority of the Security Council—or a responsibility to protect are yet accepted principles of international law.

■ 2001 Operation Enduring Freedom and the Law of Self-Defense

Article 51 recognizes the "inherent" right of a state to self-defense. The UN Charter was, naturally, designed with a World War II attack in mind: that is, an attack by one state on another by an invading military force. One question that has arisen in this body of law since 1945 has been that as to what is appropriately deemed an "armed attack." What if those conducting the attack are private groups, with little or no links to states?

Following the terrorist attacks on the United States on September 11, 2001, a US-led coalition began bombing Afghanistan on October 7. On this same day the United Kingdom and the United States each wrote to the Security Council explaining that they were acting under article 51 in the exercise of their inherent right of individual and collective self-defense. As with the NATO use of force during the Kosovo crisis, there was no explicit Security Council authorization for the use of force, despite Security Council Resolution 1368 (2001) of September 12 appearing to lay the necessary groundwork. Resolution 1368 condemned the attacks on the United States, stated that the Security Council "regards such acts, like any act of international terrorism, as a threat to international peace and security," and expressed "its readiness to take all necessary steps to respond to the terrorist attacks of 11 September 2001 and to combat all forms of terrorism, in accordance with its responsibilities under the Charter of the United Nations." The preamble of Resolution 1373 (2001) of September 28 reaffirmed the Council's unequivocal condemnation of the terror attacks and the inherent right of self-defense and explicitly drew on the chapter VII powers to require states to take far-reaching measures aimed at preventing and suppressing acts of terrorism.

Although this use of force prompted far less legal debate than had the Kosovo bombing (or the yet-to-occur Operation Iraqi Freedom), its legality was not clear-cut; this was particularly true as time went on.[44] Questions that have been raised include:

• Did the terrorist attacks on the United States constitute "armed attacks" as referred to in article 51 of the Charter, and did the Taliban government in Afghanistan support the terrorists to a degree sufficient to give it responsibility for the attacks? Michael Byers has argued that customary international law has moved on as a result of this scenario to accept that terrorist attacks constitute armed attacks,[45] whereas Marcello Kohen, for example, believes that US actions were illegal and led to no change in the law.[46]

• Given that the US-led coalition did not launch its operations for several weeks after the attacks, did this meet the customary international law requirements for the self-defense to be immediate and necessary for the objective of defense? Were attacks against the whole country of Afghanistan to the extent of removing the government—albeit unrecognized—proportional to the injury?

• Although the United States reported its actions to the Security Council, does it matter that the Council did not explicitly assume leadership for the restoration of peace and security? Article 51 recognizes the right to self-defense until the Council has taken necessary measures. Following the establishment of an interim government, Security Council Resolution 1386 (2001) authorized member states participating in the International Security Assistance Force to use all necessary means to assist the interim government to maintain security in Kabul and surrounding areas, but this arguably did not remove the ambiguity of the Council's initial position.[47]

• Given the length of the fighting in Afghanistan, for how long could the United States continue to claim to be acting in self-defense?

■ Anticipatory and Preemptive Self-Defense

Article 51 refers to the inherent right of self-defense "if an armed attack occurs." There is some difference of opinion as to how soon in relation to the armed attack the act of self-defense can begin. It does not seem reasonable that a state could not react until the bombs are actually landing on its soil. It can be argued that a right to anticipatory self-defense—that is, an act of self-defense taken in anticipation of an armed attack—exists in customary international law so long as it meets the *Caroline* standards of necessity and proportionality.

There is not, however, mainstream acceptance of a general right of anticipatory self-defense, no doubt in large part because of the obvious danger of abuse. The classic case is Israel's 1981 air strike against Iraq's Osirak atomic reactor, which was in its final stages of construction. Israel drew on international legal authorities to argue the absurdity of being expected to wait for the initial, possibly surprise attack, but the Security Council by Resolution 487 (1981) of June 19, 1981, unanimously condemned the attack as a clear violation of the UN Charter. It is possible that opinion is moving toward tolerance of anticipatory self-defense were it possible to establish a high degree of imminence and no alternative peaceful means by which to prevent the attack.[48] UN Secretary-General Kofi Annan asserted in his 2005 report *In Larger Freedom* that article 51 is sufficiently flexible to allow for self-defense against an imminent attack,[49] but a UN World Summit held in September 2005 confirmed that there is still strong resistance to anticipatory self-defense.[50]

The National Security Strategy of the United States, released on September 17, 2002, asserted a policy of preemption:

> The United States has long maintained the option of preemptive actions to counter a sufficient threat to our national security. The greater the threat, the greater is the risk of inaction—and the more compelling the case for taking anticipatory action to defend ourselves, even if uncertainty remains as to the time and place of the enemy's attack. To forestall or prevent such hostile acts by our adversaries, the United States will, if necessary, act preemptively.

> The United States will not use force in all cases to preempt emerging threats, nor should nations use preemption as a pretext for aggression. Yet in an age where the enemies of civilization openly and actively seek the world's most destructive technologies, the United States cannot remain idle while dangers gather.[51]

In terms of international law, this is an extreme form of anticipatory self-defense. According to Michael Reisman, anticipatory self-defense is a response to a palpable and imminent threat whereas preemptive self-defense is designed to arrest a development that it is not yet directly threatening but which could become a direct threat if allowed to mature.[52] Those who have advocated preemption have usually cited the extraordinary nature of the threat posed by weapons of mass destruction and the danger of nonstate actors acquiring such lethal weaponry as reasons for international law to evolve to accept preemption. The United States reaffirmed its controversial doctrine in its 2006 National Security Strategy, notably without reference to international law, but there has been little sign of any widespread acceptance of the doctrine, even by Western states.[53]

■ 2003 Operation Iraqi Freedom and Implied Security Council Authorization

It may have been in part because of strong international opposition to the US doctrine of preemption that the United States, the United Kingdom, and Australia did not rely on self-defense in their legal justification for the use of force against Iraq beginning on March 20, 2003.[54] The United States and United Kingdom wrote letters to the Security Council on the day hostilities commenced, providing legal justification for their use of force.[55] Although toward the close of its letter the United States did refer to its actions as "necessary to defend the United States and the international community from the threat posed by Iraq," the primary justification provided by both states was that of authorization by the Security Council.

The UN Security Council has over the years passed a long list of resolutions concerning Iraq.[56] Four were of particular relevance to the case made by the United States and UK, and it is worth reviewing briefly the content of each of these resolutions before considering the legal justification provided to the Security Council:

• Resolution 660 (1990) predated the Gulf War. It condemned Iraq's invasion of Kuwait and demanded that Iraq withdraw.

• Resolution 678 (1990) could be understood as an ultimatum, to the effect that if Saddam Hussein did not comply with Resolution 660 (1990) by January 15, 1991, UN member states were authorized "to use all necessary means to uphold and implement Resolution 660 (1990) and all subsequent relevant resolutions and to restore international peace and security in the area." This was the only one of the four significant resolutions to authorize the use of force, and its objective was to liberate Kuwait.

• Resolution 687 (1991) set out the terms of the cease-fire at the end of the Gulf War.

• Resolution 1441 (2002) was the last resolution passed by the Council in the lead-up to the hostilities. It asserted that Iraq was in "material breach" of previous resolutions, especially Security Council Resolution 678 (1990), and gave Iraq a final opportunity to comply. It concluded by stating that the Security Council would "remain seized of the matter."

The legal case for the use of force against Iraq by the United States, UK, and Australia was essentially that breaches of Security Council Resolution 687 (1991) had negated the basis for the cease-fire provided for in that resolution, which meant that the cease-fire was no longer effective and that the authorization for the use of force found in Security Council Resolution 678 (1990) had been reactivated. The vast majority of international lawyers agree that the legal justification provided by the United States and its allies for their use of force against Iraq in 2003 was "untenable," falling outside the range of acceptable arguments.[57] Dominic McGoldrick and Ruth Wedgwood are among the few outside government who have found the argument tenable.[58]

The most fundamental problem is the fact that UN Security Council Resolution 1441 (2003) did not explicitly authorize the use of force. Indeed, the United States and the United Kingdom had, prior to the invasion, sought an additional resolution from the Council in recognition of the fact that Resolution 1441 did not contain an authorization to use force. The UK had provided an explanation of its vote on UN Security Council Resolution 1441 (2002) that had stated quite unequivocally that "[t]here is no 'automaticity' in this Resolution. If there is a further Iraqi breach of its disarmament obligations, the matter will return to the Council."[59] The United States had similarly stated, "this Resolution contains no 'hidden triggers' and no 'automaticity' with respect to the use of force."[60] France, China, and Russia had made clear that they had only voted in favor of Resolution 1441 because it contained no automaticity to use force.

■ **The Effectiveness of the International Law on the Use of Force**

The 2003 invasion of Iraq spurred considerable scholarly discussion not only as to the legality of the attack but also as to the relevance and future of

---

Figure 6.3 The Relevance of the *Jus ad Bellum* to Cyber War

An emergent issue for the international law of the use of force is that of its applicability to *cyber war*. As societies and militaries become increasingly reliant on computers, so are they increasingly vulnerable to virtual attacks.[1] A multifaceted cyber attack by one state, or nonstate actor, against another state's information assets, economy, provision of basic services, and emergency services could be devastating, and it may be difficult to know who was responsible for the attack. The Russian government denied involvement in computer attacks on Estonia in April 2007 and in Georgia in 2008. A related issue is that of military attacks via remote-controlled weaponry such as drones. There is increasing debate regarding the implications of virtual war not only for the *jus ad bellum* but for international humanitarian law and the law of arms control.[2]

Notes
1. See, inter alia, Michael N. Schmitt, "Computer Network Attack and the Use of Force in International Law: Thoughts on a Normative Framework," *Columbia Journal of Transnational Law* 37 (1998–1999): 885–937.
2. See, inter alia, Christopher C. Joyner and Catherine Lotionte, "Information Warfare as International Coercion: Elements of a Legal Framework," *European Journal of International Law* 12 (2001): 825–865; and Scott J. Shackelford, "From Nuclear War to Net War: Analogizing Cyber Attacks in International Law," *Berkeley Journal of International Law* 27 (2009): 192–251.

---

international law.[61] A newcomer to international law could become easily disillusioned and conclude from the wars examined in this chapter that international law is weak and unenforceable. There is, unfortunately, a considerable element of truth in this, but such a hasty conclusion requires refining and qualifying. The conclusion to be drawn from the Iraq War would more accurately be that the international law on the use of force cannot be enforced against the greatest military power in the world; this is not the same as being unenforceable. The invasion of Kuwait by Iraq had unequivocally met with strong enforcement action as had its alleged failure to comply with the subsequent cease-fire resolution.

The fact that international law is unlikely to triumph if pitted against the greatest military power in the world is a sobering thought, but it is far from saying that the world would be as well off without that body of law as it is with it. Even in the case of the United States, the law provided a normative benchmark against which to measure the validity of US actions. One of the notable features of the political processes leading up to the Iraq War was the prevalence of legal debate. It was arguably not the United Nations, nor international law, but the United States whose stature was weakened by its failure to abide by international law. The United States met with worldwide condemnation for its 2003 invasion of Iraq, and US foreign policy declined dramatically in its perceived legitimacy. President Barack Obama came to power aware of the need to reaffirm the commitment of the United States to the rule of law in world affairs and to thereby help restore the "soft power" of the United States.

What then, of the impact on international law? Michael Glennon maintains that the ban on intervention found in the UN Charter has been openly violated so many times that it can no longer be regarded as authoritative,[62] but it is worth noting that noncompliance does not of itself undermine a rule of law. The International Court of Justice has stated, "If a State acts in a way prima facie incompatible with a recognized rule, but defends its conduct by appealing to exceptions or justifications contained within the rule itself, then whether or not the State's conduct is in fact justifiable on that basis, the significance of that attitude is to confirm rather than to weaken the rule."[63]

It is easy to adopt the position that all would be well if all states were to comply with all the rules of international law all the time, but given that humanitarian intervention without Security Council authorization is not clearly legal, many who would normally support this position would find it incompatible with prioritizing the protection of human rights. The international law on the use of force is the hardest test for international law, and one must be careful not to draw final conclusions on the role of international law in world politics without examining other issue areas and the experience of middle powers and of developing countries—both of the major developing countries such as China, India, and Brazil, and of the smaller states. Perhaps it is most appropriate to conclude by noting the complexity of the place of international law in world politics and the need to examine many other dimensions of the subject matter in order to develop a sophisticated appreciation of that complexity.

■ Notes

1. The text can be found in Shirley V. Scott, *International Law and Politics: Key Documents* (Boulder, CO: Lynne Rienner, 2006), pp. 3–29; or see http://www.un.org.

2. See Christopher Greenwood, "The Relationship Between *Jus ad Bellum* and *Jus in Bello*," *Review of International Studies* 9 (1983): 221–234.

3. There are some writers, including Neff, who view the UN Charter as part of the just war tradition. See Stephen C. Neff, *War and the Law of Nations. A General History* (Cambridge: Cambridge University Press, 2005), p. 5.

4. Rein Müllerson, "The Use of Force Between Its Past and Future," *International Peacekeeping* 5, no. 4-5 (July-October 1999): 115–128, esp. 115.

5. Ian Brownlie, *International Law and the Use of Force by States* (Oxford: Clarendon, 1963), p. 66.

6. H. Lauterpacht, "'Resort to War' and the Interpretation of the Covenant During the Manchurian Dispute," *American Journal of International Law* (1934): 43–60, esp. 44.

7. Brownlie, *International Law and the Use of Force by States*, p. 60.

8. 94 League of Nations Treaty Series (LNTS) 57.

9. For an historical account of the political origins of the treaty, see Robert H. Ferrell, *Peace in Their Time: The Origins of the Kellogg-Briand Pact* (New Haven, CT: Yale University Press, 1952).

10. D. J. Harris, *Cases and Materials on International Law*, 6th ed. (London: Sweet and Maxwell, 1998), p. 881n 2.

11. Ibid., fn 1.

12. On whether the term *law* has any place in the contemporary legal system, see Christopher Greenwood, "The Concept of War in Modern International Law," *International and Comparative Law Quarterly* 36 (1987): 283–305.

13. See Nikolas Stürchler, *The Threat of Force in International Law* (Cambridge: Cambridge University Press, 2007).

14. See discussion in Christine Gray, *International Law and the Use of Force*, 2nd ed. (Oxford: Oxford University Press, 2004), pp. 29ff.

15. Albrecht Randelzhofer, "Article 2(4)," in Bruno Simma, ed., *The Charter of the United Nations: A Commentary* (Oxford: Oxford University Press, 1994), p. 118.

16. Letter from Daniel Webster, US Secretary of State, to Henry Fox, British Minister in Washington, DC, April 24, 1841. 29 *British and Foreign State Papers 1840–1841*, p. 1138 (1857).

17. *Military and Paramilitary Activities in and Against Nicaragua (Nicaragua v. United States of America), Merits, Judgment, ICJ Reports 1986*, p. 103; *Oil Platforms, ICJ Reports* 2003, pp. 183, 196–198; *Congo, ICJ Reports* 2005, p. 53; and *Legality of the Threat or Use of Nuclear Weapons, ICJ Reports* 1996, p. 245.

18. *Nicaragua, ICJ Reports* 1986.

19. *Military and Paramilitary Activities in and Against Nicaragua (Nicaragua v. United States of America)*, p. 95.

20. See Vaughan Lowe et al., *The United Nations Security Council and War: The Evolution of Thought and Practice Since 1945* (Oxford: Oxford University Press, 2008).

21. Security Council Resolution 678 (1990). Some scholars have interpreted the legal basis for the use of force in the Gulf War as being Security Council sanctioned collective self-defense rather than authorization by the Security Council per se. For discussion of this point, see Christopher Greenwood, "New World Order or Old? The Invasion of Kuwait and the Rule of Law," *Modern Law Review* 55, no. 2 (March 1992): 153–186; Alissa Pyrich, "United Nations: Authorizations of Use of Force," *Harvard International Law Journal* 32 (1991): 265–274; Oscar Schachter, "United Nations Law in the Gulf Conflict," *American Journal of International Law* 85 (1991): 452–473; and Yoram Dinstein, *War, Aggression, and Self-Defence*, 4th ed. (Cambridge: Cambridge University Press, 2005), pp. 274–277.

22. For the background to the crisis see, inter alia, R. Caplan. "International Diplomacy and the Crisis in Kosovo," *International Affairs* 74, no. 4 (1998): 745–761; and M. Weller, "The Rambouillet Conference on Kosovo," *International Affairs* 75, no. 2 (1999): 211–251.

23. UN Security Council Resolutions 1160 (1998), 1199 (1998), and 1203 (1998).

24. There is no general consensus on the definition of humanitarian intervention. Ved P. Nanda, "Tragedies in Northern Iraq, Liberia, Yugoslavia, and Haiti—Revisiting the Validity of Humanitarian Intervention Under International Law, Part 1," *Denver Journal of International Law and Policy* 20, no. 2 (1992): 305–334, esp. 311. Franck and Rodley have referred to humanitarian intervention as recognition of "the right of one State to exercise an international control *by military force* over the acts of another in regard to its internal sovereignty when contrary to the laws of humanity." Thomas M. Franck and Nigel S. Rodley, "After Bangladesh: The Law of Humanitarian Intervention by Military Force," *American Journal of International Law* 67 (1973): 275–305, esp. 277 n 12.

25. Hugo Grotius, *On the Law of War and Peace: Three Books,* Book 2 (Montana: Kessinger, 2004), p. 227.

26. David J. Scheffer, "Toward a Modern Doctrine of Humanitarian Intervention," *University of Toledo Law Review* 23 (1992): 253–293, esp. 258–259.

27. Simon Chesterman, *Just War or Just Peace? Humanitarian Intervention and International Law* (Oxford: Oxford University Press, 2001), pp. 24–25.

28. Ian Brownlie, *International Law and the Use of Force by States* (Oxford: Clarendon, 1963), p. 342. See also Stephen A. Garrett, *Doing Good and Doing Well: An Examination of Humanitarian Intervention* (Westport, CT: Praeger, 1999); Brian D. Lepard, *Rethinking Humanitarian Intervention: A Fresh Legal Approach Based on Fundamental Ethical Principles in International Law and World Religions* (University Park: Pennsylvania State University Press, 2002); Jules Lobel, "Benign Hegemony? Kosovo and Article 2(4) of the UN Charter," *Chicago Journal of International Law* 1, no. 1 (Spring 2000): 19–36; John J. Merriam, "Kosovo and the Law of Humanitarian Intervention," *Case Western Reserve Journal of International Law* 33, no. 1 (Winter 2001): 111–154; Mary Ellen O'Connell, "The UN, NATO, and International Law After Kosovo," *Human Rights Quarterly* 22, no. 1 (2000): 57–89; *The Responsibility to Protect: Report of the International Commission on Intervention and State Sovereignty* (Ottawa: International Development Research Centre, 2001), available at http://www.iedrc.ca; J. L. Holzgrefe and Robert O. Keohane, *Humanitarian Intervention: Ethical, Legal, and Political Dilemmas* (Cambridge: Cambridge University Press, 2003); and Nicholas Tsagourias, "Humanitarian Intervention After Kosovo and Legal Discourse: Self-Deception or Self-Consciousness?" *Leiden Journal of International Law* 13 (2000): 11–32.

29. D. J. Harris, ed., *Cases and Materials on International Law,* 6th ed. (London: Sweet and Maxwell, 1998), p. 948. India apparently initially defended its action on grounds of humanitarian need. Barry Benjamin, "Unilateral Humanitarian Intervention: Legalizing the Use of Force to Prevent Human Rights Atrocities," *Fordham International Law Journal* 16, 1 (1992): 120–158, esp. 141.

30. Merriam, "Kosovo and the Law of Humanitarian Intervention," p. 122.

31. Julie Mertus, "Reconsidering the Legality of Humanitarian Intervention: Lessons from Kosovo," *William and Mary Law Review* 41 (2000): 1743–1787.

32. On the justifications advanced by NATO states, see Abraham D. Sofaer, "International Law and Kosovo," *Stanford Journal of International Law* 1 (2000): 1–21.

33. See the verbatim record of the hearings by the ICJ on Yugoslavia's request for the indication of provisional measures in the case concerning the Legality of Use of Force. Available at http://www.icj-cij.org.

34. Bruno Simma, "NATO, the UN, and the Use of Force: Legal Aspects," *European Journal of International Law* 10 (1999): 1–22.

35. Michael J. Glennon, "The New Interventionism: The Search for a Just International Law," *Foreign Affairs* (May/June 1999): 2–7. See also P. Hilpold, "Humanitarian Intervention: Is There a Need for a Legal Reappraisal?" *European Journal of International Law* 12, no. 3 (2001): 437–468.

36. Chesterman, *Just War or Just Peace,* p. 224.

37. Independent International Commission on Kosovo, *The Kosovo Report: Conflict, International Response, Lessons Learned* (Oxford: Oxford University Press, 2000), p. 94.

38. House of Commons, Select Committee on Foreign Affairs, Fourth Report at para. 144, available at http://www.parliament.the-stationery-office.co.uk.

39. "Speech by Mr. Robin Cook, Secretary of State for Foreign and Commonwealth Affairs, 19 July 2002," in Harris, *Cases and Materials on International Law,* pp. 957–958.

40. K. Roth, "Was the Iraq War a Humanitarian Intervention?" *Journal of Military Ethics* 5, no. 2 (2006): 84–92.

41. *The Responsibility to Protect: Report of the International Commission on Intervention and State Sovereignty,* http://www.iciss.ca.

42. Shirley V. Scott, Anthony John Billingsley, and Christopher Michaelsen, *International Law and the Use of Force: A Documentary and Reference Guide* (Santa Barbara, CA: Praeger Security International, 2009), p. 108.

43. For discussion of the relationship between humanitarian intervention and the responsibility to protect, see, inter alia, Louise Arbour, "The Responsibility to Protect as a Duty of Care in International Law and Practice," *Review of International Studies* 33 (2008): 445–458; and Carlo Focarelli, "The Responsibility to Protect Doctrine and Humanitarian Intervention: Too Many Ambiguities for a Working Doctrine," *Journal of Conflict and Security Law* 13, no. 2 (2008): 191–213.

44. See, inter alia, Eric Myjer and Nigel White, "The Twin Towers Attack: An Unlimited Right to Self-Defence?" *Journal of Conflict and Security Law* 14, no. 2 (2002): 5–18; Mary-Ellen O'Connell, "Lawful Self-Defense to Terrorism," *University of Pittsburgh Law Review* 63 (2002): 889–908; and Myra Williamson, *Terrorism, War and International Law: The Legality of the Use of Force Against Afghanistan in 2001* (Farnham, UK: Ashgate, 2009).

45. See Chapter 1, Figure 1.1.

46. Marcello G. Kohen, "The Use of Force by the United States After the End of the Cold War, and Its Impact on International Law," in Michael Byers and Georg Nolte, eds., *United States Hegemony and the Foundations of International Law* (Cambridge: Cambridge University Press, 2003), pp. 197–231.

47. Myjer and White, "The Twin Towers Attack," p. 13.

48. See, inter alia, Thomas M. Franck, *Recourse to Force: State Action Against Threats and Armed Attacks* (New York: Cambridge University Press, 2002), ch. 7; George K. Walker, "Anticipatory Collective Self-Defense in the Charter Era: What the Treaties Have Said," *Cornell International Law Journal* 31 (1998): 321–376; and David A. Sadoff, "A Question of Determinacy: The Legal Status of Anticipatory Self-Defense," *Georgetown Journal of International Law* 40, no. 2 (2009): 523–584.

49. Kofi Annan, *In Larger Freedom: Towards Development, Security, and Human Rights for All,* Report of the Secretary-General of the United Nations, 2005, p. 33, para. 124.

50. Christine Gray, "The Bush Doctrine Revisited: The 2006 National Security Strategy of the USA," *Chinese Journal of International Law* 5 (2006): 555–578, esp. 566.

51. Available at http://www.whitehouse.gov.

52. M. Reisman, "Remarks on 'Self-Defence in an Age of Terrorism,'" *American Society of International Law Proceedings* 97 (2003): 142–143.

53. See, inter alia, Rachel Bzostek, *Why Not Preempt? Security, Law, Norms, and Anticipatory Military Activities* (Aldershot, UK: Ashgate, 2008); Michael W. Doyle, *Striking First: Preemption and Prevention in International Conflict* (Princeton, NJ: Princeton University Press, 2008); Gray, "The Bush Doctrine Revisited."

54. On the reasons for the invasion see, inter alia, Tom Rick, *Fiasco: The American Military Adventure in Iraq* (New York: Penguin, 2006); and Bob Woodward, *Bush at War* (New York: Simon and Schuster, 2005).

55. Letter dated March 20, 2003, from the Permanent Representative of the United States of America to the United Nations, Addressed to the President of the Security Council, UN Document S/2003/351 (March 21, 2003). The United Kingdom and Australia sent similar letters.

56. For background on the relationship between Iraq and the Security Council, see David M. Malone, *The International Struggle Over Iraq: Politics in the UN Security Council, 1980–2005* (Oxford: Oxford University Press, 2006). More generally, see Rick Fawn and Raymond Hinnebusch, eds., *The Iraq War: Causes and Consequences* (Boulder, CO: Lynne Rienner, 2006).

57. Andrew Byrnes, "'The Law Was Warful': The Iraq War and the Role of International Lawyers in the Domestic Reception of International Law," in Hilary Charlesworth et al., *The Fluid State* (Annandale, VA: Federation Press, 2005), pp. 229–250, esp. 247.

58. Dominic McGoldrick, *From "9-11" to the Iraq War 2003: International Law in an Age of Complexity* (Oxford: Hart, 2004). Professor Christopher Greenwood, who furnished the advice to the UK government, subsequently became a judge on the International Court of Justice. Ruth Wedgwood, "The Fall of Saddam Hussein: Security Council Mandates and Preemptive Self-Defense," *American Journal of International Law* 97 (2003): 576–585.

59. Statement by Ambassador Greenstock to the Security Council, "Explanation of Vote on Security Council Resolution 1441 on Iraq, 8 November 2002," reproduced in Shirley V. Scott, *International Law and Politics: Key Documents* (Boulder, CO: Lynne Rienner, 2006), pp. 112–113.

60. Explanation of Vote by Ambassador John D. Negroponte, United States Permanent Representative to the United Nations, Following the Vote on the Iraq Resolution, Security Council, November 8, 2002, available at http://www.globalpolicy.org.

61. See, inter alia, Andrew Byrnes and Hilary Charlesworth, "The Illegality of the War Against Iraq," *Dialogue* 22 (2003): 4–9, available at http://www.assa.edu.au; Adam Roberts, "Law and the Use of Force After Iraq," *Survival* 45, no. 2 (Summer 2003): 31–56; Lori Fisler Damrosch and Bernard H. Oxman, eds., "Agora: Future Implications of the Iraq Conflict," *American Journal of International Law* 97, no. 3 (2003): 553–642; Richard A. Falk, *The Costs of War: International Law, the UN, and World Order After Iraq* (New York: Routledge, 2008); and Phil Shiner and Andrew Williams, eds., *The Iraq War and International Law* (Oxford: Hart, 2008).

62. Michael J. Glennon, *Limits of Law, Prerogatives of Power: Intervention After Kosovo* (New York: Palgrave, 2001).

63. *Case Concerning Military and Paramilitary Activities in and Against Nicaragua (Merits) ICJ Reports* 1986, p. 98.

7

Legal Argument as Political Maneuvering

IN CHAPTER 5 WE SAW THAT LEGAL POSITIVISM PROVIDES A PHILO-sophical underpinning to what can be thought of in terms of a three-tiered system of principles, rules, and concepts. Legal positivism requires that the analysis of a specific point of law, such as the legality of a state using force, be done on the basis of the components of law found within the sources of international law, thereby shunning argument based on other grounds such as morality, economics, or politics. This contributes to an image of international legal argument as objective and apolitical and means that it is often difficult for a newcomer to international law to appreciate the distinction between the image of international law conveyed in such international legal analysis and reality. As will be explored in this chapter, it is precisely because legal analysis appears apolitical that it can be brought into service in the pursuit of political objectives.

■ The Indeterminacy of International Law vs. Its Rulebook Image

Analysis of the legality of some recent uses of force in Chapter 6 showed that, even in relation to a subject area in international law that is relatively clear-cut, such as that of the use of force, it is possible to arrive at differing assessments as to the legality of a specific action. Although the majority of international lawyers assessed the use of force against Iraq in 2003 to have been illegal, there were some lawyers who considered it legal. In any particular scenario it is usually easier to make a case either for or against the legality of a specific action, but it is virtually always also possible to make a case for the opposing position; this is referred to as the *indeterminacy* of international law. It is not usually the case that both conclusions can be arrived at with equal ease, but both conclusions are usually possible. The extent to which international law is indeterminate varies across issue areas and between sources; customary international law, for example, is generally less determinate than treaty law.[1]

Recognition of the indeterminacy of international law comes as a surprise to many observers of world politics because this is not the image of law conveyed by international law rhetoric or even by most references to international law in political rhetoric. Legal argument is expressed so as to give the impression that the decision arrived at—whether for or against legality—is the only one possible. A state in dispute with another state will, for example, usually present an argument of international law that contrasts the legality of its own actions/policy position with those of the other state(s). Take, for example, the following extract from the account provided by Chinese Foreign Ministry Spokesman Zhu Bangzao of the collision between US and Chinese military planes on April 1, 2001. It would have been extraordinary if the representative of China had said that China's actions had been illegal, or if he had hinted that international law is indeterminate. Rather, the assessment of the legality of Chinese, and illegality of the US, actions are presented as if they are the only ones possible given the content of the existing sources of international law:

> The US plane suddenly veered at a wide angle towards the Chinese planes, which were closer to baseline of the Chinese side. The US plane's nose and left wing rammed the tail of one of the Chinese planes, causing it to lose control and plunge into the sea. . . .
> It should be pointed out that it was proper and in accordance with international law for Chinese military fighters to follow and monitor the US military surveillance plane within airspace over China's exclusive economic waters. . . .
> The surveillance flight conducted by the US air overran the scope of "free over-flight" according to international law. The move also violated the United Nations Convention on the Law of the Sea, which stipulates that any flight in airspace above another nation's exclusive zone should respect the rights of the country concerned.[2]

As might be expected, this statement draws a clear contrast between the purported legality of China's actions and what is presented as the clear illegality of US actions.

Let us take another example: that of US actions during the Cuban Missile Crisis of 1962. The United States wanted to ensure that the Soviet Union remove the missiles it had already installed in Cuba and not send any others. It wanted to use international law to facilitate this. But in constructing an argument contrasting the legality of US actions with the illegality of Soviet actions it ran into a basic problem: what the Soviets were doing was not obviously illegal, but any actions that the United States might take to ensure its goals were met were likely to be illegal.[3] Great effort was put into constructing a legal argument that would support the United States acting to achieve its foreign policy goals. The missiles were characterized as "offensive" rather than defensive; an immediate meeting of the Organ of Consultation of the Organization of American States was called, which passed a resolution recommending, under articles 6 and 8 of the Rio Treaty, all measures including the use of force to prevent Cuba from receiving materials from Soviet powers that threatened the peace and security of the hemisphere; the United States coined the term *quarantine* to describe what might have otherwise been regarded as an illegal blockade and worked hard diplomatically to ensure that a Soviet-proposed resolution condemning the action would not be pressed to the vote in the Security Council.[4] Although there was no explicit Security Council authorization for the US actions as might be anticipated under article 53 of the UN Charter, at least there was no explicit vote condemning the US actions. Abram Chayes, who was State Department legal counsel during the Kennedy administration and who was instrumental in crafting the legal justification for the quarantine, reflected many years later that the legal position had been very important in the diplomatic resolution of the crisis. "Having to consider the legal position carefully contributed, I think, to the wisdom of our choices."[5]

Recognition of the indeterminacy of international law is essential to gaining some appreciation of the role that international legal argument can play in world politics because it is this indeterminacy that permits it to be used as a medium of political maneuvering between states and in their relations with other international actors. Dialogues regarding questions of legality can be a mechanism by which political positions are mediated. In Chapter 5 we looked at a section of a legal analysis drawn on by Japan in support of its opposition to the creation of a sanctuary for whales in the Southern Ocean. But another eminent international lawyer, Patricia Birnie of the United Kingdom, also undertook a legal analysis of the sanctuary and declared it legal under the Charter of the IWC.[6] Naturally enough, it was the opinion of Patricia Birnie that was drawn on by many anti-whaling nations.[7]

The indeterminacy of international law means that it is possible for an international lawyer to construct a legal argument to support either side in a dispute, as opposed to working from the rules, principles, and concepts of international law to arrive ineluctably at a particular conclusion as international legal rhetoric suggests is possible. A practical example of this difference relates to the provision of legal advice to a government's foreign policy decisionmakers. Most states have attorneys within a special government agency who appraise and sort out the international legal implications of foreign policy. In Canada it is the Bureau of Legal Affairs in the Department of Foreign Affairs and Trade; in the United Kingdom it is the Legal Adviser's Department of the Foreign and Commonwealth office; in Australia it is the Legal Adviser's Branch in the Department of Foreign Affairs and Trade; and in the United States it is the Office of the Legal Adviser in the Department of State.[8] The legal adviser generally operates as an objective expounder of law before a foreign policy action is taken or a policy course selected. Once the executive branch has taken action, he or she must transform into a subjective advocate of the government's position, presenting the best legal case possible in defense of the government's policy position even if the executive has chosen a course contrary to that which he or she had advocated.[9] When told by the then British foreign secretary, Robin Cook, that the lawyers were having difficulty justifying the planned 1999 intervention in Yugoslavia, the response of the US secretary of state was, reportedly, to "get new lawyers."[10]

■ Legal Maneuvering as Political Maneuvering: The Cases Yugoslavia Brought Against the Member States of NATO in Relation to Their Bombing Campaign During the Kosovo Crisis

Sometimes a state, if in dispute with another state, will seek to have the alleged legal/illegal contrast between its behavior and that of other states with which it is in dispute confirmed by a third party such as a judicial body. This is, not surprisingly, most likely when the state concerned believes that there is a high probability that the Court will decide in favor of the legality of its actions. We will now move on to another example of legal positivism in practice. This time we will look at a set of cases brought before the International Court of Justice by Yugoslavia. This example of an attempt to have the Court confirm the illegality of the other states' actions will help us to consider further the limitations of a rulebook image of law as well as to show in more detail the operation of legal positivism as a mechanism for political interaction and maneuvering.

No doubt encouraged by the seemingly clear illegality of NATO actions, Yugoslavia on April 29, 1999, instituted proceedings (separate cases) before the ICJ against the United States, United Kingdom, France, Germany, Italy, the Netherlands, Belgium, Canada, Portugal, and Spain. Yugoslavia maintained that each of these ten states had committed acts by which it had violated a number of its legal obligations, the first mentioned in each instance being that of the obligation not to use force against another state. Yugoslavia likely saw this as an opportunity, at a minimum, to influence world opinion and delegitimize NATO's actions. Yugoslavia also filed, in each of the cases, a request for interim measures of protection, asking the Court to order the states involved to "cease immediately [their] acts of use of force" and to "refrain from any act of threat or use of force against the Federal Republic of Yugoslavia."

The International Court of Justice can issue interim measures designed to ensure that no permanent damage is done to one of the parties pending the conclusion of the case. The Court is understandably wary of doing so where it has not yet even determined whether it has jurisdiction over the case. The Court thus begins by looking to see whether it would appear that it does have jurisdiction and only indicates provisional measures if it has determined that it does have prima facie jurisdiction. In June 1999 the Court found that it did not have prima facie jurisdiction in any of the cases brought against the NATO states by Yugoslavia and on that basis declined to indicate provisional measures. In relation to the proceedings brought against the United States and Spain the ICJ found that it "manifestly lacked jurisdiction" and so dismissed the cases. As regards the other cases, the Court ruled, in effect, that it did not have an obvious basis for jurisdiction, that whether or not it did could be determined later but was not at this stage sufficiently clear for the Court to indicate provisional measures on that basis.

Let us now put into practice the law relating to the jurisdiction of the ICJ that we considered in Chapter 5 so as to understand better the process that led to the decision of the Court as regards jurisdiction and provisional measures in the *Legality of Use of Force* cases. There was no compromis involved. Yugoslavia made a written application to the Court. By article 38(2) of the Rules of Court an application instituting proceedings is required to specify as far as possible the legal grounds upon which the jurisdiction of the Court is said to be based and to specify the precise nature of the claim, as well as provide a succinct statement of the facts and grounds on which the claim is based. Yugoslavia drew on all three bases of jurisdiction other than special agreement, although it did not draw on all of them in relation to every state against which it wished to institute proceedings.

The first basis given by Yugoslavia was the compromissory clause contained in the 1948 Convention on the Prevention and Punishment of the Crime of Genocide. Yugoslavia asserted that this gave the Court a basis of jurisdiction regarding all ten states. The ICJ did not accept this argument in relation to Spain and the United States, both of which had entered reservations against article 9 of the Genocide Convention. As regards the other states, the Court ruled, in essence, that the bombing was not obviously a case of attempted genocide and that it would need to investigate further.

Second, in relation to France, Germany, Italy, and the United States, Yugoslavia tried to establish jurisdiction on the basis of article 38, paragraph 5 of the Rules of Court. None of the states gave its consent. The

United States made its position clear: "The United States has not consented to jurisdiction under Article 38, paragraph 5, and will not do so."[11]

Third, Yugoslavia drew on the optional clause in attempting to establish the jurisdiction of the ICJ in the cases brought against Belgium, Canada, the Netherlands, Portugal, Spain, and the United Kingdom. Yugoslavia had filed its acceptance of the compulsory jurisdiction of the ICJ on April 26, 1999, three days before instituting the ICJ proceedings. Vladislav Jovanovic, chargé d'affaires of the permanent mission of Yugoslavia to the United Nations, stated in a letter:

> I hereby declare that the Government of the Federal Republic of Yugoslavia recognizes, in accordance with Article 36, paragraph 2, of the Statute of the International Court of Justice, as compulsory ipso facto and without special agreement, in relation to any other State accepting the same obligation, that is on condition of reciprocity, the jurisdiction of the said Court in all disputes arising or which may arise after the signature of the present Declaration, with regard to the situations or facts subsequent to this signature, except in cases where the parties have agreed or shall agree to have recourse to another procedure or to another method of pacific settlement. The present Declaration does not apply to disputes relating to questions which, under international law, fall exclusively within the jurisdiction of the Federal Republic of Yugoslavia, as well as to territorial disputes.
>
> The aforesaid obligation is accepted until such time as notice may be given to terminate the acceptance.

The Court found that article 36(2) definitely did not establish a basis for its jurisdiction in the cases brought against Spain and the United States, both of which had made a reservation in their acceptance of the Court's jurisdiction in respect of "disputes to which the other party or parties have accepted the compulsory jurisdiction of the Court less than 12 months prior to the filing of the application bringing the dispute before the Court." As regards the others, the Court found that the legal dispute had arisen before the date specified in Yugoslavia's acceptance of article 36(2), which, because of the principle of reciprocity, applies also to the other states. Although the Court had definitely not found a basis of jurisdiction so far as either Spain or the United States were concerned, there was still a possibility of its finding jurisdiction in relation to the other states.

Because the Court did not establish prima facie jurisdiction in any of the cases, the Court declined to issue provisional measures. In the cases brought against Spain and the United States the Court found that it "manifestly lacked jurisdiction" and so dismissed the cases.

The next step was for written submissions from each side, beginning with the applicant. The Court said that Yugoslavia should submit its memorial (written pleadings) by January 5, 2000, and the remaining respondents submit their countermemorials (responses) by July 5, 2000. However, on July 5, 2000, the NATO countries for which the Court might still find jurisdiction (all but Spain and the United States) each filed preliminary objections to jurisdiction and admissibility. Hearings on the merits were then suspended and by orders of September 8, 2000, the Court fixed April 5, 2001, as the date by which Yugoslavia should present a written statement of its observations and submissions on the preliminary objections raised by the NATO countries. On January 18, 2001, Yugoslavia requested an extension, and by orders of February 21, 2001, the ICJ extended the time limit for Yugoslavia to April 5, 2002. After a further request by Yugoslavia "for a stay of proceedings or . . . for an extension by twelve months of the time period for the submission of observations on the preliminary objections" and an indication by the respondent states that they were not opposed to a stay of proceedings or to an extension of the time limit for Yugoslavia's filing of the observations and submissions, the Court fixed April 7, 2003, as the new time limit.

Hearings on the preliminary objections regarding the Court's jurisdiction to hear the case and to the admissibility of the application were held April 19–23, 2004. The Court found that it had no jurisdiction to hear the case. What proved to be the decisive objection, raised by some of the states, was the claim that the Federal Republic of Yugoslavia (FRY) had not been a party to the Statute in 1999 at the time the proceedings had been initiated. According to article 35(1) of the Statute, the Court "shall be open to the States Parties to the present Statute." By article 93 of the UN Charter,

> (1) All Members of the United Nations are ipso facto parties to the Statute of the International Court of Justice.
> (2) A State which is not a Member of the United Nations may become a party to the Statute of the International Court of Justice on conditions to be determined in each case by the General Assembly upon the recommendation of the Security Council.

The Socialist Federal Republic of Yugoslavia (SFRY) had broken up in 1991–1992; on April 27, 1992, the SFRY Assembly, the National Assembly of the Republic of Serbia, and the Assembly of the Republic of Montenegro had declared that the FRY would continue the international legal and political personality of the SFRY, and the FRY wrote to the United Nations Secretary-General that the FRY would continue the membership of the SFRY in the UN. The Security Council decided, however, by Resolution 777 (1992), that the FRY could not continue automatically the SFRY's membership. According to the Court, the legal situation as regards the status of the

FRY in the United Nations had remained ambiguous from 1992 until October 27, 2000, when the FRY made a formal application for UN membership; it was admitted by General Assembly Resolution 55/12 of November 1, 2000. The Court therefore concluded that the FRY had not been a member of the UN and party to the Statute of the Court in 1999. After considering and rejecting alternative ways by which the FRY might have had access to the Court despite not being a UN member, it concluded that the FRY had no legal right of access to the Court at the time it instituted proceedings in 1999. Having found that it had no jurisdiction to proceed to the merits, the Court nevertheless reminded the parties that they "remain in all cases responsible for acts attributable to them that violate the rights of other States."

In this example, we see how what may appear to be dry rules and procedures pertaining to the jurisdiction of the International Court of Justice became the mechanism by which the Federal Republic of Yugoslavia attempted to draw on international law in pursuit of its political objectives. There was no easy way by which Yugoslavia could force the Court to decide on the legality of NATO's use of force, despite the fact that the question appeared to be relatively clear-cut. If the Court had proceeded to hear the merits of the cases and had found that the NATO states had breached international law in their use of force, there could have been a considerable problem for those states, both abroad and at home. A 2009 poll of 20,202 respondents in twenty-one states that comprise 64 percent of the world's population found that most people in seventeen of the twenty-one states believed that their country should consistently follow international law even if it conflicts with the national interest. Interestingly, most respondents in two out of three states polled were also confident that the ICJ would treat their country fairly and impartially.[12]

We can also see that there is considerable knowledge and skill involved in legal maneuvering. There was no way that Yugoslavia would have been able to demonstrate that the Court had jurisdiction over Spain and the United States on the basis of the Genocide Convention when they had both clearly made reservations to the compromissory clause in that treaty. The number of, knowledge, skill, and experience of the international lawyers on which a government can draw is an important dimension of its capacity to achieve its objectives on the international stage. A government involved in international litigation often looks beyond its own legal team for expertise. When developing countries are represented at the ICJ, a majority of their principal legal representatives have tended to be from developed countries. Between 1999 and 2008 some 75 percent of counsel/advocates representing developing countries in cases being heard by the ICJ were from law firms or universities in developed countries.[13] This is set to change, particularly for the more wealthy developing countries, as they increase their own legal capacity. But even US trade officials preparing for dispute resolution through the World Trade Organization usually supplement their expertise with input from private firms and trade associations.[14]

International litigation is an expensive process; litigating an average case that goes to a final judgment is likely to cost millions of US dollars.[15] It is standard for each party to pay its own costs, although the ICJ has the power to make an order favoring one or the other party. In 1989 the General Assembly established the Secretary-General's Trust Fund, a system of legal aid to assist states seeking to settle disputes through the ICJ, although the fund only assists states involved in cases in which the basis of jurisdiction is an ad hoc agreement.

■ International Law, Legitimacy, and Norm Contestation

We have seen that legal maneuvering is an important form of political maneuvering. Reference to international law within political negotiations may be intended to convince the other party or parties to act in a certain way or, in the case of Yugoslavia, perhaps, to *stop* the bombing campaign. The influence may, however, be indirect, for legal discourse may achieve the desired end through enhancing or detracting from the perceived legitimacy of specific goals or policies. An even less direct objective of engaging in legal argument, particularly in litigation, is to shape norms within the international arena. A court case may not result in a decision that achieves one's immediate policy goals, but it may contribute to developing the law and norms in that issue area that could, in years to come, facilitate a momentous political and social shift. The UN human rights committees may be able to have an immediate impact on the lives of only a very small number of individuals, but the jurisprudence developed through their work is likely to influence national governments and courts and, over time, contribute to considerable improvement in the lives of large numbers of people. NGOs aim to facilitate this diffusion of norms.

A norm may or may not be part of international law, but a norm gains added influence through its incorporation into international law. The principle of the responsibility to protect is currently a political norm, although those who believe in it are attempting to demonstrate its compatibility with legal norms with a view to its one day becoming an accepted principle of international law. Norms may have very specific political ramifications. Take, for example, the principle of equal but differentiated responsibility. This is a principle of international environmental law specifying that even though all states have responsibilities towards the environment, not all states have the same responsibilities. The responsibility of developed countries is greater both because of their historical responsibility for environmental harm and because of their greater financial capacity to take action. Acceptance of this principle as a basis on which to develop climate change policy at Kyoto gave rise to a treaty in which developing countries acquired no legally binding emission reduction targets. As China rose to become the largest greenhouse gas–producing nation, it became apparent that application of this norm to the evolving treaty regime, even if fair, could potentially hinder efforts to tackle climate change. Those producing, shaping, and disseminating norms wield great power, although future applications of a norm may not always be apparent at the time of creation. Political scientists sometimes use the language of *norm entrepreneur* in recognition of the significance of that role.[16]

Let us now consider a situation in which the ICJ became involved in an attempt to shift norms in relation to nuclear weapons: the nuclear weapons advisory opinion.

On May 14, 1993, the World Health Organization requested an advisory opinion from the ICJ on whether, "in view of the health and environmental effects, . . . the use of nuclear weapons by a State in war or other armed conflict [would] be a breach of its obligations under international law including the WHO Constitution?"[17] On December 15, 1994, the UN General Assembly adopted a resolution asking the ICJ for an "urgent" advisory opinion on the question, Is the threat or use of nuclear weapons in any circumstances permitted under international law?[18]

The questions asked of the Court were legal questions, of relevance to the laws of armed conflict, environmental law, human rights law, the UN Charter, and the WHO Constitution.[19] At the same time, there could be few questions more political than those pertaining to one of the major determinants of global power relations for more than half a century. Permanent members of the Security Council perceived the question asked of the ICJ by the General Assembly as threatening their privileged status as permanent members of the UN Security Council.[20]

The Court decided to consolidate the two requests relating to the legality of nuclear weapons and, in accordance with article 66 of the Statute of the ICJ, invited states to submit written statements. Public hearings on the two questions were held from October 30 to November 14, 1995. During the proceedings the United Kingdom and France argued that because certain NGOs had been instrumental in bringing the question to the Court, it was not appropriate for the Court to answer it. The Court rejected this argument although it also rejected an application by the International Physicians for the Prevention of Nuclear War to file a brief in the case.[21]

As might be expected, nuclear and nonnuclear states tended to have polar views on the question at hand. The nuclear powers argued that there is no existing prohibition on the use or threat of use of nuclear weapons in international law, that the Treaty on the Non-Proliferation of Nuclear Weapons (NPT) legitimated the possession and thus, implicitly, the use (by them) of such weapons. Those opposed to nuclear weapons argued that the NPT, at most, acknowledged the fact of possession by the nuclear states; it is neutral as to their use; and that existing international law pointed in the direction of the illegality of the use or threat of use of nuclear weapons.[22]

On July 8, 1996, the Court delivered two opinions. It concluded that the WHO was not competent to ask the question, because, as a UN Specialized Agency, the WHO could only request advisory opinions "on legal questions arising within the scope of their activities." In response to the question of the General Assembly, the majority view was that

> the threat or use of nuclear weapons would generally be contrary to the rules of international law applicable in armed conflict, and in particular the principles and rules of humanitarian law;
> However, in view of the current state of international law, and the elements of fact at its disposal, the Court cannot conclude definitively whether the threat or use of nuclear weapons would be lawful or unlawful in an extreme circumstance of self-defence, in which the very survival of a state would be at stake.[23]

The Court was of the unanimous opinion that "[t]here exists an obligation to pursue in good faith and bring to a conclusion negotiations leading to nuclear disarmament in all its aspects under strict and effective international control."

This opinion was such that it could be acclaimed by nuclear weapon states as well as those campaigning for the elimination of nuclear weapons. If the Court had exercised its discretion not to answer the questions it would likely have been accused of failing to apply the rule of law in international relations; but in exercising its power to answer the questions the Court ran the risk of being accused of entering the political domain.[24] If, having accepted the challenge, the Court had gone on to find in favor of the legality of the threat or use of nuclear weapons, it could easily have been accused of backing the agenda of the most powerful states. Were it to have found against the legality of the threat or use of nuclear weapons the Court risked its findings being ignored and hence detracting from the credibility of international law. In a sense the Court had no option but to "tackle the fate of the earth" while at the same time giving a response that cannot but be regarded as at least "somewhat ambiguous."[25]

It may be considered to have been a little naive of those lobbying to have the question asked of the ICJ to think that, even if they were successful in having the question asked of the Court, and even if they had got all they could have hoped for and the Court had opined against the legality of nuclear weapons, the world would then miraculously be rid of these weapons. But the key individuals were more realistic; the hoped-for decision against the legality of nuclear weapons was seen as part of a broader process of "delegitimizing" nuclear weapons and weakening the resistance of the nuclear weapons powers to nuclear disarmament. The Lawyers' Committee on Nuclear Policy reasoned that even a completely negative opinion in relation to nuclear weapons could "shock the public and officials into increased action against nuclear weapons, and thus still assist the process of disarmament."[26]

The ensuing advisory opinion may have been ambiguous, but the considerable debate that it has generated[27] has brought into greater prominence issues regarding the legality—and the morality—of nuclear weapons. The immediate outcome of the opinion may not have been great, but its political significance may at some future date appear greater when viewed in historical context.

■ The Rulebook Image of International Law

It is not only in relation to determinacy that there is a mismatch between the reality of international law and the image of law conveyed both in positivist rhetoric and in references to international law in political documents. Here are some other assumptions about international law that are implicit in positivist analyses:[28]

- International law is ultimately distinguishable from, and even superior to, politics.
- International law is politically neutral or universal in the sense that it treats all states equally.
- It is possible to distinguish objectively between legal and illegal action.
- It is compulsory for a state to comply with international law.
- International law is (virtually) timeless—at least in the sense that it predates policy.
- International law is (virtually) self-contained.
- It is possible to apply the rules of law objectively so as to settle a dispute between states.
- International law is (virtually) comprehensive—it can deal with any issue that arises between states.

This set of assumptions adds up to what can be described as the "rulebook" image of international law. If a non-lawyer were presented with a large, heavy, and well-worn volume and told that it contained all the rules of international law, he or she might well believe it. According to what we can dub the "rulebook" image of international law, a decisionmaker faced with a decision as to how to act calls in the legal adviser. The legal adviser then consults the relevant page in this large volume, reads what it says must be done, and advises the decisionmaker accordingly. The decisionmaker should, of course, do as his or her advisers instruct, and if he or she does, the state will have "complied" with international law. So far as an international judiciary is concerned, the rulebook image assumes that when dealing with a dispute between two parties, judges of the International Court would, similarly, open their rulebook to the appropriate page, ascertain how each party should act in the given circumstances, and thereby settle impartially the differences between those parties. The rulebook image of international law considers that "law is 'rules,'" that these rules are politically neutral, that the judiciary is objective, and that its prime task is to apply—rather than to make—the rules.[29] International law is widely perceived as a "body of timeless absolutes, good for all seasons and all places, and postulated *a priori* in advance of actual problem situations."[30] International law is seen as a unified system with international cohesion.[31] In "international relations, most every event, including large areas of administrative activity, is considered to be classifiable as lawful or unlawful."[32]

There is some truth in this image of international law. Foreign policy decisionmakers do often consult their legal advisers, who in turn prepare a statement of the relevant law to be taken into consideration during the policymaking process. Judges of the International Court of Justice do, of course, consult the various sources of international law and endeavor to apply what they find therein to settle a dispute presented to them. International law is not as "political" as pure politics, and it does tend to be more stable than the dynamics of political relations. The indeterminacy of international law is by no means absolute; a lawyer cannot get away with justifying as legal just any action whatsoever. But, while there is some truth in the rulebook image of international law, there is an important mismatch between this image and reality. It is not that the assumptions of legal positivism do not contain an element of truth but that in their absolute sense they are not true.

Just as the notion of the possibility of a strict legal/illegal division of behavior does not correspond exactly to reality, so do these other assumptions not correspond exactly to reality. States are assumed to have sovereign equality, but, as we saw in Chapter 1, they may not, for example, have equivalent opportunity to contribute to the negotiation of a new treaty; for one reason, there may often be parallel sessions at an international conference at which a treaty is being negotiated and small delegations may not have the resources to cover all meetings.[33] There was considerable concern following the end of the Cold War at the degree to which the United States, as the world's only remaining superpower, would be able to influence the content and the operation of international law.[34]

There is a clear dynamic between policymaking and international law. Whereas the rulebook image of international law assumes that international law always precedes policy, there are many instances in which it has not done so. International law did not, for example, precede and "effortlessly resolve the problem" of Spanish–Indian relations when the Spaniards discovered the Indians. Rather, the discovery posed special problems for international jurists such as Vitoria, who reconceptualized prevailing international legal doctrines or invented new ones.[35]

The notion that international law can settle any dispute that arises between states is also manifestly untrue. International law has not always been sufficiently developed to deal with an issue in question, or a particular solution may be so important to a country that it is not prepared to accept any compromise whether mandated by international law or not. Territorial disputes tend to fall into this category. It is widely assumed, by those who have heard of its existence, that a world court can and would make an impartial determination as to the legality of the actions of two or more states in dispute and that this should then settle the dispute, presumably in favor of the state or states in the legal right. Again, it is not that there is no truth to this image, but it certainly does not tell the whole story. Even if a case reaches the ICJ and proceeds to a judgment on the merits, this may not be the end of the political story. The Tehran Hostages Crisis lasted for 444 days, between November 1979 and January 1981. During this period the United States initiated proceedings before the ICJ, and the Court both indicated provisional measures and went on to judge on the merits. But from Iran's point of view the issue at stake was much broader than that dealt with by the majority decision, and it involved a history of US interference in Iran's internal affairs. The judgment had little effect on the course of the dispute, which, once the internal instability in Iran had subsided, was finally resolved through mediation by Algeria.[36]

The rhetoric of international law proceeds as if the principles were true, but, as a system of interrelated rules, principles, and concepts, also provides for the fact that they do not wholly match reality. *Non liquet*, for example, is a term of international law that refers to a gap in the law. The possibility of the system not having provided for a particular issue is in contrast to the image of international law as complete and as having provided for any eventuality. Another example of the rules and principles of international law providing for the discrepancy between the image and reality of international law is that judges of the International Court of Justice are "independent" and elected regardless of their nationality, and yet if the Court includes upon its bench a judge of the nationality of one of the parties to a case, any other party may choose a person to sit as judge, and if the Court includes upon the bench no judge of the nationality of the parties to a case, each of those parties may choose a judge.[37]

To take a third example, the international law of territorial acquisition is in many respects out of date. Unlike in the seventeenth to the nineteenth centuries, it is no longer acceptable for a state to "acquire" a piece of territory in a colonial grab. International morality and international law have moved on.[38] Contrary to its image, international law is not timeless; it is very much a product of the political interactions of the time—or, to express it differently, there is an historical relativity of international law. The system of international law thus needs to cater to this discrepancy between the image and reality of international law in relation to territorial acquisition, and it does so by way of the intertemporal principle, which stipulates that title must be valid in accordance with the law in force at the time at which title is claimed to have been established, rather than in contemporary terms. Thus, when the International Court of Justice was asked to decide whether the territory known as the Western Sahara had been *terra nullius* at the time of its colonization by Spain, the Court premised its response by saying that the question would have to be interpreted "by reference to the law in force at that period."[39]

The pervasive image of international law does not match reality. Nevertheless, if it were not assumed to be at least largely true, there would be no basis on which to draw on international law in political maneuvering. And it is unlikely that it would continue to be assumed true if there were no element of truth in it. It is the cohesion of international law as a set of interrelated principles, rules, and concepts that lends international law its considerable degree of autonomy and that, at the same time, permits it to be used as a vehicle of political interaction.

■ Efforts to Characterize International Law as Something Other Than a Rulebook

This chapter has referred to what was termed the "rulebook" image of international law as that conveyed by international legal discourse and in most references to international law in political rhetoric. It is in recognition of the fact that international law does not match its pervasive image of being generally static, politically neutral, clear-cut, universal, self-contained, and comprehensive that a number of theorists have in recent years attempted to characterize international law as something other, or at least more, than "mere" rules. Members of the New Haven or Yale School of international law,[40] for example, have played down law as rules in favor of international law as a "comprehensive process of authoritative decisions." The New Haven approach emphasizes the dynamic nature of international law and takes into account not only rules but also the explicit discussion of values, interests, goals, and conditioning factors, prompting the criticism that, viewed from a New Haven perspective, international law becomes indistinguishable from politics or social science.[41] Jutta Brunée and Stephen Toope also expand a conceptualization of international law to encompass not only rules but "legal procedures, methodologies, institutions, and processes generating legitimacy."[42]

What can broadly be referred to as "critical legal theorists"[43] or the "newstream"[44] have, in contrast, emphasized the discrepancy between particular principles found within what has been referred to as the rulebook image of international law and reality, although they may have used different language to do so. A. Carty, for example, denied that there is a universal system of international law;[45] Martti Koskenniemi, that international law provides a nonpolitical way of dealing with disputes.[46] Koskenniemi has defined the newstream as "a critical sensibility that examines international law from a wide range of intellectual strands: philosophy, political theory, sociology, anthropology, cultural and women's studies, and so on in order to reassess its meaning, contemporary relevance, and future role."[47] Not only do critical theorists recognize that international law does not match the rulebook image of international law, but they claim that it is not capable of doing so. This gave rise to considerable introspection on the part of many of the individuals writing in the newstream genre; perhaps not surprisingly, a sense of futility pervaded much of their output.[48]

Third World Approaches to International Law (TWAIL) has been referred to as an "emergent discipline" that highlights the role that international law has played in the subordination of third world peoples but also seeks through scholarship, policy, and politics to eradicate the conditions of underdevelopment in the third world.[49] TWAIL scholars have sought to distinguish themselves from some of the pioneering Third World scholars, who included Georges Abi-Saab, F. Garcia-Amador, R. P. Anand, Mohammed Bedjaoui, and Taslim Elias; TWAIL writers retrospectively group those influential scholars together as TWAIL I and call themselves TWAIL II.[50] Critical third world scholars oppose a number of aspects of current international law which "[attempt] to confer universality on norms and practices that are European in origin, thought, and experience" such as human rights and the protection of intellectual property through the treaty on Trade-Related Aspects of Intellectual Property Rights (TRIPS).[51] Third world criticism has taken as its starting point the fact that international law was "complicit in the subjugation of non-European people."[52] The process began through the international law of territorial acquisition that from the seventeenth century to the late nineteenth century offered the legal means by which a European state could "acquire" overseas territory.

Feminist writers on international law have also stressed the fact that, in contrast to the image of law portrayed in positivist discourse, international law is not universal, nor does it treat everyone equally.[53] There are a number of schools of feminist writing in international law, which have been categorized variously as liberal feminism, cultural feminism, radical feminism, postmodern feminism, and third world feminism.[54] Feminist writers emphasize the fact that women have been almost completely excluded from international law-making arenas; the rules of international law have developed in response to the experiences of a male elite. "Feminist analysis must thus explore the unspoken commitments of apparently neutral principles of international law and the ways that male perspectives are institutionalised in it."[55] Discussions as to when the use of force is allowed, for example, tend to focus on ostensibly neutral rules contained in the UN Charter, without taking into account the impact of that use of force on the lives of women. The expulsion of Iraq from Kuwait may appear to have been brought about by a successful Security Council–authorized military operation, but it may, nevertheless, have had deleterious impacts on women. Kuwaiti women suffered significant violations of their rights after the "liberation" of Kuwait, including worse levels of rape, the detention of large numbers of domestic workers, and a continued denial of democratic rights to suffrage.[56]

What the critical theorists, third world critics, feminists, and indigenous writers on international law have in common is an appreciation of the historical—and political—relativity of international law. S. James Anaya has stressed, for example, that right from the time that the Treaty of Westphalia confirmed the state as the principal international actor, the very idea of the nation-state has made it difficult for non-European aboriginal peoples to qualify as such.

> The concept of the nation-state in the post-Westphalian sense is based on European models of political and social organisation whose dominant defining characteristics are exclusivity of territorial domain and hierarchical, centralized authority. By contrast, indigenous peoples . . . at least prior to European contact, typically have been organized primarily by tribal or kinship ties, have had decentralized political structures often linked in confederations, and have enjoyed shared or overlapping spheres of territorial control.[57]

International law is a medium of interaction between states and, to a lesser extent, other international actors. It is ineluctably embedded in a particular spatial, historical, and political context, and yet the rhetoric of international law generally conveys an image of international law as separate from politics and ahistorical, as existing ahead of any specific political scenario. Although entwined with the political context in which it operates, international law has a considerable degree of autonomy as a set of interrelated principles, rules, and concepts. We are now going to consider multilateral treaties in more detail, so as to better understand both their place as a source of international law in the framework of legal positivism and as living documents integral to particular historical and political trajectories.

▣ Notes

1. Michael Byers, *Custom, Power, and the Power of Rules: International Relations and Customary International Law* (Cambridge: Cambridge University Press, 1999), p. 37.

2. "Spokesman Zhu Bangzao Gives Full Account of the Collision Between US and Chinese Military planes (04/04/01)," Embassy of the People's Republic of China in the United States of America, http://www.china-embassy.org.

3. James G. Blight and David A. Welch, *On the Brink: Americans and Soviets Reexamine the Cuban Missile Crisis,* 2nd ed. (New York: Noonday Press, 1990), p. 40.

4. See, inter alia, Abram Chayes, "Law and the Quarantine of Cuba," *Foreign Affairs* 41 (1963): 550–557; and Leonard C. Meeker, "Defensive Quarantine and the Law," *American Journal of International Law* 57 (1963): 515–524.

5. Blight and Welch, *On the Brink,* p. 53.

6. Patricia Birnie, "Opinion on the Legality of the Designation of the Southern Ocean Whale Sanctuary by the International Whaling Commission," available at http://www.highnorth.no.

7. Nicole Garbin, "Effectiveness and Legitimacy of the International Whaling Commission," Research Report 20 (Hobart, Tasmania: Cooperative Research Centre for the Antarctic and Southern Ocean Environment, 2000), p. 18.

8. See http://www.state.gov/s/l/. See also C. C. Joyner, "International Law and the Conduct of Foreign Policy," in S. V. Scott and A. Bergin, eds., *International Law and Australian Security* (Canberra: Australian Defence Studies Centre, 1997), pp. 5–22, esp. 12.

9. Antonio Cassese, "The Role of Legal Advisers in Ensuring That Foreign Policy Conforms to International Legal Standards," *Michigan Journal of International Law* 14 (Fall 1992): 139–170. On the role of the legal adviser, see, inter alia, Richard B. Bilder, "The Office of the Legal Adviser: The State Department Lawyer and Foreign Affairs, *American Journal of International Law* 56 (1962): 633–684; *Collection of Essays by Legal Advisers of States, Legal Advisers of International Organizations, and Practitioners in the Field of International Law* (New York: United Nations, 1999); Ashley Deeks, "Inside 'L': Some Thoughts on the Office of the Legal Adviser," *Chicago Journal of International Law* 2, no. 2 (Fall 2001): 503–510; R. St. J. MacDonald, "The Role of Legal Adviser of Ministries of Foreign Affairs," *Recueil des Cours* 3 (1977): 377–482; Miriam Sapiro, "Advising the United States Government on International Law," *New York University Journal of International Law and Politics* 27, no. 3 (Spring 1995): 619–623; Stephen M. Schwebel, "Remarks on the Role of the Legal Advisor of the US State Department," *European Journal of International Law* 2, no. 1 (1991): 132–135; and Edwin D. Williamson, "International

Law and the Role of the Legal Adviser in the Persian Gulf Crisis," *New York University Journal of International Law and Politics* 23, no. 2 (Winter 1991): 361–371.

10. Cited in Edward McWhinney, "President Bush and the New US National Security Strategy: The Continuing Relevance of the Legal Adviser and International Law," *Chinese Journal of International Law* (2002): 420–435, esp. 422.

11. *Legality of Use of Force (Yugoslavia v. United Kingdom), Provisional Measures, Order of 2 June 1999, ICJ Reports* 1999, p. 925.

12. World Public Opinion.org, "People in 17 of 21 Nations Say Governments Should Put International Law Ahead of National Interest," November 2, 2009, www.worldpublicopinion.org.

13. Shirley V. Scott, "International Law and Developing Countries," in Robert Denemark, ed., *International Studies Encyclopedia,* vol. 7 (Oxford: Wiley-Blackwell, 2010), 4098–4114, esp. 4110.

14. Gregory Shaffer, Victor Mosoti, and Asif Quereshi,) *Towards a Development-Supportive Dispute Settlement System in the WTO,* International Centre for Trade and Sustainable Development Resource Paper No. 5, p. 21.

15. C. Romano, "International Justice and Developing Countries (continued): A Qualitative Analysis," *The Law and Practice of International Courts and Tribunals* 1 (2002): 539–611, esp. 552.

16. The role of norms in world politics has in recent years been the subject of considerable literature. See, for example, Zaki Laïdi, *Norms over Force: The Enigma of European Power* (New York: Palgrave Macmillan, 2008); Halim Rane, *Reconstructing Jihad amid Competing International Norms* (Houndmills, UK: Palgrave Macmillan, 2009); Simon Rushton, "The UN Secretary-General and Norm Entrepreneurship: Boutros Boutros-Ghali and Democracy Promotion," *Global Governance* 14 (2008): 95–110; Wayne Sandholtz and Wayne Sities, *International Norms and Cycles of Change* (Oxford: Oxford University Press, 2009); Kathryn A. Sikkink, Sanjeev Khagram, and James V. Riker, eds., *Restructuring World Politics: Transnational Social Movements, Networks, and Norms* (Minneapolis: University of Minnesota Press, 2002); and Nina Tannenwald, *The Nuclear Taboo: The United States and the Non-Use of Nuclear Weapons Since 1945* (Cambridge: Cambridge University Press, December 2007).

17. Health and Environmental Effects of Nuclear Weapons, WHO Resolution 46.40, UN World Health Organization, Agenda Item 33 (1993), p. 2.

18. Request for an Advisory Opinion from the International Court of Justice on the Legality of the Threat or Use of Nuclear Weapons, General Assembly Resolution 75, 49th Session, 90 mtg at 15–16, UN Document A/Res/49/75 (1994).

19. These were the bodies of law primarily drawn on in the written observations and oral hearings of the two cases. Roger S. Clark, "International Court of Justice: Advisory Proceedings on the Legality of the Threat or Use of Nuclear Weapons (Question Posed by the General Assembly): The Laws of Armed Conflict and the Use or Threat of Use of Nuclear Weapons," *Criminal Law Forum* 7 (1996): 265–298, esp. 271.

20. Kate Dewes and Commander Robert Green (Retired), "The World Court Project: How a Citizen Network Can Influence the United Nations," *Pacifica Review* 7, no. 2 (1995): 17–37, esp. 28.

21. Peter Weiss, "The World Court Tackles the Fate of the Earth: An Introduction to the ICJ Advisory Opinion on the Legality of the Threat and Use of Nuclear Weapons," *Transnational Law and Contemporary Problems* 7 (Fall 1997): 314–332, esp. 320–321.

22. Clark, "International Court of Justice: Advisory Proceedings," p. 265.

23. Para. 105(2)(E).

24. Laurence Boisson de Chazournes and Philippe Sands, "Introduction," in Laurence Boisson de Chazournes and Philippe Sands, eds., *International Law, the International Court of Justice, and Nuclear Weapons* (Cambridge: Cambridge University Press, 1999), p. 21.

25. Richard A. Falk, "Nuclear Weapons, International Law, and the World Court: A Historic Encounter," *American Journal of International Law* 91 (1997): 64–75, esp. 64.

26. Williams Epstein, Alyn Ware, and Peter Weiss, "World Court Project: How Might the Court Rule? What Effect Will That Have? Lawyers' Committee on Nuclear Policy, September 1993," cited in Ved P. Nanda and David Krieger, *Nuclear Weapons and the World Court* (Ardsley, NY: Transnational, 1998), p. 82.

27. For academic literature in response, see, inter alia, Dapo Akande, "Nuclear Weapons, Unclear Law? Deciphering the Nuclear Weapons Advisory Opinion of the International Court," *British Yearbook of International Law* 68 (1997): 165–217; Falk, "Nuclear Weapons, International Law, and the World Court," p. 64; Michael J. Matheson, "The Opinions of the International Court of Justice on the Threat or Use of Nuclear Weapons, *American Journal of International Law* 91 (1997): 417–435; Nicholas Grief, "Legality of the Threat or Use of Nuclear Weapons," *International and Comparative Law Quarterly* 46 (1997): 681–688; Kazuomi Ouchi, "The Threat or Use of Nuclear Weapons: Discernible Legal Policies of the Judges of the International Court of Justice," *Connecticut Journal of International Law* 13 (1998): 107–118; Antonio F. Perez, "The Passive Virtues and the World Court: Pro-Dialogic Abstention by the International Court of Justice," *Michigan Journal of International Law* 18 (1997): 399, 426–443; Christyne J. Vachon, "Sovereignty Versus Globalization: The International Court of Justice's Advisory Opinion on the Threat or Use of Nuclear Weapons," *Denver Journal of International Law and Policy* 26 (1998): 691–724; and Prosper Weil, "The Court Cannot Conclude Definitively . . . Non Liquet Revisited," *Columbia Journal of Transnational Law* 36 (1997): 109–119.

28. See Shirley Scott, "Beyond 'Compliance': Reconceiving the International Law–Foreign Policy Dynamic," *Australian Year Book of International Law* 19 (1998): 35–48, esp. 44–45.

29. R. Higgins, "The Identity of International Law," in B. Cheng, ed., *International Law: Teaching and Practice* (London: Stevens and Sons, 1982), p. 58.

30. E. McWhinney, *United Nations Law Making: Cultural and Ideological Relativism and International Law Making for an Era of Transition* (New York: Holmes and Meier, 1984), pp. 27–44, esp. 23.

31. O. Schachter, "International Law in Theory and Practice: General Course in Public International Law," 178 *Recueil des Cours* (1982): 22.

32. Ian Brownlie, *The Rule of Law in International Affairs: International Law at the Fiftieth Anniversary of the United Nations* (The Hague: Martinus Nijhoff, 1998), p. 16.

33. This complaint was made of the Rome diplomatic conference for an international criminal court. Fanny Benedetti and John L. Washburn, "Drafting the International Criminal Court Treaty: Two Years to Rome and an Afterword on the Rome Diplomatic Conference," *Global Governance* 5, no. 1 (1999): 1–37, esp. 29.

34. See, generally, Michael Byers and Georg Nolte, eds., *United States Hegemony and the Foundations of International Law* (Cambridge: Cambridge University Press, 2003).

35. A. Anghie, "Francisco de Vitoria and the Colonial Origins of International Law," *Social and Legal Studies* 5 (1996): 321–336.

36. Randa M. Slim, "Small-State Mediation in International Relations: The Algerian Mediation of the Iranian Hostage Crisis," in Jacob Bercovitch and Jeffrey Z. Rubin, eds., *Mediation in International Relations: Multiple Approaches to Conflict Management* (New York: St. Martin's Press in association with the Society for the Psychological Study of Social Issues, 1992), pp. 206–231.

37. Statute of the International Court of Justice, article 31(2) and (3).

38. See Joshua Castellino and Steve Allen, *Title to Territory in International Law: A Temporal Analysis* (Aldershot, UK: Ashgate, 2003).

39. *Western Sahara, Advisory Opinion, ICJ Reports* 1975, pp. 12, 38–39.

40. The New Haven School grew out of the work of scholars at the Yale Law School in New Haven, Connecticut. See, inter alia, M. S. McDougal, *Studies in World Public Order* (New Haven, CT: Yale University Press, 1960); Myres S. McDougal, "Some Basic Theoretical Concepts About International Law: A Policy-Oriented Framework of Inquiry," *Journal of Conflict Resolution* 4 (1960): 337–354; and M. S. McDougal, H. D. Lasswell, and W. M. Reisman, "Theories About International Law: Prologue to a Configurative Jurisprudence," *Virginia Journal of International Law* 8, no. 2 (1968): 188–299; Judge Rosalyn Higgins is an exponent of this approach. See her *Problems and Process: International Law and How We Use It* (New York: Oxford University Press, 1994).

41. Robert J. Beck, Anthony Clark Arend, and Robert D. Vander Lught, eds., *International Rules: Approaches from International Law and International Relations* (New York: Oxford University Press, 1996), p. 111.

42. Martha Finnemore and Stephen J. Toope, "Alternatives to 'Legalization': Richer Views of Law and Politics," *International Organization* 55, no. 3 (Summer 2000): 743–758, esp. 744. See also Jutta Brunée and Stephen J. Toope, "International Law and Constructivism: Elements of an Interactional Theory of International Law," *Columbia Journal of Transnational Law* 39 (2000): 19–74.

43. Two influential works were D. Kennedy, *International Legal Structures* (Baden-Baden: Nomos Verlagsgese Ilschaft, 1987); and M. Koskenniemi, *From Apology to Utopia* (Helsinki: Lakimiesliiton Kustannus, 1989). See also D. Cass, "Navigating the Newstream: Recent Critical Scholarship in International Law," *Nordic Journal of International Law* 65 (1996): 341–383, esp. 341; and N. Purvis, "Critical Legal Studies in Public International Law," *Harvard International Law Journal* 32 (1991): 81–127.

44. This was David Kennedy's term, first used in "A New Stream of International Law Scholarship," *Wisconsin International Law Journal* 7 (1988): 1–49.

45. A. Carty, "Critical International Law: Recent Trends in the Theory of International Law, *European Journal of International Law* 2 (1991): 66–96.

46. Martti Koskenniemi, *From Apology to Utopia: The Structure of International Legal Argument* (Helsinki: Finnish Lawyers Publishing, 1989), p. 50.

47. Martti Koskenniemi, "Introduction," *Nordic Journal of International Law* 65 (1996): 337–340, esp. 340.

48. A good example of that is the contribution by Pal Wrange to the special issue of the *Nordic Journal of International Law* devoted to the subject. In the space of only a few pages, the reader finds out that Wrange's father is dead and learns much about Wrange's personal journey to find meaning in his work as a teacher of international law, and indeed, in his life as a whole. Pal Wrange, "An Open Letter to My Students," *Nordic Journal of International Law* 65 (1996): 569–595.

49. Makau Mutua, "What Is TWAIL?" *American Society of International Law, Proceedings of the 94th Annual Meeting,* Washington, DC (2000): 31–38. See also Karin Mickelson, "Rhetoric and Rage: Third World Voices in International Legal Discourse," *Wisconsin International Law Journal* 16, no. 2 (Summer 1998): 353–419; and the special issue of the *Harvard International Law Journal* 41 (2000) devoted to research and scholarship on developing countries and their contribution to international legal theory.

50. See Antony Anghie and B. S. Chimni, "Third World Approaches to International Law and Individual Responsibility in Internal Conflicts," *Chinese Journal of International Law* 2, no. 1 (2003): 77–103, esp. 79–80.

51. Mutua, "What Is TWAIL?"

52. J. T. Gathii, "Review Essay: International Law and Eurocentricity: 1, Anti-Colonial Reconstructions of International Legal History," *European Journal of International Law* 9, no. 1 (1998): 184–211. See also Antony Anghie, *Imperialism, Sovereignty, and the Making of International Law* (Cambridge: Cambridge University Press, 2005).

53. Feminist writing came relatively late to international law. A landmark was H. Charlesworth, C. Chinkin, and S. Wright, "Feminist Approaches to International Law," *American Journal of International Law* 85 (1991): 613–645. See also D. Buss and A. Manji, eds., *International Law: Modern Feminist Approaches* (Oxford: Hart, 2005); and Catherine MacKinnon, *Are Women Human? And Other International Dialogues* (Cambridge, MA: Harvard University Press, 2006).

54. Hilary Charlesworth and Christine Chinkin, *The Boundaries of International Law: A Feminist Analysis* (Manchester: Manchester University Press, 2000), pp. 38–48. See also D. Dallmeyer, ed., *Reconceiving Reality: Women and International Law* (Washington, DC: American Society of International Law, 1993).

55. Charlesworth and Chinkin, *The Boundaries of International Law,* p. 50.

56. Ibid., pp. 260–262.

57. S. James Anaya, *Indigenous Peoples in International Law* (New York: Oxford University Press, 1996), p. 15.

8

Reading a Multilateral Treaty

A *TREATY* IS AN AGREEMENT LEGALLY BINDING UNDER INTER-
national law. In the era since World War II treaties have taken over from
custom as the most important source of international law. Treaty law addresses a wide range of issue areas including trade, the environment, human
rights, and arms control. Much of the law relating to treaties is itself found
in treaties: the Vienna Convention on the Law of Treaties (1969)[1] and the
Vienna Convention on the Law of Treaties Between States and International
Organizations or Between International Organizations (1986).[2] The Vienna
Convention on the Law of Treaties entered into force on January 27, 1980.
Although this convention is the starting point for a discussion of the law of
treaties, and much of it was a codification of customary international law,
it applies only to those treaties made after its entry into force[3] and only to
written treaties.[4] The other convention, on the law of treaties between states
and international organizations or between international organizations, has
not yet entered into force.

This chapter will focus on multilateral, as distinct from bilateral,
treaties. Multilateral treaties may be entered into by a small group of states,
they may be regional, or they may aim for universal participation. Some
multilateral treaties establish an international organization to implement the
provisions; indeed, the sole purpose of some treaties is to create an international organization. The North Atlantic Treaty Organization, for example, was established by the North Atlantic Treaty (the so-called Washington
Treaty) of April 4, 1949.[5] In these cases, the treaty functions like a constitution for the relevant IGO.

Figure 8.1 lists some of the most common subject groupings of treaties.
It is convenient to categorize treaties under subject headings—the environment, human rights, and so on—but it is important to remember that a treaty

Figure 8.1 Examples of Multilateral Treaties at a Regional and Global Level

Selected Subject Area	Example at a Regional Level	Example at a Global Level
Human rights	African Charter on Human and Peoples' Rights	Convention Against Torture and Other Cruel, Inhuman, or Degrading Treatment or Punishment
International humanitarian law	Havana Convention on Maritime Neutrality	Geneva Convention VI Relative to the Treatment of Prisoners of War
Arms control	Treaty for the Prohibition of Nuclear Weapons in Latin America and the Caribbean (Treaty of Tlatelolco)	Treaty on the Non-Proliferation of Nuclear Weapons
Trade and commercial relations	North American Free Trade Agreement	UN Convention on Contracts for the International Sale of Goods
International criminal law	European Convention on the Suppression of Terrorism	UN Convention Against Illicit Traffic in Narcotic Drugs and Psychotropic Substances
Environment	Oslo Convention on Marine Dumping	The Vienna Convention on Substances that Deplete the Ozone Layer

often falls under more than one heading. The Comprehensive Nuclear Test-Ban Treaty (CTBT), for example, can be regarded as a treaty pertaining to military security and to the environment. The 1982 Law of the Sea Treaty could perhaps be classified as a "political" treaty because it functions like a constitution for the oceans, but it also has much to say about the marine environment and is integral to the maritime security interests of a number of states.

It is easy for newcomers to international law, particularly those without a legal background, to avoid reading the texts of treaties, relying instead on secondary accounts of treaty contents. This may be for reason of convenience or out of respect for international law experts. But it is a dangerous habit; the precise wording of a legal document matters. Treaties are not difficult to comprehend, and it is usually much easier in the long run to go straight to the treaty text, using commentaries on the treaty as a supplementary source of information.

■ The Layout of a Multilateral Treaty

When reading a treaty it is useful to divide it into five main sections: the title, the preamble, the substantive clauses, the final clauses, and the testimonium.

Let's look at each in turn. Examples will be given from the Antarctic Treaty. It is recommended that readers start by locating the complete text of this treaty, as well as the Vienna Convention on the Law of Treaties. *International Law and World Politics: Key Documents*[6] is a collection of documents that contains these and many of the other treaties discussed in the following chapters and can be a handy companion to this book. Alternatively, the text of a treaty can usually be located through an Internet search engine, and glossaries of standard treaty terms can also be found online.[7]

The Title

The title of a treaty often expresses the aims of the treaty or at least its subject matter. The title may contain the term *convention, protocol, statute, covenant, charter, act, declaration, exchange of notes, agreed minute, memorandum of agreement,* or *modus vivendi* rather than *treaty* without affecting the legal status of the instrument. Although there are no set rules as to when each of these terms is to be used, each tends to be used in slightly different situations, as set out in Figure 8. 2.

Treaty titles used to be written in italics, but this practice is no longer always adhered to. It is standard practice that the first reference to a treaty in a written document is accompanied by a note specifying where the treaty text can be located. In the following chapters, references are provided to the location of treaties in the United Nations Treaty Series and/or in *International Legal Materials,* a publication of the American Society of International Law. As can be seen from the endnotes, there is a standard format for each. References to treaties in the UN Treaty Series appear as "volume number, UNTS, start page number." References to *International Legal Materials* appear as "volume number, *ILM,* start page number, year in brackets."

The Preamble

At the beginning of a treaty there is usually a preamble—a list of phrases, often couched in flowery language, that serves as an introduction. If there is later disagreement as to the interpretation of the treaty, the preamble may be looked at to help determine the "object and purpose" of the treaty. The preambular paragraphs are written in either the past tense, as in "convinced" or "assured," or in the continuous present tense, as in "hoping" or "aiming." The length of the preamble varies considerably, but recent treaties tend to have much longer preambles than older ones; the preamble to the 1948 Genocide Convention was only four paragraphs long. The Antarctic Treaty begins:

> The Governments of Argentina, Australia, Belgium, Chile, the French Republic, Japan, New Zealand, Norway, the Union of South Africa, the Union of Soviet Socialist Republics, the United Kingdom of Great Britain and Northern Ireland, and the United States of America,

Figure 8.2 The Meaning of Various Terms That Commonly Appear in the Titles of Multilateral Treaties

Agreement
A treaty of less high political significance and involving fewer states and a narrower range of subject matter than a convention. An agreement might, for example, deal with technical issues. The term *agreement* is commonly used in international economic law to indicate a broad multilateral agreement.

Charter or Statute
Reserved for treaties establishing an international institution, such as the UN Charter or Statute of the International Court of Justice. Such treaties play a role equivalent to that of a constitution. The term *charter* is occasionally used for a non–legally binding MOU (defined below).

Convention
A formal multilateral treaty. The term is used to refer to treaties created by the organs of international institutions.

Covenant
The term is more-or-less synonymous with *convention* though not as common. An example is the UN Covenant on Civil and Political Rights.

Declaration, General Act
A formal treaty or to a less formal statement of agreement.

Exchange of Notes or of Letters
The means by which states notify each other that they agree to act in a certain manner. They may constitute either a treaty or a non–legally binding MOU.

Final Act
The document that records the results of a conference convened to create an international treaty. The final act may contain the treaty or points of agreement not incorporated in the treaty.

Memorandum of Understanding
A treaty may have *Memorandum of Understanding* (MOU) in its title, but the term *MOU* usually refers to an instrument concluded between states that is not legally binding. Non–legally binding MOUs may be preferred when the parties desire confidentiality. Unlike a treaty, there is no international requirement to publish an MOU. An MOU can usually be

(continues)

Figure 8.2 continued

---

brought into operation more quickly than a treaty because most come into effect upon signature (see Anthony Aust, cited below, pp. 26–46).

Modus Vivendi
An informal agreement of a temporary or provisional nature intended to be replaced with a more detailed and formal treaty.

Procès Verbale
An information agreement containing a record of certain understandings.

Protocol
A treaty that is less formal than a convention. The term is often used to refer to an agreement concluded subsequent to a treaty, to deal with issues that arise during its operation. An optional protocol to some human rights treaties has been adopted even on the same day as the treaty, to establish additional obligations to which not all negotiating states could agree.

Treaty
Use of the term *treaty* in the title usually indicates that the subject matter of the treaty was regarded as of some gravity.

Sources: I. A. Shearer, *Starke's International Law,* 11th ed. (London: Butterworths, 1994), pp. 401–404; Anthony Aust, *Modern Treaty Law and Practice* (Cambridge: Cambridge University Press, 2000), pp. 20–25; and the *United Nations Treaty Collection Treaty Reference Guide* (1999).

Recognizing that it is in the interest of all mankind that Antarctica shall continue for ever to be used exclusively for peaceful purposes and shall not become the scene or object of international discord;

Acknowledging the substantial contributions to scientific knowledge resulting from international cooperation in scientific investigation in Antarctica;

Convinced that the establishment of a firm foundation for the continuation and development of such cooperation on the basis of freedom of scientific investigation in Antarctica as applied during the International Geophysical Year accords with the interests of science and the progress of all mankind;

Convinced also that a treaty ensuring the use of Antarctica for peaceful purposes only and the continuance of international harmony in Antarctica will further the purposes and principles embodied in the Charter of the United Nations.

The preamble usually finishes with words similar to "have agreed as follows," leading into the main treaty text.

The main treaty text may be one or two pages in length, or it may be the size of a small book. It is divided into articles. In a long treaty the articles may be grouped into chapters, sections, and parts and may include annexes. The 1982 Law of the Sea Convention consists of 320 articles divided into seventeen parts.

Substantive Articles

The substantive articles contain the obligations that the parties are assuming through the treaty. It is now common for the first article to contain key definitions, although definitions may be given elsewhere in the treaty text. Multilateral treaties now often include provisions specifying how the treaty in question is to relate to others addressing the same subject matter. A treaty may specify that the parties shall not enter into later inconsistent treaties; that an existing treaty shall not be affected; that, for parties, the treaty prevails over earlier treaties; or that compatible supplementary treaties are permitted. Disagreement over mineral resources of the seabed and ocean floor prevented a final consensus document at the Third Law of the Sea Conference. Four years of informal consultations conducted by the UN Secretary-General on several issues relating to the deep seabed mining provisions of the convention culminated on July 28, 1994, with the General Assembly adopting an agreement relating to the implementation of part XI of the 1982 UN Convention on the Law of the Sea.[8] By article 2(I) the provisions of the Agreement and part XI of the Law of the Sea Convention are to be interpreted and applied together as a single instrument: "In the event of any inconsistency between this Agreement and Part XI, the provisions of the Agreement are to prevail." If a treaty says nothing about its relationship to other treaties addressing the same subject matter, customary international law as codified by article 30 of the Vienna Convention on the Law of Treaties applies. This specifies, inter alia, that, where all the parties to the earlier treaty are parties also to the later treaty but the earlier treaty is not terminated or suspended in operation, the earlier treaty applies only to the extent that its provisions are compatible with those of the later treaty.

Final Clauses

This section of a treaty deals with the mechanics of how the treaty will function—that is, with the operation of the treaty itself as opposed to the issue being addressed by the treaty. Recent treaties contain much more in the way of formal or final clauses than earlier treaties.

The final clauses will usually include information on the following:

How long the treaty will be open for signature. It is now common for a treaty aiming at global membership to be left open for signature for a specified time after its conclusion or adoption—up to about nine months, in order to increase the number of signatories. The treaty may specify which other states—other members of the United Nations, for example—are to be allowed to sign the treaty during that time. Once the specified period is up any nonsignatory wanting to become a party has to accede rather than sign and ratify (see below).

How signatories are to express their consent to be bound by the provisions of the treaty. This usually involves signature and ratification. Ratification involves two steps. The first is that by which a state makes the internal decision to be bound by the treaty and the executive executes an instrument of ratification. The second step in the ratification process is the external one, which in the case of a multilateral treaty involves lodging the instrument of ratification with the depositary of the treaty. A state or international organization usually acts as a depositary for written instruments of ratification. Although it is usual for a state that has signed a treaty to proceed to ratification, it is not legally obliged to do so. The United States made clear its intention not to proceed to ratification of the Rome Statute of the International Criminal Court. Not all states that had signed the Environmental Protocol to the Antarctic Treaty proceeded to ratification, in that case blocking its entry into force. In the case of a protocol, there is usually a requirement that a state wishing to sign the treaty also be a party to the initial treaty.

Reservations. A multilateral treaty may specify whether it is possible for a state to accept part but not all of its provisions. The Vienna Convention defines a reservation as a "unilateral statement, however phrased or named, made by a State, when signing, ratifying, accepting, approving or acceding to a treaty, whereby it purports to exclude or to modify the legal effect of certain provisions of the treaty in their application to that State." It is gradually becoming acceptable for reservations to be made subsequent to these actions, but only if all other parties to the treaty find acceptable what is effectively a modification of the state's treaty obligation.[9] When signing or ratifying a treaty a state may also make a *declaration*. A declaration is a statement that, in legal terms, does not lessen the state's obligations under that treaty in the way that a reservation would but, for example, clarifies how that state is to interpret a particular clause.

Some treaties, such as the Convention for the Protection of the Ozone Layer and the UN Convention on the Law of the Sea, do not permit reservations. If the treaty says nothing about reservations, a state may nevertheless make a reservation so long as it is not "incompatible with the object and purpose of the treaty."[10] The question as to who has the authority to assess the acceptability of a reservation—and the implications of such a determination—is still being debated within international law.[11] It is a particular problem in respect of human rights treaties.[12]

How and when the treaty is to enter into force. Multilateral treaties usually stipulate the conditions to be met in order for the treaty to take effect as law. This might be the receipt by the depositary of a certain number of instruments of ratification, or a date, or some other requirement. In some cases the negotiating states may have agreed that the treaty would enter into force only if specific states proceed to ratification. Article XIV of the CTBT provides that a specified group of forty-four states listed in annex 2 (those with nuclear reactors on their territories) must ratify the treaty in order for it to enter into force. Although the provision was controversial, it was reasoned that the treaty must capture a certain minimum set of nuclear weapon–capable states to be effective in promoting nonproliferation objectives.[13] The Antarctic Treaty came into force on June 23, 1961, in accordance with article XIII(5) of the treaty, upon deposit of the instruments of ratification of all the signatory states. The Antarctic Treaty provided that the treaty would enter into force when the twelve signatories had all deposited their instruments of ratification. If a treaty is silent about its entry into force, this happens as soon as all negotiating states have indicated their consent to be bound by the treaty.[14]

If and how other states that have not signed the treaty may nevertheless become parties to it. This is known as *accession.* Acceding to a treaty has the same legal effect as signing and ratifying it, although in the case of the Antarctic Treaty the text provides that the implications of each will differ. States that are original signatories to the Antarctic Treaty are automatically "consultative parties" (those with the key decisionmaking responsibilities), whereas acceding states remain such only "during such times as that Contracting Party demonstrates its interest in Antarctica by conducting substantial research activity there."[15]

Withdrawal, duration, and termination of the treaty. A treaty may be terminated at any time, or a state can withdraw from it, by the consent of all the parties.[16] Most multilateral treaties specify how an individual state can withdraw if it chooses to do so, and for how long the treaty will last. Article X of the Treaty on the Non-Proliferation of Nuclear Weapons provides that:

> 1. Each State Party shall, in exercising its national sovereignty, have the right to withdraw from this Convention if it decides that extraordinary events, related to the subject-matter of this Convention, have jeopardized the supreme interests of its country. It shall give notice of such withdrawal 90 days in advance to all other States Parties, the Executive Council, the Depositary and the United Nations Security Council. Such notice shall

include a statement of the extraordinary events it regards as having jeopardized its supreme interests.

2. Twenty-five years after the entry into force of the Treaty, a conference shall be convened to decide whether the Treaty shall continue in force indefinitely, or shall be extended for an additional fixed period or periods. This decision shall be taken by a majority of the Parties to the Treaty.

If the treaty does not include provisions on withdrawal, but it can be established that the parties intended it to be possible to do so, a state may in certain circumstances be able to invoke a material breach of a treaty by another state, the impossibility of performing a treaty, or a fundamental change of circumstances (*rebus sic stantibus*), as grounds for withdrawing from, or terminating, a treaty.[17] Otherwise, a treaty is perpetual, and the unilateral denunciation of it by one state is a breach.

How and when the treaty may be modified or amended. The treaty may specify how it can be modified, which means changed only as between some parties, whereas in their relations with the other parties the original treaty provisions still apply. If the treaty says nothing about modification, article 41 of the Vienna Convention stipulates that modifications are allowed only if they do not affect the rights or obligations of the other parties to the treaty and do not contravene the object and the purpose of the treaty. *Amendment* refers to a change to the treaty that will apply to all parties. If the treaty says nothing about amendment, article 40 of the Vienna Convention applies, by which an amendment requires the consent of all the parties.

Provisions on dispute resolution. Dispute resolution provisions in a multilateral agreement set out how treaty parties are to deal with matters of contention that arise during the life of the multilateral treaty. Methods of dispute resolution may be either voluntary or compulsory, as may be any decision by a third party. Article 2(3) of the UN Charter places a basic obligation on all member states to "settle their international disputes by peaceful means in such a manner that international peace and security, and justice, are not endangered." Article 33(1) offers them a range of ways by which they might go about doing so: negotiation, enquiry, mediation, conciliation, arbitration, judicial settlement, resort to regional agencies or arrangements, or other peaceful means of their own choice. *Negotiation* is the least formal of these alternatives; it involves direct talks between the parties to the dispute. No third party is involved. This is the most common means by which states resolve their differences. One step more formal is an *inquiry;* here a third party is charged not with resolving the dispute but with ascertaining the answers to certain questions of fact, which can then be used as a basis of negotiation. *Mediation* involves a neutral third party approved by both sides to attempt to help broker a compromise. Reference of the dispute to a third party such as a commission or committee to recommend proposals for settlement is known as *conciliation*. The proposals of the conciliator are advisory only. Moving one step more formal is *arbitration,* by which each state nominates an agreed number of judges and agrees to accept the decision of those judges. The most formal method of dispute resolution in international law is *judicial settlement.*

Here is article XI of the Antarctic Treaty, which addresses dispute resolution in the regime:

> 1. If any dispute arises between two or more of the Contracting Parties concerning the interpretation or application of the present Treaty, those Contracting Parties shall consult among themselves with a view to having the dispute resolved by negotiation, inquiry, mediation, conciliation, arbitration, judicial settlement, or other peaceful means of their own choice.
> 2. Any dispute of this character not so resolved shall, with the consent, in each case, of all parties to the dispute, be referred to the International Court of Justice for settlement; but failure to reach agreement on reference to the International Court shall not absolve parties to the dispute from the responsibility of continuing to seek to resolve it by any of the various peaceful means referred to in paragraph 1 of this Article.

Several of the more recent major multilateral treaties establish their own dispute resolution mechanisms and bodies. These are typically less formal and costly than the International Court of Justice and aim for greater participation and a quicker outcome. The phenomenon has nevertheless come under debate as a perhaps unnecessary proliferation, which may weaken the unity of the international legal system as a whole and favor some fields of international law over others. This is particularly so because there is no hierarchy within the group of judicial bodies as there is in most national court systems.[18]

One of the most important differences between the World Trade Organization, established in 1995, and the General Agreement on Tariffs and Trade (GATT), which it incorporated and went beyond, was its more far-reaching provisions on dispute settlement. GATT operated on a "positive consensus" principle: consensus was required before the dispute resolution mechanism would go into operation; the procedure for dispute resolution operates much more automatically under the WTO Dispute Settlement Understanding. By article 6(1), a panel is established automatically once a complaining party so requests, unless the Dispute Settlement Body (DSB) decides by consensus not to establish a panel.[19] The report of the panel is later adopted by the DSB unless a party to the dispute formally notifies the DSB of its decision to appeal or the DSB decides by consensus not to adopt the report.[20] Members are to "comply promptly" with recommendations or rulings of the DSB.[21]

The 1982 Law of the Sea Convention offers a wide choice of methods for dispute settlement.[22] When a dispute relating to the treaty arises, states are to "proceed expeditiously" to agree on a method of dispute settlement. Annex V sets out conciliation procedures that may be used if both parties agree on the conciliation procedure. If a party does not agree to conciliation or if conciliation fails to bring about a settlement, the dispute can be submitted, at the request of any party to the dispute, to the court or tribunal having jurisdiction under section 2 of part XV.[23] Section 2 of part XV provides that parties to the convention may make a declaration regarding their choice of dispute settlement procedures: the International Tribunal for the Law of the Sea, the International Court of Justice, an arbitral tribunal established under annex VII, or a special technical arbitral tribunal established under annex VIII. If the parties to a dispute have not accepted the same procedure, a dispute is to be submitted to arbitration in accordance with Annex VII unless the parties agree otherwise.[24]

The International Tribunal for the Law of the Sea (ITLOS),[25] whose statute appears as annex VI to the Convention, was inaugurated in October 1996. The tribunal has some distinctive features of particular value to the peaceful resolution of law of the sea disputes. One is its capacity to deliver judgments in a relatively short space of time. Special chambers, including one on the marine environment, are designed in part for this purpose. Each has seven judges selected for their specialist expertise in the area. A state may still have a case heard by the full tribunal if it so wishes. The tribunal enjoys special competence to deal with requests for provisional measures. At the request of a party to a dispute, the tribunal may, as long as a prima facie case for jurisdiction can be made, prescribe, modify, or revoke provisional measures necessary to preserve the respective rights of the parties to a dispute or to prevent harm to the marine environment.[26]

The Testimonium

The final clauses are followed by the testimonium, the part below which the representatives sign, as well as by signature block and any annexes. Here is a standard testimonium:

> In witness whereof the undersigned, being duly authorised [by their respective Governments], have signed this [Agreement].
>
> Done at [place], this [ ] day of [ ], two thousand and [ ]
> For [the Government of ...]: [signature]
> For [the Government of ...]: [signature]
> [Etc.][27]

■ **Beyond the Treaty Text:**
The Antarctic Treaty and Political Process

A treaty does not come into existence as an isolated phenomenon but as part
of a political process that begins well before, and continues well after, the
finalization of the treaty text; the conclusion of the treaty is just one stage
in a longer political process by which a group of states addresses an issue
of mutual concern. Every treaty has a political and historical story to tell
and can only be understood as a political as well as a legal document if
viewed in a longer time frame and broader context. This section will illustrate the political and historical embedment of a multilateral treaty by reference to the Antarctic Treaty. In Chapter 9, we will consider the politics of
this process in more depth.

Treaty Origins: Background of the Antarctic Treaty

As we saw in Chapter 1, sovereignty is one of the most fundamental concepts both in the international states system and in the system of international law. In the case of Antarctica there has been little agreement as to
who has sovereignty over what territory. The unresolved nature of the sovereignty issue has underpinned most political questions relating to the continent. Prior to 1959 there were three groups of states with "interests" in
Antarctica. The first group could be referred to as the "South American
claimants": Chile and Argentina each asserted territorial rights over that
portion of the Antarctic continent nearest to their mainland territory. Both
states recognized the right of the other to a portion of South American
Antarctica. These rights were believed to derive from a papal bull of 1493
by which Alexander VI gave, granted, and assigned forever to Spain and its
successors, all territory from the Arctic pole to the Antarctic pole west of a
meridian 370 leagues west of the Cape Verde Islands. As successor states to
Spain in South America, Argentina and Chile believed that they had inher-
ited rights to a portion of Antarctica. From their perspective all that remained
to be done was to negotiate their mutual boundary.[28]

The second group of states with interests in Antarctica prior to 1959
consisted of the United Kingdom, France, Norway, New Zealand, and Australia. The United Kingdom originally had ambitions to acquire the entire
continent, but between the two world wars it negotiated a division of the
continent with the other states in this group. It was unable to settle the issue
with the South American claimants, however, both of whose territorial
claims overlapped that of the United Kingdom.

The third set of states with interests in Antarctica consisted of those that
had not made a formal territorial claim but that either asserted their right to do
so at a later date or had at least displayed an active interest in the continent.

This group consisted of the United States, the Soviet Union, Japan, South Africa, and Belgium.

The issue of disputed Antarctic sovereignty was most serious in relation to the Antarctic Peninsula, where the claims of Chile, Argentina, and the United Kingdom overlapped. A series of incidents in the early post–World War II years brought the UK and Argentina close to conflict.[29] In 1947 the United Kingdom proposed that the case be submitted to the International Court of Justice. The suggestion was repeated on a number of occasions, but the issue never came before the Court. In 1948 the United States, which had made no territorial claim, proposed a draft agreement by which Argentina, Australia, Chile, France, Norway, New Zealand, the United Kingdom, and the United States would be designated the administering authority of the trust territory of Antarctica.[30] The United Kingdom proposed an eight-power condominium arrangement.[31] During discussions in Santiago in 1948, a Chilean law professor, Julio Escudero Buzman, suggested that existing legal rights and interests in Antarctica be frozen for a period of five or ten years, during which activities in Antarctica would have no legal effect.[32] This idea was effectively trialed during the International Geophysical Year (IGY) of 1957–1958, for which the participating governments "reached a sort of gentleman's agreement not to engage in legal or political argumentation during that period, in order that the scientific program might proceed without impediment."[33] The arrangement appeared to work well and was formalized in the Antarctic Treaty of 1959. The treaty was proposed by the United States, which provided a draft text and a venue for the negotiations.

The Finalization of the Antarctic Treaty

The Antarctic Treaty was signed in Washington, D.C., on December 1, 1959, and entered into force on June 23, 1961, after ratification by all signatory states.[34] The treaty addresses a number of issues: scientific cooperation, the denuclearization of Antarctica, and the "freezing" of claims to territorial sovereignty in Antarctica. The treaty is sometimes listed as a *scientific treaty*,[35] and it is true that the treaty was an important contribution to the management of the continent so as to facilitate scientific endeavor. The treaty is also sometimes listed as an *arms control treaty,* notable as being the first arms control agreement to be negotiated after World War II. Article I of the treaty prohibits "any measure of a military nature, such as the establishment of military bases and fortifications, the carrying out of military manoeuvres, as well as the testing of any type of weapon." Article V prohibited "any nuclear explosions in Antarctica and the disposal there of radioactive waste material." From a political point of view, however, the treaty is most significant for its treatment of the vexed question of sovereignty in Antarctica. By article IV of the treaty:

1. Nothing contained in the present Treaty shall be interpreted as:

   a. a renunciation by any Contracting Party of previously asserted rights of or claims to territorial sovereignty in Antarctica;
   b. a renunciation or diminution by any Contracting Party of any basis of claim to territorial sovereignty in Antarctica which it may have whether as a result of its activities or those of its nationals in Antarctica, or otherwise;
   c. prejudicing the position of any Contracting Party as regards its recognition or non-recognition of any other State's rights of or claim or basis of claim to territorial sovereignty in Antarctica.

2. No acts or activities taking place while the present Treaty is in force shall constitute a basis for asserting, supporting or denying a claim to territorial sovereignty in Antarctica or create any rights of sovereignty in Antarctica. No new claim, or enlargement of an existing claim, to territorial sovereignty in Antarctica shall be asserted while the present Treaty is in force.

Article IV has functioned as the cornerstone of the Antarctic Treaty and the set of political relationships founded thereon.

The Antarctic Treaty System

With the conclusion of the treaty, what is known as the Antarctic Treaty System (ATS) came into operation. During the early years of the treaty the question of the management of Antarctic living resources was addressed in three new treaties: the 1964 Agreed Measures for the Conservation of Antarctic Fauna and Flora, the 1972 Convention for the Conservation of Antarctic Seals, and the 1980 Convention on the Conservation of Antarctic Marine Living Resources. From 1982 to 1988 consultative parties to the Antarctic Treaty negotiated a treaty dealing with a nonliving resource: minerals. The issue of who could mine Antarctica and where confronted the sovereignty issue head-on because it is usually up to the territorial sovereign to determine that.

The mineral negotiations focused considerable international attention on Antarctica and prompted certain members of the third world, led by Malaysia, to claim that the ATS was not the best or the fairest way to manage Antarctica. Particularly in the General Assembly of the United Nations, third world critics of the ATS argued that Antarctica should be the "common heritage of mankind." This was a concept that had been used in relation to outer space and the deep seabed. The third world referred to the ATS as an "exclusive club." Some believed that Antarctica should be managed by the UN; others argued that the ATS be retained but all states be able to join and all given equal decisionmaking status. Members of the ATS responded with the argument that Antarctica was already being managed in the interests of all—Antarctica was dedicated to science, and all would benefit from the scientific knowledge obtained there. The ATS did, however, allow all contracting parties to attend the minerals meetings, and several third world states, notably India and China, were granted consultative party status by the mid-1980s. There was an annual debate on the question of Antarctica in the General Assembly until 1994, but the ATS withstood this external challenge.

Meanwhile, on June 2, 1988, the Convention for the Regulation of Antarctic Mineral Resources (CRAMRA) was concluded. When Australia announced that it would not ratify this convention, however, political relations became strained because the treaty could not enter into force without Australian ratification. CRAMRA was effectively replaced by the 1992 Environmental Protocol, which, by article 7, prohibited any activity relating to mineral resources, other than scientific research. The protocol also required Antarctic activities to be subject to environmental impact assessment procedures. The protocol entered into force in January 1998, and, after a decade of negotiations, an annex on liability was concluded on June 17, 2005.[36] A secretariat for the ATS has been established in Buenos Aires.[37]

Tracing the background to, and subsequent political activity centered on, the Antarctic Treaty has sought to illustrate the fact that a multilateral treaty is the culmination of what may have been a long process of negotiation and of attempts to address an issue of concern to members of the international community. Once in place, a treaty provides a basis on which states can cooperate to manage the issue it was designed to address. We have looked briefly at the political dynamics that gave rise to the Antarctic Treaty and that have continued since. We will now look at the generic process in more detail before examining a range of multilateral treaties.

■ Notes

1. 8 *International Legal Materials (ILM)* 679 (1969); and Shirley V. Scott, ed., *International Law and Politics: Key Documents* (Boulder, CO: Lynne Rienner, 2006), pp. 58–83. The negotiating history of the Vienna Convention can be found in S. Rosenne, *The Law of Treaties* (Leyden, the Netherlands: A. W. Sijthoff, 1970). David Anderson gives his personal impressions of the negotiations in David H. Anderson, "Law-Making Processes in the UN System: Some Impressions," *Max Planck Yearbook of United Nations Law* 2 (1998): 23–50.

2. 25 *ILM* 543 (1986).

3. Vienna Convention on the Law of Treaties, article 4.

4. Ibid., article 2(1)(a).

5. 34 United Nations Treaty Series (UNTS) 243.

6. Scott, *International Law and Politics.*

7. See, for example, http://untreaty.un.org.

8. UN Document A/RES/48/263 (August 17, 1994), Annex, reproduced in 33 *ILM* 1309 (1994). See, inter alia, D. Anderson, "Efforts to Ensure Universal Participation in the United Nations Convention on the Law of the Sea," *International and Comparative Law Quarterly* 42 (1993): 654–664; D. Anderson, "Further Efforts to Ensure Universal Participation in the United Nations Convention on the Law of

the Sea," *International and Comparative Law Quarterly* 43 (1994): 886–893; Moritaka Hayashi, "The 1994 Agreement for the Universalization of the Law of the Sea Convention," *Ocean Development and International Law* 27 (1996): 31–39; and L. D. M. Nelsen, "The New Deep Seabed Mining Regime," *International Journal of Marine and Coastal Law* 10 (1995): 189–203.

9. Palitha T. B. Kohona, "Reservations: Discussion of Recent Developments in the Practice of the Secretary-General of the United Nations as Depositary of Multilateral Treaties," *Georgia Journal of International and Comparative Law* 33 (2004-2005): 415–450.

10. Vienna Convention on the Law of Treaties, article 19(c).

11. Kohona, "Reservations."

12. Roslyn Moloney, "Incompatible Reservations to Human Rights Treaties: Severability and the Problem of State Consent," *Melbourne Journal of International Law* 5 (2004): 155–168.

13. E. Arnett, "The Comprehensive Nuclear Test-Ban Treaty," *SIPRI Yearbook 1997: Armaments, Disarmament, and International Security* (Oxford: Oxford University Press, 1997), pp. 403–413, esp. 405.

14. Vienna Convention on the Law of Treaties, article 24(2).

15. Antarctic Treaty, article IX (2).

16. Vienna Convention on the Law of Treaties, article 54 (b).

17. Ibid., part V, section 3.

18. See, inter alia, Yuval Shany, "No Longer a Weak Department of Power? Reflections on the Emergence of a New International Judiciary," *European Journal of International Law* 20 (2009): 73–91.

19. Understanding on Rules and Procedures Governing the Settlement of Disputes, article 6(1).

20. Ibid., article 16(4).

21. Ibid., article 21(1).

22. See, inter alia, Natalie Klein, *Dispute Settlement in the UN Convention on the Law of the Sea* (Cambridge: Cambridge University Press, 2005).

23. United Nations Convention on the Law of the Sea (1982), article 286; 21 *ILM* 1261 (1982).

24. United Nations Convention on the Law of the Sea, article 287(5); 21 *ILM* 1261 (1982).

25. http://www.itlos.org.

26. See Shabtai Rosenne, *Provisional Measures in International Law: The International Court of Justice and the International Tribunal for the Law of the Sea* (Oxford: Oxford University Press, 2005).

27. Information taken from Anthony Aust, *Modern Treaty Law and Practice* (Cambridge: Cambridge University Press, 2000), p. 352.

28. See Shirley V. Scott, "Universalism and Title to Territory in Antarctica," *Nordic Journal of International Law* 66 (1997): 33–53.

29. This paragraph draws on Peter Beck, *The International Politics of Antarctica* (London: Croom Helm, 1986).

30. "United States Draft Agreement Placing Antarctica Under a United Nations Trusteeship," June 1948, in W. M. Bush, *Antarctica and International Law: A Collection of Inter-state and National Documents,* vol. 3 (London: Oceana, 1988), p. 462.

31. "Editorial Note," *Foreign Relations of the United States* (1948/I), p. 992.

32. "The Ambassador in Chile (Bowers) to the Secretary of State," July 19, 1948, in *Foreign Relations of the United States* (1948), p. 995. The proposal was repeated, in conversation, in August 1948. "Memorandum of Conversation, by the Under Secretary of State (Lovett), August 16, 1948," in *Foreign Relations of the United States* (1948/I), p. 1002.

33. Paul C. Daniels, "The Antarctic Treaty," in R. S. Lewis and P. M. Smith, eds., *Frozen Future: A Prophetic Report from Antarctica* (New York: Quadrangle Books, 1973), pp. 31–45, esp. 35.

34. 19 *ILM* 860 (1980); and Scott, *International Law and Politics*, pp. 705–710.

35. N. J. Rengger, *Treaties and Alliances of the World,* 5th ed. (Harlow, UK: Longman, 1990), p. 96.

36. Annex VI to the Protocol on Environmental Protection to the Antarctic Treaty, Liability Arising from Environmental Emergencies, 45 *ILM* 5 (2006). For overview and analysis, see Michael Johnson, "Liability for Environmental Damage in Antarctica: The Adoption of Annex VI to the Antarctic Environment Protocol," *Georgetown International Environmental Law Review* 19 (2006–2007): 33–55.

37. See http://www.ats.aq.

9

The Evolution of a Multilateral Treaty Regime

IN THE FINAL SECTION OF CHAPTER 8 WE LOOKED BRIEFLY AT THE political process by which the Antarctic Treaty came about and at the life of the treaty after its conclusion. In this chapter we will look in more detail at the political process of which a multilateral treaty is a part. Figure 9.1 depicts the "typical" political process centered on a multilateral treaty in terms of four principal phases: pretreaty, finalization of the multilateral treaty, operation of the treaty regime, and the supplantation or supplementation of the treaty regime.

A *multilateral treaty* is the culmination of what may have been a long political process. But it is, in another sense, only the beginning. Once the treaty document is in place it provides the central focus for the continuation of the political process that, together with the treaty itself, can now be referred to as a "regime." The term *regime* can lead to some confusion because it is used in several ways. Lawyers use it to refer to "all the law on a particular subject." Instead of talking about "all the law on human rights" a lawyer might refer to the "human rights regime"; instead of talking about the international law pertaining to arms control, reference is made to the "arms control regime," and so on. In the mid-1970s international relations theorists adopted another meaning of *regime,* referring to a process of international cooperation. Until then international cooperation had mainly been studied by analysts of international organizations. Intergovernmental organizations and international cooperation were considered more or less synonymous. But much international cooperation takes place other than through a formal organizational structure. International relations scholars began using the term *regime* to refer to a process of international cooperation, particularly in the field of economics, whether or not it involves a formal organizational

**Figure 9.1   The Typical Process of International Cooperation
Centered on a Multilateral Treaty**

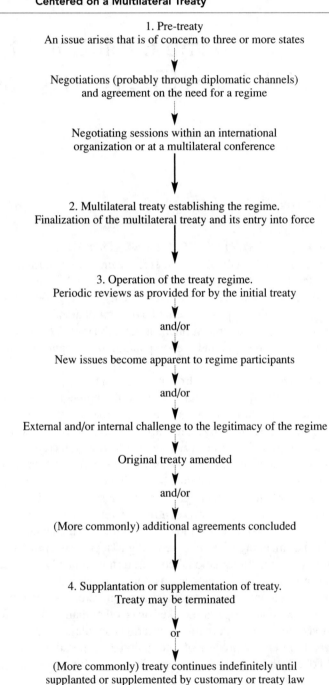

structure. The General Agreement on Tariffs and Trade (GATT), for example, was a treaty negotiated in 1947, on the basis of which several additional "negotiating rounds" were held. But there was no GATT organization, with staff and a building. GATT appeared to operate as an international organization but was not one. The "regime" concept began to be used to refer to *a pattern of cooperation* whether or not it had a formal organizational structure. GATT was a regime; so is the UN.

In the classic book on international regimes[1] the editor, Stephen Krasner, defined a regime as "principles, norms, rules and decision-making processes around which actor expectations converge in a given issue area."[2] The early writing on international regimes by political scientists did not say much about international law; it was not clearly defined as to how the rules, principles, and norms of the international (political) regime related to those of international law. The tendency to skirt around the subject of international law on the part of regime theorists has no doubt been, in part, a legacy of a general dismissal of the importance of international law by post–World War II political realists. Some leading regime theorists have sought to maintain a distinction between international law and international regimes, maintaining that formalization is not a necessary condition for the effective operation of international regimes.[3] The exact nature of the relationship between a "legal" regime and a "political" regime cannot be precisely defined, most basically because of the lack of universality in the treatment of the term by political scientists. But it is true to say that the vast majority of entities and processes to which political scientists refer as regimes—both formal international organizations and patterns of cooperation short of a formal organizational structure—have in common their foundation in a multilateral treaty. Even though a number of scholars have pointed to the possibilities of fruitful interdisciplinary interaction in the study of regimes,[4] it remains more common for disciplinary boundaries to remain, with complementary meanings attributed to the term *regime*. Thus, when political scientists refers to a regime, they are emphasizing the normative aspect of rules and norms as well as decision-making processes, social practices, and institutional structure, whereas when international lawyers refers to a regime they are focusing on the contents of one or more legal sources on a particular subject.[5]

In this book the phrase *treaty regime* is used to emphasize the fact that we are looking at the law contained in one or more multilateral treaties, in the context of the political process of which the law is a part.

■ An Issue Arises That Is of Concern to Three or More States

A multilateral treaty results from a perceived need to manage an issue of mutual concern, whether that be climate change or the treatment of refugees.

The title of the treaty will often give a good indication of the regime issue. What is of interest politically is how the issue came to be recognized as one deserving of international cooperation. Who defined it as an issue? Of course, a treaty may be a long document, and a treaty often appears to address a number of issues. But even where a multilateral treaty does address more than one issue it is usually possible, particularly if one investigates the historical record, to identify the central issue without which the treaty would not have come about. An understanding of the perception of the issue in the years immediately preceding the conclusion of the treaty can do much to help understand the evolution of that regime in later years.

■ Negotiations and Agreement on the Need for a Regime

Whereas the outsider could be excused for thinking that the primary negotiating phase is that of the international conference at which the text of the multilateral treaty is finalized, the most important negotiations have usually occurred in the months or years before that. The process of getting to the table has been referred to as the *prenegotiations*[6] to emphasize their role prior to the more formal and publicized negotiations. During the prenegotiations, participants usually reach agreement as to who is to be at the table and the boundaries within which the topic is to be discussed.[7] This was acknowledged by the Australian representative at the opening session of the Antarctic conference when he recalled that it had only been "when it became clear that there was fairly general agreement [that the best solution would be to include provisions in the Treaty that would preserve the status quo as regards territorial claims] that we believed that the calling of a Conference was justified."[8]

Much of the prenegotiations may take place at a bilateral level. Governments may be sounded out through normal diplomatic channels well ahead of the formal announcement of a multilateral conference. In this way, positions can be negotiated in an "invisible" way that does not require any party to back down publicly on its policy position. In the case of some environmental negotiations there have also been informal workshops, which participants—scientists, academics, industry representatives, and so on— attend in their personal capacities. An example of this was the Intergovernmental Panel on Climate Change. Public support for a particular course of action may also be garnered through use of the media. The negotiations may be quite rapid or take a number of sessions, spanning a number of years. The negotiation of the UN Convention on the Law of the Sea took nine years of negotiations, which followed six years of preparatory work by the UN Sea-Bed Committee.

Let us now consider the role in the negotiating phase leading up to a multilateral treaty, of the hegemon, of middle powers, of the South, and of nonstate actors. As will be seen, the respective influence of the various types of international actors depends to some extent on the issue at hand.

The Hegemon

The theory of hegemonic stability suggests, most basically, that a regime emerges when a *hegemon*—a state with preponderant power—regards such a regime as being in its best interests.[9] The United States has been a world hegemon at least since World War II; this theory thus suggests that a regime has emerged where the United States has estimated that the anticipated gains would exceed the costs of supplying the regime.[10] The theory of hegemonic stability was developed primarily in relation to trade, explaining the emergence of GATT as a multilateral trade regime in terms of US interests. The hegemonic influence of the United States would appear to have been most notable in relation to trade and arms control regimes; some scholars have argued that there is no hegemonic power for environmental issues.[11]

There have been two schools of thought regarding how the most powerful state uses its preponderant resources to create the regimes it prefers. Charles Kindleberger advanced the notion of a *benign hegemon,* which exercises positive leadership in enticing others to accept its preferences; the benign hegemon is willing to bear an undue part of the short-term costs because it will pay off in the long term in terms of prestige.[12] In the case of the 1986–1987 ozone negotiations, US negotiations involved extensive bilateral consultations in order to find the "real interests" behind states' positions; when the Soviet Union refused to accept the 1986 reference year for controlled output levels, the head of the US delegation discovered that Soviet opposition stemmed from the domestic legal constraints of a Five Year Plan, ending in 1990, that provided for a modest increase in chlorofluorocarbons (CFCs). US officials were able to design a clause that would effectively apply only to the former Soviet Union and would meet this concern but have only a minimal potential impact on CFC emissions.[13] The United States also gained leadership credibility by legislating controls at a national level before suggesting that they could be incorporated into an international treaty.

Those who believe in a coercive hegemon believe that it imposes its will whatever the preferences of others; others tolerate it because they have no choice.[14] In the negotiations for the International Criminal Court the US secretary of defense, William Cohen, apparently indicated to several allies that if they did not support the US proposal for limiting the jurisdiction of the ICC, the US might withdraw forces from bases in their territory.[15] There may, of course, be a fine line between being a benign and a coercive hegemon. In the case of the Antarctic Treaty, the United States did not necessarily "bully" the other states into signing. But the United States certainly had the greatest influence over the text of the treaty and stood to gain by its conclusion. The United States had made no territorial claim, but the terms of the treaty gave it access to the whole continent.[16] In some treaty negotiations—such as those leading to the 1951 Refugee Convention—the United States has influenced significantly the treaty negotiations but not signed the resultant treaty. Although there are plenty of examples of regimes in which the United States has played a leadership role, hegemonic stability theory has not been without its critics;[17] and it can quite readily be seen that other actors have influenced significantly the course of treaty negotiations.

Middle Powers

The term *middle power* is used to refer to those states between the most powerful and the weakest in world politics. Middle powers such as Canada, Australia, and the Scandinavian states have been active in the creation and operation of treaty regimes in the post-1945 period. Canada can take considerable credit for the conclusion of the Ottawa Convention on Land Mines. Middle-power leadership has not involved domination so much as acting as a peer of other group members. In international institutions, middle-power leadership has characteristically involved fulfilling three functions: that of a catalyst, offering the intellectual and political energy to trigger an initiative and to take the lead in dealing with that issue; as facilitators, planning, convening, and hosting formative meetings, setting agendas and priorities, and so on; and as managers—finding practical solutions to stumbling blocks in the creation or operation of regimes.[18] Great powers also do these things, but because middle powers have fewer issues with which to deal, they are able to concentrate their resources on selected issues of particular importance to them. Middle powers may have the greatest freedom in policy choices because mistakes by superpowers may have global impact, whereas smaller powers often feel they have no room to maneuver.[19]

Australia's role in providing an impetus for the final negotiations that produced the Chemical Weapons Convention is an example of the role of middle powers in treaty negotiation. In 1991 the UN General Assembly passed a resolution calling for the draft convention to be concluded in 1992. But progress within the negotiations made such an outcome appear improbable at best. Under the dedicated interest of Gareth Evans, Australian officials produced a model convention, which included compromise solutions to the outstanding areas of disagreement. Convinced that a breakthrough in the negotiations was possible, Australian officials discussed the text with officials in many state capitals, and on March 19, 1992, Evans presented to the Conference on Disarmament (CD) what he referred to as an "accelerated refinement" of the rolling text. The chairman of the negotiating committee took up the Australian initiative to produce his own chairman's text, which provided the basis for the final rounds of intense negotiations. On September 3, 1992, the annual report adopted by the CD contained the draft

Convention on the Prohibition of the Development, Production, Stockpiling, and Use of Chemical Weapons and Their Destruction. The text was unanimously endorsed by the UN General Assembly in November 1992 and was opened for signature on January 13, 1993.

The South

States of the South, also referred to as developing states or less-developed countries (LDCs), are a diverse group, but most are former colonies (with the exception of Ethiopia and Thailand) and most are poor (with the exception of the oil-producing states of the Middle East).[20] The developing world does not always have a common negotiating position but is most likely to do so where economic issues are at stake. This has included environmental negotiations, which virtually always have an economic dimension. Developing states have sometimes viewed the environmental concerns of the North as a new form of colonialism, a way by which the developed states can "pull up the development ladder behind them."[21] President George H. W. Bush proposed an initiative on forests at the Group of Seven summit in July 1990.[22] The statement by Prime Minister Mathahir Mohamad of Malaysia during UNCED appeared to encapsulate the South's response to the North's demand for a forests convention:

> Obviously the North wants to have a direct say in the management of forests in the poor South at next to no cost to themselves. The pittance they offer is much less than the loss of earnings by the poor countries and yet it is made out as a generous concession. . . .
> The poor are not asking for charity. When the rich chopped down their own forests, built their poison-belching factories and scoured the world for cheap resources, the poor said nothing. Indeed they paid for the development of the rich. Now the rich claim a right to regulate the development of the poor countries. And yet any suggestion that the rich compensate the poor adequately is regarded as outrageous. As colonies we were exploited. Now as independent nations we are to be equally exploited.[23]

Developing states have been successful in negotiating the inclusion of environment funds to facilitate their contributing to the implementation of environmental treaties. The 1990 amendments to the Montreal Protocol, for example, included a mechanism to enable developing countries' compliance with the control measures established under the protocol. Part XII of the UN Convention on the Law of the Sea similarly provides some measures specially designed to assist developing states. In taking all measures consistent with the convention to prevent, reduce, and control pollution of the environment from any sources, states are to use "the best practicable means at their disposal and in accordance with their capabilities."[24] Special mention is made of differentiation in relation to establishing global and regional rules regarding land-based sources of pollution; states are to take into account, inter alia, "the economic capacity of developing States and their need for economic development."[25] Developing states are also to be given assistance to protect and preserve the marine environment. States, directly or through competent international organizations, are to assist developing states by training scientific and technical personnel; facilitating their participation in relevant international programs; supplying necessary equipment and facilities; enhancing their capacity to manufacture such equipment; providing advice and developing facilities for research, monitoring, educational, and other programs; and assisting with the minimization of the effects of major accidents that may cause serious pollution of the marine environment and with the preparation of environmental assessments.[26] International organizations are to give preferential treatment for developing states in the allocation of appropriate funds and technical assistance and in the utilization of their specialized services.[27]

Even on environmental matters there may not always be a single voting position among developing states. In the case of the 1991 climate change negotiations, positions ranged from those of the oil producers, led by Saudi Arabia and Venezuela, which opposed possible international restraints on their major asset; to that of the Association of Small Island States, made up of twenty-five countries of the Pacific and Caribbean, whose very existence was threatened by rising sea levels.[28] It was very apparent at the 2009 conference in Copenhagen that the perceived interests in respect of climate change of the most vulnerable island states such as Tuvalu did not align with those of the richer and more rapidly developing states such as China.

Developing countries now make up more than three-quarters of membership of the World Trade Organization. During and after the Uruguay Round (1986–1994), developing countries shifted from operating as a single G77 grouping to more complex coalitions. Leading developing countries have, for example, increasingly formed pragmatic coalitions both with other developing and with developed countries on specific issues of common interest.[29]

Nonstate Actors

Nonstate actors are a third category that may be influential in treaty negotiations. Subject-matter experts often play an essential role in defining the issue, bringing the issue to the attention of governments, and suggesting solutions. The literature on treaty regimes sometimes uses the term *epistemic community* to refer to a "network of professionals with recognized expertise and competence in a particular domain and an authoritative claim to policy-relevant knowledge within that domain or issue-area."[30] The study of epistemic communities shifted attention away from the role of states in multilateral treaty negotiation to that of scientists or other professional groups who constitute a community based on shared knowledge and who may also play an important part in the creation of a regime. Of course, there may well be a degree of overlap among states and an epistemic community where, as in the case of the scientific community, much of its work is made possible by government funding.

Public-interest NGOs are a second type of nonstate actor influential in treaty negotiations; sometimes they are referred to more generally as *civil society*.[31] Public-interest NGOs are particularly apparent in the process of creating human rights, humanitarian, and environmental regimes. Without the determined efforts of NGOs, the UN Charter would have contained, at most, a "passing reference" to human rights.[32] In the campaign against land mines, to take another example, the NGO community is credited with accelerating the process and successfully seeking the transfer of negotiations from the UN Conference on Disarmament in Geneva to the convocation of "like-minded" states in Ottawa.[33]

NGOs often form a coalition to work toward a specific treaty. An umbrella NGO called the Climate Action Network coordinated the work of a number of NGOs including the World Wildlife Fund, Greenpeace, the Environmental Defense Fund, the Sierra Club, Ozone Action, and the Worldwatch Institute in working toward a convention on climate change.[34] NGOs that worked for the conclusion of a treaty to establish an international criminal court include Amnesty International, Human Rights Watch, and the Lawyers' Committee for Human Rights. At the preparatory committee stage most NGOs organized their activities through the NGO Coalition for an International Criminal Court (CICC), which grew from thirty to some eight hundred NGOs.[35]

Although the influence of NGOs on international negotiations appears to have increased in recent years it should be borne in mind that, just as there is not necessarily a clear dividing line between the views of the state and an epistemic community, so do NGOs often work in conjunction with governments.[36] As the CICC grew in strength it developed an alliance with the Like-Minded Group of States and sought to assist its efforts for a strong international criminal court by, for example, preparing researched commentaries on each issue discussed and making them available to government delegations.[37]

Industry organizations may also participate directly or indirectly in treaty negotiations. Those that became involved in negotiations for the UN Framework Convention on Climate Change included the Climate Council and the Global Climate Coalition, the American Petroleum Institute, the World Business Council for Sustainable Development, the US Council for International Business, and the International Chamber of Commerce.[38]

■ Negotiating Sessions Within an International Organization or Multilateral Conference

The text of most modern multilateral treaties has been finalized either by a UN body such as the Conference on Disarmament, or the Human Rights Council; or else at a multilateral conference specially convened for that purpose, often by a resolution of the UN General Assembly. The venue and nature of the forum are not of legal significance so long as the conclusion of the treaty has not been procured by the threat or use of force;[39] a state is under no legal obligation if its representative was coerced into giving consent to be bound by a treaty.[40] Some treaty negotiations may extend over years, with the representatives meeting for several weeks each year. Negotiations for a Chemical Weapons Convention took place over more than ten years.

If a conference is to be specially convened, the decision as to location can in itself be political. Although the host state does not formally have any impact over the conference and its outcome, it may gain stature from that role. A treaty is often known by a colloquial name that includes the city that was most important to its creation. The Convention on International Civil Aviation[41] is usually referred to as the Chicago Convention after the city in which it was adopted. The Convention on the Prohibition of the Use, Stockpiling, Production, and Transfer of Anti-Personnel Mines and Their Destruction is often referred to as the Ottawa Convention because it was conceived and opened for signature in Canada's capital city, although it was adopted in Oslo.[42] In the case of conferences not convened by the UN, the host country usually supplies the presiding officer, although this too may become a question of political debate. Once the chair has been selected, he or she is expected to be neutral. If a subject arises with which the chair has some close personal involvement, he or she may choose to have someone else in the chair while that subject is being addressed.

Delegations attending a conference are obliged to be equipped with a document known as *credentials,* which authorizes them to represent that state. An individual who is to sign a treaty requires a document known as *full powers* as evidence of authority to do so. The permanent representative of a state to the United Nations or other organization at which treaties are signed may be issued with general full powers. The practice of credentials dates from the time when communications were slower and when it would have been difficult to check if the person who appeared to be representing a government had the authority to do so. It is now usual to send a copy of credentials prior to the opening of a conference, but the original must still be submitted at the conference. A credentials committee is appointed to examine the credentials and report back. This is usually a straightforward technical exercise, but it can occasionally become a political exercise. A practice has evolved by which the credentials committee does not report back to plenary until toward the end of the proceedings, by which time their approval has lost most of its significance.[43]

The conference often begins work with a "basic text," which may have been prepared, for example, by a preparatory committee, UNEP, the ICRC, or the International Law Commission. In the case of the Antarctic Treaty, the United States had prepared the preliminary draft. But the degree to which there is already a negotiating text that is largely acceptable to the participants when the formal negotiations begin varies enormously. One extreme example of a relative lack of agreement at the opening of a diplomatic conference was the 1998 Rome Conference at which the Statute of the International Criminal Court was adopted. Despite the earlier drafting work of the preparatory committee (PrepCom), the conference began with a draft statute that still contained some 1,400 square brackets, indicating points of disagreement.[44] The third Law of the Sea conference began without any basic text.

The original draft treaty and other documents from the negotiating process are together referred to as the *travaux préparatoires*. They may become of legal significance during the life of the treaty regime. Article 32 of the Vienna Convention on the Law of Treaties provides that if a literal reading of a treaty makes interpretation of the treaty difficult, reference may be made to the preparatory work of the treaty as well as to the circumstances of its conclusion as supplementary means of interpretation.

The work of getting from the basic text to the treaty is usually undertaken by a series of committees, each of which is allocated a portion of the text. Reports are then submitted to the plenary. In the nineteenth and early twentieth centuries, French was the official language of diplomacy. English was used in addition at the 1919 peace conference. The United Nations began with five "official" languages, of which English and French were the only "working" languages into which all documents were translated. The UN and most multilateral conferences now have six official languages, all of which are working languages: Arabic, Chinese, English, French, Russian, and Spanish. It can, of course, be of considerable advantage to a state if its negotiators are able to work in their preferred language.

An international conference, unless convened by an IGO, is an independent body. One of the first tasks of an international conference is therefore to adopt the rules of procedure; this is usually done by acclamation.[45] If specific rules are to be amended, this will usually be done by simple majority voting. The first conferences with detailed rules of procedure were those of the League of Nations. These were the direct predecessors of the UN General Assembly; other international conferences have, in turn, taken the General Assembly as their model. Just as we distinguished rules pertaining to the operation of the system of international law from those dealing with all other issues of relations among states (see Chapter 5), so is it necessary, when dealing with a multilateral conference giving rise to a multilateral treaty, to distinguish between questions of *procedure* and those of *substance*. The rules of procedure may sound dry and unexciting but sometimes if a delegation does not think it will be able to command support for a particular issue of substance, it attempts to achieve the same result via the rules of procedure. Rules of procedure may therefore be an important tactical device. This is all the more so because procedural decisions are taken by a simple majority, whereas in treaty-making conferences issues of substance are usually decided by a two-thirds majority.[46]

Although the aim of many global treaties is universal membership, negotiating states often have to reconcile this goal with differences in the negotiating positions of the various states. Treaties often suffer from the so-called lowest-common-denominator factor: reflecting only that change which is acceptable to every state participating in the negotiations. In the case of the Basel Convention on the Control of Transboundary Movements of Hazardous Wastes and Their Disposal, environmental NGOs wanted the international trade in hazardous wastes made illegal but could get agreement on no more than regulation of the trade. Particularly in the case of human rights regimes, the lowest-common-denominator factor manifests itself in debate as to whether or not to permit reservations to the treaty; negotiators must decide whether to maximize "the universal application of the instrument" or to "protect its integrity."[47] No reservations are permitted to the treaty to establish the International Criminal Court or to the Montreal Protocol, but the negotiators of the Convention on the Elimination of All Forms of Discrimination Against Women decided to permit reservations other than those incompatible with the object and purpose of CEDAW.[48] Some states have, nevertheless, entered reservations to what the committee has indicated are key articles of the treaty, and other reservations are drawn so widely that their effect cannot be limited to specific provisions in the convention.[49] This is an ongoing issue for the treaty regime.[50]

■ Treaty Adoption and Entry into Force

Once the negotiations are complete, the negotiating states need to express their agreement to the finalized treaty text. This is referred to as *adopting* the text. At an international conference, adoption of the text of a treaty takes place by a vote of two-thirds of the states present and voting, unless by the same majority it is decided to apply a different rule.[51] If it is not an international conference, then adoption of the text takes place by the consent of all negotiating states. A vote is now sometimes referred to as unanimous if there are no negative votes, even if there are abstentions; if counting by majority, abstentions do not usually count. Voting by consensus—adopting a resolution without a vote although not necessarily with unanimity—is a fairly recent innovation. The best-known example of consensus voting is the third Law of the Sea conference. It had been agreed that negotiations should proceed by way of consensus in order to adopt a convention that would enjoy the widest possible support, as well as to protect the interests and views of minorities at the conference.[52] The conference proceeded by consensus until 1982 when the final text was adopted by vote, with opposition from the United States, Israel, Turkey, and Venezuela; seventeen other states, mainly European, abstained.[53] The 1995 UN Agreement on Straddling Fish Stocks and Highly Migratory Fish Stocks was adopted without a vote. The use of consensus decisionmaking by the UN Committee on the Peaceful Uses of Outer Space has been deemed a success both in terms of the treaties concluded and their wide ratification.[54]

Conferences establishing a regime usually complete their work by adopting a document known as the *final act,* which includes the text of the treaty drafted, texts of resolutions adopted, and organizational details of the conference. A treaty negotiated by the main committees of the General Assembly is usually recommended to the General Assembly for adoption, which is done by annexing the treaty to a resolution. The treaty must next be authenticated, indicating that the text, often translated into several languages, is correct. Authentication may be by signature or by initialing the text of the final act.

States that have consented to be bound by a treaty are referred to as *contracting states.* In the period between a state having expressed its consent to be bound by the treaty and entry into force of that treaty, or between a state having signed a treaty and making clear its intention not to become a party to that treaty, a state is obliged to "refrain from acts which would defeat the object and purpose" of the treaty pending its entry into force, provided that such entry into force is not unduly delayed.[55] There is often a significant period of time between the conclusion of the negotiations for a multilateral treaty and its entry into force. In the case of the Antarctic Treaty there was a two-year gap, but in some instances the time lapse may be much greater. The Geneva Conventions of 1949, for example, came into force in 1954; the 1969 Vienna Convention on the Law of Treaties did not enter into force until 1980; and the UN Law of the Sea Convention was concluded in 1982 but did not enter into force until November 1994.

Article 102 of the UN Charter provides that "every treaty and every international agreement entered into by any Member State of the United Nations after the present Charter comes into force shall as soon as possible be registered with the Secretariat and published by it." An equivalent provision in article 18 of the Covenant of the League of Nations derived from one of Woodrow Wilson's Fourteen Points and was intended to prevent a proliferation of secret treaties—the existence of which had been blamed, at least in part, for the outbreak of World War I.[56] All treaties and international agreements registered or filed and recorded with the Secretariat since 1946 are published in the *United Nations Treaty Series*. A UN publication entitled *Multilateral Treaties Deposited with the Secretary-General* is a guide to the status of the treaties for which the UN Secretary-General is the depositary. It includes information on signatures, ratifications, accessions, reservations, objections by other states to those reservations, declarations, entry into force, and so on. Both publications can be accessed at the UN Treaty Collection website.[57]

■ Aspects of Regime Life

The treaty provides the basis for a process of cooperation via which regime members manage the issue that gave rise to the treaty. In some regimes, particularly those in the environmental and nonproliferation fields, this is done by what is termed the *conference of the states parties,* a body consisting of all states that are party to the treaty. In some regimes an international organization comes into operation on entry into force of the treaty. The Chemical Weapons Convention, for example, provided for the establishment of the Organization for the Prohibition of Chemical Weapons. Particularly when a treaty establishes an international organization it may be useful for a preparatory commission (the PrepCom) to prepare for entry into force of the treaty by drafting rules of procedure, engaging staff, finding premises, and so on. In the case of the Comprehensive Nuclear Test Ban Treaty, a PrepCom was established on November 19, 1996, to set up the global verification regime and to prepare for entry into force of the treaty. Following the first conference of the states parties to the CTBT, the PrepCom will cease to exist and the Comprehensive Nuclear Test-Ban Treaty Organization will be established.

During the course of regime life the original issue will likely remain of central concern, but other matters may also need to be addressed. In some circumstances this may involve amending the original agreement, but rather than reopen aspects of the negotiations it is more typical to leave the original treaty in place and negotiate subsequent agreements or "protocols" to address subissues that arise or increase in importance during the life of the regime. The International Whaling Convention detailed industry regulations in an annex that could be revised without amending the original treaty.

As the regime operates, it may come under challenge from states either internal or external to the regime. In Chapter 8 we noted how the Antarctic regime withstood the external challenge from members of the third world as well as an internal challenge by Australia and France when they decided not to proceed with ratification of the Minerals Convention. In the case of the Treaty on the Non-Proliferation of Nuclear Weapons (NPT), the 1998 tests of India and Pakistan were widely perceived as threatening the integrity of the regime, which had been designed to accommodate only five nuclear weapon states.[58]

Regime Effectiveness

There has in recent years been considerable scholarly interest in analyzing what makes for an effective treaty regime.[59] This has been in part a reaction to the post–World War II proliferation of treaties:

> [I]n 1988 . . . we had horrible films of Iraq using poison gas against Iranian soldiers, which was a clear violation of the Geneva Protocol against chemical weapons. There was a big conference on chemical weapons in Paris shortly thereafter, and they didn't even mention Iraq in their report. Rather, their response was to create a new treaty, which became the Chemical Weapons Convention. And if there was use of chemical weapons today, I would expect their reaction to be holding another meeting in Paris and writing another treaty.[60]

Similar comments have been made about most fields of international law. In relation to the International Labor Organization, for example, Steve Charnovitz has called for a "de-emphasis on writing new conventions" to "enable the ILO to devote more time to communicating information to member countries on how to conduct more effective labor and employment programs."[61] In the field of human rights, Gudmundur Alfredsson has noted that politicians often find it easier to draft a whole new instrument than a protocol or amendments to an existing one. "In light of continuing violations, the main focus should now be on national implementation and international monitoring."[62]

The relationship between a multilateral treaty regime and the distribution of political power among those states with an interest in the subject matter may well make a significant contribution toward determining the effectiveness of the regime. The question has thus been raised as to whether the Ottawa Convention and International Criminal Court can be fully effective without US involvement.[63] US Ambassador David Scheffer commented that he considered US participation in a permanent international criminal court to be essential to its effectiveness. "History has shown that when new international institutions are started without full United States participation—like the League of Nations—they can fail. When they start with United States leadership—like the United Nations, the war crimes tribunals for the former

Yugoslavia and Rwanda, [and] the new Organization for the Prohibition of Chemical Weapons—they can succeed.[64] A similar concern has been expressed in relation to NGOs having a disproportionate influence over the negotiating process such that the resultant treaty does not reflect the "real political forces necessary to its successful implementation."[65]

The issues of compliance, transparency, verification, and dispute resolution are all relevant to the effectiveness of multilateral treaty regimes. Let's consider each in turn:

Compliance

Those seeking to enhance the effectiveness of international law understandably tend to assume that compliance is a key determinant of regime effectiveness and that the path to enhancing compliance lies in tough enforcement. Abram Chayes and Antonia Handler Chayes argued in their influential 1995 book, *The New Sovereignty: Compliance with International Regulatory Agreements,* that it is not so much the actual enforcement of legal obligations that matters most but managerial stratagems, including the enhancement of transparency and verification and the continuous review of treaty performance and compliance.[66]

There would seem to be good reasons for states complying with their obligations, not least of which is the efficiency of policy continuity. Chayes and Chayes pointed out that states do not constantly review whether or not to comply with a treaty but set up the procedures to comply and then simply keep going.[67] Particularly for those states that contributed to the negotiation of a treaty, it is likely that their perceived interests and their commitments coincide.[68] When a powerful state makes a policy decision to comply, that decision can usually be attributed largely to the concern of even powerful states that, if they flout a particular provision of international law, other states will treat them likewise on another occasion. On June 24, 1993, Angel Francisco Breard was convicted of the attempted rape and murder of Ruth Dickie in Virginia. Although Breard was a Paraguayan, the Paraguayan consular authorities did not learn about his arrest and trial until 1996. This was contrary to article 36(1)(b) of the Vienna Convention on Consular Relations of 1963,[69] which stipulates that the "authorities shall inform the person concerned without delay of his rights [to have the consular post advised of his arrest or committal to prison or custody pending trial or other form of detention]." The State Department recognized the lapse on July 7, 1997, and apologized. In 1998 the State Department released a booklet for law enforcement and other US officials that clearly presented the procedures required to comply with the Vienna Convention on Consular Relations; the forward to the booklet stated that it aimed to "help ensure that the United States can insist upon rigorous compliance by foreign governments with respect to United States citizens abroad."[70]

By article 27 of the Vienna Convention on the Law of Treaties, a party may not invoke the provisions of its internal law as justification for its failure to perform a treaty. But it is possible for a state to be in breach of international law even if not acting illegally within municipal law. This is because it is the domestic legal system of states that determines the status of international law within that system. Constitutional law varies between states. The basic division, at least in theory, is between those states that have adopted a *monist* conceptualization of the relationship between international law and municipal (domestic) law—that is, states that regard international law and municipal law as part of one system of law—and those that have adopted a *dualist* approach, regarding the two systems as separate. Monism and dualism are, however, "ideal types"; in practice, most systems contain elements of both. A state adopting a pure monist interpretation of the relationship between international law and its municipal legal system would consider treaties to be part of national law; those adopting a dualist interpretation of the relationship would assume the need for treaty terms to be somehow made into domestic law before they would carry any weight in the domestic legal system. In fact, three main categories of state can be discerned.[71]

In Belgium, Chile, Ethiopia, France, Switzerland, the Netherlands, and the United States, some form of legislative approval is required for at least some categories of treaties. Once a treaty has been approved by the state and has entered into force, it automatically becomes part of municipal law without any separate act of "incorporation" or "transformation" being required. In France and Switzerland, for example, a treaty that has been ratified and has entered into force is binding and can suspend any inconsistent national statutes. In Chile, a treaty that has been approved by congress preempts domestic law. Similarly, under article 9.4 of the Ethiopian constitution, all treaties ratified by Ethiopia are part of the laws of the country. In the United States, the Constitution provides that a treaty must have the "advice and consent" of a two-thirds vote of the Senate before it can be ratified by the president. The president is also able, however, to enter into "executive agreements," which in US law are distinguishable from treaties and so do not require Senate approval. Indeed, what in international law is termed a *treaty* may come under one of five categories in US domestic law: a treaty (requiring two-thirds Senate consent for ratification), a congressional previously authorized executive agreement, a congressional subsequently approved executive agreement, a presidential executive agreement, and a treaty authorized executive agreement. This makes the law regarding the application of treaties in the United States very complex.[72]

In the case of the second group of states, including the Federal Republic of Germany and Italy, a treaty itself has no effect in the internal legal system and requires transformation by a legislative act in order to give it municipal effect. Once legislative approval has been given, the situation is similar to that in the first category of states. In the third category of states, which includes the United Kingdom, Australia, and India, a treaty as such has no domestic effect. The terms of a treaty must be implemented or incorporated through national law, whose terms therefore may not be precisely the same as those of the treaty. Sometimes the treaty is simply appended to legislation, but usually the act of parliament will embody the treaty provisions in different terms, not necessarily even revealing their treaty source.

The main difference between these three groups of states is thus whether it is the treaty itself or the incorporating legislation that is applied by the courts. National courts can be vital to the effective implementation of international treaties, although national legal systems have varied in their degree of permeability to international law.[73] As with the question of the relationship between treaties and municipal law, the situation is not as straightforward as the monist-dualist distinction might suggest. It is not necessarily the case that judges in predominantly monist systems take treaties into account more than their counterparts in predominantly dualist systems. The US system has been one of the least permeable of national systems.[74]

The principle of *complementarity* embodied in the Rome Statute of the International Criminal Court assumes that municipal courts are the first option in judging and punishing the crimes covered by the statute. There is said to be universal jurisdiction for crimes against humanity: any state can exercise its jurisdiction over an individual, no matter where the crime was committed. A number of "terrorism" treaties—including the 1973 Convention on the Prevention and Punishment of Crimes Against Internationally Protected Persons, Including Diplomatic Agents;[75] and the 1998 International Convention on the Suppression of Terrorist Bombings[76]—oblige a state either to prosecute or extradite individuals who have committed certain offences of universal concern. Article VI of the Genocide Convention requires the state in whose territory the acts of genocide took place to try the responsible persons.

Transparency and Verification

It is now recognized that a badly designed regime cannot necessarily solve the problem it was established to address, even if all states comply perfectly with all their treaty obligations.[77] *Transparency,* the availability of regime-relevant information, appears to be a key ingredient of regime effectiveness. States are more likely to comply if the way they behave is monitored and publicized and they can see evidence that others are also adhering to their regime obligations. Promoting transparency involves fostering the acquisition, analysis, and dissemination of regular, prompt, and accurate regime-relevant information.[78] Regimes vary considerably in their degree of transparency. Most regime information systems rely on self-reporting although, in some cases, governments serve as conduits for information from substate actors—as in, for example, industry reports on CFC production under the Montreal Protocol.[79] In the Antarctic Treaty System all parties have an obligation to give notice in advance of all expeditions to and within Antarctica, on the part of its ships or nationals, and all expeditions to Antarctica organized in or proceeding from its territory; all stations in the Antarctica occupied by its nationals; and any military personnel or equipment intended to be introduced by it into Antarctica for scientific research or for any other peaceful purpose.[80]

Transparency is particularly important in promoting compliance with human rights regimes; reciprocity and systems that provide for interstate complaints are not so effective when states do not perceive their own interests as threatened by the noncompliance of another state.[81] Reporting systems have been the mainstay of the enforcement mechanisms in human rights treaties. Although the treaty bodies have experienced considerable success in attracting the participation of states, the inadequacy of committee resources has contributed to delays in processing reports.[82] Problems of delay and a lack of follow-up mechanisms have also characterized the process of individual petitioning that is available in some human rights regimes. Enhanced interest in improving the effectiveness of human rights regimes has led to debate regarding how to improve the procedure and institutions established to promote the accountability of states parties to the treaties.[83]

Verification refers to the process of checking whether a state is complying with its legal obligations. It is a politically sensitive issue because the very idea of verification clashes with the notion of sovereignty, by which a state has control over its territory and what goes on there. In the arms control field the focus is on verification because the stakes seem highest, and acceptable verification procedures have often been the key to getting the treaty negotiated in the first place. The early years of the Cold War—up to the early 1960s—saw notable failures on verification provisions during disarmament negotiations.[84] The Antarctic Treaty, by which consultative parties have the right to designate "observers" with complete freedom of access at any time to all areas of Antarctica, including all stations, and all ships and aircraft at points of discharging or embarking cargoes or personnel in Antarctica, was quite an exception. There was considerable variation in the strength of the verification provisions included in arms control treaties during the remainder of the 1960s and 1970s. The Biological Weapons Convention, for example, had little in the way of verification procedures, but the NPT contained considerable verification procedures to be undertaken by the International Atomic Energy Agency.

There have been considerable advances since the mid-1980s in developing sophisticated rules for on-site inspections and in combining various means of verification. In the case of the Chemical Weapons Convention, states have thirty days in which to reject any individual on a list of inspectors. The secretariat of the Organization for the Prohibition of Chemical Weapons must approve equipment to be used in inspections. The party in question cannot object to this. At the site, inspectors may interview staff, inspect records they deem relevant, take photos and samples, and so on. This is very sensitive because the chemical industry is used for many purposes other than weapons and there may be information a company does not want its rivals to glean for commercial reasons. Although this system may still not deliver 100 percent verification, it is a much more detailed system than was provided for in the earlier arms control treaties.

Dispute Resolution

It is standard for multilateral treaties to stipulate how any dispute "regarding the interpretation or application of the treaty" is to be settled. In practice, states are generally not bickering over the "interpretation or application" of a treaty per se but over a clash in the pursuit of their respective interests; a treaty text may then become the pivot around which one state seeks to change the policy position or actions of the state with which it has come into conflict. States may engage in considerable negotiations as to the appropriate means by which to attempt to resolve a dispute. For a state to agree to involve a third party—whether a court or an arbiter—in the resolution of a dispute is to indicate a preparedness to be at least partly flexible in its own position. Just as sovereignty is the main stumbling block to getting 100 percent verification of obligations in international law, so can it prevent states wanting to involve, or accept the decision of, a third party. In the case of the overlapping claims to Antarctica of the United Kingdom, Chile, and Argentina, the United Kingdom wanted to take the case to the ICJ but the other two sides refused. Sovereignty was an issue on which they were not prepared to compromise.

Integral to a dispute and its resolution may be the exact meaning to be given to the wording of the treaty. The Vienna Convention contains provisions regarding the interpretation of a treaty. The general rule is that a "treaty is to be interpreted in good faith in accordance with the ordinary meaning to be given to the terms of the treaty in their context and in the light of its object and purpose."[85] Where a treaty has been authenticated in two or more languages, the text is equally authoritative in each language, unless the treaty provides or the parties agree that, in case of divergence, a particular text shall prevail.[86]

■ Treaty Regimes and the Globalization of Politics

What, then, has been the political outcome of the appearance of so many new multilateral treaties in the years since World War II? We have so far viewed a multilateral treaty as a response to an issue of mutual concern. But have multilateral treaties as a whole solved the problems they were designed to address? The ozone depletion regime has been held up as a model of success. But if the mass of treaties is taken as a whole, the answer would seem to be in the negative; few treaties have completed their work and gone on to become redundant. Neither have the goals specified in the preambles of the multilateral treaties usually been achieved.

It may, however, be unreasonable to judge a regime by the idealistic-sounding goals written into the preamble of its founding treaty. According to the preamble of the Chemical Weapons Convention, for example, states parties to the convention are "determined for the sake of all mankind, to exclude completely the possibility of the use of chemical weapons." Was this a realistic aim, particularly given that a treaty is binding only on parties to that treaty? Would it really be possible for multilateral treaties to achieve all their stated objectives? A treaty may result in unintended consequences. International humanitarian law is usually assumed to have developed as a restraint on violence, but critics have argued that the laws of war have merely legitimated the violence and hence promoted it; according to Chris af Jocknick and Roger Normand, the Hague laws banned only those means and methods of combat that had no military utility while permitting new and destructive technologies, like aerial warfare, to develop unhindered.[87]

This is far from suggesting that multilateral treaties are meaningless or that state representatives are intrinsically cynical. Treaty regimes have not been totally useless, but neither have they achieved the idealistic ambitions of some of their keenest supporters, particularly NGOs. They are perhaps best thought of as management devices—means by which national decisionmakers have chosen to keep under tabs, but not necessarily solve, a broad range of issues of mutual concern. As such they can be viewed as a part of the process of increasing interconnectedness and policy coordination at a global level—that is, globalization. Multilateral treaties have become a common medium through which states coordinate policies in a wide range of issue areas.

■ Notes

1. Stephen Krasner, ed., *International Regimes* (Ithaca, NY: Cornell University Press, 1983). The chapters in this book appeared earlier as the articles in a special edition of the journal *International Organization* (Spring 1982).

2. For discussion of the conceptual issues involved in selecting a definition of a regime, see Andreas Hasenclever, Peter Mayer, and Volker Rittberger, *Theories of International Regimes* (Cambridge: Cambridge University Press, 1997), pp. 8–22.

3. Oran Reed Young, *International Cooperation: Building Regimes for Natural Resources and the Environment* (Ithaca, NY: Cornell University Press, 1989), p. 24. But compare the reference to "environmental agreements," hereafter referred

to as regimes, in Jórgen Wettestad, *Designing Effective Environmental Regimes: The Key Conditions* (Cheltenham, UK: Edward Elgar, 1999), p. 1.

4. See Anne-Marie Slaughter, Andrew S. Tulumello, and Stepan Wood, "International Law and International Relations Theory: A New Generation of Interdisciplinary Scholarship." *American Journal of International Law* 92 (1993): 367–397; and Michael Byers, *Custom, Power, and the Power of Rules: International Relations and Customary International Law* (Cambridge: Cambridge University Press, 1999).

5. International relations literature on regime theory other than that cited in the previous references includes Bas Arts, "Regimes, Non-State Actors, and the State System: A 'Structurational' Regime Model," *European Journal of International Relations* 6, no. 4 (2000): 513–542; Stephen Haggard and Beth Simmons, "Theories of International Regimes," *International Organization* 41, no. 3 (1987): 491–517; Andreas Hasenclever, Peter Mayer, and Volker Rittberger, "Integrating Theories of International Regimes," *Review of International Studies* 26, no. 1 (2000): 3–33; Marc Levy, Oran Young, and Michael Zürn, "The Study of International Regimes," *European Journal of International Relations* 1, no. 3 (1995): 267–330; and Marc W. Zacher and Brent A. Sutton, *Governing Global Networks: International Regimes for Transportation and Communication* (Cambridge: Cambridge University Press, 1995).

6. Janice Gross Stein, ed., *Getting to the Table: The Processes of International Prenegotiation* (Baltimore: Johns Hopkins University Press, 1989).

7. Ibid.

8. "Statement by Mr. Casey (Australia)," opening plenary session, in *The Conference on Antarctica, Conference Documents: The Antarctic Treaty and Related Papers* (Washington, DC: Department of State, 1960), p. 26. J. D. Myhre commented that "[o]f all the matters of substance in the 1959 Treaty, perhaps only demilitarization of Antarctica (Article I) has its origin later than 1949." J. D. Myhre, *The Antarctic Treaty System: Politics, Law, and Diplomacy* (Boulder, CO: Westview, 1986), p. 30.

9. The term was coined by Robert Keohane. David A. Lake, "Leadership, Hegemony, and the International Economy: Naked Emperor or Tattered Monarch with Potential?" *International Studies Quarterly* 37 (1993): 459–489.

10. Robert O. Keohane, "The Demand for International Regimes," in Krasner, *International Regimes.*

11. D. Humphreys, "Regime Theory and Non-governmental Organisations: The case of Forest Conservation," *Journal of Commonwealth and Comparative Politics* 34, no. 1 (1996): 90–115, esp. 91, citing Karen Litfin, "Eco-regimes: Playing Tug of War with the Nation-State," in Ronnie D. Lipschutz and Ken Conca, eds., *The State and Social Power in Global Environmental Politics* (New York: Columbia University Press, 1993).

12. Charles Kindleberger, "Dominance and Leadership in the International Economy," *International Studies Quarterly* 25 (1981): 242–254.

13. Richard Elliot Benedick, "Perspectives of a Negotiation Practitioner," in Gunnar Sjöstedt, ed., *International Environmental Negotiation* (Newbury Park, CA: Sage, 1993), p. 234.

14. For a useful review of the hegemonic stability literature, see Michael Webb and Stephen Krasner, "Hegemonic Stability Theory: An Empirical Assessment," *Review of International Studies* 15, no. 2 (1989): 183–198.

15. Michael P. Scharf, "Results of the Rome Conference for an International Criminal Court," *ASIL Insight,* August 1998, http://www.asil.org/.

16. Contrast the view, expressed in relation to Antarctica, that the theory of hegemonic stability "does not seem to be of great use in analysing this case study." Cornelis van der Lugt, "An International Environmental Regime for the Antarctic: Critical Investigations," *Polar Record* 33, no. 186 (1997): 223–238, esp. 227.

17. Webb and Krasner, "Hegemonic Stability Theory."

18. Andrew F. Cooper, Richard A. Higgott, and Kim Richard Nossal, *Relocating Middle Powers: Australia and Canada in a Changing World Order* (Vancouver: UBC Press, 1993), pp. 24–25.

19. Annette Baker Fox, "The Range of Choice for Middle Powers: Australia and Canada Compared," *Australian Journal of Politics and History* 26 (1980): 193–203, esp. 193.

20. Daniel S. Papp, *Contemporary International Relations: Frameworks for Understanding,* 6th ed. (New York: Longman, 2002), p. 196.

21. Adil Najam, "The South in International Environmental Negotiations," *International Studies* 31, no. 4 (1994): 427–464.

22. Edith Brown Weiss, "Introductory Note," 31 *International Legal Materials (ILM)* 814 (1992), p. 817.

23. UN Conference Report A/CONF.151/26/Rev.1 (Vol. III), p. 233, quoted in Karin Mickelson, "Seeing the Forest, the Trees, and the People: Coming to Terms with Developing Country Perspectives on the Proposed Global Forests Convention," in Canadian Council of International Law, *Global Forests and International Environmental Law* (London: Kluwer), p. 240.

24. United Nations Convention on the Law of the Sea, article 194(1), 21 *ILM* 1261 (1982); and Shirley V. Scott, ed., *International Law and Politics: Key Documents* (Boulder, CO: Lynne Rienner, 2006), pp. 718–805.

25. Ibid., article 207(4), 21 *ILM* 1261 (1982).

26. Ibid., article 202, 21 *ILM* 1261 (1982).

27. Ibid., article 203, 21 *ILM* 1261 (1982).

28. Richard Elliot Benedick, "Perspectives of a Negotiation Practitioner," in Sjöstedt, *International Environmental Negotiation,* p. 236.

29. S. E. Rolland, "Developing Country Coalitions at the WTO: In Search of Legal Support," *Harvard International Law Journal* 48 (2007): 483–551. See also Fatoumata Jawara and Aileen Kwa, *Behind the Scenes at the WTO: The Real World of Trade Negotiations—The Lessons of Cancun* (London: Zed, 2004).

30. Peter M. Haas, "Introduction: Epistemic Communities and International Policy Coordination," *International Organization* 46, no. 1 (Winter 1992): 3.

31. See, inter alia, Humphreys, "Regime Theory and Non-governmental Organisations"; Richard Price, "Reversing the Gun Sights: Transnational Civil Society Targets Land Mines," *International Organization* 52 (1998): 613–644; Susan Carr and Roger Mpande, "Does the Definition of the Issue Matter? NGO Influence and the International Convention to Combat Desertification in Africa," *Journal of Commonwealth and Comparative Politics* 34, no. 1 (1996): 143–166.

32. John P. Humphrey, "The UN Charter and the Universal Declaration of Human Rights," in Evan Luard, ed., *The International Protection of Human Rights* (New York: Praeger, 1967), pp. 39–58, esp. 39–40.

33. Ruth Wedgwood, "Legal Personality and the Role of Non-Governmental Organizations and Non-State Political Entities in the United Nations System," in Rainer Hofmann, ed., *Non-State Actors as New Subjects of International Law: International Law—From the Traditional State Order Towards the Law of the Global Community.* Proceedings of an International Symposium of the Kiel Walther-Schücking Institute

of International Law, March 25 to 28, 1998 (Berlin: Ducker and Humblot, 1999), pp. 21–36, esp. 25.

34. Chiara Giorgetti, "The Role of Nongovernmental Organizations in the Climate Change Negotiations," *Colorado Journal of International Environmental Law and Policy* 9 (1998): 115–137, esp. 127.

35. Fanny Benedetti and John L. Washburn, "Drafting the International Criminal Court Treaty: Two Years to Rome and an Afterword on the Rome Diplomatic Conference," *Global Governance* 5 (1999): 1–37, esp. 21.

36. Humphreys, "Regime Theory and Non-governmental Organisations."

37. Benedetti and Washburn, "Drafting the International Criminal Court Treaty," p. 21.

38. Giorgetti, "The Role of Nongovernmental Organizations in the Climate Change Negotiations," pp. 131–132.

39. Vienna Convention on the Law of Treaties, article 52, 1155 United Nations Treaty Series (UNTS) 336.

40. Ibid., article 51, 1155 UNTS 336.

41. 15 UNTS 295.

42. Anthony Aust, *Modern Treaty Law and Practice* (Cambridge: Cambridge University Press, 2000), p. 23.

43. The information in this paragraph draws on Robbie Sabel, *Procedure at International Conferences: A Study of the Rules of Procedure of Conferences and Assemblies of International Inter-governmental Organisations,* 2nd ed. (Cambridge: Cambridge University Press, 2006), pp. 58–61.

44. UN Document A/CONF.183/2/Add.1 (1998). Cited in Philippe Kirsch and John T. Holmes, "The Rome Conference on an International Criminal Court: The Negotiating Process," *American Journal of International Law* 93 (1999): 2–12, esp. 3.

45. Sabel, *Procedure at International Conferences,* p. 25.

46. Ibid., p. 4.

47. Rebecca J. Cook, "Reservations to the Convention on the Elimination of All Forms of Discrimination Against Women," *Virginia Journal of International Law* 30, no. 3 (1990): 643–713, esp. 673. See also C. Chinkin and J. P. Gardner, *Human Rights as General Norms and a State's Right to Opt Out: Reservations and Objections to Human Rights Conventions* (London: BIICL, 1997); and C. Redgwell, "Universality or Integrity? Some Reflections on Reservations to General Multilateral Treaties," *British Yearbook of International Law* 64 (1993): 245–282.

48. Article 28(2). This is in accordance with article 19 of the Vienna Convention on the Law of Treaties.

49. See Chinkin and Gardner, *Human Rights as General Norms and a State's Right to Opt Out;* M. Coccia, "Reservations to Multilateral Treaties on Human Rights," *California Western International Law Journal* 15, no. 1 (Winter 1985): 1–15; J. K. Gamble Jr., "Reservations to Multilateral Treaties: A Macroscopic View of State Practice," *American Journal of International Law* 74, no. 2 (1980): 372–394; Ryan Goodman, "Human Rights Treaties, Invalid Reservations, and State Consent," *American Journal of International Law* 96, no. 3 (July 2002): 531–560; Daniel N. Hytton, "Default Breakdown: The Vienna Convention on the Law of Treaties: Inadequate Framework on Reservations," *Vanderbilt Journal of Transnational Law* 27, no. 2 (May 1994): 419–451; P. H. Imbert, "Reservations and Human Rights Conventions," *Human Rights Review* 6, no. 1 (Spring 1981): 28–60; Catherine J. Redgwell, "Reservations to Treaties and Human Rights Committee General Comment No. 24 (52)," *International and Comparative Law Quarterly* 46, no. 2 (April 1997): 390–412; William A. Schiabas, "Reservations to Human Rights Treaties:

Time for Innovation and Reform," *Canadian Yearbook of International Law* 32 (1994): 39–81; and E. F. Shenman, "The US Death Penalty Reservation to the International Covenant on Civil and Political Rights: Exposing the Limitations of the Flexible System Governing Treaty Formation," *Texas International Law Journal* 29 (1994): 69–93.

50. See Division for the Advancement of Women, Convention on the Elimination of All Forms of Discrimination Against Women, "Reservations to CEDAW," http://www.un.org.

51. Vienna Convention on the Law of Treaties, article 9(2).

52. T. T. B. Koh, "Negotiating a New World Order for the Sea," in Alan K. Henrikson, ed., *Negotiating World Order: The Artisanship and Architecture of Global Diplomacy* (Wilmington, DE: Scholarly Resources, 1986), p. 41.

53. See Barry Buzan, "Negotiating by Consensus: Developments in Technique at the United Nations Conference on the Law of the Sea, *American Journal of International Law* 75, no. 2 (1981): 324–348; and Tommy T. B. Koh and Shanmugam Jayakumar, "The Negotiating Process of the Third United Nations Conference on the Law of the Sea," in Myron H. Nordquist, ed., *United Nations Convention on the Law of the Sea 1982: A Commentary,* vol. 1 (Dordrecht, the Netherlands: Martinus Nijhoff, 1985).

54. Eilene Galloway, "Consensus Decisionmaking by the United Nations Committee on the Peaceful Uses of Outer Space," *Journal of Space Law* 7, no. 3 (1979): 3–13.

55. Vienna Convention on the Law of Treaties, article 18(b).

56. Ursula Knapp, "Article 102," in Bruno Simma, ed., *The Charter of the United Nations: A Commentary* (Oxford: Oxford University Press, 1994), p. 1104.

57. Available at http://treaties.un.org.

58. T. Graham Jr. and D. B. Shaw, "Nearing a Fork in the Road: Proliferation or Nuclear Reversal?" *Nonproliferation Review* 6, no. 1 (1998), available online at http://cns.miis.edu.

59. See, inter alia, Helmut Breitmeier, Oran Young, and Michael Zürn, *Analyzing International Environmental Regimes: From Case Study to Database* (Cambridge, MA: MIT, 2006); Andreas Hasenclever, Peter Mayer, and Volker Rittberger, *Theories of International Regimes* (Cambridge: Cambridge University Press, 1997); Carsten Helm and Detlef Sprinz, "Measuring the Effectiveness of International Environmental Regimes," *Journal of Conflict Resolution* 44, no. 5 (2000): 630–652; Jeffrey Kucik and Eric Reinhardt, "Does Flexibility Promote Cooperation? An Application to the Global Trade Regime," *International Organization* 62, no. 3 (2008): 477–505; Edward L. Miles et al., eds., *Environmental Regime Effectiveness* (Cambridge, MA: MIT, 2002); Ronald B. Mitchell, "Problem Structure, Institutional Design, and the Relative Effectiveness of International Environmental Agreements," *Global Environmental Politics* 6, no. 3 (2006): 72–89; and Hugh Ward, "International Linkages and Environmental Sustainability: The Effectiveness of the Regime Network," *Journal of Peace Research* 43, no. 2 (2006): 149–166.

60. Cited in James Kitfield, "Is Arms Control Dead?" *National Journal,* July 14, 2001, p. 2224. Compare comments on compliance with the Biological Weapons Convention in an Interview with John R. Bolton, Under Secretary of State for Arms Control and International Security, Center for Nonproliferation Studies, Monterey Institute of International Studies, http://cns.miis.edu.

61. Steve Charnovitz, "The International Labour Organization in Its Second Century," *Max Planck Yearbook of United Nations Law* 4 (2000): 147–184, esp. 174.

62. Gudmundur Alfredsson, "Concluding Remarks: More Law and Less Politics," in Gudmundur Alfredsson, Jonas Grimheden, Bertram G. Ramcharan, and Alfred de Zayas, eds., *International Human Rights Monitoring Mechanisms: Essays in Honour of Jakob Th. Möller* (The Hague: Martinus Nijhoff, 2001), p. 918.

63. See, for example, Peter Malanczuk, "The International Criminal Court and Landmines: What Are the Consequences of Leaving the US Behind?" *European Journal of International Law* 11 (2000): 77–90.

64. David Scheffer, "US Policy and the Proposed Permanent International Criminal Court," address before the Carter Center, Atlanta, Georgia, November 13, 1997, available at www. state.gov.

65. Wedgwood, "Legal Personality and the Role of Non-Governmental Organizations and Non-State Political Entities in the United Nations System," pp. 25–26.

66. Abram Chayes and Antonia Handler Chayes, *The New Sovereignty: Compliance with International Regulatory Agreements* (Cambridge, MA: Harvard University Press, 1995).

67. Ibid., p. 4.

68. Ibid., pp. 4–7.

69. Vienna Convention on Consular Relations, 596 UNTS 261.

70. Department of State Publication 10518, *Consular Notification and Access: Instructions for Federal, State, and Local Law Enforcement and Other Officials Regarding Foreign Nationals in the United States and the Rights of Consular Officials to Assist Them,* January 1998, archived at http://www.state.gov.

71. These categories are taken from Francis G. Jacobs and Shelley Roberts, eds., *The Effect of Treaties in Domestic Law* (London: Sweet and Maxwell, 1987), pp. xxivff.

72. Ibid., p. 141.

73. See, inter alia, Eyal Benvenisti, "Judicial Misgivings Regarding the Application of International Law: An Analysis of Attitudes of National Courts," *European Journal of International Law* 4 (1993): 159–183; and Karen Knop, "Here and There: International Law in Domestic Courts," *International Law and Politics* 32 (2000): 501–535. For identification and exploration of the rationales offered by national court judges in support of references to international human rights law, see Reem Bahdi, "Globalization or Judgment: Transjudicialism and the Five Faces of International Law in Domestic Courts," *George Washington International Law Review* 34, no. 3 (2002): 555–603.

74. Thomas M. Franck and Gregory H. Fox, eds., *International Law Decisions in National Courts* (New York: Transnational, 1996), p. 5.

75. 13 *ILM* 41 (1974).

76. 37 *ILM* 249 (1998).

77. George W. Downs, David M. Rocke, and Peter N. Barsoom, "Is the Good News About Compliance Good News About Cooperation?" *International Organization* 50, no. 3 (1996): 379–406.

78. Ronald B. Mitchell, "Sources of Transparency: Information Systems in International Regimes," *International Studies Quarterly* 42 (1998): 109–130, esp. 109.

79. Ibid., pp. 116–117.

80. The Antarctic Treaty, article VII (5).

81. A point made by V. Leary, *International Labour Conventions and National Law* (The Hague: Martinus Nijhoff, 1982), p. 17. See also Robert Blackburn and Jørg Polakiewicz, eds., *Fundamental Rights in Europe: The European Convention*

on Human Rights and Its Member States, 1950–2000 (Oxford: Oxford University Press, 2001), p. 11.

82. James Crawford, "The UN Human Rights Treaty System: A System in Crisis?" in Philip Alston and James Crawford, eds., *The Future of UN Human Rights Treaty Monitoring* (Cambridge: Cambridge University Press, 2000).

83. See Philip Alston and James Crawford, eds., *The Future of UN Human Rights Treaty Monitoring* (Cambridge: Cambridge University Press, 2000); and Anne F. Bayefsky, ed., *The UN Human Rights Treaty System in the 21st Century* (The Hague: Kluwer Law International, 2000).

84. See Harald Müller, "The Evolution of Verification: Lessons from the Past for the Present," *Arms Control* 14 (1993): 333–356.

85. Vienna Convention on the Law of Treaties, article 31(1).

86. Ibid., article 33(1).

87. Chris af Jochnick and Roger Normand, "The Legitimation of Violence: A Critical History of the Laws of War," *Harvard International Law Journal* 35 (1994): 49–95.

10

International Law and Arms Control

DISARMAMENT IS THE REDUCTION, OR ELIMINATION THROUGH negotiation of an international agreement, of the means of waging war.[1] The Hague Conferences of 1899 and 1907 had the declared aim of ensuring universal peace and bringing about a reduction of "excessive" armaments,[2] although the disarmament goals of those conferences were not achieved. The Covenant of the League of Nations also "recognise[d] that the maintenance of peace requires the reduction of national armaments to the lowest point consistent with national safety and the enforcement by common action of international obligations." Disarmament efforts under the auspices of the League culminated in the 1932 Disarmament Conference, convened in Geneva and attended by representatives of sixty states. Although it appeared to be moving toward agreement on certain topics, the conference was suspended in 1936 without having formalized a convention text.[3] Once Adolph Hitler was known to be rearming Germany in defiance of the Versailles Treaty, disarmament was effectively off the international agenda.

In comparison with the Covenant of the League of Nations, the UN Charter did not make much reference to disarmament. Whereas many after World War I believed that the war had been caused by the prewar arms race, the dominant belief in relation to World War II was that it could have been avoided if the great powers had maintained and been prepared to use adequate military force.[4] The "regulation of armaments" is nevertheless one of the subjects on which the General Assembly may make recommendations to members or to the Security Council.[5] The Security Council, assisted by the Military Staff Committee, was to formulate plans "to be submitted to the Members of the United Nations for the establishment of a system for the regulation of armaments."[6]

During the Cold War, the phrase *arms control* came into use to refer to rules for limiting competition in armaments between the two superpowers, the United States and Soviet Union; the term is now used more broadly to refer to means of trying to constrain reciprocal threats by regulating the acquisition, testing, numbers, ratios, types, location, deployment, spread, or use of current or prospective armaments; this may, but need not necessarily, include disarmament—the actual reduction or elimination of armaments.[7] Each of the weapons of mass destruction—nuclear, biological, and chemical—has its own global treaty, and in this chapter we will look at each in turn. Arms control treaties play an important role in the international management of security threats, despite the more diffuse nature of post–Cold War security threats and the increased significance of nonstate actors not parties to treaties. Figure 10.1 lists examples of global treaties on arms control.

■ Treaty on the Non-Proliferation of Nuclear Weapons, 1968

The Non-Proliferation Treaty (NPT)[8] is the centerpiece of multilateral efforts at arms control. Richard Butler has described it as "supplemental to" and "comparable in stature to" the UN Charter.[9] In 1963 John F. Kennedy commented in a well-known statement,

> personally I am haunted by the feeling that by 1970, unless we are successful, there may be ten nuclear powers instead of four, and by 1975, fifteen or twenty. . . . I see the possibility in the 1970s of the President of the

Figure 10.1 Some Global Treaties on Arms Control

1963	Treaty Banning Nuclear-Weapon Tests in the Atmosphere, in Outer Space, and Under Water (PTBT)
1968	Treaty on the Non-Proliferation of Nuclear Weapons (NPT)
1971	Treaty on the Prohibition of the Emplacement of Nuclear Weapons and Other Weapons of Mass Destruction on the Sea Bed and Ocean Floor and in the Subsoil Thereof (Seabed Treaty)
1972	The Convention on the Prohibition of the Development, Production, and Stockpiling of Bacteriological (Biological) and Toxin Weapons and on Their Destruction (BWC)
1977	Treaty on Principles Governing the Activities of States in the Exploration and Use of Outer Space, Including the Moon and Other Celestial Bodies (Outer Space Treaty)
1977	Agreement Governing the Activities of States on the Moon and Other Celestial Bodies (Moon Agreement)
1993	Convention on the Prohibition of the Development, Production, Stockpiling, and Use of Chemical Weapons and on Their Destruction (CWC)
1996	Comprehensive Nuclear Test-Ban Treaty (CTBT)

United States having to face a world in which fifteen or twenty or twenty-five nations may have these weapons. I regard that as the greatest possible danger and hazard.[10]

The NPT was concluded in June 1968 and entered into force on March 5, 1970.[11] The crux of the nonproliferation obligations are found in articles I and II. By article I, nuclear weapons states undertook "not to transfer to any recipient whatsoever nuclear weapons or other nuclear explosive devices or control over such weapons or explosive devices directly, or indirectly; and not in any way to assist, encourage, or induce any non-nuclear-weapon State to manufacture or otherwise acquire nuclear weapons or other nuclear explosive devices, or control over such weapons or explosive devices." Conversely, by article II, non-nuclear-weapon states undertook "not to receive the transfer from any transferor whatsoever of nuclear weapons or other nuclear explosive devices or of control over such weapons or explosive devices directly, or indirectly; not to manufacture or otherwise acquire nuclear weapons or other nuclear explosive devices; and not to seek or receive any assistance in the manufacture of nuclear weapons or other nuclear explosive devices." A "nuclear-weapon state" was defined in article IX(3) as "one which has manufactured and exploded a nuclear weapon or other nuclear explosive device prior to 1 January 1967." Five states met this definition: the United States, the Soviet Union, the United Kingdom, France, and China. France and China did not sign.

The NPT provisions were obviously inequitable. Not only did the then non-nuclear-weapon states (NNWS) pledge never to become nuclear powers but, by article III(1), each NNWS party undertook to accept IAEA safeguards to verify its compliance with the treaty. The treaty did, though, recognize the right of each party to develop nuclear energy for peaceful purposes; indeed, by article V, parties undertake to ensure that the potential benefits from peaceful applications of nuclear explosions are made available to non-nuclear weapon states at a low charge and on a nondiscriminatory basis.

The inequity was mediated a bit further by article VI, by which nuclear-weapon states were to "undertake . . . to pursue negotiations in good faith on effective measures relating to cessation of the nuclear arms race at an early date and to nuclear disarmament, and on a treaty on general and complete disarmament under strict and effective international control." Article VI was something of a quid pro quo for NNWS. The alleged failure of the nuclear-weapon states to comply with their obligations in article VI has been a source of ongoing dissatisfaction within the regime.

The trade-off between nuclear-weapon states and non-nuclear-weapon states went a little further. The NPT was accompanied by UN Security

Council Resolution 255 of June 19, 1968, which welcomed "the intention expressed by certain States that they will provide or support immediate assistance, in accordance with the Charter, to any non-nuclear-weapon State Party to the Treaty on the Non-Proliferation of Nuclear Weapons that is a victim of an act or an object of a threat of aggression in which nuclear weapons are used." China and France, which were not at that time parties to the NPT, are not bound by this resolution. Declarations that nuclear-weapon states will come to the assistance of a NNWS threatened with nuclear weapons are known as "positive security assurances." In the years since the conclusion of the NPT, all five nuclear-weapon-states parties to the treaty have issued "negative assurances": guarantees that they will refrain from using nuclear weapons against non-nuclear-weapon states that are parties to the NPT. Security Council Resolution 984 (1995) reinforced the 1968 commitment and took note of the unilateral assurances given by nuclear-weapon states against the use of nuclear weapons.[12]

The post–Cold War years have been ones of particular challenge for the NPT regime. It has come under external challenge from "second generation" or "opaque" states—such as Israel, India, Pakistan, North Korea, Argentina, Brazil, and South Africa—that developed nuclear weapons subsequent to the conclusion, and in defiance of, the NPT. Incorporating a date into the definition of a nuclear weapon state in the NPT meant that if and when other states openly conducted tests—as did India and Pakistan in 1998—they were still not eligible to join the treaty regime as nuclear-weapon states. Until the tests by India and Pakistan, not one new state had declared itself to be a nuclear state.[13] Indeed, the 2000 Review Conference called on India and Pakistan to join the regime as non-nuclear-weapon states. Following the 1998 tests the Indian prime minister declared that India was "now a nuclear weapon State. This is a reality that cannot be denied. It is not a conferment that we seek; nor is it a status for others to grant. It is an endowment to the nation by our scientists and engineers."[14] On October 10, 2008, the United States and India signed the Agreement for Cooperation Between the Government of the United States of America and the Government of India Concerning Peaceful Uses of Nuclear Energy. India undertook to separate its civil and military nuclear facilities and to place all its civil nuclear facilities under International Atomic Energy Agency safeguards and would be able to engage in nuclear trade with the United States without India becoming party to the NPT.[15]

Iraq signed the NPT in 1968 and ratified it the following year. As part of the 1991 cease-fire agreement between Iraq and the United Nations, UN Security Council Resolution 687 of April 3, 1991, required Iraq to "unconditionally accept the destruction, removal, or rendering harmless, under international supervision" of all nuclear, chemical, and biological weapons-related assets. It authorized the IAEA and created the United Nations Special

Commission (UNSCOM) to conduct on-site inspections at facilities suspected of being part of an Iraqi nuclear weapons program. The IAEA had regularly inspected Iraq's declared nuclear facilities but had never found diversions of nuclear material from declared sites to illegal nuclear activities.[16] The IAEA discovered a large and advanced Iraqi secret complex for producing nuclear material necessary for manufacturing a nuclear weapon, thereby calling into question the adequacy of its own system of safeguards,[17] and leading to the development by the IAEA of a strengthened safeguards system that was better equipped to detect undeclared nuclear materials. After years of strained relations between UNSCOM and the Iraqi regime, the UN arms inspectors were in December 1998 denied access to Iraq. The work of UNSCOM was officially terminated by Resolution 1284 (1999),[18] and UNSCOM was replaced by the United Nations Monitoring, Verification, and Inspection Commission (UNMOVIC).

UNMOVIC began inspections in late 2002. Security Council Resolution 1441, adopted November 8, 2002,[19] stated that Iraq was in material breach of its disarmament obligations under Resolution 687; it directed UNMOVIC and the IAEA to report immediately any interference by Iraq with their inspection duties. Maintaining that Iraqi cooperation with the inspections was inadequate, the United States and United Kingdom in mid-February 2003 embarked on a diplomatic campaign to gain Security Council authorization for the use of force against Iraq. When it became clear that there was little support for such a resolution, the United States offered Iraq's president, Saddam Hussein, an ultimatum: if he and his sons did not leave Iraq within forty-eight hours there would be military conflict.[20] Saddam rejected the ultimatum, and on March 19 President George W. Bush announced that war had begun. A subsequent search of Iraq failed to locate any weapons of mass destruction.

In 1993 the Democratic People's Republic of Korea (DPRK, i.e., North Korea) announced its intention to exercise its legal right to withdraw from the NPT and refused to allow international inspections of its nuclear facilities despite mounting evidence of attempts to develop nuclear weapons. In 1994 North Korea signed the so-called Agreed Framework with the US, by which the DPRK was to freeze its nuclear program and remain a party to the NPT.[21] In exchange, the United States, the Democratic Republic of Korea (ROK; South Korea), and Japan founded the Korean Peninsula Energy Development Organization (KEDO) in March 1995 to build two light-water reactors for North Korea as well as to finance and supply North Korea with shipments of heavy fuel oil as an interim energy source. In October 2002 North Korea admitted that it had continued a uranium-enrichment program after the 1994 Agreed Framework went into effect. KEDO took steps to put pressure on North Korea to eliminate its program, including the suspension of oil deliveries.[22] North Korea responded by ousting international inspectors and moving to restart a plutonium facility that had been closed under the 1994 agreement and then, on January 10, 2003, announced that it would withdraw from the NPT.[23]

A Review and Extension Conference for the NPT took place in New York from April 17 to May 12, 1995. Article X of the NPT had provided that a conference would be convened twenty-five years after entry into force of the treaty "to decide whether the Treaty shall continue in force indefinitely, or shall be extended for an additional fixed period or periods." This decision was to be taken by a majority of the parties to the treaty. NNWS were reluctant to agree to the indefinite extension of the treaty, fearing that they would then lose their leverage over the nuclear-weapons states. Opposition to indefinite extension on the part of non-nuclear states stemmed from objections regarding the discriminatory nature of the NPT. Indonesia claimed, for example, that

> an indefinite extension would mean the permanent legitimisation of nuclear weapons and the five privileged powers would be permitted to keep their nuclear arsenals while others are barred forever from acquiring them. It will thus lead to a permanent division of the world into nuclear-haves and have-nots, ratify inequality in international relations and relegate the vast majority of non-nuclear nations into a second class status.[24]

In contrast, some observers have not regarded the obvious inequity in the treaty as a problem. "Sincere indignation over the double standard implies a utopian assumption that greater equality of States breeds peace; historical support for this view is, at best, ambiguous."[25] The NPT was extended indefinitely on May 12, 1995, as the third in a package of three decisions. Decision One related to strengthening the review process for the treaty. As from 1997, for example, ten-day PrepCom meetings were to be held in each of the four years preceding quinquennial review conferences. Decision Two involved agreement on a statement of "principles and objectives for nuclear non-proliferation." This called, inter alia, for a reaffirmed commitment by the nuclear-weapon states to article VI, involving a program of action that included the completion of a Comprehensive Test Ban Treaty no later than 1996, the immediate commencement and early conclusion of negotiations on a convention banning production of fissionable material for nuclear weapons, and the "determined pursuit" by the nuclear-weapons states of "systematic and progressive efforts to reduce nuclear weapons globally, with the ultimate goal of eliminating those weapons."

China supported the 1995 decision to extend indefinitely the NPT. China had originally opposed the treaty as discriminatory. During the 1960s and 1970s China publicly endorsed the spread of nuclear weapons as a way of countering the nuclear superpower duopoly, although it appears to have stood by its declarations that it would not help other states in their efforts to develop nuclear weapons.[26] In the 1980s China gradually moved toward embracing the regime, and it acceded to the NPT on March 9, 1992. Since then China has declared its commitment to nonproliferation although during this period China has been a significant nuclear proliferator. Of greatest concern to arms controllers has been the nation's unsafeguarded transfers and exports of highly enriched uranium, heavy water, nuclear reactors, nuclear weapon designs, and ballistic missiles to Pakistan, North Korea, and Iran.[27]

In an attempt to inject fresh ideas into multilateral efforts at disarmament, an eight-nation New Agenda Coalition was formed in June 1998, following the indefinite extension of the NPT and coming a month after the South Asian tests. This coalition, composed of Brazil, Egypt, Ireland, Mexico, New Zealand, Slovenia (which has since left the coalition), South Africa, and Sweden, built to some extent on the efforts of the Canberra Commission—a group of eminent scientists, disarmament experts, military strategists, and statesmen formed by the Australian government in October 1995 to develop "concrete and realistic steps for achieving a nuclear weapons-free world." That commission's 1996 report had reiterated the theme that nuclear nonproliferation and nuclear disarmament cannot be pursued separately.[28] The New Agenda Coalition was influential in achieving the Thirteen Steps paragraph in the Final Document of the 2000 Review Conference, agreed by consensus, which provides a set of "practical steps for the systematic and progressive efforts to implement Article VI of the Treaty." The coalition has in the years since 2000 continued its efforts to have nuclear disarmament accepted as a realistic policy option. Those favoring full nuclear disarmament were in 2009 heartened by a statement by US President Barack Obama that the United States would pursue the eventual elimination of nuclear weapons.[29]

Iran signed the NPT in 1968, ratified it two years later, and signed a safeguards agreement with the IAEA in 1974. In June 2003 the director-general of the IAEA reported that Iran had failed to meet its obligations under its Safeguards Agreement with respect to the reporting of nuclear material, the subsequent processing and use of that material, and the declaration of facilities where the material was stored and processed. The West has been concerned that Iran is developing a nuclear weapon capability and has engaged in extensive diplomacy in an endeavor to curb Iran's ambitions even though Iran's civilian nuclear power program is not in breach of the treaty. Iran refused to halt enrichment despite the Security Council's demand in Resolution 2696 (2006) that it do so, along with several sets of political inducements and UN sanctions.[30]

In September 2005, North Korea agreed to a framework agreement by which it would end its nuclear program in exchange for aid and security guarantees. It then refused to participate in further multilateral talks and did not carry out the agreement.[31] In July 2006, North Korea tested several long-range ballistic missiles, and in early October it declared that it had conducted a nuclear test.[32] The UN Security Council responded with Resolution 1718, which demanded that North Korea not conduct any further nuclear test or launch a ballistic missile and imposed economic sanctions on North Korea. After intensive "Six Power" talks, North Korea agreed in February 2007 to shut down and seal its reactor at Yongbyon, provide a complete and correct declaration of all its nuclear programs, and allow IAEA inspections to resume, in return for fuel and other assistance.[33]

Problems arose during the implementation of the agreement, including intelligence reports that North Korea was assisting Syria to construct an undeclared nuclear reactor.[34] Negotiations with US officials on a regime to verify North Korea's commitment to end its nuclear program failed in December 2008; it launched a multistage Taepodong-2 missile in April 2009 and conducted an underground nuclear test the following month. Security Council resolution 1874 (2009) strengthened the sanctions regime.

It was disappointing that the 2005 Review Conference was the "biggest failure in the history of this Treaty,"[35] particularly given that the regime was under challenge from North Korea and Iran, and to a lesser extent Syria. In September 2007, Israel conducted an airstrike on a Syrian site believed to be a partly constructed nuclear reactor. It was with some relief that states parties were able to agree to a consensus final document at the 2010 Review Conference. The conference noted inter alia the Secretary-General's five-point proposal for nuclear disarmament, including consideration of negotiations for a nuclear weapons convention. Momentum is building within civil society for a treaty to eliminate the use, production, trade, and stockpiling of nuclear weapons.

■ Convention on the Prohibition of the Development, Production, and Stockpiling of Bacteriological (Biological) and Toxin Weapons and on Their Destruction, 1972

Biological warfare is

> the intentional use of disease-causing microorganisms or other entities that can replicate themselves (e.g., viruses, infectious nucleic acids and prions) against humans, animals or plants for hostile purposes. It may also involve the use of toxins: poisonous substances produced by living organisms, including micro-organisms (e.g., botulinum toxin), plants (e.g., ricin derived from castor beans) and animals (e.g., snake venom). If they are utilized for warfare purpose, the synthetically manufactured counterparts of these toxins are biological weapons.[36]

Biological weapons can kill at an equivalent rate to nuclear weapons, although without damaging infrastructure. This is the subject of the 1972 Biological Weapons Convention.[37]

The 1925 Geneva Protocol for the Prohibition of the Use in War of Asphyxiating, Poisonous, or Other Gases, and of Bacteriological Methods of Warfare[38] prohibited the use of biological weapons but did not outlaw their development, production, or possession. The next major development in the international management of biological weapons was the Biological Weapons Convention (BWC), negotiated between 1969 and 1971, which was opened for signature in 1972 and entered into force in 1975.[39] Article I provides:

> Each State Party to this Convention undertakes never in any circumstance to develop, produce, stockpile or otherwise acquire or retain:
> (1) Microbial or other biological agents, or toxins whatever their origin or method of production, of types and in quantities that have no justification for prophylactic, protective or other peaceful purposes;
> (2) Weapons, equipment or means of delivery designed to use such agents or toxins for hostile purposes or in armed conflict.

The second paragraph of article 1 contains a major loophole: the parties to the BWC undertake never to acquire or retain biological weapons "that have no justification for prophylatic, protective or other peaceful purposes"; in practice it is virtually impossible to distinguish programs with purely defensive purposes from those designed with offensive use in mind. By article II, each state party undertakes to destroy, or to convert to peaceful purposes, any existing stockpiles of agents, toxins, weapons, equipment, and means of delivery specified in article I. The convention specified in article XII that a review conference was to be held within five years after entry into force. The first review conference took place in 1980, the next in 1986, and since then they have been held at five-year intervals.

In contrast to both the NPT that preceded it and the Chemical Weapons Convention that was to follow, the BWC contains no verification measures. Article VI provided for enforcement only insofar as any state party finding that another state party is acting in breach of the convention may lodge a complaint with the Security Council; all states parties are to cooperate with any investigation that the Security Council may initiate as a result of such a complaint. The absence of effective verification measures facilitated conclusion of the Convention, as did the unilateral renouncement of biological weapons by the United States in 1969 and its decision in 1970 to destroy its stockpiles. In 1970 the United States announced that military programs for biological agents and toxins would be limited to research and development for defensive purposes.[40]

Ongoing developments in biotechnology and genetic engineering, which, although with great potential to improve the quality of life, could also be turned into deadly weapons, generated in the post–Cold War years momentum to negotiate a protocol on verification. At the 1986 review conference, parties had decided to take a series of confidence-building measures to compensate, in part at least, for the absence of meaningful verification provisions.[41] Further impetus came from the discovery of a major clandestine Soviet biological weapons program and the information regarding the Iraqi program that emerged following the Gulf War. The 1991 third review conference created VEREX, an ad hoc group of governmental experts to identify and examine potential verification measures from a scientific and technical standpoint. Between 1995 and 2001 an ad hoc group of some fifty states worked further on the issue of verification, and, at the fourth review conference in 1996, the group received a mandate to negotiate a legally binding instrument. Formal talks on a verification protocol began in 1995.

The administration of US President Bill Clinton played a key role in the post–Cold War push for a verification mechanism within the regime,[42] but in 2001 the George W. Bush administration formally rejected the draft protocol, stating that it was "forced to conclude that the mechanisms envisioned for the protocol would not achieve their objectives, that no modification of them would allow them to achieve their objectives, and that trying to do more would simply raise the risk to legitimate United States activities." This effectively marked the withdrawal of the United States from the negotiations. The US administration had three basic objections to the protocol. First was that, as written, and if implemented, it would compromise the US biodefense preparations. Inspections would enable the development of countermeasures to frustrate the defenses that the US was preparing. Second, inspections would compromise the intellectual property assets of the US pharmaceutical and biotech industries. Third, there was the undermining of the US system of export controls and the multilateral framework of export controls known as the Australia Group to prevent the export both of dual-use items and others that could be used in an offensive biological weapons program.[43] In response to the view that a flawed protocol was better than no protocol, the United States undersecretary of state for arms control and international security, John Bolton, responded that it was "worse than nothing, that this attitude could have led to a protocol that would have simply rewarded hypocrisy by permitting countries that are willing to lie about compliance with the BWC to sign the protocol and then to lie about compliance."[44] At the fifth review conference, which met from November 19 to December 12, 2001, the United States proposed the termination of the existing diplomatic process to strengthen compliance with the treaty; the conference adjourned without even reaching agreement on a final declaration.[45] With negotiations regarding verification at an impasse, the sixth review conference in 2006 was nevertheless able to agree on a final declaration that included an article-by-article review of the treaty, a new intersessional process, and the establishment of an implementation support unit (ISU). Located within the Geneva branch of the United Nations Office for Disarmament Affairs,[46] the ISU could be interpreted as a step toward a permanent treaty organization such as the Organization for the Prohibition of Chemical Weapons.

■ **Convention on the Prohibition of the Development, Production, Stockpiling, and Use of Chemical Weapons and on Their Destruction, 1993**

Chemical weapons are the topic of the 1993 Chemical Weapons Convention (CWC).[47] Such weapons are nothing new; the Greeks used sulphur mixtures on the battlefield as long ago as 431 B.C.[48] International attempts to limit or prevent their usage date from a 1675 Franco-German agreement not to use poisoned bullets.[49] The Hague Convention of 1899 prohibited the use of projectiles "the object of which is diffusion of asphyxiating or deleterious gases." The 1925 Geneva Protocol for the Prohibition of the Use of Asphyxiating, Poisonous, or Other Gases, and Bacteriological Methods of Warfare banned the use of chemical weapons in war but not the development, production, or possession of such weapons. It had been anticipated that chemical weapons would be banned simultaneously with biological weapons, but in the lead-up to the 1972 convention several Western countries proposed proceeding with the agreement only for the less militarily useful biological weapons, arguing that they required less rigorous verification provisions.[50]

Formal negotiations for the CWC began in the Conference on Disarmament in 1984. The basis for negotiations was the so-called rolling text, an evolving draft that was updated annually with provisionally agreed elements and those on which disagreement remained. Progress toward a treaty was slow. States disagreed over whether the ban should be total as well as the nature of verification provisions. If very stringent, they appeared as intrusive on national sovereignty; if too lax, the regime would not be deemed effective. Developing countries demanded that all discriminatory export control measures for weapons-related chemicals be abolished. Negotiations gained impetus with the Gulf War and with the submission by Australia of a complete draft convention in 1992.[51] The Conference on Disarmament adopted the final text on September 3, 1992, and it was opened for signature on January 13, 1993. The CWC entered into force on April 29, 1997.

The CWC was the first multilateral treaty to provide for the elimination of an entire category of weapons of mass destruction. By article I of the CWC, each state party undertakes never to develop, produce, otherwise acquire, stockpile, or retain chemical weapons, or transfer, directly or indirectly, chemical weapons to anyone. Each state party also undertakes to destroy chemical weapons it owns or possesses and any chemical weapons production facilities it owns or possesses. By article IV(6) destruction is to begin no later than two years after entry into force of the convention and to finish no later than ten years after its entry into force.

Pursuant to article VIII of the CWC, the Organization for the Prohibition of Chemical Weapons (OPCW) was established in The Hague upon entry into force of the CWC in 1997,[52] "to achieve the object and purpose of this Convention, to ensure the implementation of its provisions, including those for international verification of compliance with it, and to provide a forum for consultation and cooperation among State Parties."[53] The OPCW comprises the conference of the states parties, the main body of the OPCW made up of all states that have ratified the convention, as well as the Executive Council, consisting of forty-one elected representatives from states that have ratified the convention, the Technical Secretariat, and the Scientific Advisory Board. According to the OPCW, there were four remaining possessor states party to the convention at the end of 2008: India, Libya, the Russian Federation, and the United States of America.[54]

The CWC is notable for its far-reaching verification provisions. A routine monitoring regime involves submission by states parties to the OPCW of initial and annual declarations, visits, and systematic inspections of declared chemical weapons storage, production, and destruction facilities. But it is the system of *challenge inspections* that is of particular note. Under this system, a state party may request an inspection to be conducted of any facility or location in the territory or under the jurisdiction of any other state party, in order to clarify and resolve questions of possible noncompliance.[55] Within twelve hours of the submission of a request to conduct a challenge inspection, the Executive Council is to decide whether the request is abusive, frivolous, or inconsistent with the convention. If the council decides that the request is valid, the OPCW conducts a challenge inspection of the facility or location in question. The inspected state party has the obligation to provide access for the inspection, although it also has the right to take measures to protect sensitive installations, and to prevent disclosure of confidential information and data unrelated to the CWC.[56]

■ Comprehensive Nuclear Test-Ban Treaty, 1996

A global halt to nuclear weapons test explosions was first proposed by Indian Prime Minister Jawaharlal Nehru in April 1954[57] after a US thermonuclear test exposed a Japanese fishing trawler and more than 200 Marshall Islanders to radioactive fallout.[58] Following the dangerous standoff during the 1962 Cuban Missile Crisis, talks began in 1963 for a comprehensive nuclear test ban. The negotiators failed to agree on the number of on-site verification inspections, and a limited test-ban treaty was concluded instead. This was the 1963 Treaty Banning Nuclear Weapon Tests in the Atmosphere, in Outer Space, and Under Water, known as the Partial Test-Ban Treaty (PTBT).[59] Under this agreement nuclear testing was allowed to continue underground. The Threshold Test-Ban Treaty of 1974 limited the yield of underground nuclear weapon tests to 150 kilotons. Although little progress was made toward a comprehensive test-ban treaty during the Cold War, this objective was far from forgotten, having been raised at every NPT review conference. Many states believed that article VI of the NPT placed the nuclear states under a legal obligation to take positive steps toward the conclusion of a comprehensive test-ban treaty. At the 1975, 1980, 1985, and 1990 review conferences NNWS made clear that they expected the disarmament obligations found in article VI to begin through a comprehensive treaty. The idea of a comprehensive test-ban treaty remained a central objective of nuclear disarmament and arms control campaigners throughout the 1960s, 1970s, and 1980s. As the finalized treaty's preamble was later to say, it was believed that "by constraining the development and qualitative improvement of nuclear weapons and ending the development of advanced new types of nuclear weapons," a comprehensive test ban constitutes "an effective measure of nuclear disarmament and non-proliferation in all its aspects."

The end of the Cold War appeared to offer new opportunities for progress toward nuclear disarmament. In 1991 parties to the PTBT held an amendment conference to discuss a proposal to convert the PTBT into an instrument banning all nuclear-weapon tests. The proposal was not accepted, but the initiative contributed to the pressure for a comprehensive test-ban treaty. Negotiations for this treaty began in the Conference on Disarmament in January 1994. As the 1995 NPT review and extension conference loomed, nuclear-weapons states came under increased pressure to show how they had complied with article VI. Lack of a comprehensive test-ban treaty had come to be seen as indicative of a lack of real effort. At the 1995 review and extension conference the NPT was indefinitely extended as part of a politically binding package of three decisions. The "Principles and Objectives of Nuclear Non-Proliferation and Disarmament" contained a paragraph calling for a comprehensive test-ban treaty no later than 1996 (to be followed by a fissile material cut-off treaty). The final draft of the Comprehensive Test-Ban Treaty (CTBT) was adopted by the General Assembly on September 10, 1996, and opened for signature on September 24, 1996.[60]

Article I of the CTBT contains the basic obligation on states "not to carry out any nuclear weapon test explosion or any other nuclear explosion, and to prohibit and prevent any such nuclear explosion at any place under its jurisdiction or control; as well as to refrain from causing, encouraging, or in any way participating in the carrying out of any nuclear weapon test explosion or any other nuclear explosion." Under article XIV the CTBT is to enter into force 180 days after the date of deposit of the instruments of ratification by all states listed in annex 2, "but in no case earlier than two years after its opening for signature." Annex 2 contains the forty-four states members of the Conference on Disarmament operating nuclear reactors.[61]

The role of the Comprehensive Nuclear Test-Ban Treaty Organization, which will come into existence following the first conference of the states parties to the CTBT, is, according to article II of the treaty, "to achieve the object and purpose of [the] Treaty, to ensure the implementation of its provisions, including those for international verification of compliance with it, and to provide a forum for consultation and cooperation among States Parties." Article IV sets out the general verification provisions. The verification regime is to include an international monitoring system, consultation and clarification, on-site inspections, and confidence-building measures. The International Monitoring System, whose purpose is to detect and identify nuclear explosions prohibited under the treaty, is to consist of 50 primary and 120 auxiliary seismological stations to detect seismic activity, as well as 80 radionuclide stations to identify radioactive particles released during a nuclear explosion and 60 infrasound and 11 hydroacoustic stations to pick up the sound of a nuclear explosion in the atmosphere or under water, respectively.[62] Provision is also made for on-site inspections if consultations have not been able to clarify an ambiguous event.

When negotiations for the CTBT began in 1994, India was an enthusiastic supporter. By the conclusion of the negotiations in 1996, India was the fiercest critic of the CTBT. Together with Iran it blocked consensus on a final CTBT text, the Indian representative telling the General Assembly that India would "never sign this unequal Treaty, not now, nor later."[63] The shift was in part because of concern with the nuclear programs of China and Pakistan, but it also had a lot to do with India's dissatisfaction with the outcome of the 1995 NPT review and extension conference. India took the position that because the NPT extension conference had not adequately addressed the disarmament issue, the CTBT represented the next, and possibly the only remaining, opportunity to extract a stronger disarmament commitment.[64] It was after India announced that it would not subscribe to the CTBT that the final draft treaty contained the 44-state requirement for entry into force. A previous draft had made entry into force contingent on ratification by the 37 states that would host facilities for the CTBT's International Monitoring System. India had withdrawn its monitoring stations from the network and so would no longer have been on the list of states whose signature was required for entry into force. India resented being placed in a situation in which it was effectively forced to either join a regime with which it had expressed its profound dissatisfaction, or shoulder responsibility for the whole treaty not entering into force.

There was some hope that India's attitude toward the CTBT would change after the completion of its 1998 tests. Moderates in the Indian government believed that signing would remove Indian isolation and that India had sufficient data to conduct the subcritical and computer simulation experiments permitted under the treaty. Critics of the CTBT within India maintained that India needed to do more tests; they objected to the US Stockpile Stewardship Program, which they believed would permit the more advanced nuclear-weapons states to introduce modifications into existing weapon designs.[65]

The UK, France, and Russia, as well as all the European and Western bloc countries, strongly support entry into force of the CTBT. Ten key states must ratify the convention before it can enter into force, one of which is the United States. The CTBT was a key foreign policy objective of the Clinton administration, and the United States was the first state to sign the CTBT. And yet on October 13, 1999, the US Senate voted to reject ratification of the CTBT, and in 2001 the United States boycotted a conference to encourage support for the CTBT. Nuclear states have nevertheless put unilateral moratoriums on nuclear tests. Russia has not conducted a nuclear test since 1991, the United States since 1992. France began a moratorium in 1992 but ended it in 1995 to begin a series of tests at Mururoa Atoll. It resumed its moratorium in early 1996. China placed a moratorium on its nuclear tests in 1996. The Obama administration has indicated its support for ratification of the CTBT.

■ **A Multilateral Arms Control Treaty on Cyberspace?**

There is growing debate regarding how to lessen the risks of cyberwar. Russia has on a number of occasions proposed an arms control treaty on cyberspace along the lines of others, such as the CWC, that would ban a country from secretly embedding malicious codes or circuitry that could be later activated in the event of war. The UK and United States have taken the view that coordinated law enforcement is the key and have promoted as a model the Council of Europe Convention on Cybercrime.[66]

■ **Regional Treaties Establishing Nuclear-Weapons-Free Zones**

The Antarctic Treaty (1959), Outer Space Treaty (1967), Moon Agreement (1979), and Seabed Treaty (1971) all denuclearized their respective locations. Several nuclear-weapons-free zones have also been established by treaty in populated areas, which prohibit in their respective delimited areas the possession of nuclear weapons, their development, production, introduction, or deployment. The first was the 1967 Treaty of Tlatelolco for Latin America and the Caribbean, followed by the 1985 Treaty of Rarotonga establishing a nuclear-weapon-free zone in the South Pacific, the 1995 Treaty of Bangkok for Southeast Asia, and the 1996 Treaty of Pelindaba for an African Nuclear-Weapon-Free Zone. All of these have now entered into force. The Semipalatinsk Treaty on a Nuclear-Weapon-Free Zone in Central Asia was opened for signature on September 8, 2006.[67]

■ US–Soviet Union Bilateral Treaties on Nuclear Arms Control

During the Cold War, the prospect of nuclear war between the superpowers threatened to destroy the world. As well as the multilateral efforts to manage weapons of mass destruction, a series of bilateral arms reduction treaties was concluded between the USSR and the United States.

In 1969 the United States and the Soviet Union initiated bilateral negotiations on restricting their strategic nuclear arsenals (weapons with an intercontinental range). The Strategic Arms Limitation Talks (SALT) resulted in the signing in 1972 of both the US-Soviet Treaty on the Limitation of Anti-Ballistic Missile Systems (the ABM Treaty) and the US-Soviet Interim Agreement. An ABM system is any system designed to counter strategic ballistic missiles (or their elements) in flight trajectory.[68] The ABM Treaty prohibited the development of an antiballistic missile system to protect the whole of either country or of an individual region, except where expressly permitted. The ABM Treaty became the centerpiece of bilateral strategic arms control because the doctrine of mutually assured destruction (MAD) relied on each side having strong offensive capabilities while itself remaining vulnerable to attack. The Interim Agreement, designed to last until a more detailed and far-reaching agreement could be negotiated, froze for five years the aggregate number of fixed land-based intercontinental ballistic missile launchers and ballistic missile launchers on submarines, although it did not prevent both sides from pursuing developments—such as multiple-warhead missiles—not covered by the treaty.

The SALT negotiations resumed in 1977. The 1979 US-Soviet Treaty on the Limitation of Strategic Offensive Arms, known as SALT II, capped armaments at a level higher than that existing at the time of their negotiation, thus keeping in check the arms race, although not requiring any actual disarmament. Unlike SALT I, SALT II provided for quantitative parity. Although it was not ratified by the US Senate, both sides complied for several years with the new limits placed on the size of their arsenals. With the assumption to office of President Ronald Reagan in 1981, the SALT negotiations were renamed the Strategic Arms Reduction Talks (START). After nine years of negotiations, the two sides signed the Treaty on the Reduction and Limitation of Strategic Offensive Arms, which came to be known as the START I Treaty. Unlike SALT, which had limited the future growth of strategic nuclear arms, START required reductions in existing levels of strategic nuclear arms to 1,600 launchers and 6,000 warheads for each side. It entered into force on December 5, 1994. The 1987 Intermediate-Range Nuclear Forces (INF) Treaty provided for the elimination of all nuclear missiles with a range of between 310 and 3,400 miles.[69] The ban on intermediate-range missiles is of unlimited duration.

The end of the Cold War led to new proposals for negotiated arms reductions, even to some unilateral disarmament as tactical and battlefield nuclear weapons became of much less importance to security in Europe. Presidents George H. W. Bush and Boris Yeltsin signed the US-Russian Treaty on Further Reduction and Limitation of Strategic Offensive Arms, or START II, in Moscow on January 3, 1993. Both sides undertook to deploy no more than 3,000 to 3,500 strategic nuclear warheads on their land-based intercontinental ballistic missiles, submarine-launched ballistic miles, and heavy bombers. Following the dissolution of the USSR, the START, INF, and ABM treaties were effectively changed into multilateral agreements with Belarus, Kazakhstan, Russia, and Ukraine as successor states to the former Soviet Union.[70] In September 1997 representatives of the United States, Russia, Belarus, Kazakhstan, and Ukraine signed a package of agreements including the START II extension protocol, which extended the deadline for the completion of START II reductions from January 1, 2003, to December 31, 2007. The United States ratified the original START II agreement in January 1996 but has not ratified a 1997 protocol extending the treaty's implementation deadline and other concurrently negotiated treaties. Having postponed a vote on START II ratification several times, the Russian Duma approved ratification of START II, its extension protocol, and concurrently negotiated agreements on April 14, 2000, but made the exchange of instruments of ratification contingent on US ratification of the extension protocol and other, concurrently negotiated, agreements.[71]

The United States and Russia agreed in 2000 to begin negotiating START III but agreed subsequently to strategic reductions outside the START framework. On December 13, 2001, President George W. Bush gave the requisite six months' notice of US withdrawal from the ABM Treaty in order to continue development of its controversial missile defense program.[72] And yet on May 24, 2002, Presidents Bush and Putin signed the Treaty on Strategic Offensive Reductions (SORT), setting out commitments to reduce their deployed strategic warheads to less than 2,200 each by 2012.[73] In announcing the successful conclusion of the six-month negotiations, Bush claimed that the treaty would "liquidate the legacy of the cold war."[74]

START I expired on December 5, 2009. On March 27, 2010, Presidents Barack Obama and Dmitry Medvedev announced agreement on the terms of the New START Treaty. This would be a legally binding and verifiable agreement to reduce both sides' deployed strategic nuclear warheads to 1,550, a figure 74 percent lower than the limit of the 1991 START Treaty and 30 percent lower than the deployed strategic warhead limit of the 2002 Moscow Treaty.[75]

As is true with other types of treaties, arms control agreements may not have been 100 percent successful, and verification provisions can never be 100 percent foolproof. But arms control treaties have constituted a very important part of the post–World War II security framework. This is why any perceived indications of a lack of respect for arms control, whether on the part of North Korea when announcing that it would withdraw from the NPT, or on the part of the United States in withdrawing support for the verification provisions under negotiation in the biological weapons regime, prompts strong reaction from the international community and arms control experts. Few would deny the importance to the structures of world politics of this group of bilateral and multilateral treaties.

▓ Notes

1. Robert J. Mathews and Timothy L. H. McCormack, "The Relationship Between International Humanitarian Law and Arms Control," in Helen Durham and Timothy L. H. McCormack, eds., *The Changing Face of Conflict and the Efficacy of International Humanitarian Law* (The Hague: Martinus Nijhoff, 1999), pp. 65–98, esp. 78.

2. Jozef Goldblat, *Arms Control: A Guide to Negotiations and Agreements* (London: Sage, 1994), p. 11.

3. Ibid., pp. 15–20.

4. Jozef Goldblat, "Contribution of the UN to Arms Control," in Dimitris Bourantonis and Marios Evriviades, eds., *A United Nations for the Twenty-First Century: Peace, Security, and Development* (The Hague: Kluwer, 1996), pp. 243–257, esp. 244.

5. Charter of the United Nations, article 11(1).

6. Charter of the United Nations, articles 26 and 47(1).

7. Ramesh Thakur and William Maley, "The Ottawa Convention on Landmines: A Landmark Humanitarian Treaty in Arms Control," *Global Governance* 5 (1999): 273–302, esp. 274.

8. 729 United Nations Treaty Series (UNTS) 161; and Shirley V. Scott, ed., *International Law and Politics: Key Documents* (Boulder, CO: Lynne Rienner, 2006), pp. 117–122.

9. Richard Butler, *Fatal Choice: Nuclear Weapons and the Illusion of Missile Defense* (Crows Nest, New South Wales: Allen and Unwin, 2001), p. 52.

10. Quoted in Michael Reiss, *Without the Bomb: The Politics of Nuclear Nonproliferation* (New York: Columbia University Press, 1988), p. 16.

11. For the details of the process by which the NPT was negotiated, see United Nations, *Review of the Multilateral Treaty-Making Process* (New York: United Nations, 1985), pp. 220–221.

12. The texts of the negative security assurances can be found in *The United Nations and Nuclear Non-Proliferation* (New York: United Nations, 1995). See also George Bunn, "The Legal Status of US Negative Security Assurances to Non-Nuclear Weapon States," *The Nonproliferation Review* (Spring-Summer 1997): 1–17.

13. Benjamin Frankel, ed., *Opaque Nuclear Proliferation: Methodological and Policy Implications* (London: Frank Cass, 1991), p. 18.

14. "Statement to Parliament by Prime Minister Vajpayee, 27 May 1998," available at http://www.acronym.org.uk.

15. The text is available at http://www.state.gov. See, inter alia, P. R. Chari, ed., *Indo-US Nuclear Deal: Seeking Synergy in Bilateralism* (London: Routledge, 2009); and R. P. Rajagopalan, "Indo-US Nuclear Deal: Implications for India and the Global Nuclear Regime," Special Report no. 62 (New Delhi: Institute for Peace and Conflict Studies, 2008), available at http://ipcs.org.

16. Bill Monahan, "Giving the Non-Proliferation Treaty Teeth: Strengthening the Special Inspection Procedures of the International Atomic Energy Agency," *Virginia Journal of International Law* 33, no. 1 (Fall 1992): 161–196.

17. Ibid.

18. See, inter alia, R. Butler, *The Greatest Threat: Iraq, Weapons of Mass Destruction, and the Crisis of Global Security* (New York: Public Affairs, 2000); and the review of that by David Malone, "Iraq: No Easy Response to 'The Greatest Threat,'" *American Journal of International Law* 95 (2001): 235–245; Chantal de Jonge Oudraat, "UNSCOM: Between Iraq and a Hard Place," *European Journal of International Law* 13, no. 1 (2002): 139–152; Scott Ritter, *Endgame: Solving the Iraq Problem Once and For All* (New York: Simon and Schuster, 1999); and the review of that by Brian Urquhart, "How Not to Fight a Dictator," *New York Review of Books,* May 6, 1999, p. 25; and "The Lessons and Legacy of UNSCOM: An Interview with Ambassador Richard Butler," *Arms Control Today,* June 1999, pp. 3–9.

19. For more detail on the background to the resolution, see Sean D. Murphy, "Contemporary Practice of the United States," *American Journal of International Law* 96 (2002): 956–962.

20. See Sean D. Murphy, "Contemporary Practice of the United States," *American Journal of International Law* 97 (2003): 419–432.

21. Marian Nash (Leigh), "United States–Democratic People's Republic of Korea," *American Journal of International Law* 89 (1995): 372–375.

22. Paul Kerr, "KEDO Suspends Oil Shipments to North Korea," *Arms Control Today,* December 2002, available at http://www.armscontrol.org; and Stephen Lunn, "Halt N-Program or Lose Oil, N Korea Told," *Weekend Australian,* November 16–17, 2002, p. 15.

23. Glen Kessler, "US Plays Down North Korean Move," *Washington Post,* January 11, 2003, available at http://washingtonpost.com.

24. *Nuclear Proliferation News,* ACRONYM Consortium, Issue No. 23, May 3, 1995, http://csf.colorado.edu.

25. R. K. Betts, "Paranoids, Pygmies, Pariahs, and Nonproliferation," *Foreign Policy* 26 (Spring 1977): 157–183, esp. 158. See also Richard Betts, "Paranoids, Pygmies, Pariahs, and Nonproliferation Revisited," *Security Studies* 2 (Spring/Summer 1993): 100–126.

26. Quoted in Mingquan Zhu, "The Evolution of China's Nuclear Nonproliferation Policy," *Nonproliferation Review* 4, no. 2 (Winter 1997): 40–48, esp. 43.

27. Mohan Malik, "Chinese Perspectives on Nuclear Non-proliferation and Asian Security," in Carl Ungerer and Marianne Hanson, eds., *The Politics of*

Nuclear Non-proliferation (St. Leonards, New South Wales: Allen and Unwin in association with the Department of International Relations Research School of Pacific and Asian Studies, Australian National University, 2001), pp. 132–157. See also Steven Dolley, "China's Record of Proliferation Misbehavior," *Issue Brief* (Washington, DC: Nuclear Control Institute, September 29, 1997), available at http://www.nci.org/ib92997.htm; Ming Zhang, *China's Changing Nuclear Posture: Reactions to the South Asian Nuclear Tests* (Washington, DC: Carnegie Endowment for International Peace, 1999); and Zhu, "The Evolution of China's Nuclear Nonproliferation Policy."

28. J. Dhanapala, "A Strengthened Review Process for the NPT," *Fordham International Law Journal* 20 (1997): 1532–1542, esp. 1538.

29. An excerpt of the speech is found in John R. Crook, ed., "Contemporary Practice of the United States Relating to International Law," *American Journal of International Law* 103 (2009): 575–608, esp. 600–602.

30. UN Security Council Resolutions 1737 (2006), 1747 (2007), 1803 (2008), and 1835 (2008).

31. John R. Crook, ed., "Contemporary Practice of the United States Relating to International Law," *American Journal of International Law* 101 (2007): 478–508, esp. 499.

32. Ibid., pp. 185–230, esp. 216–218.

33. Ibid., p. 499.

34. John R. Crook, ed., "Contemporary Practice of the United States Relating to International Law," *American Journal of International Law* 102 (2008): 860–901, esp. 887.

35. Harald Müller, "The 2005 NPT Review Conference: Reasons and Consequences of Failure and Options for Repair," prepared for the Weapons of Mass Destruction Commission, www.wmdcommission.org.

36. Adam Daniel Rotfeld, "Introduction" to "Biotechnology and the Future of the Biological and Toxin Weapons Convention," *SIPRI Fact Sheet,* November 2001, http://projects.sipri.

37. Convention on the Prohibition of the Development, Production, and Stockpiling of Bacteriological (Biological) and Toxin Weapons and on Their Destruction, 11 *International Legal Materials (ILM)* 309 (1972), http://www.opbw.org.

38. *American Journal of International Law* 25 (1931): supplement 94-6.

39. 11 *ILM* 309 (1972); and Scott, *International Law and Politics,* pp. 129–133.

40. Goldblat, *Arms Control,* p. 93.

41. Ibid., p. 229.

42. Scott Keefer, "International Control of Biological Weapons," *ILSA Journal of International and Comparative Law* 6 (1999): 107–141, esp. 108.

43. Interview with John R. Bolton, Undersecretary of State for Arms Control and International Security, Center for Nonproliferation Studies, Monterey Institute of International Studies, at http://cns.miis.edu.

44. Ibid.

45. Seth Brugger, "BWC Conference Suspended After Controversial End," *Arms Control Today,* January/February 2002, available at http://www.armscontrol.org.

46. See http://www.unog.ch.

47. 32 *ILM* 804 (1993); and Scott, *International Law and Politics,* pp. 134–166.

48. Amy E. Smithson, "Chemical Weapons: The End of the Beginning," *Bulletin of the Atomic Scientists,* October 1992, pp. 37–43, esp. 37.

49. Ibid.

50. Goldblat, *Arms Control,* pp. 93–96.

51. "The Chemical Weapons Convention: A Guided Tour of the Convention on the Prohibition of the Development, Production, Stockpiling, and Use of Chemical Weapons and on Their Destruction," http:www.opcw.org.

52. See http://www.opcw.org.

53. Convention on the Prohibition of the Development, Production, Stockpiling, and Use of Chemical Weapons and on Their Destruction, article VIII(1).

54. "Report of the OPCW on the Implementation of the Convention on the Prohibition of the Development, Production, Stockpiling, and Use of Chemical Weapons and on Their Destruction in 2008," Organization for the Prohibition of Chemical Weapons Report C-14/4, December 2, 2008, p. 1.

55. Convention on the Prohibition of the Development, Production, Stockpiling, and Use of Chemical Weapons and on Their Destruction, article IX(8).

56. Ibid., article IX(11).

57. Rebecca Johnson and Daryl Kimball, "Who Needs the Nuclear Test Ban?" *Disarmament Diplomacy* 59 (July-August 2001), available at http://www.acronym.org.uk.

58. Dinshaw Mistry, "Domestic-International Linkages: India and the Comprehensive Test Ban Treaty," *Nonproliferation Review,* Fall 1998, pp. 25–38, esp. 26–27.

59. 480 UNTS 43.

60. 35 *ILM* 1443 (1996); and Scott, *International Law and Politics,* pp. 167–197.

61. Or, more precisely, states that formally participated in the 1996 session of the Conference on Disarmament and that appear in table 1 of the December 1995 edition of "Nuclear Research Reactors in the World" and table 1 of the April 1996 edition of "Nuclear Power Reactors in the World," both compiled by the International Atomic Energy Agency.

62. The details are found in Part 1 of the accompanying Protocol to the Comprehensive Nuclear Test-Ban Treaty.

63. Mistry, "Domestic-International Linkages," p. 25.

64. Ibid., p. 29.

65. Gaurav Kampani, "In Praise of Indifference Toward India's Bomb," *Orbis,* Spring 2001, pp. 241–257, esp. 248.

66. John Markoff and Andrew E. Kramer, "US and Russia Differ on a Treaty for Cyberspace," *New York Times,* June 28, 2009, available at www.nytimes.com. See, inter alia, David Elliott, "Weighing the Case for a Convention to Limit Cyberwarfare," www.armscontrol.org.

67. The text is available at http://cns.miis.edu. For background and analysis, see Marco Roscini, "Something Old, Something New: The 2006 Semipalatinsk Treaty on a Nuclear Weapon-Free Zone in Central Asia," *Chinese Journal of International Law* 7, no. 3 (2008): 593–624. On nuclear-weapon-free zones in general, see Scott Parrish and Jean du Preez, "Nuclear-Weapon-Free Zones: Still a Useful Disarmament and Non-Proliferation Tool?" paper prepared for the Weapons of Mass Destruction Commission, www.wmdcommission.org.

68. Goldblat, *Arms Control,* p. 56.

69. The text can be found at http://www.armscontrol.org.

70. By a 1997 MOU on Succession to the ABM Treaty, for example, the United States, Russia, Belarus, Kazakhstan, and Ukraine were designated parties to the ABM Treaty.

71. "START II and Its Extension Protocol at a Glance," fact sheet prepared by the Arms Control Association and available at http://www.armscontrol.org; and "START II Ratification: A Chronology," compiled by Scott Parrish, at http://cns .miis.edu.

72. See, inter alia, Charles L. Glaser and Steve Fetter, "National Missile Defense and the Future of US Nuclear Weapons Policy," *International Security* 26, no. 1 (2001): 40–92; David Edward Grogan, "Power Play: Theater Ballistic Missile Defense, National Ballistic Missile Defense, and the ABM Treaty," *Virginia Journal of International Law* 39, no. 4 (1999): 799–879; and Keith Wilson, "Why Are the Missiles (and Missile Defence) Called Peace-Keepers? Corroding the Concept of Peaceful Use," *Leiden Journal of International Law* 14, no. 4 (2001): 759–828.

73. "United States (U.S.)-Russian Federation: The Moscow Treaty (Treaty Between the United States of America and The Russian Federation on Strategic Offensive Reductions)," May 24, 2002, 41 *ILM* 799 (2002).

74. Patricke Tyler, "Pulling Russia Closer," *New York Times,* www.nytimes .com, May 14, 2002.

75. The White House, Office of the Press Secretary, "Key Facts About the New START Treaty," March 26, 2010, available at http://www.whitehouse.gov.

11

International
Human Rights Law

ALTHOUGH IT HAS ANCIENT ORIGINS AND THERE WERE SOME human rights–related mechanisms within the League of Nations system, international human rights law is primarily a post–World War II phenomenon. The development of a comprehensive system of human rights protection was given much impetus by the horrors of Nazi persecution of the Jews and other atrocities during World War II. Particularly as it operates at a global level, international human rights law is intimately related to the United Nations system. All the global instruments have their origins in the UN. The second-mentioned goal of the UN is to "reaffirm faith in fundamental human rights, in the dignity and worth of the human person, in the equal rights of men and women and of nations large and small." The most substantive human rights obligation in the Charter is found in article 56, by which members pledge to take "joint and separate action in cooperation with the Organization for the achievement of . . . universal respect for, and observance of, human rights and fundamental freedoms for all without distinction as to race, sex, language, or religion."[1]

This was to be done "[w]ith a view to the creation of conditions of stability and well-being which are necessary for peaceful and friendly relations among nations," illustrating the fact that the development of international human rights law, especially in its early days, was not as distinct from the more mainstream objectives of states as is often thought. As we saw in Chapter 3, the primary function attributed to the UN was the maintenance of world peace. Human rights abuse, especially on a large scale, was regarded as a potential threat to that peace. The violent treatment by the Nazis of their own population was considered ultimately inseparable from German aggression beyond its borders. The drafters of the UN Charter emphasized social justice and human rights as the foundations for a stable international order.[2] This notion is reiterated in the preamble to a number of human rights treaties. The Convention on the Rights of the Child, for example, states in the preamble that "recognition of the inherent dignity and of the equal and inalienable rights of all members of the human family is the foundation of freedom, justice and peace in the world." The International Convention on the Elimination of all Forms of Racial Discrimination "reaffirm[s] that discrimination between human beings on the grounds of race, colour or ethnic origin is an obstacle to friendly and peaceful relations among nations and is capable of disturbing peace and security among peoples and the harmony of persons living side by side even within one and the same State." See Figure 11.1.

■ The Universal Declaration of Human Rights, 1948

The UN Charter indicated the new interest in international human rights, but the 1948 Universal Declaration of Human Rights of (UDHR)[3] is usually regarded as the foundation of international human rights law. As a declaration, it is not a legally binding instrument but rather is hortatory or recommendatory in nature. The UDHR has nevertheless been of great influence, both on national constitutions and case law and as an impetus for the further development of human rights law at an international level. Some lawyers have sought to argue that it has become customary international law—but, even though there may not be much opposition to its principles, and some of it may have been binding by custom, few would accept that the

**Figure 11.1 Some Landmarks in the Evolution of
          Global International Human Rights Law**

1948	Convention on the Prevention and Punishment of the Crime of Genocide
1948	Universal Declaration of Human Rights
1951	Convention Relating to the Status of Refugees
1965	International Convention on the Elimination of All Forms of Racial Discrimination
1966	International Covenant on Economic, Social, and Cultural Rights
1966	International Covenant on Civil and Political Rights
1973	International Convention on the Suppression and Punishment of the Crime of Apartheid
1979	Convention on the Elimination of All Forms of Discrimination Against Women
1984	Convention Against Torture and Other Cruel, Inhuman, or Degrading Treatment or Punishment
1989	Convention on the Rights of the Child
2006	Convention of the Rights of Persons with Disabilities

actual practice by states with the UDHR as a whole has been such as to satisfy the requirement of "general, uniform and consistent practice." The UDHR was drafted by a committee chaired by Eleanor Roosevelt; the committee reported to the Commission on Human Rights, which, in turn, sent the draft to the UN General Assembly. There the UDHR was scrutinized by the Third Committee of the Assembly and adopted by the General Assembly, all in a remarkably short space of time. The Cold War, the women's lobby, and the tradition of Latin American socialism all influenced the wording of the UDHR, but the primary influence was the Holocaust; the UDHR was adopted to avoid any similar abomination.[4]

In Nazi Germany there had been a breakdown in the dividing line between the persons and the state. The UDHR was an assertion that "the interests of the individual [come] before those of the State and that the State should not be allowed to deprive the individual of his dignity and his basic rights."[5] Rights set out in the UDHR include civil and political rights such as those to life, liberty, security of person, freedom from arbitrary arrest, the presumption of innocence, freedom of opinion and expression and of peaceful assembly and association; as well as economic, social, and cultural rights including social security, forming and joining trade unions, rest and leisure, and participating in the cultural life of the community.

The twentieth anniversary of the adoption of the Universal Declaration of Human Rights was marked by an International Conference on Human Rights, held in Tehran, Iran, from April 22 to May 13, 1968. The Proclamation of Tehran affirmed the faith of the conference in the principles of the UDHR and urged all peoples and governments to dedicate themselves to those principles and to redouble their efforts to "provide for all human beings a life consonant with freedom and dignity and conducive to physical, mental, social and spiritual welfare." In referring to "new standards and obligations to which States should conform," the proclamation also made reference to the two recently concluded international covenants.

▦ The International Covenant on Civil and Political Rights and the International Covenant on Economic, Social, and Cultural Rights, 1966

The UDHR was the springboard for two treaties. The 1966 International Covenant on Civil and Political Rights (ICCPR)[6] built on the civil and political rights found in the UDHR, although it did not include the right to property, nationality, or asylum. The 1966 International Covenant on Economic, Social, and Cultural Rights (ICESCR)[7] built on the second group of rights found in the UDHR, although it did not include a right to property as had been found in article 17 of the Universal Declaration. This pattern of a declaration followed by a legally binding treaty has been standard in international human rights law. The UDHR and the two covenants considered together are often referred to as the International Bill of Rights. The covenants did not enter into force until 1976.

Both covenants contain some of the same or similar provisions. Article 1 of each is identical. It reaffirms the principle that the right of self-determination is universal and calls upon all states to respect and promote the realization of that right; it also provides that "all peoples may, for their own ends, freely dispose of their natural wealth and resources."[8] Article 3 of both covenants requires states to undertake to ensure the equal right of men and women to the enjoyment of all the rights set out in the covenant.

The ICCPR established the Human Rights Committee to which states parties to the covenant submit reports on the measures they have adopted that give effect to the rights recognized in the covenant.[9] The committee studies the reports and makes "general comments."[10] There is also an optional procedure by which states may grant other states that have also accepted the provision the right to bring a complaint against them before the committee.[11] Should the matter referred to the committee not be resolved to the satisfaction of the states parties concerned, the committee may, with the prior consent of the parties concerned, appoint an ad hoc conciliation commission.[12] The First Optional Protocol to the ICCPR provides for individual complaints to the Human Rights Committee.[13] A number of conditions must have been met:

- The state having jurisdiction over that individual is a party to the protocol (art. 1);
- The individual has exhausted all available domestic remedies (except where the application of the remedies has been unreasonably prolonged) (art. 5(2)(b));
- The communication must not be anonymous, or an abuse of the right of submission of such communications or be incompatible with the provisions of the covenant (art. 3);
- The matter is not examined under another procedure of international investigation or settlement (art. 5(2)).

The Second Optional Protocol to the ICCPR,[14] aiming at the abolition of the death penalty, was adopted by the General Assembly on December 15, 1989.

A state party to the ICCPR undertakes to take steps "to the maximum of its available resources, with a view to achieving progressively the full realization of the rights recognized in the . . . Covenant."[15] This obligation under the ICESCR is a much weaker legal obligation than that required of a state in relation to the ICCPR, by article 2(1) of which a state party undertakes to "respect and to ensure to all individuals within its territory and subject to its jurisdiction the rights recognized in the present Covenant." States are to submit reports, which, since 1987, have been considered by a Committee on Economic, Social, and Cultural Rights (CESCR), responsible to ECOSOC. The committee prepares "general comments" in response.

The CESCR began calling for an Optional Protocol to establish an individual complaint mechanism akin to that functioning in relation to the ICCPR. On December 10, 2008, the UN General Assembly adopted the Optional Protocol to the ICESCR, which provides, inter alia, that states recognize the competence of the committee to receive and consider communications submitted by or on behalf of individuals or groups of individuals claiming to be victims of a violation of any of the rights set out in the covenant by that state party. It also creates an inquiry procedure, by which the committee may investigate grave or systematic violations of the covenant.[16]

Apart from these two covenants, there are a large number of more specific global human rights treaties, some of which preceded, some of which paralleled, and some of which have followed the negotiation of the covenants.

■ Convention on the Prevention and Punishment of the Crime of Genocide, 1948

The twentieth century has been referred to as the "century of genocide."[17] The Holocaust involved the systematic extermination of between five and six million Jews as well as the murder of large numbers of Gypsies, Russian and Polish prisoners of war, East European slave laborers, and Germans who were physically disabled or mentally retarded.[18] The term genocide was invented by a Polish lawyer, Raphael Lemkin, from the Greek *genos,* meaning "race," and the Latin *cide,* meaning "killing," to refer to the destruction of a nation or of an ethnic group.[19] Lemkin began his work in the 1930s, horrified by the fact that a Turkish official who had ordered the massacre of hundreds of thousands of Armenians had not been brought to trial whereas the young man who had allegedly assassinated him was.[20] In his 1944 book entitled *Axis Rule in Occupied Europe,* Lemkin detailed the techniques developed by the Germans to carry out political, social, economic, biological, physical, religious, and moral genocide, which he referred to as "one of the most complete and glaring illustrations of the violation of international law and the laws of humanity."

The decision of the Nuremberg Tribunal not to accept jurisdiction over crimes against humanity in times of peace prompted Lemkin to embark on an intensive campaign to draft and bring into force an international agreement that would define genocide as an international crime subject to universal jurisdiction.[21] The text of the convention was drawn up by an ad hoc committee of ECOSOC, drawing on preparatory work undertaken by the UN Secretariat, which drew on experts in the field as well as the comments of member states and the Commission on Human Rights. Not all members of the Sixth Committee had agreed with the idea of drafting a multilateral treaty. The United Kingdom's representative, for example, argued that a convention would not deter state-initiated genocide and that if a significant number of states resisted ratifying such a convention it would cast doubt on the claim that genocide was an internationally recognized crime. The UK proposed that the General Assembly affirm that genocide was a crime entailing national and international responsibility and that member states should be urged to incorporate the principles of the Secretariat's draft into their domestic law.[22] Of particular importance to bringing about the convention was the "exceptional dedication" of several experts and appeals of many NGOs.[23] The General Assembly adopted the text of the Genocide Convention in 1948; it entered into force in 1951.[24]

Article I of the Genocide Convention established genocide as an international crime, "whether committed in time of peace or in time of war." Genocide is defined in article II as:

> acts committed with the intent to destroy, in whole or in part, a national, ethnical, racial, or religious group and includes any of the following:
>
>   (a) Killing members of the group;
>   (b) Causing serious bodily or mental harm to members of the group;
>   (c) Deliberately inflicting on the group conditions of life calculated to bring about its physical destruction in whole or in part;
>   (d) Imposing measures intended to prevent births within the group;
>   (e) Forcibly transferring children of the group to another group.

Notable about this definition is the element of intent and the breadth of actions encompassed by the term *genocide:* it is not just about killing. In an article published in the *American Journal of International Law* in 1947, Lemkin explained:

> The crime of genocide involves a wide range of actions, including not only the deprivation of life but also the prevention of life (abortions, sterilizations) and also devices considerably endangering life and health (artificial infections, working to death in special camps, deliberate separation of families for depopulation purposes and so forth). All these actions are subordinated to the criminal intent to destroy or to cripple permanently a human group. The acts are directed against groups, as such, and individuals are selected for destruction only because they belong to these groups. In view of such a phenomenon the terms previously used to describe an attack upon

nationhood were not adequate. Mass murder or extermination wouldn't apply in the case of sterilization because the victims of sterilizations were not murdered, rather a people was killed through delayed action by stopping propagation. Moreover, mass murder does not convey the specific losses to civilization in the form of the cultural contributions which can be made only by groups of people united through national, racial or cultural characteristics.[25]

There have been proposals to amend the definition of the convention so as to include negligent as well as intentional genocide, and to encompass other types of groups—particularly economic and political—omitted from this definition.[26] Political groups were included in a 1946 General Assembly resolution, but the Soviets blocked attempts to include political groups in the convention's definition of genocide.[27]

By articles III and IV of the convention, persons who commit genocide, conspire to commit genocide, directly and publicly incite others to commit genocide, attempt to commit genocide, or who are complicit in genocide are to be punished "whether they are constitutionally responsible rulers, public officials or private individuals." The war crimes trials at Nuremburg had established that subordinates were not able to plead "superior orders" but were individually responsible for their role in the Holocaust. By article V the contracting parties undertake to enact legislation to give effect to the provisions of the convention and to provide effective penalties for persons guilty of genocide or the related acts specified in article III.

Many states have ratified the convention with reservations, particularly to the compromissory clause. The United States ratified the convention only in 1986, and even then it made two reservations, five "understandings," and one "declaration."[28] One of the reservations requires the consent of the United States to the submission of any dispute to the International Court of Justice. A reservation by the United States to article IX can, on the basis of the principle of reciprocity, be drawn on by another state in the event that the United States attempts to invoke ICJ jurisdiction against it on the basis of the Genocide Convention. Hence, the effect of the US reservation is much broader than it appears.

Despite the existence of the Genocide Convention, the Nazi Holocaust was not the last genocide of the twentieth century. Others included that of the Tutsis in Burundi from 1993 to 1998 and in Rwanda in 1994.[29] During the 1990s, supporters of an international criminal court argued that, even if it is ultimately not possible to prevent genocide, the least we can do is to establish a permanent international criminal court so that potential perpetrators of genocide recognize that there is a good chance that they will be brought to justice. Genocide is one of four crimes over which the International Criminal Court has jurisdiction.

■ Convention Relating to the Status of Refugees, 1951, and the Protocol Relating to the Status of Refugees, 1967

There have been mass migrations throughout human history. During World War II, the Nazi attempt to exterminate the Jews, their invasion of other states, and the sovietization of Eastern Europe led to millions of displaced people. The Office of the United Nations High Commissioner for Refugees (UNHCR) was established by General Assembly Resolution 428(V) of December 14, 1950,[30] and the Convention Relating to the Status of Refugees was concluded the following year.[31] The regime founded on the 1951 Refugee Convention is generally classified as a human rights regime, but it is important to be aware that the treatment of refugees is an intensely political issue; international refugee law has been shaped by the perceived security implications of mass movements of people across borders.[32]

The United States, which after World War II took in many Eastern Europeans, regarding them as examples of the failure of communism,[33] was the principal architect of the postwar refugee regime.[34] Article 1 of the 1951 Refugee Convention defined a *refugee* as a person

> [who] owing to [a] well-founded fear of being persecuted for reasons of race, religion, nationality, membership of a particular social group or political opinion, is outside the country of his nationality and is unable or, owing to such fear, is unwilling to avail himself of the protection of that country; or who, not having a nationality and being outside the country of his former habitual residence as a result of such events, is unable or, owing to such fear, is unwilling to return to it.

The 1951 definition began with the words "[a]s a result of events occurring before 1 January 1951," and each contracting party was to make a declaration at the time of signature, ratification, or accession, as to whether it was going to apply these words to "events occurring in Europe before 1 January 1951" or to "events occurring in Europe or elsewhere before 1 January 1951." Perhaps not surprisingly, the USSR and Eastern bloc rejected the convention. "Indeed for at least the next three decades the Soviet Union perceived the UNHCR to be a tool of Western political ambitions."[35] The 1967 Protocol to the Convention[36] removed the temporal and geographical restrictions of the refugee definition.

The most important protection that the convention accords those qualifying as refugees under article 1 is contained in the convention's prohibition of expulsion or return ("refoulement"). By article 33(1), no contracting state shall expel or return a refugee to the frontiers of territories where their life or freedom would be threatened on account of their race, religion, nationality, membership of a particular social group, or political opinion. No reservations are permitted to article 33.[37] By article 31(1), the contracting states are not to impose penalties, on account of illegal entry or presence, on refugees who, coming directly from a territory where their life or freedom was threatened in the sense of article 1, enter or are present in their territory without authorization, provided they present themselves without delay to the authorities and show good cause for their illegal entry or presence. Furthermore, by article 31(2), contracting states "shall not apply to the movements of such refugees restrictions other than those which are necessary and such restrictions shall only be applied until their status in the country is regularised or they obtain admission into another country."

Since the late 1960s, when a major proportion of the international refugee population began to come from the less developed world, Western governments have been less enthusiastic about welcoming refugees. Many countries began to practice deterrence policies by, for example, turning back potential asylum seekers before they entered a country—and hence before they are able to apply for refugee status. Other deterrence tactics have included the denial or limitation of welfare benefits to asylum seekers, limited access to appeal procedures regarding the determination of their refugee status, and the use of negative propaganda and language.[38]

The Refugee Convention does not address the problem of *internally displaced people* that, in terms of numbers, is an even greater problem than that of conventional refugees.[39] There are more than eleven million internally displaced persons (IDPs) in Africa alone. The Guiding Principles on Internal Displacement, promulgated in 1998, describe IDPs as

[p]ersons or groups of persons who have been forced or obliged to flee or to leave their homes or places of habitual residence, in particular as a result of or in order to avoid the effects of armed conflict, situations of generalized violence, violations of human rights or natural or human-made disasters, and who have not crossed an internationally recognized State border.

In 2001 the UNHCR began a series of global consultations on international protection with the aim of revitalizing the 1951 convention framework.[40] A ministerial meeting of states parties to the 1951 convention and/or 1967 protocol held in Geneva in December 2001 adopted a Declaration of States Parties by which the contracting states reaffirmed their commitment to implement their obligations under the 1951 convention and/or its 1967 protocol "fully and effectively"[41] and expressed the belief that the regime should be developed further, in a way that "complements and strengthens the 1951 Convention and its Protocol."[42]

Issues of concern to the UNHCR in recent years include that of the extent to which its mandate should extend to those affected by environmental change and in particular climate change; the nexus between asylum and migration; how to prevent and respond to statelessness—whether or not those involved are refugees; and how to deal with smuggling, trafficking, and protracted refugee situations.[43]

■ International Convention on the Elimination of All Forms of Racial Discrimination, 1965

On November 20, 1963, the General Assembly adopted the United Nations Declaration on the Elimination of All Forms of Racial Discrimination. Article 1 of the declaration proclaims that

> [d]iscrimination between human beings on the grounds of race, colour or ethnic origin is an offence to human dignity and shall be condemned as a denial of the principles of the Charter of the United Nations, as a violation of the human rights and fundamental freedoms proclaimed in the Universal Declaration of Human Rights, as an obstacle to friendly and peaceful relations among nations and as a fact capable of disturbing peace and security among peoples.

The Human Rights Commission drafted the treaty at the request of the General Assembly. The Sub-Commission on the Prevention of Discrimination and Protection of Minorities began the work on the convention, taking as a basis for its work the draft prepared by the US member of the subcommission. The Human Rights Commission dealt with the draft prepared by the subcommission and then passed it on to the Third Committee, which forwarded a final text to the General Assembly.[44] *Racial discrimination* is defined in article 1 as "any distinction, exclusion, restriction or preference based on race, colour, descent or national or ethnic origin which has the purpose or effect of nullifying or impairing the recognition, enjoyment or exercise, on an equal footing, of human rights and fundamental freedoms." By article 2, states parties "condemn racial discrimination and undertake to pursue by all appropriate means and without delay a policy of eliminating racial discrimination in all its forms and promoting understanding among all races." States are

> (a) . . . to engage in no act or practice of racial discrimination against persons, groups of persons or institutions and to ensure that all public authorities and public institutions, national and local, shall act in conformity with this obligation;
> (b) . . . not to sponsor, defend or support racial discrimination by any persons or organizations;
> (c) . . . take effective measures to review governmental, national and local policies, and to amend, rescind or nullify any laws and regulations which have the effect of creating or perpetuating racial discrimination wherever it exists;
> (d) . . . prohibit and bring to an end, by all appropriate means, including legislation as required by circumstances, racial discrimination by any persons, group or organization;

(e) . . . encourage, where appropriate, integrationist multiracial organizations and movements and other means of eliminating barriers between races, and to discourage anything which tends to strengthen racial division.

Other provisions intended to assist in the elimination of racial discrimination include preventing, prohibiting, and eradicating all racial segregation and apartheid (article 3); condemning all racial propaganda and dissemination of ideas based on racial superiority or hatred (article 4); guaranteeing the right of every individual to equality before the law (article 5); and adopting immediate and effective educational measures to promote understanding, tolerance, and friendship among nations and racial or ethnical groups (article 7).[45]

The Committee on the Elimination of Racial Discrimination (CERD) was the first United Nations human rights instrument to set up an international monitoring system, including a procedure for individual complaints. The details of this are set out in part II of the convention.[46] Established in 1969, CERD consists of eighteen independent experts elected by the states parties after being nominated by states. The committee receives the periodic reports of states (article 9) and inquires into and helps settle complaints about one state by another (articles 11 to 13). Article 14 is an optional clause about individual complaints:

A State Party may at any time declare that it recognizes the competence of the Committee to receive and consider communications from individuals or groups of individuals within its jurisdiction claiming to be victims of a violation by that State Party of any of the rights set forth in this Convention. No communication shall be received by the Committee if it concerns a State Party which has not made such a declaration.

After exhausting available local remedies, an individual must first seek a review at the domestic level by a national body nominated by the state in its optional declaration. If unsatisfied with the outcome of that review, the individual has six months to bring the matter before the committee. The committee must first find the complaint to be admissible (not be anonymous and to have exhausted local remedies unless the application of the remedies has been too prolonged) and, having received any written communications from the state concerned, will make "suggestions and recommendations" to that state.

■ Convention on the Elimination of All Forms of Discrimination Against Women, 1979

The Commission on the Status of Women laid the foundations for the Convention on the Elimination of All Forms of Discrimination Against Women (CEDAW)[47] with a number of instruments to deal with specific political, social, and cultural concerns of women. Such early initiatives included the 1953 Convention on the Political Rights of Women, the 1957 Convention on the Nationality of Married Women, the 1962 Convention on Consent to Marriage, Minimum Age for Marriage, and Registration of Marriages, and the 1967 Declaration on the Elimination of Discrimination Against Women. These generated international interest in women's human rights: the scholarly literature on women's human rights increased as the number of legal instruments increased.[48] CEDAW was opened for signature on March 1, 1980, and entered into force only eighteen months later, on September 3, 1981.

Articles 2 and 3 contain the crux of the obligations assumed by states under this convention. By article 2, states parties "condemn discrimination against women in all its forms" and "agree to pursue by all appropriate means and without delay a policy of eliminating discrimination against women." Article 3 requires states to "take in all fields, in particular in the political, social, economic and cultural fields, all appropriate measures, including legislation, to ensure the full development and advancement of women." *Discrimination against women* is defined in the convention as "any distinction, exclusion or restriction made on the basis of sex which has the effect or purpose of impairing or nullifying the recognition, enjoyment or exercise by women, irrespective of their marital status, on a basis of equality of men and women, of human rights and fundamental freedoms in the political, economic, social, cultural, civil or any other field." "Temporary special measures aimed at accelerating de facto equality between men and women" and special measures aimed at protecting maternity (i.e., affirmative action measures) are not to be regarded as discrimination.[49]

The particular actions required of states are specified in more detail in the other substantive provisions. They include taking appropriate measures

- To suppress all forms of traffic in women and exploitation of prostitution of women (art. 6);
- To ensure to women, on equal terms with men and without any discrimination, the opportunity to represent their governments at the international level and to participate in the work of international organizations (art. 8);
- To eliminate discrimination against women in order to ensure to them equal rights with men in the field of education (art. 10), in the field of employment (art. 11), in the field of health care (art. 12), and in other areas of economic and social life (art. 13); in rural areas (art. 14); in all matters relating to marriage and family relations (art. 16); and
- To accord women equality with men before the law (art. 15).

CEDAW established the Committee on the Elimination of Discrimination Against Women, whose main role is to receive and consider reports of state parties.[50] The frequency of meetings has since 2007 been increased to three times a year; the committee meets in three-week sessions. There was no provision in the convention for the consideration of complaints from states or from individuals. The committee has considered the issue of reservations, which have been of particular concern in this regime. Several states have reservations that indicate acceptance of the convention only to the extent compatible with Islamic *sharia* or traditional customs and practices. The Vienna Convention on the Law of Treaties stipulates that reservations should not be incompatible with the object and purpose of a treaty. The committee has decided that articles 2 and 16 of the convention are central to the objects and purposes of CEDAW, and has encouraged states to withdraw reservations to those articles.

An Optional Protocol to CEDAW was adopted by the Commission on the Status of Women on March 12, 1999, and by the General Assembly on October 6, 1999.[51] The Optional Protocol contains two procedures. The first allows individual women, or groups of women, under the jurisdiction of a state party to the protocol, to submit claims of violations of rights under the CEDAW to the Committee on the Elimination of Discrimination Against Women; the second enables the committee to initiate inquiries into situations of grave or systematic violations of women's rights under the CEDAW.

■ Convention Against Torture and Other Cruel, Inhuman, or Degrading Treatment or Punishment, 1984

The Convention Against Torture[52] followed a 1975 General Assembly Declaration on the Protection of All Persons from Being Subjected to Torture and Other Cruel, Inhuman, or Degrading Treatment or Punishment. The convention proved much more difficult to achieve than had the declaration, particularly as regards the implementation provisions.[53] The text was drafted by a working group set up by the Commission on Human Rights, which received a draft international convention proposed by Sweden as well as one from the International Association of Penal Law. NGOs, including the International Commission of Jurists, Amnesty International, and the International Association of Penal Law, had for some time been calling for an international convention on torture.[54] The General Assembly adopted the Convention on December 10, 1984.

Torture is defined in article 1 as

> any act by which severe pain or suffering, whether physical or mental, is intentionally inflicted on a person for such purposes as obtaining from him or a third person information or a confession, punishing him for an act he or a third person has committed or is suspected of having committed, or intimidating or coercing him or a third person, or for any reason based on discrimination of any kind, when such pain or suffering is inflicted by or at the instigation of or with the consent or acquiescence of a public official

or other person acting in an official capacity. It does not include pain or suffering arising only from, inherent in or incidental to lawful sanctions.

Article 2 of the convention provides:

> 1. Each State Party shall take effective legislative, administrative, judicial or other measures to prevent acts of torture in any territory under its jurisdiction.
> 2. No exceptional circumstances whatsoever, whether a state of war or a threat of war, internal political instability or any other public emergency, may be invoked as a justification of torture.
> 3. An order from a superior officer or a public authority may not be invoked as a justification of torture.

The convention established the Committee Against Torture.[55] This consists of ten elected members, acting in their personal capacity. States parties are to submit a report on the measures they have taken to give effect to their undertakings under the convention within one year of entry into force of the convention for the state involved and thereafter submit supplementary reports every four years. The committee deals with complaints by one state party against another and, if the state involved has declared its acceptance, of communications from or on behalf of individuals subject to its jurisdiction. In December 2002 the General Assembly adopted an Optional Protocol to the convention,[56] to establish a preventive system of regular visits to places of detention.

The Convention Against Torture came into prominence with the efforts of the administration of George W. Bush to legally justify behaviors prohibited under the convention.[57] The Committee Against Torture in November 2008 expressed its deep concerns regarding routine and widespread use of torture in China.[58] Speaking on the twenty-fifth anniversary of the convention, the committee chair said that it was regrettably not possible to say that torture had decreased over the past quarter of a century. Obstacles to realizing the objectives of the convention include the refusal of governments to clearly define and criminalize torture and to investigate and ensure that perpetrators of torture are brought to justice.[59]

■ Convention on the Rights of the Child, 1989

The Convention on the Rights of the Child (CRC)[60] has been ratified by more countries than any other human rights instrument; it has almost universal membership.[61] Proposals for a global treaty on children's rights had been mooted as early as at a conference organized by the League of Nations in 1924. In 1959 the General Assembly adopted the Declaration on the Rights of the Child. But the 1979 UN "Year of the Child" was the final impetus for the Human Rights Commission sponsoring a forum that met for one week each year to produce a convention on the rights of the child. The General Assembly adopted the convention, without a formal vote, on November 20, 1989, and it entered into force on September 2, 1991.

A key phrase in the treaty is that of the "best interests of the child." "In all actions concerning children, whether undertaken by public or private social welfare institutions, courts of law, administrative authorities or legislative bodies, the best interests of the child shall be a primary consideration" (article 3(1)). The bulk of the text in the substantive part of the convention is devoted to specifying the various rights of the child. These include the right to life (article 6); the right to a name from birth, to acquire a nationality, and, as far as possible, to know and be cared for by his or her parents (article 7); the right of a child who is separated from one or both parents to maintain personal relations and direct contact with both parents on a regular basis, except if it is contrary to the child's best interests (article 9); the right to express his or her own views in all matters affecting the child, the views to be given due weight in accordance with the age and maturity of the child (article 12); the right to the enjoyment of the highest attainable standard of health and to facilities for the treatment of illness and rehabilitation of health (article 24); the right to education (article 28); the right to be protected from economic exploitation, hazardous work, or work that interferes with the child's education or is detrimental to the child's health or physical, mental, spiritual, moral, or social development (article 32); and the right to rest and leisure, play and recreational activities, and to participate fully in cultural and artistic life (article 31). The state is to implement the various rights included in the convention, by "all appropriate legislative, administrative, and other measures" (article 4).

The convention established the Committee on the Rights of the Child, which receives and examines state reports on the measures taken to implement the convention and the progress that has been made in furthering the enjoyment of rights under it.[62] The committee may make suggestions and general recommendations to any state party concerned and report to the General Assembly, together with comments, if any, from states parties. There are two optional protocols to the convention: on the involvement of children in armed conflict and on the sale of children, child prostitution, and child pornography.[63] These protocols were adopted by the General Assembly in May 2000. In June 2009 the Human Rights Council established an open-ended working group to explore the possibility of adding an optional protocol to the regime to enable individuals to bring matters before the committee, as happens within the CERD, ICCPR, CAT, CEDAW, and CRPD regimes.

▓ Vienna Declaration and Programme of Action, 1993

By General Assembly Resolution 45/155 of December 18, 1990, the United Nations decided to hold a world conference on human rights in order to review and assess the progress that had been made in the field of human rights and to identify potential future obstacles and ways to overcome them.[64] The resultant Vienna Declaration and Programme of Action[65] reaffirmed the commitment of all states to observe and protect human rights and fundamental freedoms for all. "Human rights and fundamental freedoms are the birthright of all human beings; their protection and promotion is the first responsibility of Governments" (section I(1)). The Declaration and Programme of Action reiterated that enhancement of international cooperation in the field of human rights is essential for the full achievement of the purposes of the United Nations. Section II(18) of the declaration recommended that the General Assembly consider, as a matter of priority, the establishment of a High Commissioner for Human Rights "for the promotion and protection of all human rights." The General Assembly created the position on December 20, 1993, by Resolution 48/151.[66]

▓ Convention on the Rights of Persons with Disabilities, 2006

The Convention on the Rights of Persons with Disabilities (CRPD)[67] reaffirms that persons with disabilities have the same human rights as everyone else, including the right to life, liberty, and security of the person; equal recognition before the law and legal capacity; and freedom from torture. States have obligations to promote, protect, and ensure those rights, including through adopting legislation and administrative measures to promote the human rights of persons with disabilities; adopting legislative and other measures to abolish discrimination; and stopping any practice that breaches the rights of persons with disabilities.

Article 3 sets out a list of principles that underpin the convention. These include respect for inherent dignity; individual autonomy, including the freedom to make one's own choices and independence of person; non-discrimination; full and effective participation and inclusion in society; respect for difference and acceptance of persons with disabilities as part of human diversity and humanity; equality of opportunity; accessibility; equality between men and women; respect for the evolving capacities of children with disabilities; and respect for the right of children with disabilities to preserve their identities.

The convention established the Committee on the Rights of Persons with Disabilities, a body of independent experts tasked with reviewing the periodic reports of states parties on the steps they have taken to implement the convention. The optional protocol, adopted at the same time as the convention, provides for an individual complaints mechanism as well as a procedure by which the committee can investigate grave or systematic violations by a state party to the optional protocol of any of the provisions of the convention. The convention also established a Conference of States Parties that meets regularly to guide implementation of the convention, including electing members of the Committee on the Rights of Persons with Disabilities and debating and adopting proposed amendments to the convention.

The convention was drafted between 2002 and 2006 by the Ad Hoc Committee on a Comprehensive and Integral International Convention on the Protection and Promotion of the Rights and Dignity of Persons with Disabilities, a committee of the United Nations General Assembly with the participation of NGOs. The convention entered into force on May 3, 2008.

▓ International Convention for the Protection of All Persons from Enforced Disappearance, 2006

The International Convention for the Protection of All Persons from Enforced Disappearance[68] was adopted by the UN General Assembly on December 20, 2006, and opened for signature on February 6, 2007. According to article 1, "no exceptional circumstances whatsoever, whether a state of war or a threat of war, internal political instability or any other public emergency, may be invoked as a justification for enforced disappearance." *Enforced disappearance* is defined in article 2 as "the arrest, detention, abduction or any other form of deprivation of liberty by agents of the State or by persons or groups of persons acting with the authorization, support or acquiescence of the State, followed by a refusal to acknowledge the deprivation of liberty or by concealment of the fate or whereabouts of the disappeared person, which place such a person outside the protection of the law." Enforced disappearance is on the increase in some parts of the world. It is used by governments to silence dissent, eliminate political opposition, and persecute ethnic, religious, and political groups.[69] The International Coalition Against Enforced Disappearances is a global network of NGOs working for the early ratification and effective implementation of the convention.[70]

▓ Regional Human Rights Treaty Regimes

The global human rights treaties are complemented by regional treaty regimes, the most complex of which is the European system.[71] The European Convention for the Protection of Human Rights and Fundamental Freedoms,[72] also known as the European Convention on Human Rights, was drafted by the Council of Europe, opened for signature on November 4, 1950, and entered into force on September 3, 1953.[73] The convention was intended to enforce the rights contained in the Universal Declaration of Human Rights. Thirteen basic rights of individuals are contained in the original convention, including the right to life (article 2), the prohibition of torture (article 3), and the right to a fair trial (article 6). Other rights or freedoms have been added in a series of protocols; Protocol No. 13, for example, concerns "the abolition of the death penalty in all circumstances."[74] The convention is of particular importance for its system of rights enforcement; the original European Court of Human Rights was set up in 1959, and the court in its current form dates from 1998.[75] It has delivered over 10,000 judgments.

The convention is a product of the Council of Europe rather than of the European Union or its predecessors, but the EU has used the convention as a benchmark for the development of human rights protection within the union.[76] The convention was a strong influence on the text of the 2000 European Union Charter of Fundamental Rights, which sets out the whole range of civil, political, economic, and social rights of European citizens and all persons resident in the European Union and which came into effect upon entry into force of the Treaty of Lisbon on December 1, 2009.

The rights covered in the European Convention on Human Rights are primarily civil and political rights; the European Social Charter of 1961 and its protocols address economic and social rights.[77] The revised Social Charter was opened for signature in 1996 and entered into force in 1999. Compliance with the European Social Charter is monitored by the European Committee of Social Rights.

The Organization of American States was established at the Ninth International Conference of American States, held in Bogotá, Colombia, in 1948. As well as conclude the Charter of the Organization of American States, the states of the American region meeting in Bogotá adopted the American Declaration of the Rights and Duties of Man.[78] This is similar in content to, but preceded by several months, the Universal Declaration of Human Rights. This declaration includes ten articles setting out the duties of the citizen, including to "acquire at least an elementary education" and to "render whatever civil and military service his country may require for its defence and preservation, and, in case of public disaster, to render such services as may be in his power."

The next major step in creating a regional human rights system was the 1959 establishment by the Organization of American States of the Inter-American Commission on Human Rights.[79] It was agreed on by a resolution of the Fifth Meeting of Consultation of Ministers of Foreign Affairs rather than by treaty, reflecting reluctance on the part of the countries involved to take legally binding obligations as regards human rights.[80] The Inter-American Commission on Human Rights began work the following year. In its early years it was concerned primarily with preparing country reports, for which it conducted on-site investigations.[81] With the return of more countries to a democratic form of government and with the 1978 entry into force of the American Convention on Human Rights,[82] the individual complaint procedure became a more prominent part of its work in the 1980s.

The 1969 American Convention on Human Rights focuses on civil and political rights, although articles 26 and 42 are dedicated to the progressive development of economic, social, and cultural rights. The Additional Protocol to the American Convention on Human Rights in the Area of Economic, Social, and Cultural Rights came into effect on November 16, 1999. The American Convention on Human Rights provided for a compulsory individual petition procedure (article 44) and created the Inter-American Court of Human Rights.[83] This court has an advisory and contentious jurisdiction. The right of individual petition to the commission is mandatory in the convention; by article 44 any person, group of persons, or nongovernmental entity legally recognized in one or more member states of the Organization of American States may lodge petitions with the commission containing denunciations or complaints of violation of the convention by a state party. The commission also has jurisdiction over petitions filed by individuals from states not party to the convention, as they relate to the American Declaration. Once the commission's procedures have been completed, the commission or the state concerned can submit the matter to the Inter-American Court of Human Rights so long as the state concerned has accepted the court's jurisdiction. Compared to the European system, the issues that have been dealt with by both the commission and the court have concerned gross, rather than ordinary, violations of human rights, including forced disappearance, killing, torture, and the arbitrary detention of political opponents.[84]

The newest of the three regional systems is that of the African Union. Also known as the Banjul Charter, the African Charter on Human Rights and Peoples' Rights[85] was adopted unanimously on June 17, 1981, by the Organization of African Unity and entered into force in 1986. The preamble takes into consideration "the virtues of [the African] historical tradition and the values of African civilization, which should inspire and characterize . . . reflection on the concept of human and peoples' rights." The charter covers civil and political rights, and by article 22(1) recognizes the right of all peoples "to their economic, social and cultural development." African society is said to place more emphasis on the community than on the individuals within the community. This, together with a Marxist influence,[86] led to inclusion in the African Charter of "peoples" rights.[87] Also notable is that it imposes duties on the individual;[88] article 27 provides that the individual has duties toward his family and society, the state and other legally recognized communities, and the international community. So-called clawback clauses do, however, serve to limit the rights provided for in the charter;[89] the profession and free practice of religion is, for example, "subject to law and order." Article 14 guarantees the right to property; the right "may only be encroached upon in the interest of public need and in accordance with the provisions of appropriate laws."

The African Charter provided for the establishment of the African Commission on Human and Peoples' Rights to monitor the convention. The commission met for the first time in 1987.[90] On June 8, 1998, the Organization of African Unity adopted the Protocol to the African Charter on Human and Peoples' Rights on the Establishment of an African Court on Human and People's Rights.[91] The African Court issued its first judgment on December 15, 2009.

The Convention Governing the Specific Aspects of Refugee Problems in Africa 1969[92] is notable for its definition of refugees, which is broader than that of the 1951 convention; it includes "every person who, owing to external aggression, occupation, foreign domination or events seriously disturbing public order in either part or the whole of his country of origin or nationality, is compelled to leave his place of habitual residence in order to seek refuge in another place outside his country of origin or nationality." The 1990 African Charter on the Rights and Welfare of the Child entered into force in 1999; the African Union in 2003 adopted the Protocol to the African Charter on Human and Peoples' Rights on the Rights of Women in Africa (the Maputo Protocol)[93] and on October 22, 2009, approved the African Union Convention for the Protection and Assistance of Internally Displaced Persons in Africa (the Kampala Convention).[94]

■ Human Rights in Sociopolitical Context

There have been critics of the human rights movement from within the movement itself. Feminists have critiqued the notion of "human" rights, pointing out that the supposed gender neutrality of human rights documents and rhetoric has disguised a masculine bias in the selective promotion and protection of human rights. If, for example, the original International Bill of Rights had really been addressed to all human beings, why was a separate women's convention required? Just how do human rights relate to women's rights?[95] Similarly, the 1948 Universal Declaration "utterly failed to encompass the circumstances and worldviews of indigenous peoples, and . . . never considered their participation in the norm-creating processes as essential to establish the claim of universality."[96]

There has in recent years been considerable debate regarding the duty of states, regardless of their political, economic, and cultural systems, to promote rights versus their relativity to a particular religious and cultural tradition.[97] Is it possible to elucidate rights that are truly universal, or has the development of international human rights law been a process of Western imperialism?[98] The Final Declaration and Programme of Action of the World Conference of Human Rights, held in Vienna in 1993, proclaimed all human rights to be "universal, indivisible and interdependent and interrelated." Although it explicitly stipulated that "it is the duty of States, regardless of their political, economic and cultural systems, to promote and protect all human rights and fundamental freedoms," this was preceded by the qualification that "the significance of national and regional particularities and various historical, cultural and religious backgrounds must be borne in mind."[99]

The debate as to the universality of rights is not a new phenomenon arising from the globalizing of world politics but has for centuries taken place within Western thought itself.[100] The particular rights that have been incorporated into international human rights law are historically contingent and may evolve in tandem with other strands of sociopolitical change. This is evident, in part, from the ongoing definitional debates that surround several human rights treaty regimes—how, for example, to define the terms *genocide*[101] or *refugees*.[102]

The temporal relativity of rights is also evident in the notion of "generations" of human rights. Civil and political rights are sometimes referred to as *first-generation* human rights; economic, social, and cultural rights are referred to as *second-generation* rights. The importance of the 1993 conference declaring all human rights to be indivisible stemmed from the fact that civil and political rights are associated with the eighteenth-century Declaration on the Rights of Man whereas economic, social, and cultural rights derived from the growth of socialist ideals in the late nineteenth and early twentieth centuries and the impact of the labor movement.[103] Whereas the former Soviet States had believed in the supremacy of economic, social, and cultural rights, Western states have given priority to civil and political rights.

Third-generation rights are usually deemed those that will benefit groups and peoples rather than just individuals,[104] including the right to self-determination and the right to development. The right to development was declared by the General Assembly in its 1986 Declaration on the Right to Development[105] and recognized in the African Charter of Human and Peoples' Rights.[106] Article 24 of the African Charter on Human and Peoples' Rights refers to the right of peoples "to a general satisfactory environment favourable to their development." The right "to live in a healthy environment" was referred to in the Additional Protocol to the American Convention on Human Rights in the Area of Economic, Social, and Cultural Rights.

The human rights of indigenous peoples are sometimes referred to as *fourth-generation* rights.[107] Indigenous peoples were not expressly included in the text of any United Nations human rights instrument before the 1989 Convention on the Rights of the Child;[108] article 30 of that convention provides that a child "who is indigenous shall not be denied the right, in community with other members of his or her group, to enjoy his or her own culture, to profess and practise his or her own religions, or to use his or her own language." The International Labor Organization had, however, acted before this, its Convention 107 of 1957[109] having been primarily a response to reports of labor discrimination in Latin America.[110] Article 2 of the Convention Concerning the Protection and Integration of Indigenous and Other Tribal and Semi-Tribal Populations in Independent Countries accorded governments the "primary responsibility for developing co-ordinated and systematic action for the protection of the populations concerned and their progressive integration into the life of their respective communities."

The convention came to be criticized for having adopted a 1950s-style paternalistic or integrationist approach toward indigenous peoples[111] and so was revised and replaced by ILO Convention 169 of 1989.[112] Article 2 of the Convention Concerning Indigenous and Tribal Peoples in Independent Countries (Convention 169) recognized the responsibility of governments for "developing, with the participation of the peoples concerned, coordinated and systematic action to protect the rights of [indigenous and tribal peoples] and to guarantee respect for their integrity." Article 3(1) of the convention provides that indigenous and tribal peoples shall enjoy the full measure of human rights and fundamental freedoms "without hindrance or discrimination."

The UN Declaration on the Rights of Indigenous Peoples[113] was adopted in 2007 "as a standard of achievement to be pursued." Article 1 recognizes that indigenous peoples have the right to the full enjoyment, as a collective or as individuals, of all human rights in international human rights law. Articles 3 and 4 recognize the right of indigenous peoples to self-determination and to autonomy or self-government in matters relating to their internal and local affairs. The nonbinding declaration, which had been some twenty years in the making, was adopted by 143 votes to 4 (Australia, Canada, New Zealand, and the United States), with 11 abstentions. Australia has subsequently reversed its position and endorsed the declaration.[114]

■ Conclusion

Long-standing questions for international human rights law include that as to the relative desirability of a widely ratified treaty but with relatively weak or indeterminate provisions versus a much tighter treaty with fewer states parties. Along similar lines is the question of the extent to which there is a direct correlation between treaty ratification and practical respect for human rights. Although international human rights norms do appear to have had some effect on the behavior of states toward their citizens,[115] ascertaining just how much effect and through what processes is a challenging task. James Cavallaro and Stephanie Brewer have pointed out, for example, that although the European Court of Human Rights is undoubtedly influential in Western Europe, it is facing fresh challenges in ensuring respect for its decisions by newer members of the Council of Europe that suffer from large-scale endemic human rights abuses and that may be resistant to supranational courts; the growth of human rights bodies with binding legal authority does not ineluctably translate into better human rights on the ground.[116] The influence of international courts and treaty bodies may often lie in their empowering local activists and bringing greater transnational attention to the issue rather than through direct impact on the behavior of governments. And where a human rights violation takes place in the private sphere or under the control of local authorities, it may take time for a national government to effect change even if it is committed to doing so. The existence of a body of international human rights law by no means guarantees improved respect for human rights but can make an important contribution toward achieving that goal.

▓ Notes

1. For background, see John P. Humphrey, "The UN Charter and the Universal Declaration of Human Rights," in Evan Luard, ed., *The International Protection of Human Rights* (London: Thames and Hudson, 1967), pp. 39–58, esp. 39–46.

2. Ian Brownlie, ed., *Basic Documents on Human Rights,* 3rd ed. (Oxford: Clarendon, 1993), p. 1. Reflecting in 1950 on the causes for international law coming to give individual rights, Sir Hersch Lauterpacht suggested that they included "the realisation of the dangers besetting international peace as the result of the denial of fundamental human rights." H. Lauterpacht, *International Law and Human Rights* (London: Stevens and Sons, 1950), p. 62.

3. General Assembly Resolution 217 A(III), December 10, 1948, UN Doc A/810, p. 71; and Shirley V. Scott, ed., *International Law and Politics: Key Documents* (Boulder, CO: Lynne Rienner, 2006), pp. 335–340. See also Jochen von Bernstorff, "The Changing Fortune of the Universal Declaration of Human Rights: Genesis and Symbolic Dimensions of the Turn to Human Rights in International Law," *European Journal of International Law* 19 (2008): 903–924; Gudmundur Alfredsson and Asbjørn Eide, eds., *The Universal Declaration of Human Rights: A Common Standard of Achievement* (The Hague: Martinus Nijhoff, c1999); and Asbjørn Eide et al., eds., *The Universal Declaration of Human Rights: A Commentary* (London: Scandinavian University Press, 1992).

4. Johannes Morsink, *The Universal Declaration of Human Rights: Origins, Drafting, and Intent* (Philadelphia: University of Pennsylvania Press, 1999), p. 37. See also Susan Waltz, "Universalising Human Rights: The Role of Small States in the Construction of the Universal Declaration of Human Rights," *Human Rights Quarterly* 23 (2001): 44–72.

5. Hernan Santa Cruz, Chilean delegate to the Third Committee, cited in Morsink, *The Universal Declaration of Human Rights,* p. 38.

6. 6 *International Legal Materials (ILM)* 368 (1967); and Scott, *International Law and Politics,* pp. 371–388. See also M. Bossuyt, *Guide to the Travaux Préparatoires of the International Covenant on Civil and Political Rights* (Dordrecht, the Netherlands: Martinus Nijhoff, 1987).

7. 6 *ILM* 360 (1967); and Scott, *International Law and Politics,* pp. 396–405.

8. See Sally Morphet, "Article 1 of the Human Rights Covenants: Its Development and Current Significance," in Dilys M. Hill, ed., *Human Rights and Foreign Policy: Principles and Practice* (Houndmills, UK: Macmillan, 1989), pp. 67–88.

9. See http://www2.ohchr.org. See also P. R. Ghandhi, *The Human Rights Committee and the Right of Individual Communication: Law and Practice* (Aldershot, UK: Ashgate, 1998).

10. International Covenant on Civil and Political Rights, article 40(4).

11. Ibid., article 41.

12. Ibid., article 42.

13. 6 *ILM* 383 (1967); and Scott, *International Law and Politics,* pp. 388–391.

14. 29 *ILM* 1465 (1990); and Scott, *International Law and Politics,* pp. 392–395.

15. International Covenant on Economic, Social, and Cultural Rights, article 2(1).

16. 48 *ILM* 262 (2009). For background and analysis, see the Introductory Note by Tara J. Melish, 48 *ILM* 256 (2009).

17. Roger Smith, "Human Destructiveness and Politics: The Twentieth Century as an Age of Genocide," in Isidor Wallimann and Michael Dobkowski, eds., *Genocide and the Modern Age: Etiology and Case Studies of Mass Death* (Westport, CT: Greenwood, 1987), pp. 21–39; and Israel W. Charny, "The Study of Genocide," in Israel Charny, ed., *Genocide: A Critical Bibliographic Review* (New York: Facts on File, 1988), pp. 1–19. See also M. Levine, "Why Is the Twentieth Century the Century of Genocide?" *Journal of World History* 11, no. 2 (2000): 305–336; and Samuel Totten, William S. Parsons, and Israel Charny, eds., *Century of Genocide: Eyewitness Accounts and Critical Views* (New York: Garland, 1997).

18. Donald L. Niewyk, "Holocaust: The Jews," in Totten, Parsons, and Charny, *Century of Genocide,* p. 136.

19. Raphael Lemkin, *Axis Rule in Occupied Europe* (New York: Howard Fertig, 1973), p. 79.

20. Remarks of Henry T. King Jr., in Henry T. King Jr., Benjamin B. Ferencz, and Whitney R. Harris, "Origins of the Genocide Convention," *Case Western Reserve Journal of International Law* 40, no. 1-2 (2008): 13–34, esp. 14.

21. Richard W. Edwards, "Contributions of the Genocide Convention to the Development of International Law," *Ohio Northern University Law Review* 8 (1981): 300–320.

22. Matthew Lippman, "The Convention on the Prevention and Punishment of the Crime of Genocide: Fifty Years Later," *Arizona Journal of International and Comparative Law* 15, no. 2 (1998): 427–428, esp. 449.

23. *The United Nations and Human Rights, 1945–1995* (New York: United Nations, 1995), p. 20.

24. 78 United Nations Treaty Series (UNTS) 277; and Scott, *International Law and Politics,* pp. 221–224. See also Paola Gaeta, ed., *The UN Genocide Convention: A Commentary* (Oxford: Oxford University Press, 2009).

25. Raphael Lemkin, "Genocide as a Crime Under International Law," *American Journal of International Law* 41, no. 1 (1947): 145–151, esp. 147.

26. See David Luban, "Calling Genocide by Its Rightful Name: Lemkin's Word, Darfur, and the UN Report," *Chicago Journal of International Law* 7 (2006): 303–320.

27. Lippman, "The Convention on the Prevention and Punishment of the Crime of Genocide," p. 452.

28. See "Counterpoint," *Case Western Reserve Journal of International Law* 18 (1986): 277–282.

29. Howard Ball, *Prosecuting War Crimes and Genocide: The Twentieth Century Experience* (Lawrence: University Press of Kansas, 1999), p. 219.

30. www.unhcr.org.

31. 189 UNTS 137; and Scott, *International Law and Politics,* pp. 341–354. For the travaux préparatoires, see A. Takkenberg and C. C. Tahbaz, *The Collected Preparatoires of the 1951 Convention Relating to the Status of Refugees,* 3 vols. (Amsterdam: Dutch Refugee Council, 1990).

32. Gil Loescher, "Refugee Movements and International Security," *Adelphi Papers* 268 (Summer 1992); and see Gil Loescher, "Refugees and Foreign Policy," in Hill, *Human Rights and Foreign Policy,* pp. 130–139.

33. See James C. Hathaway, "A Reconsideration of the Underlying Premise of Refugee Law," *Harvard International Law Journal* 31, no. 1 (Winter 1990): 129–183; Dennis Gallagher, "The Evolution of the International Refugee System," *International Migration Review* 23, no. 3 (1989): 579–598, esp. 594; and Tom J. Farer, "How the International System Copes with Involuntary Migration: Norms, Institutions, and State Practice," *Human Rights Quarterly* 17 (1995): 72–100.

34. Gil Loescher, "The International Refugee Regime: Stretched to the Limit?" *Journal of International Affairs* 47, no. 2 (1994): 351–377, esp. 356.

35. Alex Cunliffe, "The Refugee Crises: A Study of the United Nations High Commission for Refugees," *Political Studies* 43 (1995): 278–290, esp. 281.

36. 606 UNTS 267; and Scott, *International Law and Politics,* pp. 355–358.

37. Convention Relating to the Status of Refugees, article 42, and Protocol Relating to the Status of Refugees, article VII.

38. Lisa Hassan, "Deterrence Measures and the Preservation of Asylum in the United Kingdom and United States," *Journal of Refugee Studies* 13, no. 2 (2000): 184–204, esp. 186. See also M. Fullerton, "Failing the Test: Germany Leads Europe in Dismantling Refugee Protection," *Texas International Law Journal* 36 (2001): 231–276; and M. J. Gibney, *The Ethics and Politics of Asylum: Liberal Democracy and the Response to Refugees* (Cambridge: Cambridge University Press, 2004).

39. See Simon Bagshaw, "Responding to the Challenge of Internal Forced Migration: The Guiding Principles," in Ryszard Cholewinski and Richard Perruchoud, *International Migration Law: Developing Paradigms and Key Challenges* (The Hague: T. M. C. Asser, 2007), pp. 189–202; Roberta Cohen, "The Global Crisis of Internal Displacement," in James Daniel White and Anthony J. Marsella, eds., *Fear of Persecution: Global Human Rights, International Law, and Human Well-Being* (Lanham, MD: Lexington, 2007), pp. 15–32; and Catherine Phuong, *The International Protection of Internally Displaced Persons* (Cambridge: Cambridge University Press, 2005).

40. See Erika Feller, Volker Türk, and Frances Nicholson, eds., *Refugee Protection in International Law: UNHCR's Global Consultations on International Protection* (Cambridge: Cambridge University Press, 2003).

41. Article 1, "Declaration Reaffirming the Commitment of Signatory States to the 1951 Refugee Convention," available at http://www.hrea.org.

42. Preamble article 7, ibid.

43. See, inter alia, Philippe Leclerc, ed., "Nationality and Reduction of Statelessness: International, National and Regional Perspectives," special edition of *Refugee Survey Quarterly* 25, no. 3 (2006): 5–261; Gil Loescher, Alexander Betts, and James Milner, *The United Nations High Commissioner for Refugees (UNHCR): The Politics and Practice of Refugee Protection into the Twenty-first Century* (New York: Routledge, 2008); J. McAdam and B. Saul, "An Insecure Climate for Human Security? Climate-Induced Displacement and International Law," in A. Edwards and C. Ferstman, eds., *Human Security and Non-Citizens: Law, Policy, and International Affairs* (Cambridge: Cambridge University Press, 2010); Matthew Gibney, *The Ethics and Politics of Asylum: Liberal Democracy and the Response to Refugees* (New York: Cambridge University Press, 2004); Matthew E. Price, *Rethinking Asylum: History, Purpose, and Limits* (Cambridge: Cambridge University Press, 2009); and Silvia Scarpa, *Trafficking in Human Beings: Modern Slavery* (Oxford: Oxford University Press, 2008).

44. See Egon Schwelb, "The International Convention on the Elimination of All Forms of Racial Discrimination, *International and Comparative Law Quarterly* 15 (1966): 996–1059.

45. 5 *ILM* 352 (1966); and Scott, *International Law and Politics,* pp. 359–370.

46. See http://www2.ohchr.org.

47. 19 *ILM* 33 (1980); and Scott, *International Law and Politics,* pp. 406–417. See, inter alia, N. Burrows, "The 1979 Convention on the Elimination of All Forms of Discrimination Against Women," *Netherlands International Law Review* 32 (1985): 419–460; K. Engle, "International Human Rights and Feminism: When Two Discourses Meet," *Michigan Journal of International Law* 13, no. 515 (Spring 1992): 517–610; Elizabeth Evatt, "Finding a Voice for Women's Rights: The Early Days of CEDAW," *George Washington International Law Review* 34, no. 3 (2002): 515–553; M. Galey, "Promoting Nondiscrimination Against Women," *International Studies Quarterly* 23, no. 2 (1979); and A. R. Lars, *Guide to the Travaux Preparatoires of the UN Convention on the Elimination of All Forms of Discrimination Against Women* (Dordrecht, the Netherlands: Martinus Nijhoff, 1993). See also "CEDAW Success Stories," http://www.unifem.org.

48. Engle, "International Human Rights and Feminism," p. 521.

49. Convention on the Elimination of All Forms of Discrimination Against Women, article 4.

50. See http://www2.ohchr.org . See also Hanna Beate Schöpp-Schilling, ed., *The Circle of Empowerment: Twenty-five Years of the UN Committee on the Elimination of Discrimination Against Women* (New York: Feminist Press, 2007).

51. "United Nations General Assembly: Optional Protocol to the Convention on the Elimination of All Forms of Discrimination Against Women, October 15, 1999, 39 *ILM* 281 (2000). See Laboni Amena Hoq, "The Women's Convention and Its Optional Protocol: Empowering Women to Claim Their Internationally Protected Rights," *Columbia Human Rights Law Review* 32, no. 3 (2001): 677–726; and Emilia Della Torre, "Women's Business: The Development of an Optional Protocol to the United Nations Women's Convention," *Australian Journal of Human Rights* 6, no. 2 (2000): 181–193.

52. 23 *ILM* 1027 (1984); Scott, *International Law and Politics,* pp. 225–237. See, inter alia, Peter R. Baehr, "The General Assembly: Negotiating the Convention on Torture," in David P. Forsythe, *The United Nations in the World Political Economy:*

Essays in Honour of Leon Gordenker (London: Macmillan, 1989), pp. 36–53; J. Herman Burgers and Hans Danelius, *The United Nations Convention Against Torture: A Handbook on the Convention Against Torture and Other Cruel, Inhuman, or Degrading Treatment or Punishment* (Dordrecht, the Netherlands: Martinus Nijhoff, 1988); and Manfred Nowak and Elizabeth McArthur, *The United Nations Convention Against Torture: A Commentary* (Oxford: Oxford University Press, 2008).

53. J. Herman Burgers, "An Arduous Delivery: The United Nations Convention Against Torture (1984)," in Johan Kaufmann, ed., *Effective Negotiation: Case Studies in Conference Diplomacy* (The Hague: Martinus Nijhoff, 1989), pp. 45–52, esp. 46.

54. *Review of the Multilateral Treaty-Making Process* (New York: United Nations, 1985), p. 206.

55. See http://www2.ohchr.org. See also Chris Ingelese, *The UN Committee Against Torture: An Assessment* (The Hague: Kluwer Law International, 2001); and Amrita Mukherjee, *Torture and the United Nations: Charter and Treaty-based Monitoring* (London: Cameron May, 2008).

56. 42 *ILM* 26 (2003).

57. See Karen J. Greenberg and Joshua L. Dratel, eds., *The Torture Papers: The Road to Abu Ghraib* (New York: Cambridge University Press, 2005); Philippe Sands, *Torture Team: Rumsfeld's Memo and the Betrayal of American Values* (New York: Palgrave Macmillan, 2008); and Michael Otterman, *American Torture: From the Cold War to Abu Ghraib and Beyond* (Melbourne: Melbourne University Press, 2007).

58. Committee Against Torture, "Consideration of Reports Submitted by States Parties Under Article 19 of the Convention: Concluding Observations of the Committee Against Torture," December 12, 2008, http://daccess-dds-ny.un.org.

59. "'We Cannot Say That Torture Has Decreased,' Reveals UN Committee Against Torture on Key Anniversary," Office of the High Commissioner for Human Rights, http://www.ohchr.org.

60. 28 *ILM* 1448 (1989); and Scott, *International Law and Politics,* pp. 418–438. See also Sharon Detrick, *A Commentary on the United Nations Convention on the Rights of the Child* (The Hague: Martinus Nijhoff, 1999); and A. Glenn Mower Jr., *The Convention on the Rights of the Child: International Law Support for Children* (Westport, CT: Greenwood, 1997).

61. *The United Nations and Human Rights, 1945–1995* (New York: United Nations, 1995), p. 84.

62. See www2.ohchr.org. See also Geraldine Van Bueren, "Committee on the Rights of the Child: Overcoming Inertia in This Age of No Alternatives," in Malcolm Langford, ed., *Social Rights Jurisprudence: Emerging Trends in International and Comparative Law* (Cambridge: Cambridge University Press, 2008), pp. 569–587.

63. 39 *ILM* 1285 (2000).

64. For an overview of the conference, see that prepared by the Centre for Human Rights in Geneva for the *Human Rights Law Journal* 14, no. 9-10 (November 30, 1993): 346–352. See also Adama Dieng, "Introduction," *International Commission of Jurists Review* 50 (June 1993): 3–7.

65. Reproduced in the *Human Rights Law Journal* 14, no.9-10 (November 30, 1993): 352–363.

66. See Andrew Clapham, "Creating the High Commissioner for Human Rights: The Outside Story," *European Journal of International Law* 5 (1994): 556–568.

67. 46 *ILM* 443 (2007).

68. Text is available at http://www2.ohchr.org. See Tullio Scovazzi and Gabriella Citronic, *The Struggle Against Enforced Disappearance and the 2007 United Nations Convention* (The Hague: Martinus Nijhoff, 2007).

69. Amnesty International, "Seven More Ratifications Needed for Enforced Disappearance Convention to Enter into Force," August 28, 2009, http://www .amnesty.org.

70. See http://www.icaed.org.

71. Dinah Shelton, *Regional Protection of Human Rights* (Oxford: Oxford University Press, 2008).

72. European Convention on Human Rights and Fundamental Freedoms 213 UNTS 221.

73. On the negotiation of the European Convention on Human Rights see G. Marston, "The UK's Part in the Preparation of the European Convention on Human Rights," *International and Comparative Law Quarterly* 42 (1993): 796–826; and A. H. Robertson and J. G. Merrills, *Human Rights in Europe,* 3rd ed. (Manchester, UK: Manchester University Press, 1993), chapter 1.

74. 41 *ILM* 515 (2002).

75. The webpage of the court is http://www.echr.coe.int.

76. Ann Sherlock, *The European Union and the European Convention on Human Rights* (Oxford: Oxford University Press, 2010).

77. See Règis Brillat, "The European Social Charter," in G. Alfredsson et al., eds., *International Human Rights Monitoring Mechanisms* (The Hague: Martinus Nijhoff, 2001), pp. 601–606; and Donna Gomien, David Harris, and Leo Zwaak, *Law and Practice of the European Convention on Human Rights and the European Social Charter* (Strasbourg, France: Council of Europe, 1996).

78. Organization of American States Resolution XXX, OAS Off. Rec. OEA/ Ser.L/V/I.4 Rev. (1965).

79. See http://www.cidh.oas.org/. On the creation of the commission, see C. Medina Quiroga, *The Battle of Human Rights: Gross Systematic Violations and the Inter-American System* (Dordrecht, the Netherlands: Martinus Nijhoff, 1988).

80. Christina Cerna, "The Inter-American Commission on Human Rights: Its Organization and Examination of Petitions and Communications," in David J. Harris and Stephen Livingstone, eds., *The Inter-American System of Human Rights* (Oxford: Clarendon, 1998), pp. 65–114, esp. 66.

81. Ibid.

82. 9 *ILM* 673 (1970).

83. See http://www.corteidh.or.cr.

84. See David Harris, "Regional Protection of Human Rights: The Inter-American Achievement," in Harris and Livingstone, *The Inter-American System of Human Rights,* pp. 1–29; and James L. Cavallaro and Stephanie Erin Brewer, "Reevaluating Regional Human Rights Litigation in the Twenty-First Century: The Case of the Inter-American Court," *American Journal of International Law* 102 (2008): 768–827, esp. 774.

85. 21 *ILM* 59 (1982). For background and commentary, see Theo van Boven, "The Relations Between Peoples' Rights and Human Rights in the African Charter," *Human Rights Journal* 7, no. 2-4 (1986): 183–194; Malcolm D. Evans and Rachel

Murray, eds., *The African Charter on Human and Peoples' Rights: The System in Practice, 1986–2006*, 2nd ed. (Cambridge: Cambridge University Press, 2008); Michelo Hansungule, "The African Charter on Human and Peoples Rights: A Critical Review," *African Yearbook of International Law* 8 (2000): 265–331; Christof Heyns and Magnus Killander, "The African Regional Human Rights System," in Felipe Gomez Isa and Koen de Feyer, eds., *International Protection of Human Rights: Achievements and Challenges* (Bilbao, Spain: University of Deusto, 2006), available at http://www.ssrn.com/; and Isaac Nguema, "Human Rights Perspectives in Africa: The Roots of a Constant Challenge," *Human Rights Law Journal* 11, no. 3–4 (1990): 261–283.

86. Michelo Hansungule, "The African Charter on Human and Peoples Rights: A Critical Review," *African Yearbook of International Law* 8 (2000): 265–331, esp. 273.

87. For discussion of how to define *peoples* see Yoram Dinstein, "Collective Human Rights of Peoples and Minorities, *International and Comparative Law Quarterly* 25 (January 1976): 102–120.

88. Part 1, chapter II, articles 27–29.

89. Cees Flinterman and Catherine Henderson, "The African Charter on Human and Peoples' Rights," in R. Hanski and M. Suksi, eds., *An Introduction to the International Protection of Human Rights: A Textbook* (Turku, Finland: Abo Akademi University Institute for Human Rights, 1997).

90. See, inter alia, Evelyn Ama Ankumah, *The African Commission on Human and Peoples' Rights: Practice and Procedures* (The Hague: Martinus Nijhoff, 1996); and Oji Umozurike, "The Complaint Procedures of the African Commission on Human and People's Rights," in Gudmundur Alfredsson, Jonas Grimheden, Bertram G. Ramcharan, and Alfred de Zayas, eds., *International Human Rights Monitoring Mechanisms: Essays in Honour of Jakob Th. Möller* (The Hague: Martinus Nijhoff, 2001), pp. 707–712.

91. Protocol to the African Charter of Human and People's Rights, OAU Doc. OAU/LEG/EXP/AFCHPRPROT (2). See, inter alia, Makau Mutua, "The African Human Rights Court: A Two-Legged Stool?" *Human Rights Quarterly* 21, no. 2 (1999): 342–363; and Gino J. Naldi and Konstantinos Magliveras, "Reinforcing the African System of Human Rights: The Protocol on the Establishment of a Regional Court of Human and Peoples' Rights," *Netherlands Quarterly Human Rights* 16 (1998): 431–456.

92. 1001 UNTS 45, also available at http://heiwww.unige.ch. The convention entered into force on June 20, 1974. For the background to the convention, see Ivor Jackson, *The Refugee Concept in Group Situations* (The Hague: Martinus Nijhoff, 1999). For discussion, see Eduardo Arboleda, "Refugee Definition in Africa and Latin America: The Lessons of Pragmatism," *International Journal of Refugee Law* 3, no. 2 (1991): 185–205; and George Okoth-Obbo, "Thirty Years On: A Legal Review of the 1969 OAU Refugee Convention," *African Yearbook of International Law* (2001): 3–69.

93. Adrien Katherine Wing, "Women's Rights and Africa's Evolving Landscape: The Women's Protocol of the Banjul Charter," in Jeremy I. Levitt, ed., *Africa: Mapping New Boundaries in International Law* (Oxford: Hart, 2008), pp. 13–34.

94. The text of the treaty and status information is available at http://www.africa-union.org/root/au/Documents/Treaties/treaties.htm.

95. See, inter alia, C. Bunch, "Women's Rights as Human Rights: Toward a Revision of Human Rights," *Human Rights Quarterly* 12 (1990): 486–498; Rebecca J.

Cook, ed., *Human Rights of Women: National and International Perspectives* (Philadelphia: University of Pennsylvania Press, 1994); Engle, "International Human Rights and Feminism"; and V. Spike Peterson and Laura Parisi, "Are Women Human? It's Not an Academic Question," in Tony Evans, ed., *Human Rights Fifty Years On: A Reappraisal* (Manchester, UK: Manchester University Press, 1998), pp. 132–160.

96. Richard Falk, *Human Rights Horizons* (New York: Routledge, 2000), p. 51.

97. See, inter alia, Christina Cerna, "Universality of Human Rights and Cultural Diversity: Implementation of Human Rights in Different Socio-Cultural Contexts," *Human Rights Quarterly* 16 (1994): 740–782; Jack Donnelly, ed., *Universal Human Rights in Theory and Practice,* 2nd ed. (Ithaca, NY: Cornell University Press, 2003); Neil Englehart, "Rights and Culture in the Asian Values Argument: The Rise and Fall of Confucian Ethics in Singapore," *Human Rights Quarterly* 22, no. 2 (2000): 548–568; Makau Mutua, "Savages, Victims, and Saviors: The Metaphor of Human Rights," *Harvard International Law Journal* 42 (2001): 201; Fali S. Nariman, "The Universality of Human Rights," *International Commission of Jurists Review* 50 (June 1993): 8–22; A. Pollis, "Cultural Relativism Revisited: Through a State Prism," *Human Rights Quarterly* 18, no. 2 (1996): 316–344; Alison Dundes Renteln, *International Human Rights: Universalism Versus Relativism* (Newbury Park, CA: Sage, 1990); Ferdinand Teson, "International Human Rights and Cultural Relativity," *Virginia Journal of International Law* 25 (1985): 869–898; and G. J. H. van Hoof, "Asian Challenges to the Concept of Universality: Afterthoughts on the Vienna Conference on Human Rights," in Peter R. Baehr, Fried van Hoof, Liu Nanlai, Tao Zhenghua, and Jacqueline Smith, eds., *Human Rights: Chinese and Dutch Perspectives* (The Hague: Martinus Nijhoff, 1996), pp. 1–15.

98. For discussion of this and other challenges to the universality of human rights, see D. Otto, "Everything Is Dangerous: Some Post-Structural Tools for Rethinking the Universal Knowledge Claims of Human Rights Law," *Australian Journal of Human Rights* 5, no. 1 (1998): 17–47.

99. Vienna Declaration and Programme of Action Adopted at the World Conference on Human Rights, A/CONF.157/24, June 25, 1993, section I, para. 5.

100. See, for example, Chris Brown, "Universal Human Rights: A Critique," in Tim Dunne and Nicholas J. Wheeler, eds., *Human Rights in Global Politics* (Cambridge: Cambridge University Press, 1999), p. 103.

101. See, for example, George J. Andreopoulos, ed., *Genocide: Conceptual and Historical Dimensions* (Philadelphia: University of Pennsylvania Press, 1994).

102. See, for example, E. Arboleda and I. Hoy, "The Convention Refugee Definition in the West: Disharmony of Interpretation and Application," *International Journal of Refugee Law* 5, no. 1 (1993): 66–90.

103. Matthew C. R. Craven, *The International Covenant on Economic, Social, and Cultural Rights: A Perspective on Its Development* (Oxford: Clarendon, 1995), p. 8.

104. See P. H. Kooijmans, "Human Rights Universal Panacea? Some Reflections on the So-Called Human Rights of the Third Generation," *Netherlands International Law Review* 37 (1990): 315–329.

105. UN General Assembly Resolution 41/128, December 4, 1986.

106. For literature on the right to development, see, inter alia, Daniel Aguirre, *The Human Right to Development in a Globalized World* (Aldershot, UK: Ashgate, 2008); A. Rosas, "The Right to Development," in A. Eide, C. Krause, and A. Rosas,

Economic, Social, and Cultural Rights: A Textbook (Dordrecht, the Netherlands: Martinus Nijhoff, 2001), pp. 247–255; and Argun Sengupta, "On the Theory and Practice of the Right to Development," *Human Rights Quarterly* 24 (2002): 837–889.

107. See, inter alia, S. James Anaya, *Indigenous Peoples in International Law* (New York: Oxford University Press, 1996); and the collection of essays in S. James Anaya, ed., *International Law and Indigenous Peoples* (Abingdon, UK: Ashgate, 2003).

108. *The United Nations and Human Rights, 1945–1995* (New York: United Nations, 1995), p. 102.

109. Convention No. 107, "Convention Concerning the Protection and Integration of Indigenous Populations and Other Tribal and Semi-Tribal Populations in Independent Countries," International Labor Organization, *Conventions and Recommendations Adopted by the International Labour Conference, 1919–1966* (Geneva: International Labor Office, 1966), pp. 901–908.

110. Russel Lawrence Barsh, "Indigenous Peoples: An Emerging Object of International Law," *American Journal of International Law* 80 (1986): 369–385, esp. 370.

111. Convention No. 169, "Convention Concerning Indigenous and Tribal Peoples in Independent Countries," in International Labor Conference, *Conventions and Recommendations, 1919–1937* (Geneva: International Labor Office, 1937), pp. 1436–1447. See also Julian Burger and Paul Hunt, "Towards the International Protection of Indigenous Peoples' Rights," *Netherlands Quarterly of Human Rights* 12, no. 1 (1994): 405–423, esp. 406.

112. International Labor Organization Convention Concerning Indigenous and Tribal Peoples in Independent Countries (No. 169), 72 ILO Official Bulletin 59. See S. James Anaya, "Indigenous Peoples and Their Demands Within the Modern Human Rights Movement," in Yael Danieli, Elsa Stamatopoulou, and Clarence J. Dias, *The Universal Declaration of Human Rights: Fifty Years and Beyond* (New York: Baywood, 1999), pp. 149–161, esp. 156–158; L. Swepston, "The Indigenous and Tribal Peoples Convention (No. 169): Eight Years After Adoption," in C. Price Cohen, ed., *The Human Rights of Indigenous Peoples* (Ardsley, NY: Transnational, 1998), pp. 17–36; and Alexandra Xanthaki, *Indigenous Rights and United Nations Standards, Self-Determination, Culture, and Land* (New York: Cambridge University Press, 2007).

113. UN General Assembly A/RES/61/295, 46 ILM 1013 (2007).

114. United Nations Declaration on the Rights of Indigenous Peoples Adopted by the General Assembly, September 13, 2007, http://www.un.org.

115. See Thomas Risse, Stephen C. Ropp, and Kathryn Sikkink, eds., *The Power of Human Rights: International Norms and Domestic Change* (New York: Cambridge University Press, 1999).

116. Cavallaro and Brewer, "Reevaluating Regional Human Rights Litigation in the Twenty-First Century."

12

International Humanitarian Law

THE PHRASE *INTERNATIONAL HUMANITARIAN LAW* (IHL) DENOTES "a set of rules which seek, for humanitarian reasons, to limit the effects of armed conflict. It protects persons who are not or are no longer participating in the hostilities and restricts the means and methods of warfare."[1] Here we reach the *jus in bello,* the laws of war, that we set aside in Chapter 6 when examining the *jus ad bellum.* International humanitarian law is now regarded largely as a field of international law separate from that of arms control, which establishes controls over the production, testing, stockpiling, transfer, and deployment of weaponry by which conflict might be conducted.[2] There is nevertheless some overlap; even though arms control treaties do not directly address what happens when there is armed conflict, treaties relating to international humanitarian law that limit or prohibit weaponry could also be classified as arms control treaties. The Landmines Convention, to take one example, could be classified either as an addition to IHL or to the treaties on arms control.[3] The ICRC has played an integral role in the evolution of IHL and manages an online database containing the texts of treaties and their current status.[4] See Figure 12.1.

Laws governing the conduct of war are much older than those seeking to prevent states from initiating war; ancient societies of various civilizations had legal codes with humanitarian provisions similar to those found in the modern laws of war. Wars between Egypt and Sumeria in the second millennium B.C., for example, were governed by a complex set of rules obligating belligerents to distinguish combatants from civilians.[5] The Laws of Manu, the greatest of the ancient Hindu codes, prohibited Hindus from using poisoned arrows.[6] In the nineteenth century there began a process of codifying what we now refer to as "international humanitarian law." Modern

Figure 12.1 Some Landmarks in the Evolution of International Humanitarian Law

1856	Paris Declaration on Maritime War
1864	Geneva Convention on Wounded and Sick
1868	Declaration Renouncing the Use, in Time of War, of Explosive Projectiles Under 400 Grammes Weight (The St. Petersburg Declaration)
1899	Hague Conventions and Declarations
1907	Hague Conventions and Declaration
1925	Geneva Protocol for the Prohibition of the Use in War of Asphyxiating, Poisonous, or Other Gases, and of Bacteriological Methods of Warfare
1929	Geneva Convention for the Amelioration of the Condition of the Wounded and Sick in Armies in the Field
1948	United Nations Convention on the Prevention and Punishment of the Crime of Genocide
1949	The Geneva Conventions
1954	Hague Convention for the Protection of Cultural Property in the Event of Armed Conflict
1976	Convention on the Prohibition of Military or Any Other Hostile Use of Environmental Modification Techniques
1977	Protocols Additional to the Geneva Conventions
1980	Convention on Prohibitions or Restrictions on the Use of Certain Conventional Weapons Which May Be Deemed to Be Excessively Injurious or to Have Indiscriminate Effects (CCW)
1998	Rome Statute of the International Criminal Court
2008	Convention on Cluster Munitions

IHL has two streams: that pertaining to limitations or prohibitions of specific means and methods of warfare (the Hague laws), and that regarding the protection of civilians and those no longer fighting (the Geneva laws). This distinction has been less useful since the 1977 Protocols Additional to the Geneva Conventions, which address both issues.

Perhaps more so than in any other issue area of international law, the relevant treaty regimes in international humanitarian law need to be understood in the context of customary international law on the subject. This was expressly recognized in the *Martens Clause,* which first appeared in the preamble to the 1899 Hague Convention II and has appeared in similar wording in other treaties. The preamble to the 1907 Hague Convention IV stated that:

> Until a more complete code of the laws of war has been issued, the high contracting parties deem it expedient to declare that, in cases not included in the Regulations adopted by them, the inhabitants and the belligerents remain under the protection and the rule of the principles of the law of nations, as they result from the usages established among civilized peoples, from the laws of humanity, and the dictates of the public conscience.

In 2005 the ICRC published a review of customary international humanitarian law,[7] intended to assist in identifying such law. The three-volume study, the product of over ten years' research, is to be periodically updated by a team based at the Lauterpacht Center for International Law at the University of Cambridge.[8]

Another fundamental principle underpinning IHL stipulates that parties to a conflict and members of their armed forces do not have an unlimited choice of methods and means of warfare.[9] The *principle of military necessity* stipulates that "only that degree and kind of force, not otherwise prohibited by the law of armed conflict, required for the partial or complete submission of the enemy with a minimum expenditure of time, life, and physical resources may be applied."[10]

The first modern effort to ban weapons that caused unnecessary suffering was the St. Petersburg Declaration of 1868, a response to the development of a bullet that exploded on contact with a hard surface. The preamble stated what became known as the *principle of unnecessary suffering,* which has underpinned attempts at limiting battlefield armaments:

> Considering . . . [t]hat the only legitimate object which States should endeavour to accomplish during war is to weaken the military forces of the enemy;
> That for this purpose it is sufficient to disable the greatest possible number of men;
> That this object would be exceeded by the employment of arms which uselessly aggravate the sufferings of disabled men, or render their death inevitable;
> That the employment of such arms would, therefore, be contrary to the laws of humanity.[11]

▣ The 1899 and 1907 Hague Conventions and Declarations

The first Hague Peace Conference was held at the initiative of Tsar Nicholas II of Russia, with the aim of limiting armaments.[12] Representatives of twenty-six states concluded conventions relating to the peaceful settlement of disputes, the laws and customs of war on land, and maritime warfare, as well as declarations prohibiting the launching of projectiles and explosives from balloons, using projectiles diffusing asphyxiating gases, and using expanding bullets.

The second Hague Peace Conference, aimed at limiting armaments, was attended by representatives of forty-four states. The conference adopted thirteen conventions and one declaration. Those relevant to international humanitarian law are:

- Hague Convention III, Concerning the Opening of Hostilities
- Hague Convention IV, Concerning the Laws and Customs of War on Land and Annex to the Convention: Regulations Concerning the Laws and Customs of War on Land

- Hague Convention V, Concerning the Rights and Duties of Neutral Powers and Persons in Case of War on Land
- Hague Convention VI, Concerning the Status of Enemy Merchant Ships at the Outbreak of Hostilities
- Hague Convention VII, Concerning the Conversion of Merchant Ships into Warships
- Hague Convention VIII, Concerning the Laying of Automatic Submarine Contact Mines
- Hague Convention IX, Concerning Bombardment by Naval Forces in Times of War
- Hague Convention XI, Concerning Certain Restrictions with Regard to the Exercise of the Right of Capture in Naval War
- Hague Convention XIII, Concerning the Rights and Duties of Neutral Powers in Naval War

The conventions vary in their contemporary importance. Convention III has been completely disregarded, for example, but Hague Convention IV and annexed regulations, which revised the laws of land warfare embodied in the second Hague Convention of 1899, remains of importance.[13] Article 23(e) of the regulations annexed to the fourth Hague Convention of 1907 reiterated the principle of unnecessary suffering that had been expressed in the preamble to the 1868 St. Petersburg Declaration, forbidding the employment of "arms, projectiles, or material calculated to cause unnecessary suffering." Because it was recognized that the convention did not represent a complete code of the law of land warfare, the Martens Clause was included in its preamble. The International Military Tribunal at Nuremberg, Germany, in 1946 recognized the 1907 Hague Convention IV as declaratory of customary international law.[14]

■ The Geneva Conventions of 1949

The well-known Geneva Conventions are:

- Geneva Convention I, for the Amelioration of the Condition of the Wounded and Sick in Armed Forces in the Field[15]
- Geneva Convention II, for the Amelioration of the Condition of the Wounded, Sick, and Shipwrecked Members of Armed Forces at Sea[16]
- Geneva Convention III, Concerning the Treatment of Prisoners of War[17]
- Geneva Convention IV, Concerning the Protection of Civilian Persons in Time of War[18]

The focus of these conventions was the protection of victims of war. Sponsored by the ICRC, they grew out of pre–World War II efforts to draft new conventions as well as the experiences of that war in demonstrating inadequacies in the existing law. The First Geneva Convention was a new and enlarged version of a 1929 Geneva Convention on the wounded and sick. It provides, inter alia, that members of the armed forces and other categories provided for in article 13, who are wounded or sick, "shall be respected and protected in all circumstances." The Third Geneva Convention defines *prisoners of war,* for not all persons who take part in international armed conflict are entitled to prisoner-of-war status. The convention sets out how prisoners of war must be treated and that, by article 118, they are to be released and repatriated without delay after the cessation of active hostilities.

The Fourth Geneva Convention was the first international agreement in the laws of war to exclusively address the treatment of civilians—those who "find themselves, in case of a conflict or occupation, in the hands of a Party to the conflict or Occupying Power of which they are not nationals."[19] It provides, inter alia, that such "protected persons are entitled, in all circumstances, to respect for their persons, their honour, their family rights, their religious convictions and practices, and their manners and customs. They shall at all times be humanely treated, and shall be protected especially against all acts of violence or threats thereof and against insults and public curiosity."[20]

Some consideration was given to the laws of war for internal conflicts. This resulted in a common article 3 in the 1949 conventions, which extended some fundamental humanitarian protections to noncombatants "in the case of armed conflict not of an international character." The 1949 conventions entered into force in 1954 and now have virtually universal participation. It is likely that most, if not all, of their provisions have attained the status of customary international law.[21]

Protocols Additional to the Geneva Conventions are:

• Protocol Additional to the Geneva Conventions of 12 August 1949, and Relating to the Protection of Victims of International Arms Conflicts, 1977[22]
• Protocol Additional to the Geneva Conventions of 12 August 1949, and Relating to the Protection of Victims of Non-International Armed Conflicts, 1977[23]
• Protocol Additional to the Geneva Conventions of 12 August 1949, and relating to the Adoption of an Additional Distinctive Emblem, 2005[24]

The 1977 protocols to the Geneva Conventions, again sponsored by the ICRC, were an attempt to respond to issues that had become increasingly apparent since the conclusion of the Geneva Conventions, both in terms of reaffirming some customary IHL and further developing international humanitarian law.[25] One major problem was that war had increasingly become an intrastate rather than interstate phenomenon in the years since World War II and only the common article 3 of the 1949 conventions had applied specifically to civil wars. A second problem was that although the 1949 Geneva Conventions had updated international law regarding the protection of civilians and those no longer fighting, limitations or prohibitions of specific means and methods of warfare were becoming increasingly dated. Much of the preparatory work for the protocol was undertaken by the ICRC, which presented the Diplomatic Conference on the Reaffirmation and Development of International Humanitarian Law with two draft protocols from which to work. The conference held four sessions in Geneva between 1974 and 1977.

The two protocols represent some merging of the Hague and Geneva streams of international humanitarian law. The first protocol (Protocol of 8 June 1977 Additional to the Geneva Conventions of 12 August 1949, and Concerning the Protection of Victims of International Armed Conflicts) dealt with international conflict. It is divided into several parts, addressing the wounded, sick, and shipwrecked; medical transportation; missing and dead persons; methods and means of warfare, combatant and prisoner-of-war status; and the civilian population. Article 48 codified the *principle of distinction:*

> In order to ensure respect for and protection of the civilian population and civilian objects, the Parties to the conflict shall at all times distinguish between the civilian population and combatants and between civilian objects and military objectives and accordingly shall direct their operations only against military objectives.

Military objectives were defined in article 52(2). Article 51(5) prohibits "an attack which may be expected to cause incidental loss of civilian life, injury to civilians, damage to civilian objects, or a combination thereof, which would be excessive in relation to the concrete and direct military advantage anticipated," thereby codifying the *principle of proportionality.* "When a choice is possible between several military objectives for obtaining a similar military advantage, the objective to be selected shall be that the attack on which may be expected to cause the least danger to civilian lives and to civilian objects."[26]

IHL therefore recognizes that some civilian casualties may occur in the course of attacks against legitimate military objectives; states are not categorically prohibited from harming civilians. Military commanders are required to weigh the value of innocent civilian lives in relation to the capture or destruction of a particular military objective; failure to do so can constitute a war crime. In making such decisions commanders will also take into account the increased danger to which their own forces may be exposed in order to minimize civilian casualties.

Since the adoption of the 1977 additional protocols, virtual technologies have made it much easier to review what may have been difficult decisions in the heat of battle, raising public expectations and prompting the increasing involvement of lawyers in targeting and other strategic decisionmaking.[27] This is true in relation, for example, to the use by the United States since 2004 of drones—powered aerial vehicles that are piloted remotely— to target terrorist leaders in Pakistan. Critics have claimed that they breach the principles of distinction, necessity, proportionality, and humanity.[28]

Chapter II of section III (Treatment of Persons in the Power of a Party to the Conflict) provides measures relating to women and children. Article 76(1) provides that "[w]omen shall be the object of special respect and shall be protected against rape, forced prostitution and any other form of indecent assault." More recently, Security Council Resolution 1820 (2008) condemned sexual violence during armed conflict and demanded that all parties to armed conflict immediately take appropriate measures to protect civilians, including women and girls, from all forms of sexual violence. The Council called for greater inclusion of women at all stages of peace processes.[29]

The second protocol (Protection of Victims of Non-International Armed Conflicts) builds on the common article 3 in the Geneva Conventions. It was the first international treaty devoted exclusively to the protection of persons affected by noninternational armed conflict. Strongest support for the protocol came from Europe and North America whereas the struggle for independence on the part of national liberation movements led to much third world opposition.[30] The difficulty of reaching agreement produced a much shorter document than the first protocol. It has separate parts on humane treatment (of all persons who do not take a direct part or who have ceased to take part in hostilities); wounded, sick, and shipwrecked; and the civilian population.

The third additional protocol, adopted in 2005, authorizes use of a red crystal in addition to the red cross and red crescent emblems used by medical and rescue workers.[31]

■ Convention on Prohibitions or Restrictions on the Use of Certain Conventional Weapons Which May Be Deemed to Be Excessively Injurious or to Have Indiscriminate Effect, 1980

The Convention on Prohibitions or Restrictions on the Use of Certain Conventional Weapons Which May Be Deemed to Be Excessively Injurious or to Have Indiscriminate Effects (CCW)[32] resulted from the efforts of the ICRC and was adopted at a conference convened by the United Nations.

The CCW bans or restricts the use of specific weapons or means of warfare that pose special risks of causing indiscriminate damage to civilians or unnecessary suffering. Annexed protocols each deal with a specific type of conventional weapon, and article 8 provides for the addition of further annexed protocols. Protocols address fragmentation weapons undetectable by X-ray (protocol I); mines, booby-traps, and other devices (protocol II, which was amended in 1996); incendiary weapons (protocol III); blinding laser weapons (protocol IV, adopted in 1995); and explosive remnants of war (protocol V, adopted in 2003). The framework convention was amended in December 2001 to make all existing protocols applicable to noninternational armed conflict.

■ Convention on the Prohibition of the Use, Stockpiling, Production, and Transfer of Anti-Personnel Mines and Their Destruction (Ottawa Convention), 1997

The first widespread use of land mines as a means of curtailing attack was in World War I. Driven by improvements in land mine technology, which made them much cheaper to produce, use expanded greatly. Land mines fail the double test of discrimination between combatants and civilians and balance between military necessity and proportionality;[33] by far the majority of victims are civilians, and it is usually after the conflict that they are killed or injured.

It was in the 1970s that land mines were placed on the international policy agenda. Protocol II of the 1980 CCW dealt with land mines but stopped short of actually banning the mines and had no impact on countries using mines during internal conflicts.[34] The 1996 review conference of the CCW amended protocol II so as to further tighten restrictions on the production, use, and transfer of antipersonnel mines but still stopped short of a ban. Disappointed by this outcome, Canada took the lead in efforts to have a total ban on antipersonnel mines. A conference in Ottawa on October 4–5, 1996, attended by NGOs and representatives of seventy-four countries, set in train the so-called Ottawa Process, which led to the Ottawa Convention.[35] It is notable because it was brought about through the efforts not of a superpower or coalition of great powers but of a coalition of states led by Canada and of NGOs led by the International Campaign to Ban Landmines (ICBL), with the strong support of the UN Secretary-General.[36]

Article 1 lists the general obligations:

1. Each State Party undertakes never under any circumstances:

   a. To use anti-personnel mines;
   b. To develop, produce, otherwise acquire, stockpile, retain or transfer to anyone, directly or indirectly, anti-personnel mines;
   c. To assist, encourage or induce, in any way, anyone to engage in any activity prohibited to a State Party under this Convention.

2. Each State Party undertakes to destroy or ensure the destruction of all anti-personnel mines in accordance with the provisions of this Convention.

Article 7 of the Ottawa Convention requires states parties to submit an annual report to the UN Secretary-General on the measures taken to meet its obligations. At the first meeting of the states parties in Mozambique, states decided to make these reports publicly available, including on the Internet.[37] The state-based reporting system is complemented by the work of the ICBL, which in June 1998 established Landmine Monitor to monitor and document compliance with the 1997 Treaty.[38]

The use of antipersonnel mines decreased greatly after conclusion of the treaty; according to Landmine Monitor the number of states using land mines decreased from some fifteen states in 1997 to two—Myanmar and Russia—by 2009. The number of states producing land mines fell from thirty-eight to thirteen in the same period, and the use by nonstate groups also decreased.[39] Success has been tempered by the fact that the United States, Russia, and China did not become parties. President Bill Clinton gave two reasons for the United States not to sign: first, that the United States would have to remove its antipersonnel land mines from the demilitarized zone along the border between North Korea and South Korea; and second, that the convention would have banned US antitank mines as well as antipersonnel mines.[40]

The Cartagena (Spain) Summit was held November 30–December 4, 2009, to review ten years of progress under the treaty. The United States was represented at the summit, which was the first time that it participated formally at a meeting of states parties to the treaty. The US delegation at the summit announced that the Obama administration was in the process of a comprehensive review of US land mines policy.[41] Despite not being party to the convention, the United States has not used antipersonnel mines since 1991, not exported them since 1992, and not produced them since 1997.[42]

■ **The Rome Statute of the International Criminal Court, 1998**

One of the most significant developments in both international humanitarian law and public international law as a whole since 1945 has been the creation of an international criminal court. The earliest recorded precedent for an international criminal court or tribunal was the 1474 trial of the Burgundian governor of Breisach, Peter von Hagenback. He was brought before a court made up of twenty-eight judges from Alsace, Switzerland, and other states within the Holy Roman Empire when it was found that his troops had raped and killed innocent civilians and pillaged their property during the occupation of Breisach. Hagenback argued that he had been following the orders of his superiors, but his defense was rejected and he was sentenced to death. There appears then to have been a gap of nearly four centuries before the first proposal to set up a permanent international criminal court was made by Gustave Moynier, a founder of the Red Cross.[43]

Although some commentators have reservations about the criminal prosecution of the perpetrators of mass atrocity,[44] the mainstream view is that trying alleged war criminals can further the goals of justice by assigning specific individual guilt and avoiding collective guilt. Seeing justice done is generally thought to facilitate a society's healing and enable it to move forward. It is through the trial process that records are made of the nature of, and responsibility for, the crimes committed. Howard Ball has written that "[w]ithout the thousands of pages of documents and tribunal judgments, the victims' suffering and the horrid deeds of the killers will in part rest in the hands of the 'revisionists,' persons who say that the Jewish Holocaust [for example] never occurred. And the perpetrators will have accomplished one of their goals: to erase all memory of the victims."[45]

Attempts to create an international criminal court were made in the aftermath of World War I.[46] Sections 227 to 230 of the Versailles Peace Treaty mandated the establishment of an international war crimes tribunal, and war crimes clauses were included in the various peace treaties. But the political will to push for strict enforcement of these provisions was weak, and the victorious Western allies allowed Germany to try its alleged war criminals in Germany's Supreme Court; of the 900 Germans identified by the Allies, 888 were acquitted or had the charges dismissed without trial.[47] In 1937 the League of Nations finalized the text of a convention to establish an international criminal court in which to try persons accused of crimes defined in the Convention for the Prevention and Punishment of Terrorism, but the treaty never entered into force.[48]

After World War II, the Nuremberg Tribunal and the International Military Tribunal for the Far East were established as ad hoc tribunals, with the charter of the "Tokyo Tribunal" based largely on the Nuremberg charter. These tribunals were controversial because they were sometimes seen as "victors' justice": the victorious Allies were the judges, and the defendants were citizens of the defeated Axis powers. The tribunals appeared to be judging people for crimes that had not existed as legal crimes at the time of the actions.[49] The vital legacy of Nuremberg is the principle that individuals, whether government officials or others, are accountable for acts deemed unacceptable to common standards of international law and morality.

In 1946 the UN General Assembly decided that the important principles and precedents created by the Nuremberg charter and judgments of the Nuremberg Tribunal should serve as the basis for the further codification of international law,[50] and in 1948 the Assembly asked the International Law Commission (ILC) to examine the possibility of creating a permanent International Criminal Court. The ILC decided in 1950 "that the establishment of an international judicial organ for the trial of persons charged with genocide or other crimes over which jurisdiction will be conferred upon that organ by international conventions is desirable,"[51] and on December 12, 1950, the General Assembly by Resolution 489(V) established a committee to prepare one or more preliminary draft conventions and proposals relating to the establishment and the statute of an international criminal court. A second committee, established two years later, prepared a revised draft statute. A major stumbling block in the 1953 draft statute was the absence of an internationally accepted definition of the crime of aggression.

No further action was taken during the Cold War years; an international criminal court whose goals included the punishment of aggressive warfare was seen during these years as a threat to national sovereignty.[52] The end of the Cold War provided an opportunity for the United Nations to resume its work toward an international criminal court. In 1989 Trinidad and Tobago proposed that efforts at drafting a statute be resumed so as to create an international judicial institution capable of dealing with the increase in international drug trafficking. The General Assembly requested the ILC to do so and, prompted by the widespread atrocities being committed in the war in the former Yugoslavia, asked that the ILC complete the drafting as a matter of priority.

By resolution 827 (1993), the UN Security Council established the International Tribunal for the Prosecution of Persons Responsible for Serious Violations of International Humanitarian Law Committed in the Territory of the Former Yugoslavia Since 1991 (ICTY).[53] Acting under Chapter VII of the UN Charter, the Security Council further decided "that all States shall cooperate fully with the International Tribunal and its organs in accordance with the present resolution and the Statute of the International Tribunal." The ICTY is based in The Hague.

The following year, the Security Council established the International Criminal Tribunal for Rwanda (ICTR)[54] "for the sole purpose of prosecuting persons responsible for genocide and other serious violations of international humanitarian law committed in the territory of Rwanda and Rwandan citizens responsible for genocide and other such violations committed in the territory of neighbouring States, between January 1, 1994 and December 31, 1994."[55] The Tribunal is based in Arusha in the United Republic of Tanzania, although the Tribunal shares an appeals chamber with the ICTY in The Hague. The ICTR began work in 1998.

The ICTY and ICTR have contributed considerably to the development of IHL. The ICTR conviction of former mayor Jean-Paul Akayesu of genocide and crimes against humanity for his encouragement of the rape of Tutsi women in Rwanda, represented the first time that rape had been found to be an act of genocide, and it laid a foundation for later prosecutions for sexual crimes by both tribunals.[56] The ICTY case against Dragolujub Kunarac, Radomir Kovac, and Zoran Vukovic gave rise to the first convictions for sexual enslavement as a crime against humanity.[57] In the case against Radislav Krstic, the Appeals Chamber upheld a previous ICTY finding that the executions of 7,000–8,000 Bosnian Muslims in and around the town of Srebrenica had constituted acts of genocide.[58]

Senior Serb leadership involved in the Yugoslav conflict to have appeared before the ICTY have included former president Slobodan Milosevic, whose death brought his trial to an end in March 2006, and former Bosnian Serb leader Radovan Karadzic. Notable cases heard by the ICTR have included those involving Jean Kambanda, former prime minister of Rwanda, whose conviction for genocide was in 2000 upheld by the Appeals Chamber,[59] and of Ferdinand Nahimana and two other former media executives, who in 2007 lost their appeal against their conviction for genocide for their dissemination of hate speech before and during the Rwandan genocide.[60]

Meanwhile, in 1994 the ILC submitted a draft statute for an international criminal court to the General Assembly. The ILC recommended that the General Assembly "convene an international conference of plenipotentiaries to study the draft Statute and to conclude a convention on the establishment of an International Criminal Court." The General Assembly created a preparatory committee to achieve a draft treaty that a diplomatic conference would be able to negotiate into a final text in a matter of weeks. The PrepCom met for six difficult sessions in 1996–1998.

A five-week diplomatic conference convened in Rome in mid-1998. During negotiations, states tended to align with one of three groups. The "like-minded group," which had promoted the establishment of an international criminal court and generally favored a strong and independent court, was composed of middle powers and developing states. The second group consisted of the permanent members of the Security Council, which wanted a strong role for the Council vis-à-vis the proposed court and the exclusion of nuclear weapons from the types of weapons prohibited by the statute. The third group of states—including India, Mexico, and Egypt—insisted that nuclear weapons be included among those prohibited by the statute. Meanwhile, NGOs generally pressed for a strong court, an independent prosecutor, sensitivity to gender concerns, and jurisdiction over internal armed conflict.[61]

The relationship of national courts and processes to that of the proposed ICC was, naturally, one of the most sensitive issues during the negotiations. The ILC had incorporated into its draft statute the principle of *complementarity,* by which the Court operates only if a national jurisdiction is unwilling or unable genuinely to carry out an investigation or prosecution. The Rome Statute makes clear that the Court is not intended to have primacy over national courts but rather to be complementary to national criminal jurisdictions.[62]

The International Criminal Court has jurisdiction over individuals, not states, in respect of four crimes: *genocide,* defined as per the Genocide Convention; *crimes against humanity* (including murder, extermination, enslavement, deportation or forcible transfer of the population, imprisonment or other severe deprivation of physical liberty in violation of fundamental rules of international law, torture, sexual violence, and so on, when committed as part of a widespread or systematic attack directed against any civilian population); *war crimes* (including most of the serious violations of international humanitarian law mentioned in the 1949 Geneva Conventions and their protocols, such as rape, sexual slavery, enforced prostitution, forced pregnancy, and other forms of sexual violence, whether committed during an international or internal conflict); and *aggression* (once a provision defining this crime and setting out the conditions for the exercise of such jurisdiction is adopted).[63]

Although it would be reasonable to expect that the crime of waging a war of aggression would be perpetrated by a state, the final judgment of the Nuremberg Tribunal in October 1946 held that "crimes against international law are committed by men, not by abstract entities, and only by punishing individuals who commit such crimes can the provisions of international law be enforced."[64] Several resolutions of the General Assembly declared the criminality of aggressive war, and a succession of four special committees of the General Assembly sought to define aggression. Finally, General Assembly Resolution 3314 (XXIX) of December 14, 1974, defined an act of aggression as "the use of armed force by a State against the sovereignty, territorial integrity or political independence of another State, or in any other manner inconsistent with the Charter of the United Nations."[65] General Assembly resolutions are not a source of international law, and this definition in any case remains controversial. The Rome Conference delegated the definition of aggression to the preparatory committee and its subordinate special working group.[66] On June 12, 2010, the first Review Conference on the Rome Statute adopted amendments to the Statute concerning the definition of, and exercise of jurisdiction over, the crime of aggression.[67] This was a momentous development, though the amendments cannot be activated before 2017.

Drug trafficking, which had provided the impetus for the renewed efforts to create an international criminal court, was not included because most delegations took the view that it was not of the same nature as the other crimes to be included, that the Court would not have the resources to undertake the necessary investigations, and that it could eventually flood the Court.[68] Similarly, whereas some states were particularly keen to have terrorism included within the jurisdiction of the Court, it could have unduly politicized the Court, particularly because there was no widely accepted definition of the crime.[69]

Article 13 provides for three "trigger mechanisms" by which a case can come before the Court: (1) if referred to the Prosecutor by a State Party; (2) on the initiative of the prosecutor with the authorization of a Pre-Trial Chamber; or (3) if referred to the prosecutor by the Security Council acting under Chapter VII of the UN Charter. But article 12 contains preconditions to the exercise of jurisdiction by the ICC in a case initiated by either of the first two triggers. The state on the territory of which the crime was committed and/or the state of which the person accused of the crime is a national must be a party to the Rome Statute or have accepted the jurisdiction of the Court. Where a case is referred to the Court by the Security Council, the Court will have jurisdiction—even if the crime was committed in nonstate parties by nationals of nonstates parties and in the absence of consent by the territorial state or the state of nationality of the accused.

The ICC does not have retrospective jurisdiction (article 11). On becoming a party to the Rome Statute a state may declare that for a period of seven years, it does not accept the jurisdiction of the Court with respect to war crimes when a crime is alleged to have been committed by its nationals or on its territory (article 124). States parties are obliged to cooperate with a request for assistance from the Court in relation to its investigation and prosecution of crimes (article 86). Such assistance may involve, for example, the taking of evidence, the provision of records, the protection of victims and witnesses, or the arrest and surrender of an individual on its territory. The Court, which is situated in the Hague, may order imprisonment for up to thirty years or life, fines, and forfeiture of the proceeds of a crime (article 77).

The United Nations Diplomatic Conference of Plenipotentiaries on the Establishment of an International Criminal Court adopted the Rome Statute on July 17, 1998, by a vote of 120–7 with 21 abstentions.[70] The United States, despite having been active in the preparation of the treaty text, voted against its adoption, together with Israel, China, Iraq, Yemen, Libya, and Qatar. The primary point to which the United States took issue was that the Court would be able to assume jurisdiction without the express permission of the Security Council.[71] The United States argued that the Security Council has prime responsibility for the maintenance of the peace and that an independent court might interfere with Security Council efforts to contain threats to the peace. The United States has also argued that the ICC is taking jurisdiction over nonstates parties in violation of article 34 of the Vienna Convention on the Law of Treaties, because the ICC has jurisdiction over a listed crime if it is committed on the territory of a state party to the

Rome Statute even if the state of which the accused is a national is not a party;[72] defenders of the Rome Statute would respond by saying that when an alien commits a crime on the territory of another state, prosecution of that person is never dependent on the consent of the state of nationality;[73] territorial jurisdiction over crimes is firmly established in international law.[74] The United States is party to a number of antiterrorism treaties that empower states parties to investigate and prosecute perpetrators of any nationality found within their territory. The United States expressed concern that the Rome Statute would allow politicized prosecutions of its peacekeepers and hence inhibit its involvement in multinational operations.[75]

Despite voting against adoption of the treaty text, the United States signed just before the December 31, 2000, deadline for doing so. President Clinton was quoted as saying that "[w]ith signature, we will be in a position to influence the evolution of the court. Without signature, we will not."[76] Then, by letter to the UN Secretary-General of the United Nations of April 27, 2002, the US undersecretary of state for arms control and international security in the George W. Bush administration, John Bolton, briefly stated the intention of the United States not to become a party to the treaty. "Accordingly, the United States has no legal obligations arising from its signature on December 31, 2000. The United States requests that its intention not to become a party, as expressed in this letter, be reflected in the depositary's status lists relating to this treaty."[77]

Following entry into force of the Rome Statute on July 1, 2002, the United States came under criticism for negotiating more than 100 bilateral treaties, dubbed "impunity agreements" by critics, by which states have agreed not to transfer US nationals, government officials, or military personnel to the ICC without US authorization. The 2002 US American Servicemembers' Protection Act essentially prohibits US support for, or cooperation with, the International Criminal Court.

In the early years of the operation of the Court, the governments of Uganda, the Democratic Republic of Congo, and the Central African Republic referred situations to the prosecutor and by Resolution 1593 (2005) the UN Security Council referred the situation in Darfur to the prosecutor of the ICC. The United States abstained rather than veto the resolution. The first trial—of Congolese militia leader Thomas Lubanga—began on January 26, 2009. In March 2009, the president of Sudan, Omar al Bashir, became the first incumbent head of state to have a warrant issued for his arrest.

■ Hybrid Criminal Tribunals
In order to create judicial mechanisms that would be quicker, more cost effective, and better address the needs to the postconflict societies than the

ICTY, ICTR, and ICC, a new experiment in international criminal law has been the creation of what are known as hybrid, or mixed, tribunals.[78] Hybrid tribunals generally employ both national and international staff and incorporate both international and domestic law in their statutes. Examples include those established in Timor-Leste, Sierra Leone, Cambodia, Kosovo, and Lebanon.

The Special Court for Sierra Leone (SCSL)[79] in June 2003 issued an arrest warrant for Charles Taylor, the then President of Liberia, who was subsequently arrested and transferred to the court. In May 2004 the SCSL handed down a landmark decision rejecting Taylor's claim of immunity as an incumbent Head of State.[80] In February 2008 the Appeals Chamber of the SCSL ruled that forced marriages in the context of an armed conflict could constitute a crime against humanity and upheld the first convictions for the conscription of child soldiers.[81]

■ Convention on Cluster Munitions, 2008

Cluster munitions are munitions designed to disperse or release explosive submunitions or bomblets. The bomblets may be distributed over a large area and sometimes fail to explode on impact. They cannot discriminate between military and civilians and often cause large numbers of death and injuries after fighting has ceased. Awareness heightened after their use by Israel when fighting Hezbollah in southern Lebanon in 2006. Frustrated at the slow-moving progress toward the abolition of cluster munitions under the CCW, Norway in November 2006 announced an alternative process. The "Oslo process" resulted in the Convention on Cluster Munitions,[82] adopted on May 30, 2008, by 107 states at a diplomatic conference in Dublin, Ireland, and entered into force on August 1, 2010. The convention prohibits the use, production, stockpiling, and transfer of cluster munitions. Even after the conclusion of the convention, some states—including some key states—planned to continue discussions on a protocol on cluster munitions to the CCW.[83]

■ Notes

1. http://www.icrc.org.
2. Adam Roberts and Richard Guelff, eds., *Documents on the Laws of War,* 2nd ed. (Oxford: Clarendon, 1989), p. 17.
3. See Ramesh Thakur and William Maley, "The Ottawa Convention on Landmines: A Landmark Humanitarian Treaty in Arms Control?" *Global Governance* 5 (1999): 273–302.
4. See http://www.icrc.org.
5. Chris af Jochnick and Roger Normand, "The Legitimation of Violence: A Critical History of the Laws of War," *Harvard International Law Journal* 35, no. 1 (Winter 1994): 49–95, esp. 60.

6. Roberts and Guelff, *Documents on the Laws of War,* p. 29.

7. Jean-Marie Henckaerts and Louise Doswald-Beck, eds., *Customary International Humanitarian Law* (Cambridge: Cambridge University Press, 2005).

8. For progress, check the website of the center, http://www.lcil.cam.ac.uk.

9. This is no. 6 in the "Fundamental Rules of International Humanitarian Law Applicable in Armed Conflicts," reprinted in Roberts and Guelff, *Documents on the Laws of War,* p. 470.

10. Roberts and Guelff, *Documents on the Laws of War,* p. 5.

11. "Declaration Renouncing the Use, in Time of War, of Explosive Projectiles Under 400 Grammes Weight," in ibid., pp. 30–31.

12. For texts and commentary, see J. B. Scott, ed., *The Hague Conventions and Declarations of 1899 and 1907,* 3rd ed. (New York: Oxford University Press, 1918).

13. Fleck, *The Handbook of Humanitarian Law in Armed Conflicts.*

14. Roberts and Guelff, *Documents on the Laws of War,* p. 44.

15. 75 UNTS 31.

16. 75 UNTS 85.

17. 75 UNTS 135; and Shirley V. Scott, ed., *International Law and Politics: Key Documents* (Boulder, CO: Lynne Rienner, 2006), pp. 441–487.

18. 75 UNTS 267; and Scott, *International Law and Politics,* pp. 489–517.

19. Geneva Convention IV, Concerning the Protection of Civilian Persons in Time of War, article 4.

20. Ibid., article 27.

21. Fleck, *The Handbook of Humanitarian Law in Armed Conflicts,* p. 24.

22. 1125 United Nations Treaty Series (UNTS) 3; 16 *International Legal Materials (ILM)* 1391 (1977); and Scott, *International Law and Politics,* pp. 518–566.

23. 1125 UNTS 609; 16 *ILM* 1442 (1977); and Scott, *International Law and Politics,* pp. 567–576.

24. 45 *ILM* 558 (2006).

25. See Y. Sandoz, C. Swinarski, and B. Zimmermann, eds., *Commentary on the Additional Protocols of 8 June 1977 to the Geneva Conventions of 12 August 1949* (Geneva: ICRC and Martinus Nijhoff, 1987).

26. Protocol of 8 June 1977 Additional to the Geneva Conventions of 12 August 1949, and Concerning the Protection of Victims of International Armed Conflicts, Article 57(3).

27. This paragraph draws on Jack M. Beard, "Law and War in the Virtual Era," *American Journal of International Law* 103, no. 3 (2009): 409–445.

28. See Philip Alston, "Promotion and Protection of All Human Rights, Civil, Political, Economic, Social, and Cultural Rights, Including the Right to Development: Report of the Special Rapporteur on Extrajudicial, Summary, or Arbitrary Executions on His Mission to the United States," May 28, 2009, Human Rights Council UN Document A/HRC/11/2/Add.5, available at http://www2.ohchr.org.

29. See Sanam Naraghi Anderlini, *Women Building Peace: What They Do, Why It Matters* (Boulder, CO: Lynne Rienner, 2007).

30. For the negotiating history of the protocol see D. Forsythe, "Legal Management of International War: The 1977 Protocol on Non-International Armed Conflicts," *American Journal of International Law* 72 (1978): 272–295.

31. See Jean-Francois Queguiner, "Commentary on the Protocol Additional to the Geneva Conventions of 12 August 1949, and Relating to the Adoption of an Additional Distinctive Emblem (Protocol III)," *International Review of the Red*

Cross 89, no. 865 (2007): 175–207, available at http://www.icrc.org, or see Queguiner's "Introductory Note to the Additional Protocol" at 45 *ILM* 555 (2006).

32. 1342 UNTS 137; 19 *ILM* 1523.

33. Thakur and Maley, "The Ottawa Convention on Landmines," p. 278.

34. The inadequacies of the protocol are canvassed in Yvette Politis, "The Regulation of an Invisible Enemy: The International Community's Response to Land Mine Proliferation," *Boston College International and Comparative Law Review* 22, no. 2 (1999): 465–493, esp. 472–475.

35. 36 *ILM* 1509 (1997).

36. See Shawn Roberts, "No Exceptions, No Reservations, No Loopholes: The Campaign for the 1997 Convention on the Prohibition of the Development, Production, Stockpiling, Transfer, and Use of Anti-Personnel Mines and on Their Destruction," *Colorado Journal of International Environmental Law and Policy* 9, no. 2 (Summer 1998): 371–391. See also Stephen Biddle, J. Klare, J. Wallis, and I. Oelrich, "Controlling Anti-personnel Landmines," *Contemporary Security Policy* 19, no. 3 (December 1998): 27–71.

37. "Mine Ban Treaty Transparency Reporting," *Landmine Monitor*, available at http://www.icbl.org.

38. See http://www.icbl.org.

39. "Major Findings 1999–2009," *Landmine Monitor*, http://lm.icbl.org.

40. Christian M. Capece, "The Ottawa Treaty and Its Impact on US Military Policy and Planning," *Brooklyn Journal of International Law* 25, no. 1 (1999): 183–204, esp. 183–184. See also Lynn Sellers Bickley, "US Resistance to the International Criminal Court: Is the Sword Mightier Than the Law?" *Emory International Law Review* 14 (2000): 213–276; and Jodi Preusser Mustoe, The 1997 Treaty to Ban the Use of Landmines: Was President Clinton's Refusal to Become a Signatory Warranted?" *Georgia Journal of International and Comparative Law* 27, no. 3 (1999): 541–569.

41. "US Statement at the Cartagena Summit on a Mine-Free World," December 1, 2009, http://www.state.gov.

42. "US: Obama Rejection of Mine Ban Treaty 'Reprehensible,'" *Human Rights Watch*, November 25, 2009, http://www.hrw.org, accessed November 26, 2009.

43. See Christopher Keith Hall, "The First Proposal for a Permanent International Criminal Court," *International Review of the Red Cross* 322 (March 1998): 57–74.

44. See Mark J. Osiel, "Why Prosecute? Critics of Punishment for Mass Atrocity," *Human Rights Quarterly* 22, no. 1 (2000): 118–147.

45. Howard Ball, *Prosecuting War Crimes and Genocide: The Twentieth Century Experience* (Lawrence: University Press of Kansas, 1999), pp. 224–225.

46. Benjamin B. Ferencz, "An International Criminal Code and Court: Where They Stand and Where They're Going," *Columbia Journal of Transnational Law* 30 (1992): 375–399, esp. 382.

47. Ball, *Prosecuting War Crimes and Genocide*, p. 24. See also James F. Willis, *Prologue to Nuremberg: The Politics and Diplomacy of Punishing War Criminals of the First World War* (Westport, CT: Greenwood, 1982).

48. Michael P. Scharf, "The Jury Is Still Out on the Need for an International Criminal Court," *Duke Journal of Comparative and International Law* 1 (1991): 135–168, esp. 137.

49. See Arnold C. Brackman, *The Other Nuremberg* (New York: Morrow, 1987); Robert E. Conot, *Justice at Nuremberg* (New York: Harper and Row, 1983); and Richard H. Minear, *Victor's Justice: The Tokyo War Crimes Trial* (Princeton, NJ: Princeton University Press, 1971).

50. General Assembly Resolution 95(I), UN Document A/236 (1946).

51. The vote was 8 to 1 with 2 abstentions. 43rd Meeting of the International Law Commission, Friday, June 9, 1950. *Yearbook of the International Law Commission, 1950*, vol. I, p. 23.

52. Robert Rosenstock, "Symposium: Should There Be an International Tribunal for Crimes Against Humanity?" *Pace International Law Review* 6 (1984): 84. See also Ferencz, "An International Criminal Code and Court," pp. 383–384.

53. http://www.icty.org. See, inter alia, Pierre Hazan, *Justice in a Time of War: The True Story Behind the International Criminal Tribunal for the Former Yugoslavia* (College Station: Texas A&M University Press 2004); Rachel Kerr, *The International Criminal Tribunal for the Former Yugoslavia: An Exercise in Law, Politics, and Diplomacy* (Oxford: Oxford University Press, 2004); and William A. Schabas, *The UN International Criminal Tribunals: The Former Yugoslavia, Rwanda, and Sierra Leone* (Cambridge: Cambridge University Press, 2006).

54. http://www.ictr.org.

55. Security Council resolution 955 (1994). See, inter alia, L. J. van den Herik, *Contribution of the Rwanda Tribunal to the Development of International Law* (Leiden: Brill, 2005); Nicholas A. Jones, *The Courts of Genocide: Politics and the Rule of Law in Rwanda and Arusha* (Abingdon: Routledge, 2010); and Kingsley Moghalu, *Rwanda's Genocide: The Politics of Global Justice* (New York: Palgrave Macmillan, 2005).

56. Both Akayesu and the prosecutor appealed, but the Appeals Chamber dismissed all of the challenges of Akayesu. *The Prosecutor v. Jean-Paul Akayesu*, Case No. ICTR-96-4-A, June 1, 2001.

57. Case No. IT-96-23-T and IT-96-23/1-T, February 23, 2001.

58. *Prosecutor v. Krstic*, Case No. IT-98-33-A, Judgment, April 19, 2004.

59. *Jean Kambanda v. The Prosecutor*, Case No. ICTR 97-23-A, October 19, 2000.

60. *Prosecutor v. Nahimana, Barayawiza and Ngeze*, Case No. ICTR-99-52-A, Judgment, November 28, 2007.

61. Cited in Philippe Kirsch and John T. Holmes, "The Rome Conference on an International Criminal Court: The Negotiating Process," *American Journal of International Law* 93, no. 2 (1999): 2–12, esp. 4–5.

62. See John T. Holmes, "The Principle of Complementarity," in Roy S. Lee, ed., *The International Criminal Court: The Making of the Rome Statute* (New York: Springer, 1999), p. 41; Jo Stigen, *The Relationship Between the International Criminal Court and National Jurisdictions: The Principle of Complementarity* (Leiden, the Netherlands: Martinus Nijhoff, 2008); Mauro Politi and Federica Gioia, eds., *The International Criminal Court and National Jurisdictions* (Aldershot, UK: Ashgate, 2008); and Mohamed M. El Zeidy, *The Principle of Complementarity in International Criminal Law: Origin, Development, and Practice* (Leiden, the Netherlands: Martinus Nijhoff, 2008).

63. The Rome Statute of the International Criminal Court, articles 5 to 8; and Scott, *International Law and Politics*, pp. 248–314.

64. Ferencz, "An International Criminal Code and Court," pp. 552–553, quoting the *Judgment of the International Military Tribunal for the Trial of German Major War Criminals: The Law of the Charter*, available at http://avalon.law.yale.edu.

65. General Assembly Resolution 3314 (XXIX) (1974), article 1.

66. Final Act of the United Nations Diplomatic Conference of Plenipotentiaries on the Establishment of the International Criminal Court (17 July 1998), annex I, para. F.

67. See, inter alia, Sergey Sayapin, "The Definition of the Crime of Aggression for the Purpose of the International Criminal Court: Problems and Perspectives," *Journal of Conflict and Security Law* 13 (2008): 353–391.

68. Andreas Zimmermann, "Article 5 Crimes Within the Jurisdiction of the Court," in Otto Triffterer, ed., *Commentary on the Rome Statute of the International Criminal Court: Observers' Notes, Article by Article* (Baden-Baden, Germany: Nomos Verlagsgesellschaft, 1999), pp. 97–106, esp. 99.

69. Ibid.

70. 37 *ILM* 999 (1998). See, inter alia, M. Cherif Bassiouni, *The Statute of the International Criminal Court* (Ardsley, NY: Transnational, 2002); Yves Beigbeder, *Judging War Criminals* (New York: St. Martin's, 1999); and Leila Nadya Sadat, *The International Criminal Court and the Transformation of International Law* (Ardsley, NY: Transnational, 2002).

71. For a succinct explanation as to why the United States voted no, see Michael P. Scharf, "Results of the Rome Conference for an International Criminal Court," *ASIL Insight,* http://www.asil.org. See also Marcella David, "Grotius Repudiated: The American Objections to the International Criminal Court and the Commitment to International Law," *Michigan Journal of International Law* 20 (1999): 337–412; David J. Scheffer, "The United States and the International Criminal Court," *American Journal of International Law* 93 (1999): 12–22; and Sarah B. Sewall and Carl Kaysen, eds., *The United States and the International Criminal Court: National Security and International Law* (Lanham, MD: Rowman and Littlefield, 2000).

72. Sharon A. Williams, "Article 12 Preconditions to the Exercise of Jurisdiction," in Triffterer, *Commentary on the Rome Statute of the International Criminal Court,* p. 340.

73. Ibid.

74. Although not to the exclusion of the active and passive personality principles. Antonio Cassese, "The Statute of the International Criminal Court: Some Preliminary Reflections," *European Journal of International Law* 10 (1999): 144–171, esp. 160.

75. For analysis of this objection see Marten Zwanenburg, "The Statute for an International Criminal Court and the United States: Peacekeepers Under Fire?" *European Journal of International Law* 10 (1999): 124–143.

76. "US President 'Makes History' in Last-Minute Assent to War Crimes Court," *Sydney* (Australia) *Morning Herald,* January 2, 2001, p. 9.

77. 41 *ILM* 1014 (2002). For discussion, see Curtis A. Bradley, "US Announces Intent Not to Ratify International Criminal Court Treaty," *ASIL Insight,* May 2002, available at http://www.asil.org.

78. David Cohen, "'Hybrid' Justice in East Timor, Sierra Leone, and Cambodia: 'Lessons Learned' and Prospects for the Future," *Stanford Journal of International Law* 1 (2007): 1–38.

79. http://www.sc-sl.org/.

80. *Prosecutor v. Taylor,* Case No. SCSL-2003-01-I, Decision on Immunity from Jurisdiction, May 31, 2004.

81. *Prosecutor v. Brima, Kamara and Kanu,* Case No. SCSL-2004-16-A, Judgment, February 22, 2008, paras. 175–203 and 298–306.

82. See http://www.clusterconvention.org.

83. Karen Hulme, "The 2008 Cluster Munitions Convention: Stepping Outside the CCW Framework (Again)," *International and Comparative Law Quarterly* 58 (2009): 219–227.

13

International Law
and the Environment

AS WITH INTERNATIONAL HUMAN RIGHTS LAW, INTERNATIONAL
environmental law is primarily a product of the post–World War II years.
Two of the legal documents vitally important to the evolution of international environmental law are not treaties but declarations: nonbinding statements of agreed principles and intent. These are the Stockholm Declaration of 1972,[1] which was one of three nonbinding instruments adopted by the first Conference on the Human Environment, held in Stockholm, Sweden,[2] and the Declaration on Environment and Development, held in Rio de Janeiro, Brazil. Principle 21 of the Stockholm Declaration has become a principle of customary international law. It states:

> States have, in accordance with the Charter of the United Nations and the principles of international law, the sovereign right to exploit their own resources pursuant to their own environmental policies, and the responsibility to ensure that activities within their jurisdiction or control do not cause damage to the environment of other States or of areas beyond the limits of national jurisdiction.

The 1992 Rio Conference produced a suite of documents, including the 800-page Agenda 21, intended to provide a global framework for environmental and developmental policies, and the Rio Declaration on Environment and Development—a counterpart to the Stockholm Declaration on the Human Environment.[3] The Rio Declaration is a statement of twenty-seven key environmental principles; Principle 7, for example, is the *principle of common but differentiated responsibility to the environment*. Building on the concept of the "common heritage of mankind," this principle specifies that even though all countries are responsible for global environmental problems, some countries are more responsible than others:[4]

States shall cooperate in a spirit of global partnership to conserve, protect and restore the health and integrity of the Earth's ecosystem. In view of the different contributions to global environmental degradation, States have common but differentiated responsibilities. The developed countries acknowledge the responsibility that they bear in the international pursuit of sustainable development in view of the pressures their societies place on the global environment and of the technologies and financial resources they command.

As the examples of regime development in this chapter will show, North-South issues have been central to the development of international environmental law.[5]

Principle 15 of the Rio Declaration expresses a widely accepted definition of the *precautionary principle,* the essence of which is the idea of taking action to address an environmental threat ahead of a disaster[6]: "In order to protect the environment, the precautionary approach shall be widely applied by States according to their capabilities. Where there are threats of serious or irreversible damage, lack of full scientific certainty shall not be used as a reason for postponing cost-effective measures to prevent environmental degradation."

Principle 4 of the Rio Declaration endorses the concept of *sustainable development,* which had been enunciated by the 1987 Brundtland Report, *Our Common Future:* "In order to achieve sustainable development, environmental protection shall constitute an integral part of the development process and cannot be considered in isolation from it."[7]

Thirty years after Stockholm, and ten years after the Rio Earth Summit, the World Summit on Sustainable Development was held in Johannesburg, South Africa, to review progress since Rio. In addition to the 10,000 delegates, some 8,000 representatives of major organizations (representing women, children and youth, indigenous people, NGOs, local authorities, workers and trade unions, business and industry, scientific and technological communities, and farmers) were accredited to the Summit; the Civil Society Global Forum ran parallel to the summit. The summit produced the Johannesburg Declaration on Sustainable Development, by which the "representatives of the peoples of the world" reaffirmed the commitment to sustainable development, as well as the more detailed Johannesburg Plan of Implementation,[8] which set out a number of specific targets by which to make sustainable development a reality. Under "poverty eradication," for example, governments agreed to halve, by 2015, the proportion of the world's people whose income is less than $1 a day and the proportion of people who suffer from hunger and, by the same date, to halve the proportion of people without access to safe drinking water. These agreements were complemented by the commitment by governments and other stakeholders to a broad range of partnership activities and initiatives to implement sustainable development at the national, regional, and international levels. Businesses became involved in more than ninety partnership initiatives launched at the summit, in a range of sectors including energy, water, agriculture, and biodiversity.[9]

Although there had been some international agreements relating to the environment prior to Stockholm, they were comparatively few. Stockholm was a springboard for the development of international environmental law. By the time of the United Nations Conference on Environment and Development in June 1992, there were more than 870 legal instruments in which at least some provisions are concerned with environmental issues[10] (see Figure 13.1). It was partly in reaction to the years of negotiating the detailed and comprehensive Law of the Sea Convention—which was ultimately rejected by the United States—and partly due to the difficulties of getting far-reaching commitments to environmental action that the standard in environmental negotiations has become that of negotiating a framework convention followed by one or more protocols.[11] The Vienna Convention on the Protection of the Ozone Layer was followed by the Montreal Protocol, the Framework Convention on Climate Change was followed by the Kyoto Protocol, and so on. Most of the environmental treaty regimes have established at least two institutions: a conference of the parties (COP) and a secretariat, though the precise role played by each varies between regimes.

**Figure 13.1 Some Key Global Treaties Establishing
               Environmental Treaty Regimes**

1972	Convention for the Protection of the World Cultural and Natural Heritage
1973	Convention on International Trade in Endangered Species of Wild Fauna and Flora
1979	Convention on the Conservation of Migratory Species of Wild Animals
1979	Convention on Long Range Transboundary Air Pollution
1982	United Nations Convention on the Law of the Sea, Part XII
1985	Vienna Convention for the Protection of the Ozone Layer
1986	Convention on Early Notification of a Nuclear Accident
1989	Convention on the Control of Transboundary Movements of Hazardous Wastes and Their Disposal
1992	UN Framework Convention on Climate Change
1992	Convention on the Protection and Use of Transboundary Watercourses and Lakes
1992	Convention on Biological Diversity
1994	UN Convention to Combat Desertification
2001	Stockholm Convention on Persistent Organic Pollutants

■ The Ozone Depletion Regime

The ozone depletion treaty regime was founded on the Vienna Convention for the Protection of the Ozone Layer[12] and the Montreal Protocol on Substances that Deplete the Ozone Layer.[13] With the Montreal Protocol having in 2009 achieved universal ratification and with human-induced ozone depletion having in recent years been decreasing, the ozone depletion regime is regarded as one of the most successful environmental regimes.[14] Aspects of the regime—including its application of the precautionary approach, financial mechanisms, and institutional arrangements—have influenced other regimes.

The stratospheric ozone layer first became a subject of concern in 1970 when it was feared that supersonic transportation may cause it damage. Concern reappeared in 1974 when two scientists suggested that the chlorine in chlorofluorocarbons (CFCs) could destroy ozone molecules and deplete the ozone layer.[15] CFCs were invented in 1928 by DuPont and General Motors chemists who were seeking a nontoxic heat transfer fluid for refrigeration. They came to be widely used, not only in refrigeration and air-conditioning, but also as blowing foams, solvents, sterilants, freezing agents, surface treatment agents, and propellants for aerosol spray cans. Ozone destruction permits increased levels of UV-B radiation to reach Earth's surface, causing increases in skin cancers and other damaging health and environmental effects. The strength of the scientific evidence against CFCs was a factor that contributed to the success of the treaty-making efforts.[16]

In response to the scientific findings, the United States and several other countries—including Canada and Sweden—took unilateral action to control aerosol emissions of CFCs in the 1970s. Several international organizations also became involved in the CFC/ozone issue, including the World Meteorological Organization and the Organization for Economic Cooperation and Development. In response to growing concern, the United Nations Environment Programme (UNEP) in 1981 established an ad hoc working group of legal and technical experts charged with the task of drafting a global framework convention for the protection of the ozone layer. By article 2 of the 1985 Vienna Convention, the parties agreed to "take appropriate measures in accordance with the provisions of this Convention and of those protocols in force to which they are party to protect human health and the environment against adverse effects resulting or likely to result from human activities which modify or are likely to modify the ozone layer." No specific controls on production and use could be agreed at Vienna, but the Convention legitimized stratospheric ozone depletion as an international environmental issue and provided a framework—including an agreement to cooperate in scientific research and to exchange information—within which further negotiation could take place.[17]

Scientific understanding of stratospheric ozone continued to evolve, and by 1987 there was much stronger evidence of the ozone-depleting role of CFCs and other ozone-depleting substances (ODS) and hence greater public concern and international consensus on the need to take decisive action. Although the two largest manufacturers of CFCs were initially opposed to international restrictions on CFCs, Imperial Chemical Industries (ICI) and DuPont came to favor controls once they saw the opportunity for increased profits through the marketing of new, more profitable substitutes.[18] The Montreal Protocol, adopted and opened for signature on September 16, 1987, provided for the production and consumption of the controlled chemicals to be limited to 80 percent of 1986 levels by July 1, 1993, and to 50 percent of 1986 levels by July 1, 1998.[19] Scientific findings that were released soon after the crafting of the Montreal Protocol indicated not only that these reductions would be inadequate to eliminate the existing hole in the ozone layer but that they would not even reduce ozone depletion.[20] Both the convention and the protocol provide that there shall be regular meetings of the parties to the respective instruments,[21] and, at the 1990 London meeting,[22] the parties amended the protocol to strengthen existing measures for the control of substances covered by the original protocol and agreed on controls for additional substances.[23]

Ozone depletion had initially been an issue of concern to certain developed countries that manufactured and used CFCs. But by the time of the London meeting, developed countries realized that their efforts would be to no avail if the large, highly populated, developing countries were not actively involved in the treaty regime. The realization that any regime relating to protection of the ozone layer must include highly populated states, whether or not they were significant consumers or producers of ozone-depleting substances, was particularly important "because it marked one of the few times that the industrialized world needed the cooperation and participation of the Third World."[24] It was not clear at this stage whether some of the largest developing countries would come on board. India and China argued strongly that it was unfair for industrialized countries to expect developing countries to forego CFC-containing technologies or to pay more for substitutes and thereby enrich the chemical industries that had created the problem in the first place.[25] Developing countries wanted to retain access to CFCs or to get assistance to acquire substitutes.

Article 5(1) of the Montreal Protocol allowed developing countries to delay for ten years their compliance with the control measures, and to exceed the target percentage reductions at any point if such action is deemed necessary in order to satisfy basic domestic needs. Concerned at the precedent it would set, the United States and other industrialized states were at first strongly opposed to establishing a fund to assist the developing countries in their transitions from CFC technologies.[26] But, after intense bargaining at the London conference, key developing states became parties to the protocol; in return, developed states agreed to provide financial incentives and technical cooperation through a multilateral fund. Parties to the protocol are required to "take every practicable step, consistent with the programmes supported by the financial mechanism, to ensure . . . that the best available, environmentally safe substitutes and related technologies" are expeditiously transferred to certain developing countries. This was the first time that the national governments of developed countries voted to provide developing countries with financial assistance for reaching environmental goals.[27]

The Multilateral Fund for the Implementation of the Montreal Protocol began operations in 1991. It pays the agreed incremental costs incurred by developing countries in phasing out their consumption and production of ozone-depleting substances.[28] By mid-2009, the fund had supported the transfer of technology and capacity building through more than 6,000 projects and activities in 147 developing countries.[29] States with "economies in transition," including those of Central and Eastern Europe, receive assistance from the Global Environmental Facility.[30]

The protocol has been further adjusted and amended at several meetings of the parties since London. Details of adjustments, amendments, and other decisions of the parties to the Montreal Protocol and the Vienna Convention can be found in the regime handbooks, available from the UNEP Ozone Secretariat.[31]

■ The Climate Change Regime

The phrase *greenhouse effect* refers to the gradual warming of Earth's atmosphere.[32] Carbon dioxide, water vapor, methane, and nitrous oxide act as a blanket around the Earth; their increased emission by people and the steady reduction in the number of trees to absorb carbon dioxide means that heat has been increasingly less able to escape the solar system, thereby raising the Earth's temperature. Scientists believe that even a warming of two degrees Celsius could have dramatic effects on Earth's climate, affecting rainfall, wind, cloud cover, ocean currents, sea levels, growing seasons, and polar ice caps. Although there might be an occasional positive effect from such change, the overall impact is negative. The solution to the greenhouse effect appears clear, although it is not easy to achieve: "(1) stop the burning of fossil fuels, (2) stop the destruction of the world's rain forests, and (3) replant those areas that have already been destroyed."[33]

The success of the Montreal Protocol encouraged international negotiations on the larger concern of global climate change.[34] The climate change regime was one of the most quickly established of all international regimes.

In December 1988 the UN General Assembly passed a resolution calling for the adoption of a framework convention on climate change.[35] The World Meteorological Organization and the United Nations Environment Programme (UNEP) then established the Intergovernmental Panel on Climate Change (IPCC) in 1988 to assess the scientific basis and impact of climate change and to make recommendations. Its first scientific report was published in 1990. In the same year the General Assembly established the Intergovernmental Negotiating Committee to draft a framework treaty. The United Nations Framework Convention on Climate Change[36] was opened for signature at the UN Conference on Environment and Development (UNCED) and entered into force on March 21, 1994.[37]

The Climate Change Convention incorporated the principle of common but differentiated responsibility: although all parties share certain common responsibilities in the context of global warming, developed countries have a particular onus to act. Articles 4(2)a and 4(2)b oblige developed states (annex 1 countries) to adopt national policies that "will demonstrate that developed countries are taking the lead in modifying longer-term trends in anthropogenic emissions consistent with the objective of the convention" and to provide detailed reports on such policies "with the aim of returning individually or jointly to their 1990 levels . . . of carbon dioxide and other greenhouse gases not controlled by the Montreal Protocol." The Alliance of Small Island States, Australia, Canada, and New Zealand supported the inclusion of time-tabled emission reductions in the treaty text, but the United States and some oil-producing countries argued that any introduction of specific emission reductions would be premature.[38] The convention left the negotiation of the limits on emission standards and implementation procedure to the COP. The convention included a financial mechanism as well as an implementation and dispute settlement mechanism.

By the mid-1990s it was becoming clear that developed countries, in particular the United States, would not meet their emission reduction targets of 1990 levels by the year 2000;[39] scientific opinion also indicated that earlier agreed targets would not be enough to significantly reduce climate change. Business NGOs became more active in the regime and were quite influential, particularly in the United States, in discouraging any move on the part of governments toward controlled emission standards.[40] No protocol was negotiated at the first conference of the parties in Berlin, Germany, in 1995, but the parties did adopt the so-called Berlin Mandate, a decision that they would adopt a protocol or another legal instrument to strengthen the commitments of the annex 1 parties.[41]

In the lead-up to the third COP, the United States, with 4 percent of the world's population, more than 20 percent of the world's wealth, and producing more than 20 percent of greenhouse emissions,[42] made it known that it expected the developing nations as well as the industrialized nations to participate in setting "realistic and binding goals." The European Union took a strong line, proposing uniform binding targets of a 15 percent reduction in greenhouse gas emissions by 2010 (based on 1990 levels). The European Union planned to meet its proposed target of a net 10 percent decrease by averaging emission levels across the whole EU "bubble." Thus Greece, Ireland, Portugal, Spain, and Sweden were to be permitted to increase their emission levels, but this would be countered by the closing of the former East Germany's outdated heavy industry and Britain's change from coal-fired to natural gas power stations. The Group of 77 accepted the European target as appropriate for the industrialized nations, but the developing countries made it quite clear that they would not commit themselves to reduce their own emissions of greenhouse gases.

The Kyoto Protocol to the United Nations Framework Convention on Climate Change[43] was adopted by the third COP on December 11, 1997, and entered into force on February 16, 2005. The individual emission targets of states were tailored in a way to meet a global outcome of a 5.2 percent reduction below 1990 levels in greenhouse gases by 2012. Three non-EU annex 1 (developed) countries were to be allowed emissions growth above their 1990 levels: Australia (+8 percent), Iceland (+10 percent), and Norway (+1 percent) The EU received a collective emissions target of –8 percent; the United States, –7 percent; and Japan, –6 percent.[44] In addition to individual emission targets, the protocol allowed for other mechanisms to help reduce emissions, including the "clean development mechanism" (CDM),[45] joint implementation (JI), and emissions trading. These were designed to help annex 1 countries achieve their reductions more cheaply than they could at home, by doing so in other countries. Emissions trading, for example, would allow companies to be able to sell excess permits on the open market, where they could be bought by companies that failed to meet emission targets. The Kyoto Protocol also included stronger reporting obligations and a system to address noncompliance.[46]

US President Clinton signed the protocol but said that he would not submit it to the Senate for ratification unless several changes were made. His successor, George W. Bush, strengthened US opposition to the Kyoto Protocol, insisting that developing countries make "meaningful" contributions to future reductions in greenhouse gas emissions. To critics, this position appeared to reject the principle of common but differentiated responsibility with which the United States had agreed under article 3(1) of the UN Framework Convention on Climate Change (UNFCCC).[47]

A UN climate change conference was held in Bali, Indonesia, December 3–15, 2007, representing both the thirteenth annual meeting of the conference of the parties to the UNFCCC (COP 13) and the third COP serving as the meeting of parties to the 1997 Kyoto Protocol. The conference adopted the "Bali Roadmap," which launched an adaptation fund and includes the Bali Action Plan,[48] setting out a two-year process aimed at completing negotiations for a post-2012 protocol to the convention at the fifteenth conference of states parties.

By the time the fifteenth COP to the UNFCCC and fifth COP to the Kyoto Protocol convened in Copenhagen, Denmark, on December 7, 2009, however, there was pervasive doubt that agreement could yet be reached on a legally binding agreement. China had well and truly overtaken the United States as the world's biggest producer of carbon dioxide emissions.[49] Its attitude and actions would be critical to the success of global efforts to prevent catastrophic climate change both in a direct sense and because of the influence on climate change skeptics and decisionmakers in other countries, particularly the United States.

Negotiations between the United States, China, Brazil, South Africa, and India led by US President Barack Obama in the closing days of the Copenhagen conference gave rise to the Copenhagen Accord,[50] a political agreement recognizing the need to keep global warming to below two degrees Celsius and providing for a Copenhagen Green Climate Fund through which developed countries would assist developing states with the financial costs of adaptation and mitigation. Developing countries signatories to the accord agreed to implement nationally appropriate mitigation actions; significantly, those supported by technology, finance, and capacity building were to be subject to international measurement, reporting, and verification. Due to opposition from some developing countries, including Tuvalu and Bolivia, the conference did no more than "note" the Copenhagen accord, which therefore has no legal status within the current international law climate change framework but may be an important step toward another legally binding treaty. There were many outspoken critics of the accord. Meanwhile, global emissions of greenhouse gases continue to increase.

■ The Basel Regime

One reason sometimes given for the success of the ozone depletion regime is that the United States campaigned so strongly for it, having already introduced its own domestic legislation that could then be used as a blueprint for an international agreement. The so-called Basel regime provides an interesting contrast to the ozone depletion regime in this respect, because the major impetus for its creation was concern on the part of the developing world and environmental NGOs.

The Convention on the Control of Transboundary Movements of Hazardous Wastes and Their Disposal was concluded in 1989 in Basel, Switzerland, and entered into force in 1992.[51] It was the first global attempt to deal with the problem of toxic trade and was negotiated under the auspices of the

UNEP. Between the 1940s and the 1980s there was an enormous increase in the volume of hazardous waste generated annually worldwide, particularly by the United States and Western Europe. Because more stringent environmental regulations increased costs of local disposal, producers increasingly looked elsewhere to dispose of waste. Some was exported to other industrialized countries, but more waste was increasingly sent to the developing world. Africa was particularly targeted in the mid 1980s, as was the South Pacific, the Caribbean, and Latin America. As opposition to the trade in these countries increased by the early 1990s, Asia and Eastern and Central Europe were increasingly targeted.[52] Although the receipt of considerable foreign exchange was an obvious attraction, the trade caused many problems. The developing countries often had inadequate or no means by which to safeguard the waste, and it could easily cause considerable environmental damage and endanger health. This was particularly so if the waste was mislabeled and the recipient misinformed or deceived regarding the product. For example, the European Community sent radioactive milk to Jamaica in 1987, and a US company sold fertilizer mixed with copper smelter dust containing high levels of lead to Bangladeshi farmers.[53]

In the early 1980s the UNEP began drafting guidelines on the waste trade. The work was completed in 1985, the Cairo Guidelines were adopted by the UNEP Governing Council in 1987,[54] and the General Assembly endorsed the guidelines in December 1987. In 1987 UNEP began work on what became the Basel Convention. The text was negotiated during five working sessions between late 1987 and early 1989 by an ad hoc working group of legal and technical experts with a mandate to prepare a global convention on the control of transboundary movements of hazardous wastes. Informal negotiations conducted by the executive director with governments, IGOs, NGOs, and industry also played an important part in the success of the preparatory process.[55] The three main types of actors involved in the negotiations were developed countries, developing countries, and a grouping of environmental NGOs called the International Toxic Waste Action Network. Developing countries were opposed to the trade, which they regarded as not only environmentally damaging but also damaging to their long-term economies.

The Basel Convention does not ban all transboundary movement of hazardous waste, but it does impose controls and limitations on the trade. A party is not to permit hazardous or other wastes to be exported to, or imported from, a nonparty and, by article 4, may elect to prohibit the import of hazardous wastes for disposal; other parties are then to prohibit the export of wastes to that party. If a party has not prohibited the import of wastes, its written consent to a specific import must be obtained. By article 9, parties are to ensure that the transboundary movement of hazardous wastes and other wastes only be allowed if: (1) the state of export does not have the technical capacity and the necessary facilities, capacity, or suitable disposal sites in order to dispose of the wastes in an environmentally sound and efficient manner; (2) the wastes are required as a raw material for recycling or recovery industries in the state of import; or (3) the transboundary movement in question is in accordance with other criteria to be decided by the parties.

In the belief that the Basel Convention had not gone far enough, the Organization of African Unity provided in the 1991 Bamako (Mali) Convention that "all Parties shall take appropriate legal, administrative and other measures within the area under their jurisdiction to prohibit the import of all hazardous wastes, for any reason, into Africa from non-Contracting Parties. Such import shall be deemed illegal and a criminal act."[56]

In December 1992 Costa Rica, Honduras, El Salvador, Guatemala, and Nicaragua signed a regional agreement requiring parties to prohibit the import and transit of hazardous wastes to Central America.[57] Individual countries, including Poland, Ukraine, and the Philippines, have imposed national bans on hazardous waste imports.[58]

In September 1995 the Basel Convention was amended to ban hazardous waste exports for final disposal and recycling from what are known as annex 7 countries (members of the OECD, the EU, and Liechtenstein) to non–annex 7 countries. This was a major breakthrough for environmentalists but has to be ratified by three-quarters of the states parties in order to enter into force. This has generally been understood to mean three-quarters of those states parties present in 1995, but an alternative interpretation is that it will not enter into force until ratified by three-quarters of parties at the current time.

In December 1999 the conference of the parties adopted the Basel Protocol on Liability and Compensation for Damage Resulting from Transboundary Movements of Hazardous Waste and Their Disposal (this has not yet entered into force). The COP is continuing to seek ways to promote minimizing the generation of hazardous and other waste as well as its transboundary movement.

■ Convention on Biological Diversity, 1992

The Convention on Biological Diversity (CBD),[59] the first global agreement specifically devoted to the conservation and sustainable use of biological diversity, was negotiated between 1987 and 1992 under the auspices of the UNEP. The convention was adopted on May 22, 1992, in Nairobi, Kenya, and opened for signature at the UNCED. *Biodiversity* means the variability within and among living organisms and the systems they inhabit. Biodiversity supports the ecosystem functions essential for life on Earth, such as the provision of fresh water, soil conservation, and climate stability as well as providing products such as food, medicines, and materials for industry. The rate of biodiversity loss has been increasing at an unprecedented rate.

The Convention on Biological Diversity does not focus on saving specific species facing extinction but takes a holistic approach to maintaining genetic diversity. *Diversity* is understood to include diversity within species, among species, and of ecosystems. The convention incorporates the precautionary principle in that it is a step toward lessening harmful impacts of human activity despite the fact that scientists recognize that they do not yet know all the scientific implications of reduced diversity or the extent to which diversity has already been reduced, particularly in the oceans.

As a framework convention, it does not go far in setting out substantive rules. Primary responsibility remains at the national level; each state party is, "in accordance with its particular conditions and capabilities," to "develop national strategies, plans or programmes for the conservation and sustainable use of biological diversity" and to "integrate, as far as possible and as appropriate, the conservation and sustainable use of biological diversity into relevant sectoral or cross-sectoral plans, programmes and policies" (article 6). Areas beyond national jurisdiction are to be addressed, as appropriate, either by states acting individually or through "competent international organizations." The CBD entered into force in late 1993.

The conference of the parties to the Convention on Biological Diversity adopted the Cartagena (Spain) Protocol on Biosafety on January 29, 2000, and it entered into force on September 11, 2003.[60] The protocol provides an international regulatory framework for the safe transfer, handling, and use of living modified organisms resulting from modern biotechnology. Negotiations are underway for a protocol addressing the subject of access to genetic resources and the fair and equitable sharing of benefits arising out of their utilization.

■ Stockholm Convention on Persistent Organic Pollutants, 2001

The Stockholm Convention on Persistent Organic Pollutants,[61] which came about as a result of the 1992 Earth Summit, is designed to eliminate or severely restrict the production and use of certain toxic pesticides and industrial chemicals including aldrin, chlordane, DDT, dieldrin, endrin, and dioxins. Such chemicals are termed "persistent" because they do not break down in the environment; they accumulate in the body fat of people and animals and can travel great distances on wind and water currents. Although the exact nature and extent of toxic chemical threats remains unknown, it is believed that many people around the world now carry enough persistent organic pollutants (POPs) in their body fat to cause serious health problems, including reproductive and developmental problems, cancer, and immune system disruption.

As with other environmental treaties, a network of NGOs played an active role in the negotiations. In early 1998 a small group of NGOs formed the International POPs Elimination Network (IPEN).[62] IPEN coordinated NGO conferences and workshops at the five negotiating sessions from 1998 to 2000. The treaty was adopted on May 22, 2001, and entered into force on May 17, 2004. IPEN is now a network of more than 700 public-interest NGOs working for the elimination of POPs on an expedited yet socially equitable basis.

Article 1 states, "Mindful of the precautionary approach as set forth in Principle 15 of the Rio Declaration on Environment and Development, the objective of this Convention is to protect human health and the environment from persistent organic pollutants." Chemicals are listed in annexes to the convention. Some are to be immediately banned, whereas the use of others is to be significantly curtailed. Developed countries commit to providing financial assistance to help developing countries in the implementation of the convention. The treaty established the POPs Review Committee to evaluate additional chemicals with a view to their inclusion in the regime.

■ The Law of the Sea and Protection of the Marine Environment

In Chapters 10–13 we have considered separately some of the key treaties in several fields of international law. In practice, however, legal instruments rarely function as discrete entities but as part of a network of interrelated treaties. To get some sense of that, we will survey a group of treaties that bear on the subject of the marine environment. The body of international law designed to protect the marine environment has evolved into an extensive web of multilateral treaties that has witnessed some notable successes. Operational discharges of oil from ships have been greatly reduced, in many cases sewage and industrial discharges have been controlled, and a ban on ocean disposal of radioactive waste has reduced radionuclide contamination of the marine environment. Much of the existing international law on the marine environment evolved in response to disasters; there is now a recognized need to try to preempt if not prevent disasters through coordinated global action.

The 1982 Law of the Sea Convention is the starting point for considering any aspect of existing oceans law. Although comprehensive in the sense of dealing with all areas of marine protection, the 1982 convention is supplemented by many other, more detailed, agreements, some of which predated it and some of which are more recent than the convention. We begin by looking briefly at the background to the 1982 convention before moving on to the treaty itself and then to other treaties that also protect the marine environment.

The 1930, 1958, and 1960
Conferences on the Law of the Sea

The law of the sea was unsettled between the end of the fifteenth century and the beginning of the nineteenth century. There were two contending schools of thought. The first, Mare Clausum (Closed Sea), held that the sea and its resources are capable of being subject to appropriation and dominion. The second school of thought, expounded by Hugo Grotius, argued that things that cannot be seized or enclosed cannot become property. It was the Grotian view, by which no one can claim exclusive rights over fisheries or navigation on the high seas, that came gradually to predominate in the eighteenth century.[63] By the beginning of the nineteenth century, Britain was the champion of the idea of the "freedom of the seas," subject only to a coastal state's right to claim a narrow belt of the sea offshore its coast for the purpose of fishing and protecting its neutrality.[64] Foreign vessels retained a right of "innocent passage" through those waters. The only accepted extensions of these rights were some claims to exclusive fishing rights beyond territorial waters, made on the basis of long uninterrupted usage. The principle of freedom of the seas was clearly in the interests of a major trading and colonial power.

By 1930 the international law of the sea was nearing the end of the two centuries of relative stability. The Hague Codification Conference in 1930, which followed years of work by a committee of experts, sought to clarify a standard width of territorial waters, but its participants were unable to agree on the exact extent of the territorial sea. The fact that only ten of the participating states accepted the three-mile limit as favored by Britain was evidence of the challenge to its supremacy. The "traditional" law of the sea had developed primarily in response to issues of transport, communications, and fisheries. Following World War II, these issues were transformed; new fishing methods increased markedly the total volume of fishing, necessitating new conservation measures. It also became technically possible and economically feasible to exploit other resources of the sea, and to use the oceans for military deployment and the dumping of waste materials, also raising a number of new management issues.

One of the first postwar changes to the traditional law of the sea was the emergence of the continental shelf doctrine. The *continental shelf* was a term used by geologists and geographers to refer to the area of comparatively shallow water bordering a continent and separating it from the drop to the deep ocean floor. The depth and width of the shelf and its surface range considerably. In the first of two "Truman proclamations" made in September 1945, US President Harry Truman asserted sovereign rights of jurisdiction and control over the natural resources of the subsoil and seabed of its continental shelf.[65] Although the wording of the proclamation included all "natural resources," there is little doubt that the motivation for Truman's action was the emerging offshore oil industry.[66] The declaration was to in no way affect the legal status of the high seas above the continental shelf. In his second proclamation, Truman provided for the establishment of conservation zones for the protection of fisheries in "certain areas of the high seas contiguous to the United States." In those areas fished by nationals of other countries as well as the United States, zones were to be established by agreement, and joint regulations and controls would be put into effect.

Although it was the relative shallowness of the water over the continental shelf that facilitated the exploitation of oil reserves and so prompted the Truman proclamations, the geographical phenomenon of a shelf became the convenient basis for a general extension of coastal states' rights beyond the territorial limit. More than twenty nations followed suit during the next eight years, many of which had no immediate interest in mining developments, and some of which did not even have a continental shelf in the geological sense.[67] The precise nature of the claims varied according to motivations, from mere jurisdiction over resources of the seabed, to actual ownership of the bed and the seas above the shelf. The first country to claim a 200-mile zone was Chile, which on June 23, 1947, proclaimed national sovereignty over the continental shelf off its coasts and islands and over the seas above the shelf to a distance of 200 miles.[68] The Chilean proclamation was motivated primarily by the perceived needs of its new offshore whaling operations. Peru promulgated its declaration of a 200-mile zone on August 1, 1947, in an effort to protect its fisheries; a number of other declarations followed. The Truman proclamation claiming to be based solely on that which was "reasonable and just" met little opposition,[69] but the more extensive claims of the South American states prompted international protest.

Preparatory work for the 1958 Law of the Sea Conference had been undertaken by the International Law Commission, which had prepared seventy-three draft articles that the conference transformed into four treaties: the Convention on the High Seas, the Convention on Fishing and Conservation of the Living Resources of the High Seas, the Convention on the Territorial Sea, and the Convention on the Continental Shelf. Neither the 1958 conference nor the second Conference on the Law of the Sea held two years later, was able to agree on the limits of the territorial sea or on the coastal states' exclusive fishing rights.

With the decolonization process of the 1960s and 1970s, many newly independent states became dissatisfied with the existing law of the sea, which they believed to be the product of European experience.[70] On November 1, 1967, Arvid Pardo, the Maltese ambassador to the United Nations, made a landmark speech to the First Committee of the UN General Assembly. Pardo drew attention to the immense resources of the seabed and ocean floor beyond the limits of national jurisdiction and proposed that the seabed and ocean floor be used exclusively for peaceful purposes and that the area and its resources be considered the "common heritage of mankind." He suggested that a constitution or charter be adopted dealing with ocean space as an organic and ecological whole.[71] The United Nations responded by establishing the Seabed Committee to develop a legal regime for the exploration and exploitation of the resources of the ocean floor area.

The 1982 Law of the Sea Convention

The third UN Law of the Sea Conference was a vast diplomatic and legal undertaking. By the time negotiations began in December 1973, only 27 out of 111 coastal states still claimed a 3-mile territorial sea; 52 claimed a territorial sea of 12 miles. The United Nations Convention on the Law of the Sea (LOSC)[72] established the right of every state to a 12-mile territorial sea and also included the right of ships of all states to innocent passage through the territorial sea. LOSC established that adjacent to the territorial sea there be an exclusive economic zone (EEZ) of not more than 200 nautical miles from the baselines from which the breadth of the territorial sea is measured. All states retain high seas freedom of navigation within the EEZ while coastal states acquire jurisdiction over vessels only to apply international rules for enforcement purposes. The coastal state has sovereign rights over living and mineral resources within this zone, as well as jurisdiction with regard to the protection and preservation of the marine environment. The coastal state was to fix a total allowable catch of different species within the EEZ and, if unable to harvest that entire catch, allocate the surplus to third states (article 62). The first priority was to go to landlocked and geographically disadvantaged states, second to developing countries, and third to other countries including the traditional fishing nations (articles 62, 69, and 70).

The Convention consists of the following parts:

Part I: Introduction
Part II: Territorial Sea and Contiguous Zone
Part III: Straits Used for International Navigation
Part IV: Archipelagic States
Part V: Exclusive Economic Zone

Part VI: Continental Shelf
Part VII: High Seas
Part VIII: Regime of Islands
Part IX: Enclosed or Semi-Enclosed Seas
Part X: Right of Access of Land-Locked States to and from the Sea and
    Freedom of Transit
Part XI: The Area
Part XII: Protection and Preservation of the Marine Environment
Part XIII: Marine Scientific Research
Part XIV: Development and Transfer of Marine Technology
Part XV: Settlement of Disputes
Part XVI: General Provisions
Part XVII: Final Provisions

There are also nine annexes:

Annex I: Highly Migratory Species
Annex II: Commission on the Limits of the Continental Shelf
Annex III: Basic Conditions of Prospecting, Exploration, and
    Exploitation
Annex IV: Statute of the Enterprise
Annex V: Conciliation
Annex VI: Statute of the International Tribunal for the Law of the Sea
Annex VII: Arbitration
Annex VIII: Special Arbitration
Annex IX: Participation by International Organizations

LOSC entered into force on November 16, 1994, one year after the deposit of the sixtieth instrument of ratification of or accession to the convention. Several key Western states did not become parties to the convention, however, because they were not happy with the provisions in Part XI relating to exploitation of the deep seabed. Consultations initiated by the UN Secretary-General with the objective of increasing regime participation resulted in the 1994 Agreement Relating to the Implementation of Part XI of the Convention.[73] Depite this, the United States remains outside the LOSC regime.

The LOSC and Protection of the Marine Environment

The most fundamental environmental obligation states accept under the LOSC regime is to "protect and preserve" the marine environment. To this end states are to take, individually or jointly as appropriate, all measures consistent with the convention necessary to prevent, reduce, and control pollution of the marine environment from any source.[74] Part XII focuses on the protection and preservation of the marine environment, although provisions relating to protection of the marine environment are scattered throughout the convention. The principle that states have the responsibility to ensure that activities within their jurisdiction or control do not cause damage to the environment of other states or of areas beyond the limits of national jurisdiction is reiterated in the 1982 convention as it relates to pollution of the marine environment.[75]

In providing for international rules and national legislation to prevent, reduce, and control pollution of the marine environment within zones of national jurisdiction and on the high seas, LOSC distinguishes between flag states, port states, and coastal states, although in practice a state may, of course, often fall into more than one category. The 1982 convention leaves no doubt that the "freedom of the high seas" no longer includes the freedom to pollute them. Flag states are to ensure that vessels flying their flag or of their registry are prohibited from sailing until they comply with relevant international rules and standards and they are to provide the vessels with a certificate to that effect.[76] The 1982 convention marked a major change from customary international law, in that it also accorded jurisdiction to port states and coastal states. A port state—a state whose ports are visited by a vessel—may, under article 211(3), establish particular requirements for the prevention, reduction, and control of pollution of the marine environment as a condition for the entry of foreign vessels into its ports. Coastal states may adopt laws and regulations for the prevention, reduction, and control of marine pollution from foreign vessels operating in their territorial waters and EEZs as long as the rules do not hamper the right of innocent passage through the territorial sea. Under article 211(6)(a) a coastal state may apply to the International Maritime Organization (IMO) to have a certain area designated a special marine area protected from shipping. Two such sensitive areas that have been approved by the IMO are the Great Barrier Reef in Australia and the archipelago of Sabana-Camaguey in Cuba. Under the LOSC provisions on the marine environment, the flag state retains primary enforcement responsibility, but port states and coastal states are also given powers of inspection, detention, and instituting proceedings against a vessel in violation of marine pollution laws.

Despite the fact that a high proportion of marine pollution originates from land-based sources, the negotiating states wanted latitude to weigh environmental objectives against the needs of their economies.[77] Whereas the convention requires states to adhere to minimum international standards established by international organizations as regards pollution from ships, dumping, and seabed installations, they are only required to "take into account" internationally agreed rules, standards, and recommended practices and procedures in adopting laws and regulations to prevent, reduce, and control pollution of the environment from land-based sources.[78] They are also to "take other measures as may be necessary to prevent, reduce and control such pollution."[79]

Part XII of LOSC reinforced, and in some instances effectively superseded, the 1958 Geneva Conventions on the Law of the Sea and the 1972 Action Plan resulting from the Stockholm Conference. LOSC deals with the broad spectrum of ocean issues, but most provisions are of a very general nature. In this sense the treaty provides a framework for a complex web of more detailed treaty law, some of which predated, and some of which is more recent than, the 1982 convention.

The bulk of the instruments that fill in the LOSC framework for the marine environment have been sponsored by one of the two major institutions working to protect and preserve the marine environment: the International Maritime Organization, formerly called the Intergovernmental Maritime Consultative Organization (IMCO), and the UNEP.

The UNEP Regional Seas Programme and Other Regional Agreements

Although many environmental problems such as climate change are truly global, their particular nature and relative importance tends to vary from region to region; each sea has its own special characteristics. Under the Regional Seas Programme of UNEP,[80] launched in 1974, states in a particular region formulate a region-specific "action plan" that identifies areas of cooperation. In most cases a regional seas convention has been concluded to provide the legal framework for a regional action plan. Technical protocols address specific problems such as oil spills or conservation of a specific habitat. The Regional Seas Programme has been considered a great success. There are other regional treaties and programs for marine environmental protection, such as the OSPAR Commission for the North Atlantic and North Sea, not formally part of the Regional Seas Programme. The first international convention specifically concerned with land-based marine pollution was the 1974 Paris Convention on the Prevention of Marine Pollution from Land-Based Sources, concluded by states bordering the North Sea and the Northern Atlantic.

The IMO and Global Treaties to Protect the Marine Environment

In the late 1960s there were several major tanker accidents, such as the 1967 incident in which the *Torrey Canyon* ran aground at the entrance to the English Channel, spilling its entire cargo of 120,000 tons of crude oil. This was the biggest oil pollution incident ever recorded up to that time.[81] Such accidents posed major questions regarding their prevention and management and prompted the IMO to conclude a number of conventions relating to accidental pollution of the seas by ships. Some related directly to protection of the marine environment whereas others, such as the 1974 International Convention for the Safety of Life at Sea (SOLAS),[82] did so indirectly by addressing shipping safety concerns.

In terms of tonnage of oil entering the oceans, routine operations such as the cleaning of oil cargo tanks and the disposal of engine-room wastes posed an even bigger threat to the marine environment than accidents; at the time when IMCO first began operations it was normal practice simply to wash cargo tanks out with water and pump the resulting mixture of oil and water into the sea.[83] The IMCO assumed responsibility for the administration of the 1954 Convention for the Prevention of Pollution of the Sea by Oil (OILPOL)[84] and went on to sponsor a number of global and regional single-issue treaties designed to minimize ocean pollution from ships. The OILPOL Convention prohibited the dumping of oily wastes within a certain distance of land and in "special areas" where the danger to the environment was especially acute.

The International Convention for the Prevention of Pollution from Ships (MARPOL 73/78)[85] addresses pollution of the oceans by ships through both normal operations and accidents. MARPOL has a series of annexes, the sixth of which limits the main air pollutants contained in ships' exhaust gas and regulates shipboard incineration; the annex was revised in 2008. The IMO is now addressing the issue of the contribution of shipping in climate change. Shipping has been estimated to contribute over 2 percent of global carbon dioxide emissions. The 1969 International Convention for Civil Liability for Oil Pollution Damage and the 1971 International Convention on the Establishment of an International Fund for Compensation for Oil Pollution Damage established a system of liability and compensation for oil pollution damage caused by ships. In 1989 the International Convention on Salvage was adopted under IMO auspices. It was designed to create an incentive for salvors to take measures to protect the environment, even if those measures may have no useful result. In 1996 IMO members concluded the International Convention on Liability and Compensation for Damage in Connection with the Carriage of Hazardous and Noxious Substances by Sea.[86]

The 1990 London International Convention on Oil Pollution Preparedness, Response, and Cooperation (OPRC) is designed to facilitate international cooperation in the event of a major oil pollution incident. The OPRC Convention requires states to take certain precautionary measures such as having oil pollution emergency plans on ships, as well as national and regional systems for preparedness and response. It upholds the widely, though not universally, accepted principle of "polluter-pays": that is, the costs of

pollution should be borne by the person or organization responsible for causing the pollution and consequential costs.[87] OPRC 1990 has more than 100
contracting parties, representing 68 percent of the world's tonnage, and is
considered a great success. The 2000 Protocol on Preparedness, Response,
and Cooperation to Pollution Incidents by Hazardous and Noxious Substances extends the regulatory framework to cover releases of hazardous
and noxious substances.

Other relatively recent additions to the suite of IMO conventions relating to the marine environment include the 2004 Convention for the Control
and Management of Ships' Ballast Water and Sediments and the 2009 International Convention for the Safe and Environmentally Sound Recycling
of Ships. The latter attempts to balance protection of the marine environment with commercial and safety considerations.

■ Conclusion: Complementary and Overlapping Environmental Regimes

Although, as we have seen, there is a considerable amount of treaty law devoted to addressing specific issues of concern regarding the marine environment, there are many others that are not necessarily usually listed as
treaties on the marine environment but that also have a bearing on the subject. Marine living resources are often grouped in a separate category, but
the questions of how much of a particular species to catch and where are
clearly also pertinent to the marine environment more generally. The Basel
Convention helps protect the marine environment through regulating the
transboundary movement of hazardous wastes. The CBD is relevant because fifteen of the thirty-three types of animal life (phyla) are found only
in the oceans;[88] even the deep seabed is high in biodiversity.[89] Climate
change is also having a noticeable impact on the marine environment. Sea-
water is warming and becoming more acidic. As the oceans absorb increasing amounts of carbon dioxide, carbonic acid is formed, disrupting
processes of calcification used by coral and other organisms that are, in turn,
destroyed.

A principal challenge for international environmental law is that of forg-
ing and sustaining links between the many treaty regimes. Some of this is
already in train. Efforts are being directed toward developing effective links
between the Basel regime, the POPs regime, and the Rotterdam Convention on the Prior Informed Consent Procedure for Certain Hazardous Chemicals and Pesticides in International Trade.[90] Similarly, there is likely to be
increased interaction between the ozone depletion regime and the climate
change regime in part because there is little point in, for example, taking action to improve the ozone depletion issue but through so doing inadvertently

exacerbating global warming. Climate change is underscoring the interrelated nature of the global environment and the need to think in holistic terms.

■ Notes

1. 11 *International Legal Materials (ILM)* 1416 (1972).

2. The other two were a resolution on institutional and financial arrangements, and an action plan.

3. Edith Brown Weiss, "Introductory Note," 31 *ILM* 814 (1992), p. 816.

4. Paul G. Harris, "Common but Differentiated Responsibility: The Kyoto Protocol and United States Policy," *NYU Environmental Law Journal* 7 (1999): 27–48, esp. 30. See also Duncan French, "Developing States and International Environmental Law: The Importance of Differentiated Responsibilities," *International and Comparative Law Quarterly* 49 (January 2000): 35–60; and panel discussion on common but differentiated responsibility in the American Society of International Law, *Proceedings of the 96th Annual Meeting,* March 13–16, 2002, pp. 358–368.

5. See, inter alia, C. K. Mensah, "The Role of Developing Countries," in L. Campiglio, *The Environment After Rio: International Law and Economics* (London: Graham and Trotman, 1994), pp. 33–52; M. A. L. Miller, *The Third World in Global Environmental Politics* (Boulder, CO: Lynne Rienner, 1995); N. Middleton, P. O'Keefe, and S. Moyo, *The Tears of the Crocodile: From Rio to Reality in the Developing World* (London: Pluto, 1993); and John Ntambirweki, "The Developing Countries in the Evolution of an International Environmental Law," *Hastings International and Comparative Law Review* 14 (1991): 905–928.

6. See, inter alia, M. Fitzmaurice, *Contemporary Issues in International Environmental Law* (Cheltenham, UK: Edward Elgar, 2009); D. Freestone and Ellen Key, eds., *The Precautionary Principle and International Law: The Challenge of Implementation* (The Hague: Kluwer, 1996); Arie Trouwborst, *Evolution and Status of the Precautionary Principle in International Law* (The Hague: Kluwer Law International, 2002).

7. See Nico Schrijver, *The Evolution of Sustainable Development in International Law: Inception, Meaning, and Status* (Leiden, the Netherlands: Martinus Nijhoff, 2008).

8. See http://www.un.org.

9. For details, see http://www.basd-action.net.

10. Weiss, "Introductory Note," p. 814.

11. James K. Sebenius, "Designing Negotiations Toward a New Regime: The Case of Global Warming," *International Security* 15, no. 4 (Spring 1991): 110–148, esp. 114.

12. Vienna Convention for the Protection of the Ozone Layer, March 22, 1985, 26 *ILM* 1516 (1987).

13. Montreal Protocol on Substances that Deplete the Ozone Layer, September 16, 1987, 26 *ILM* 1541 (1987).

14. "Upgrading Ozone Layer Treaty to Assist in Combating Climate Change Key Issue at International Meeting in Egypt," November 2, 2009, http://www.unep.org.

15. A pathfinding study by Mario Molina and Sherwood Rowland in 1974 suggested that the release of chlorofluorocarbons might be leading to the depletion of

the ozone layer. See M. J. Molina and F. S. Rowland, "Stratospheric Sink for Chlorofluoromethanes: Ahlorine Atom Catalyzed Destruction of Ozone," *Nature* 249 (1974): 810.

16. Edward A. Parson, "Protecting the Ozone Layer," in Peter M. Haas, Robert O. Keohane, and Marc A. Levy, eds., *Institutions for the Earth: Sources of Effective International Environmental Protection* (Cambridge, MA: MIT Press, 1993), p. 29.

17. Peter M. Morrisette, "The Evolution of Policy Responses to Stratospheric Ozone Depletion," *Natural Resources Journal* 29 (1989): 793–820.

18. D. Bryk, "The Montreal Protocol and Recent Developments to Protect the Ozone Layer," *Harvard Environmental Law Review* 15 (1995): 275–298, esp. 293.

19. For discussion and analysis, see James T. B. Tripp, "The Montreal Protocol: Industrialised and Developing Countries Sharing the Responsibility for Protecting the Stratospheric Ozone Layer," *International Law and Politics* 20 (1988): 733–752.

20. Lori B. Talbot, "Recent Developments in the Montreal Protocol on Substances that Deplete the Ozone Layer: The June 1990 Meeting and Beyond," *International Lawyer* (Spring 1992): 145–181, esp. 147.

21. Article 6 of the convention; article 11 of the protocol.

22. Amendment to the Montreal Protocol on the Substances that Deplete the Ozone Layer, 29 *ILM* 537 (1991).

23. For the story and analysis of the London negotiations, see, inter alia, R. E. Benedick, *Ozone Diplomacy: New Directions in Safeguarding the Planet* (Cambridge, MA: Harvard University Press, 1991), chapter 3; and J. A. Mintz, "Progress Toward a Healthy Sky: An Assessment of the London Amendments to the Montreal Protocol on Substances that Deplete the Ozone Layer," *Yale Journal of International Law* 16, no. 2 (Summer 1991): 571–582.

24. David D. Caron, "Protection of the Stratospheric Ozone Layer and the Structure of International Environmental Lawmaking," *Hastings International and Comparative Law Review* 14 (1991): 761.

25. E. R. DeSombre and J. Kauffman, "The Montreal Protocol Multilateral Fund: Partial Success Story," in Robert O. Keohane and Marc A. Levy, eds., *Institutions for Environmental Aid: Pitfalls and Promises* (Cambridge, MA: MIT Press, 1996), pp. 89–126, esp. 95.

26. Miller, *The Third World in Global Environmental Politics,* p. 79.

27. "The Ozone Layer: The Lady Turned," *Economist,* July 7, 1990, p. 43.

28. "Backgrounder: Basic Facts and Data on the Science and Politics of Ozone Protection," United Nations Environment Programme, October 5, 2001, p. 8.

29. Multilateral Fund for the Implementation of the Montreal Protocol, "Achievements," http://www.multilateralfund.org.

30. See http://thegef.org.

31. See http://ozone.unep.org/.

32. Margot B. Peters, "An International Approach to the Greenhouse Effect: The Problem of Increased Atmospheric Carbon Dioxide Can Be Approached by an Innovative International Agreement," *California Western International Law Journal* 20, no. 1 (1989–1990): 67–89, esp. 68.

33. Ibid., p. 70.

34. Talbot, "Recent Developments in the Montreal Protocol on Substances that Deplete the Ozone Layer," p. 181. The ozone depletion regime is still looked at as a useful model. See, e.g., J. Abdel-Khalik, "Prescriptive Treaties in Global Warming:

Applying the Factors Leading to the Montreal Protocol," *Michigan Journal of International Law* 22 (Spring 2001): 489–521.

35. United Nations General Assembly, "Resolution on the Protection of the Global Climate," General Assembly Resolution 43/53, A/RES/43/53, January 27, 1989.

36. 31 *ILM* 849 (1992); and Shirley V. Scott, ed., *International Law and Politics: Key Documents* (Boulder, CO: Lynne Rienner, 2006), pp. 600–619.

37. The homepage of the secretariat can be found at http://unfccc.int.

38. Peter G. G. Davies, "Global Warming and the Kyoto Protocol," *International and Comparative Law Quarterly* 47 (1998): 446–461, esp. 448.

39. David Driesen, "Free Lunch or Cheap Fix? The Emissions Trading Idea and the Climate Change Convention," *Boston College Environmental Affairs Law Review* 26, no. 1 (1998): 1–88, esp. 18.

40. Tony Brenton, *The Greening of Machiavelli: The Evolution of International Environmental Politics* (London: Royal Institute of International Affairs and Earthscan, 1994), p. 168.

41. Decision 1/CP.1 (UN Document Fccc/CP/1995/7/Add.1). For an account and evaluation of the first COP, see S. Oberthür and H. Ott, "The First Conference of the Parties," *Environmental Law and Policy* 25/4/5 (1995): 144–156.

42. Cameron Forbes, "US Plays Greenhouse Game Hard as Possible," *Australian,* October 8, 1997, p. 13.

43. 37 *ILM* 22 (1998); and Scott, *Internationl Law and Politics,* pp. 620–640.

44. Media Release, Minister for Foreign Affairs, Alexander Downer, December 12, 1997.

45. The website of the Clean Development Mechanism is http://cdm.unfccc.int.

46. See O. Yoshida, "Soft Enforcement of Treaties: The Montreal Protocol's Noncompliance Procedure and the Functions of Internal International Institutions," *Colorado Journal of International Environmental Law and Policy* 10, no. 1 (1999): 95–141.

47. See discussion in Harris, "Common but Differentiated Responsibility."

48. Decision 1/CP.13, adopted at COP 13 in Bali, December 2007, available at http://unfccc.int.

49. John Vidal and David Adam, "China Overtakes US as World's Biggest CO_2 Emitter," *Guardian,* June 19, 2007, available at www.guardian.co.uk.

50. Available at http://unfccc.int/.

51. 28 *ILM* 657 (1989); and Scott, *International Law and Politics,* pp. 579–599. The webite of the secretariat is http://www.basel.int.

52. J. Clapp, "The Toxic Waste Trade with Less-Industrialised Countries: Economic Linkages and Political Alliances," *Third World Quarterly* 15, no. 3 (1994): 505–518, esp. 507.

53. Ibid.

54. Iwona Rummel-Bulsa, "The Basel Convention: A Global Approach for the Management of Hazardous Wastes," *Environmental Policy and Law* 24, no. 1 (1994): 13–18, esp. 13.

55. Ibid., p. 14.

56. "Bamako Convention on the Ban of the Import into Africa and the Control of Transboundary Movement and Management of Hazardous Wastes Within Africa," http://www.tufts.edu.

57. Jennifer R. Kitt, "Waste Exports to the Developing World: A Global Response," *Georgetown International Environmental Law Review* 7 (1995): 485–514, esp. 504.

58. Ibid.

59. 31 *ILM* 818 (1992); and Scott, *International Law and Politics,* pp. 641–660. The homepage of the convention is at http://www.cbd.int.

60. 39 *ILM* 1027 (2000); and Scott, *International Law and Politics,* pp. 661–679.

61. 40 *ILM* 532 (2001); and Scott, *International Law and Politics,* pp. 680–702. The website of the convention is at www.pops.int.

62. See http://www.ipen.org.

63. T. T. B. Koh, "Negotiating a New World Order for the Sea," in Alan K. Henrikson, ed., *Negotiating World Order: The Artisanship and Architecture of Global Diplomacy* (Wilmington, DE: Scholarly Resources, 1986), pp. 33–45, esp. 33–34.

64. For discussion of the origins of the 3-mile territorial waters, see Wyndham L. Walker, "Territorial Waters: The Cannon Shot Rule," *British Year Book of International Law 1945,* 210–231; and H. S. K. Kent, "The Historical Origins of the Three-Mile Limit," *American Journal of International Law* 48 (1954): 537–553.

65. Proclamation No. 2667 and No. 2668, "Policy of the United States with Respect to the Natural Resources of the Subsoil and Sea Bed of the Continental Shelf," September 28, 1945, *Federal Register* 10 (1945): 12303–12304.

66. A. L. Hollick, "United States Oceans Policy: The Truman Proclamations," *Virginia Journal of International Law* 17, no. 1 (1976): 23–55, esp. 23.

67. Only four states were actually engaged in off-shore drilling operations by 1954. R. Cullen, *Australian Federalism Offshore* (Melbourne: University of Melbourne Press, 1985), p. 7.

68. M. Whiteman, *Digest of International Law* 14 (Washington, DC: US Department of State, 1965), pp. 794–796.

69. B. A. Helmore, "The Continental Shelf," *Australian Law Review* 27 (1954): 732–734, esp. 732.

70. Koh, "Negotiating a New World Order for the Sea," p. 36.

71. See also Arvid Pardo, "Who Will Control the Seabed?" *Foreign Affairs* 47, no. 1 (October 1968): 123–137.

72. United Nations Convention on the Law of the Sea, 21 *ILM* 1261 (1982); and Scott, *International Law and Politics,* pp. 718–805.

73. 33 *ILM* (2004) 1309; and Scott, *International Law and Politics,* pp. 806–823.

74. United Nations Convention on the Law of the Sea, 21 *ILM* 1261 (1982), article 194 (1).

75. Ibid., article 194(2).

76. Ibid., article 217.

77. P. W. Birnie and A. E. Boyle, *International Law and the Environment* (Oxford: Clarendon, 1992), p. 307.

78. United Nations Convention on the Law of the Sea, 21 *ILM* 1261 (1982), article 207(1).

79. Ibid., article 207(2).

80. http://www.unep.org/regionalseas/.

81. "IMO—The First Fifty Years," http://www.imo.org.

82. "International Convention for the Safety of Life at Sea," November 1, 1974, 1184 United Nations Treaty Series (UNTS) 2.

83. "IMO—The First Fifty Years."

84. "International Convention for the Prevention of Pollution of the Sea by Oil," May 12, 1954, 327 UNTS 3.

85. Protocol Relating to the 1973 International Convention for the Prevention of Pollution from Ships. 17 *ILM* 546 (1978).

86. 35 *ILM* 1406 (1996).

87. See discussion in P. Sands, *Principles of International Environmental Law, Vol. I: Frameworks, Standards, and Implementation* (Manchester: Manchester University Press, 1995), pp. 213–217.

88. *The Ocean Our Future: The Report of the Independent World Commission on the Oceans* (Cambridge: Cambridge University Press, 1998), p. 99.

89. Lyle Glowka, "Beyond the Deepest of Ironies: Genetic Resources, Marine Scientific Research, and International Seabed Area," in Jean-Pierre Beurier, Alexandre Kiss, and Said Mahmoudi, *New Technologies and Law of the Marine Environment* (The Hague: Kluwer, 2000), p. 77. On the relationship of the Convention on Biological Diversity to the Law of the Sea Convention, see Rüdiger Wolfrum and Nele Matz, "The Interplay of the United Nations Convention on the Law of the Sea and the Convention on Biological Diversity," *Max Planck Yearbook of United Nations, Law* 4 (2000): 445–480.

90. 38 *ILM* 1 (1999). The homepage of the convention is http://www.pic.int.

14

The Future Role of International Law in World Politics

IN THIS BOOK WE HAVE EXAMINED THE OPERATION OF THE SYS-tem of international law, viewed as a largely autonomous subsystem within world politics. We will begin this chapter by reviewing briefly some of the major themes that have surfaced during this discussion. We will then be ready to consider some of the questions international lawyers are currently asking about the future role of international law in world politics.

■ Five Themes Concerning the Current Operation of the System of International Law

A System of Interrelated Ideas

International law is, in essence, a system of interrelated ideas. In Chapter 1 we defined international law as a system of interrelated rules, principles, and concepts that governs relations among states and, increasingly, international organizations, individuals, and other actors in world politics. In defining international law, we could have chosen to emphasize that international law is a process more so than a static entity,[1] or that the system of international law incorporates international institutions such as the International Court of Justice. Although it is true that international law is dynamic and that it does incorporate institutional structures, the essence of international law is its ideas. What is interesting from a political perspective is how political actors draw on the intangible components of international law as a medium of interaction and as a mechanism by which to mediate their power relationships. The vast majority of disputes between political actors in world politics are settled peacefully; international law facilitates the reconciliation of otherwise conflicting policy agendas.

A State-Based System of Law

International law is a primarily state-based system of law. The two most important sources of international law are treaties and custom. Both of these emerge through the actions of states. The vast majority of the content of international law accords rights and responsibilities to states. The International Court of Justice decides contentious cases between states only, and states are the primary enforcement agents of international law, though they sometimes act through intergovernmental organizations. This is not to say that nonstate actors—such as nongovernmental organizations, multinational corporations, and individuals—do not influence the creation, implementation, enforcement, and dispute resolution processes in international law. The direct role of these nonstate actors within international law is increasing, as exemplified by the International Criminal Court, which has jurisdiction over individuals rather than states. In terms of the formal operation of the system of international law, states and intergovernmental organizations made up of states nevertheless still retain a preeminent position.

Entwined with World Politics

International law is entwined with world politics. International law is closely related to the broader political system in which it functions. This could not help but be the case when there is such a strong degree of overlap between the major actors in world politics and those in international law and when some of the most basic concepts in international law, notably sovereignty, are also political concepts. International law is a medium of political interaction and negotiation as well as a source of authority and legitimacy. Political actors draw on the rules, concepts, and principles of international law to justify their actions and to persuade other actors to behave in certain ways favorable to themselves. The relative power of states and the policy goals that each is pursuing thus cannot help but influence the content of international law and its implementation. The fact that the rules, principles, and concepts of international law are evolving in a logical relationship with each other and that lawyers constantly seek to distinguish the meanings of those terms from those of their political or moral counterparts nevertheless acts as a force for stability both within international law and beyond that, in world politics more generally.

An Autonomous System of Interrelated Rules, Principles, and Concepts

Although international law is entwined with world politics, it has a considerable degree of autonomy as a system of interrelated rules, principles, and concepts. Thinking of international law as a system of interrelated rules, principles, and concepts can facilitate our recognition of the considerable autonomy enjoyed by the system of international law. It is the specific definition attributed to concepts such as sovereignty and statehood within a relatively autonomous system of interrelated ideas that gives them authority as legal concepts and so allows them to function as a mechanism of interaction in world politics. If international law did not enjoy internal coherence it would all too easily merge into its political surroundings and its influence be dissipated.

In Chapter 5 the system of ideas that constitutes international law was represented as a pyramid to emphasize the importance to the unity of the system of its foundation philosophy. One of the key functions fulfilled by the philosophy underpinning the system is that of explaining why states should comply with international law. Internal to international law must be an explanation of the basis of legal obligation: why it is that a state must do as international law dictates. We have seen that, according to legal positivism, a state must comply because it has consented to the relevant law; consent is the source of legal obligation.

If the system is to retain coherence, the notion that international law derives from the will of states must also underpin other rules in the system. Thus, for example, the International Court of Justice has jurisdiction over a case only if it believes that the states involved have given consent. Of course, it is not always clear-cut as to when a state has given its consent. It sometimes suits one party to a dispute to have a case heard by the Court, in which case it is likely to attempt to demonstrate the consent by the other party. International law remains at every stage entwined with world politics.

Expansion Since 1945
A characteristic feature of world politics since 1945 has been the rapid expansion of the system of public international law. The expansion of international law has more than one dimension. There has been an increase in the breadth of subject matter addressed by international law. Although international humanitarian law predates World War II, international human rights law and international environmental law have emerged since 1945.

International law has also expanded in terms of the sheer quantity of rules, principles, and concepts found within the system. The multilateral treaty has been the primary vehicle for such expansion. Also, there has been an increase in the number of actors involved in international law. The number of states has increased due to decolonization and, more recently, the dissolution of the Soviet Union and Yugoslavia. Nonstate actors are playing an active role in the system of international law, albeit often an informal one.

The period of rapid growth of the system of international law is now being followed by one in which there is greater emphasis on enhancing the effectiveness of existing treaty regimes. Pick up a book on recent developments in any field of public international law and you may well find a comment to the effect that it is now time to consolidate the international law in this field, to find ways of making specific treaty regimes more effective rather than to continually negotiate new treaties. In relation to human rights, for example, "[t]he conceptual battle is over, and the focus has shifted to . . . implementation."[2]

■ The Future of International Law

We are now ready to take an informed position on some key questions concerning the future of international law.

Is there a danger that the rapid growth of international law will lead to its fragmentation? We have seen that international law is an interrelated system of principles, norms, and concepts. As this system expands rapidly and both international law and international lawyers become increasingly specialized, so is there a danger that a compartmentalized international law will have internal inconsistencies and contain contradictory norms. According to Gerhard Hafner, international law has become increasingly fragmented since the end of the Cold War, jeopardizing its credibility, reliability, and authority.[3] Tensions are set to increase between global legal regimes promoting, on the one hand, free trade, and on the other, the environment or human rights. The relationship between EU law and international law is an issue likely to come into increasing prominence.[4]

International dispute resolution bodies have an important role in helping prevent tensions crystallizing into outright contradictions, but more than one president of the International Court of Justice has expressed concern that the introduction of subject-specific international courts and tribunals, such as those on human rights and law of the sea, may exacerbate the problems of fragmentation.[5] Indeed, the International Criminal Tribunal for the Former Yugoslavia in 1999 determined that the ICJ had incorrectly interpreted the law on state responsibility and articulated its own position; the ICJ subsequently revisited the question and reaffirmed its own interpretation.[6]

The ILC considered the topic of fragmentation from 2002 to 2006. The analytical study resulting from its work played down the novelty of the problem and appeared intended to defuse any feelings of alarm.[7] The study suggested that one practical path toward resolving emerging conflicts might be through the further refinement of, and—somewhat ironically perhaps—through increased differentiation and specialization within, the law of treaties. The ILC also produced a "set of practical guidelines to help think about and deal with the issue of fragmentation in legal practice."[8]

Is it useful to use constitutional language in analyzing developments within international law? International lawyers are increasingly using constitutional language in their discussions of international law.[9] Within a domestic or municipal legal system, a constitution sets out the political principles and rules most fundamental to that system, including those pertaining to the composition and functions of the organs of government. It implies a hierarchy of laws, for constitutional norms usually prevail over an inconsistent ordinary law. Constitutional law is particularly difficult to amend and is a source of stability to the system it underpins. A constitution does, though, evolve to a limited extent over time in order to meet the needs of a changing political context, but at the same time provides checks and balances to this process to guard against abuses of power by the institutions of government.

In contrast to these features of a constitution-based legal system and polity, international law has generally been described as the product of a decentralized process of law creation. As emphasized by writers on fragmentation, international legal regimes have developed in specific subject areas, often in relative isolation from regimes in other subject areas. And yet there are clearly some aspects of international law that can be viewed in constitutional terms. Article 103 of the UN Charter, to take one example, has a hierarchical role within international law, for it states that in the event of a conflict between the obligations of the members of the United Nations under the Charter and those under any other international agreement, their obligations under the Charter prevail.

Some scholars are using the language of constitutionalism in relation to specific regimes of international law; others are stepping back to consider broader and philosophical questions. Debate is likely to continue as to whether, on the one hand, the study of constitutionalization and international law should be or is about developing new tools for understanding what already exists or whether it is a normative project, aiming to build a grand new global order modeled on what is sometimes found at a national level.

Can international law save the world from catastrophic climate change? Climate change is the quintessential global issue. What is needed is to halt the ever-increasing emissions of greenhouse gases and associated land uses such as clearing native forests. Given that emissions of greenhouse gases do not respect national boundaries, success in saving the world from the worst effects of climate change requires coordinated action at the global level. Multilateral treaty making has been the principal vehicle by which governments have sought to coordinate their actions to address the threat of catastrophic climate change. And yet, if measured against what scientists advise is required, these efforts have to date proven inadequate to the challenge. Greenhouse gas emissions continue to increase, the United States and China accepted no reduction targets under the Kyoto Protocol, and even if all states were to comply with their obligations under the Kyoto Protocol the reduction in emissions would be inadequate.[10] Multilateral treaty negotiations are often slow and leave states free to choose whether or not to accept what may in any case have been a lowest common denominator outcome. Climate change requires such far-reaching changes in such a short time frame that it arguably requires a more authoritarian governance mechanism than that offered by the multilateral treaty.[11]

The international law approach to addressing a global issue is bottom-down. According to Barry Rabe, debate regarding climate policy for two decades focused on international diplomacy seeking the one best system by which to reduce emissions; meanwhile, much of value has been taking place at the substate level; the formal engagement of a government in the international realm of policy is not a good indicator of policy development or of emissions reductions at the local level.[12] Some states within the United States have entered into agreements on climate change with other countries; California, for example, in 2006 entered into an agreement on climate change cooperation with Great Britain.[13] Local governments have not just responded to policy goals set at the national or international level but are taking initiatives in their own right,[14] and civil society groups are playing an important role. It is possible that a bottom-up approach may prove more successful, and international lawyers should be exploring innovative approaches by which to address this vital issue.

What does the rise of China and India mean for international law? In 1941 Henry Luce published a famous article in which he referred to the "American century."[15] The United States was the dominant influence on international law in the twentieth century and, as the world's only superpower in the closing years of that century and the early years of the present century, aroused concern among the international law community that its influence could be too great.[16] Concern increased during the administration of George W. Bush (2001–2009), which was widely deemed to have an undesirable attitude toward international law.[17]

We are currently witnessing a global shift of power toward Asia. Although still often classified as a developing country, China has become an economic powerhouse and is increasing in military power, raising the question as to whether US-China relations may in coming decades be fraught with rivalry and even friction. The United States has been strengthening relations with India, whose economy is also changing and growing rapidly. Although the Asian region is no newcomer to international law—the Japanese Society of International Law predates the American Society of International Law, for example—international law is increasing in prominence within the Asian region. The Asian Society of International Law was recently established.[18] A leading figure in its establishment, Onuma Yasuaki, has written of a coming multipolar and multicivilizational world, in which Western values will no longer necessarily dominate the international legal system.[19] The attitude of China toward international law and the nature of its engagement will be crucial influences on the international law of the future. The *Chinese Journal of International Law* has become an important publication in the field.[20]

Can international law provide for peaceful change in the international order? A related question is that as to whether international law can facilitate peaceful change to a new international distribution of power. International law not only reflects the international distribution of power but on an ongoing basis reinforces that distribution. This is most obviously the case in relation to the Security Council, in which five states have veto power over any substantive decisions. The structure of the Council mirrors the nature of the international order at the close of World War II, but it also contributes to the contemporary reality. The veto power in the Security Council is an important component of the so-called P5—the United States, Russia, France, United Kingdom, and China—and those states are, not surprisingly, reluctant to relinquish that power or to share it with additional states, whether that be India, Brazil, or Japan. And yet, as each decade passes, the discrepancy between the contemporary world and that of 1945 cannot but increase.

War has traditionally been the process through which a new international order comes into being. Writing in 1930, J. L. Brierly asserted that if war is to be eliminated, international law must provide an alternative means of revising the established international order.[21] According to Brierly, the analogy to war in the domestic sphere is neither the crimes nor the disputes of individuals, but revolution. The alternative to revolution has been the legislature. It is not that we need a "servile imitation of a national legislature" at the international level but that there must be "some ordered process whereby we can satisfy the demand for change which is the mark of any living human society." The UN Charter, which gives the P5 a veto not only over substantive decisions but over Charter amendments, arguably fails to provide the alternative to war called for by Brierly.

Notes

1. See, for example, R. Higgins, *Problems and Process: International Law and How We Use It* (New York: Oxford University Press, 1994).

2. Christof Heyns and Frans Viljoen, "The Impact of the United Nations Human Rights Treaties on the Domestic Level," *Human Rights Quarterly* 23 (2001): 483–535, esp. 483.

3. Gerhard Hafner, "Pros and Cons Ensuing from Fragmentation of International Law," *Michigan Journal of International Law* (2004): 849–863.

4. See, inter alia, Albert Posch, "The *Kadi* Case: Rethinking the Relationship Between EU Law and International Law?" *Columbia Journal of European Law* online 15, no. 1 (2009), http://www.cjel.net.

5. Martti Koskenniemi and Paivi Leino, "Fragmentation of International Law? Postmodern Anxieties," *Leiden Journal of International Law* 15 (2002): 553–579.

6. See Jeffrey L. Dunoff and Joel P. Trachtman, eds., *Ruling the World? Constitutionalism, International Law, and Global Governance* (Cambridge: Cambridge University Press, 2009), pp. 6–7.

7. "Fragmentation of International Law: Difficulties Arising from the Diversification and Expansion of International Law—Report of the Study Group of the International Law Commission," General Assembly, A/CN.4/L.682, April 4, 2006. See also Anne-Charlotte Martinueau, "The Rhetoric of Fragmentation: Fear and Faith in International Law," *Leiden Journal of International Law* 22 (2009): 1–28.

8. "Fragmentation of International Law: Difficulties Arising from the Diversification and Expansion of International Law—Report of the Study Group of the International Law Commission," General Assembly, A/CN.4/L.702, July 18, 2006.

9. See, inter alia, Jeffrey L. Dunoff and Joel P. Trachtman, eds., *Ruling the World? Constitutionalism, International Law, and Global Governance* (New York: Cambridge University Press, 2009); Vicki C. Jackson, *Constitutional Engagement in a Transnational Era* (New York: Oxford University Press, 2009); Jan Klabbers, Anne Peters, and Geir Ulfstein, *The Constitutionalization of International Law* (Oxford: Oxford University Press, 2009); and Ronald St. John Macdonald and Douglas M. Johnston, eds., *Towards World Constitutionalism: Issues in the Legal Ordering of the World Community* (Leiden, the Netherlands: Martinus Nijhoff, 2005).

10. Intergovernmental Panel on Climate Change, *Climate Change 2007: Mitigation of Climate Change—Contribution of Working Group III to the Fourth Assessment Report of the Intergovernmental Panel on Climate Change* (Cambridge: Cambridge University Press, 2007), p. 32.

11. Shirley V. Scott, "Climate Change and Peak Oil as Threats to International Peace and Security: Is it Time for the Security Council to Legislate?" *Melbourne Journal of International Law* 9, no. 2 (2008): 495–514.

12. Barry G. Rabe, "Beyond Kyoto: Climate Change Policy in Multilevel Governance Systems," *Governance: An International Journal of Policy, Administration, and Institutions* 20 (2007): 423.

13. John R. Crook, "Contemporary Practice of the United States Relating to International Law," *American Journal of International Law* (2006): 918–962, esp. 933.

14. See, inter alia, Michele M. Betsill and Harriet Bulkeley, "Cities and the Multilateral Governance of Global Climate Change," *Global Governance* 12 (2006): 141; Harriet Bulkeley et al., "Environmental Governance and Transnational Municipal Networks in Europe," *Journal of Environmental Policy and Planning* 5 (2003): 235; and Paul Wapner, "Horizontal Politics: Transnational Environmental Activism and Global Cultural Change," *Global Environmental Politics* 2 (2002): 37.

15. Henry Luce, "The American Century," *Life*, February 17, 1941. The essay was reproduced, with responses, in *Diplomatic History* 23 (1990): 159–171. See also Nicholas Guyatt, *Another American Century? The United States and the World Since 9/11* (London: Zed, 2003).

16. See, for example, Michael Byers and George Nolte, eds., *United States Hegemony and the Foundations of International Law* (Cambridge: Cambridge University Press, 2003).

17. See, inter alia, Amy Bartholomew, ed., *Empire's Law: The American Imperial Project and the "War to Remake the World"* (London: Pluto, 2006); Nico Krische, "International Law in Times of Hegemony: Unequal Power and the Shaping of the International Legal Order," *European Journal of International Law* 16 (2005): 369–408; and Philippe Sands, *Lawless World: America and the Making and Breaking of Global Rules from FDR's Atlantic Charter to George W. Bush's Illegal War* (New York: Viking, 2005).

18. See its website at http://law.nus.edu.sg/asiansil/.

19. Onuma Yasuaki, "Towards an Intercivilizational Approach to Human Rights," *Asian Yearbook of International Law* 7 (2001-2002): 21–81; and "A Transcivilizational Perspective on Global Legal Order in the Twenty-First Century: A Way to Overcome West-centric and Judiciary-centric Deficits in International Legal Thoughts," in Macdonald and Johnston, *Towards World Constitutionalism*.

20. See http://chinesejil.oxfordjournals.org.

21. J. L. Brierly, "International Law and Resort to Armed Force," *Cambridge Law Journal* 4 (1930-1932): 308–319.

Acronyms

ABM	antiballistic missile
ATS	Antarctic Treaty System
BWC	Convention on the Prohibition of the Development, Production, and Stockpiling of Bacteriological (Biological) and Toxin Weapons and on Their Destruction (Biological Weapons Convention)
CAT	Convention Against Torture and Other Cruel, Inhuman, or Degrading Treatment or Punishment
CCW	Convention on Prohibitions or Restrictions on the Use of Certain Conventional Weapons Which May Be Deemed to Be Excessively Injurious or to Have Indiscriminate Effects
CD	Conference on Disarmament
CDM	clean development mechanism
CEDAW	Convention on the Elimination of All Forms of Discrimination Against Women
CERD	International Convention on the Elimination of All Forms of Racial Discrimination
CESCR	Committee on Economic, Social, and Cultural Rights
CFC	chlorofluorocarbon
CICC	Coalition for an International Criminal Court
COP	Conference of the Parties
COPUOS	Committee on the Peaceful Uses of Outer Space
CRAMRA	Convention for the Regulation of Antarctic Mineral Resources
CRC	Convention on the Rights of the Child
CRPD	Convention of the Rights of Persons with Disabilities

CTBT	Comprehensive Nuclear Test-Ban Treaty
CWC	Convention on the Prohibition of the Development, Production, Stockpiling, and Use of Chemical Weapons and on Their Destruction (Chemical Weapons Convention)
DPRK	Democratic People's Republic of Korea
DSB	Dispute Settlement Body
ECOSOC	Economic and Social Council
EEZ	exclusive economic zone
EU	European Union
FMCT	Fissile Material Cut-Off Treaty
FRY	Federal Republic of Yugoslavia
GA	General Assembly
GATT	General Agreement on Tariffs and Trade
GEF	Global Environment Facility
GEMS	Global Environmental Monitoring System
HRC	Human Rights Council
IAEA	International Atomic Energy Agency
IALANA	International Association of Lawyers Against Nuclear Arms
ICBL	International Campaign to Ban Landmines
ICC	International Criminal Court
ICCPR	International Covenant on Civil and Political Rights
ICESCR	International Covenant on Economic, Social, and Cultural Rights
ICJ	International Court of Justice
ICRC	International Committee of the Red Cross
ICRW	International Convention for the Regulation of Whaling
ICTR	International Criminal Tribunal for Rwanda
ICTY	International Criminal Tribunal for the Former Yugoslavia
IDP	internally displaced person
IGO	intergovernmental organization
IGY	International Geophysical Year
IHL	international humanitarian law
ILC	International Law Commission
ILM	International Legal Materials
ILO	International Labor Organization
IMCO	Intergovernmental Maritime Consultative Organization
IMO	International Maritime Organization
INF	Intermediate-Range Nuclear Forces (Treaty)
INGO	international nongovernmental organization
IPB	International Peace Bureau

IPCC	Intergovernmental Panel on Climate Change
IPEN	International POPs Elimination Network
IPPNW	International Physicians for the Prevention of Nuclear War
ITLOS	International Tribunal for the Law of the Sea
IWC	International Whaling Commission
KEDO	Korean Peninsula Energy Development Organization
LDC	less-developed country
LNTS	League of Nations Treaty Series
LOSC	United Nations Convention on the Law of the Sea
MAD	mutually assured destruction
MARPOL	International Convention for the Prevention of Pollution from Ships
MNC	multinational corporation
MNE	multinational enterprise
MOU	memorandum of understanding
NATO	North Atlantic Treaty Organization
NGO	nongovernmental organization
NNWS	non-nuclear-weapon state
NPT	Treaty on the Non-Proliferation of Nuclear Weapons
NWFZs	nuclear-weapon-free zones
NWS	nuclear-weapon state
OAS	Organization of American States
ODS	ozone-depleting substances
OILPOL	Convention for the Prevention of Pollution of the Sea by Oil
ONUC	United Nations Operation in the Congo
OPCW	Organization for the Prohibition of Chemical Weapons
OPRC	International Convention on Oil Pollution Preparedness, Response, and Cooperation
PCIJ	Permanent Court of International Justice
POP	persistent organic pollutant
PTBT	Treaty Banning Nuclear Weapon Tests in the Atmosphere, in Outer Space, and Under Water (Partial Test-Ban Treaty)
ROK	Democratic Republic of Korea
SALT	Strategic Arms Limitation Talks
SCSL	Special Court for Sierra Leone
SOFA	status of forces agreement
SOLAS	International Convention for the Safety of Life at Sea
SORT	Strategic Offensive Reductions Treaty
START	Strategic Arms Reduction Talks
TRIPS	Trade-Related Aspects of Intellectual Property Rights
TWAIL	Third World Approaches to International Law

UDHR	Universal Declaration of Human Rights
UKTS	United Kingdom Treaty Series
UN	United Nations
UNCED	United Nations Conference on Environment and Development
UNCLOS	United Nations Conference on the Law of the Sea
UNEF	United Nations Emergency Force
UNEP	United Nations Environment Programme
UNESCO	United Nations Educational, Scientific, and Cultural Organization
UNHCR	United Nations High Commissioner for Human Rights
UNITAF	Unified Task Force
UNMISET	United Nations Mission of Support in East Timor
UNMOVIC	United Nations Monitoring, Verification, and Inspection Commission
UNOSOM	United Nations Operation in Somalia
UNSCOM	United Nations Special Commission
UNTAG	United Nations Transition Assistance Group
UNTS	United Nations Treaty Series
UNTSO	United Nations Truce Supervision Organization
WHO	World Health Organization
WTO	World Trade Organization

For Further Reference

■ Online

www.eisil.org

The Electronic Information System for International Law is a collaborative project created by the American Society of International Law with useful information, documents, and links to a vast array of online sources of information in the various subfields of international law.

www.ppl.nl

This will give you access to the online catalog of the Peace Palace Library in The Hague as well as much up-to-the-minute reference information.

www.un.org

The United Nations website is the starting point for exploring any aspect of international law related to the work of the United Nations.

www.un.org/law/avl

Holdings of the United Nations Audiovisual Library of International Law include documents and audiovisual materials relating to the negotiation and adoption of significant legal instruments under the auspices of the United Nations and a collection of lectures on virtually every subject of international law.

http://fletcher.tufts.edu/multilaterals.html

The Multilaterals Project, begun in 1992, is an ongoing project at the Fletcher School of Law and Diplomacy, Tufts University. It is an ideal starting point for locating the text of any multilateral treaty.

http://internationallawobserver.eu/
The International Law Observer blog is dedicated to reports, commentary, and the discussion of topical issues of public international law as well as EC/EU-law.

http://jurist.law.pitt.edu/
Jurist is a web-based legal news and real-time legal research service based at the University of Pittsburgh School of Law. It includes news and commentary on international law.

http://opiniojuris.org/
A blog on international law and international relations, based in the United States but including contributors from elsewhere.

http://treaties.un.org/
The United Nations Treaties Collection is a valuable resource for treaty texts and information on their status.

▓ Books

Anaya, S. James. *International Human Rights and Indigenous Peoples* (Austin, TX: Wolters Kluwer Law & Business, 2009).

Armstrong, David, ed. *Routledge Handbook of International Law* (London: Routledge, 2009).

Armstrong, David, Theo Farrell, and Helene Lambert. *International Law and International Relations* (Cambridge: Cambridge University Press, 2007).

Aust, A. *Modern Treaty Law and Practice,* 2nd ed. (Cambridge: Cambridge University Press, 2007).

Barker, J. Craig. *International Law and International Relations* (London: Continuum, 2000).

Beck, Robert J., Anthony Clark Arend, and Robert D. Vander Lugt, eds. *International Rules: Approaches from International Law and International Relations* (New York: Oxford University Press, 1996).

Birnie, P. W., A. E. Boyle, and C. Redgwell. *International Law and the Environment,* 3rd ed. (Oxford: Oxford University Press, 2009).

Brownlie, Ian. *Principles of Public International Law,* 7th ed. (Cambridge: Cambridge University Press, 2008).

Burns, Richard D. *Arms Control: From Antiquity to the Nuclear Age* (Westport, CT: Praeger Security International, 2009).

Byers, M. *Custom, Power, and the Power of Rules: International Relations and Customary International Law* (Cambridge: Cambridge University Press, 1999).

Byers, M., ed. *The Role of International Law in World Politics: Essays in International Relations and International Law* (Oxford: Oxford University Press, 2000).

Charlesworth, H., and Jean-Marc Colcaud, eds. *Fault Lines of International Legitimacy* (New York: Cambridge University Press, 2009).

Dinstein, Y. *War, Aggression, and Self-Defence,* 4th ed. (Cambridge: Cambridge University Press, 2005).

Fleck, Dieter, ed., in collaboration with Michael Bothe. *The Handbook of Humanitarian Law in Armed Conflict,* 2nd ed. (Oxford: Oxford University Press, 2007).

Harris, D. J. *Cases and Materials on International Law,* 6th ed. (London: Sweet and Maxwell, 2004).

Henkin, Louis. *How Nations Behave: Law and Foreign Policy* (New York: Council on Foreign Relations and Columbia University Press, 1979).

Janis, Mark W. *International Law,* 5th ed. (New York: Aspen, 2008).

Joyner C. C. *International Law in the Twenty-first Century: Rules for Global Governance* (Lanham, MD: Rowman and Littlefield, 2005).

Klabbers, J. *An Introduction to International Institutional Law,* 2nd ed. (Cambridge: Cambridge University Press, 2009).

Ku, Charlotte, and Paul F. Diehl, eds. *International Law: Classic and Contemporary Readings,* 3rd ed. (Boulder, CO: Lynne Rienner, 2009).

Merrills, J. G. *International Dispute Settlement,* 4th ed. (Cambridge: Cambridge University Press, 2005).

Noyes, John E., Laura A. Dickinson, and Mark W. Janis. *International Law Stories* (New York: Foundation Press/Thomson/West, 2007).

O'Connell, Mary Ellen. *The Power and Purpose of International Law: Insights from the Theory and Practice of Enforcement* (Oxford: Oxford University Press, 2008).

Scott, Shirley V., ed. *International Law and Politics: Key Documents* (Boulder, CO: Lynne Rienner, 2006).

Simma, B., ed. *The Charter of the United Nations: A Commentary.* 2 vols. (Oxford: Oxford University Press, 2002).

Simmons, Beth A., and Richard H. Steinberg, eds. *International Law and International Relations* (Cambridge: Cambridge University Press, 2006).

Steiner, Henry J., and Philip Alston. *International Human Rights in Context: Law, Politics, Morals,* 3rd ed. (Oxford: Oxford University Press, 2008).

Index

ABM Treaty, 4
Abolition of Forced Labor Convention (1957), 61*n66*
Acheson, Dean, 14
Afghanistan: use of Uniting for Peace Resolution in, 107; US-led coalition bombing of, 109
African Charter on Human Rights and Peoples' Rights (1981), 229, 230, 231
African Charter on the Rights and Welfare of the Child (1990), 230
African Commission for Human and Peoples' Rights, 66
African Court, 66
African Union, 31, 229, 230
Agreed Measures for the Conservation of Antarctic Fauna and Flora (1964), 156
Alien Tort Claims Act of 1789, 9
Al-Qaida, 7
American Convention on Human Rights (1969), 229
American Declaration of the Rights and Duties of Man, 228
Amnesty International, 63, 169, 223
Annan, Kofi, 7, 37, 110
Antarctica: denuclearization of, 155–156; proposed condominium arrangement for, 155; sovereignty issue, 155–156

Antarctic Treaty (1959), 154–157, 173; background, 154–155; establishment of nuclear-free zone and, 203–204; finalization of, 155–156; origins, 154–155; seen as arms control treaty, 155; transparency in, 179; verification issues, 179
Antarctic Treaty System (ATS), 156–157; claims by third world, 156, 157
Anti-Ballistic Missile Treaty (1972), 204–206
Argentina: Antarctic Treaty dispute resolution and, 180; interest in Antarctica, 154; as second-generation nuclear state, 192
Arms control: defining, 190; international law and, 189–206; New Agenda Coalition, 195; Treaty on the Non-Proliferation of Nuclear Weapons and, 190–196
Association of Small Island States, 168, 269
Australia: acceptance of optional clause on ICJ jurisdiction, 87; case against by Nauru, 15; greenhouse gas emissions in, 270; interest in Antarctica, 154; justification for use of force in Iraq, 111; lack of domestic effect of multilateral treaties, 178; Legal Adviser's Branch, 124; as middle power in

307

About the Book

THE COPENHAGEN CLIMATE CHANGE CONFERENCE. IRAN'S PLANS to build nuclear weapons. Ongoing armed conflict in Congo, Iraq, and Afghanistan. Debates about the responsibility to protect. In each of these headline events the complex relationship of international law and world politics comes into play. The second edition of *International Law in World Politics*—thoroughly updated and now including a full chapter on the use of force—introduces the concepts, the rules, and the functioning of international law in a way that is accessible to students of political science.

Shirley Scott covers such core topics as the nature of legal argument, the negotiation and implementation of multilateral treaties, and the place of both intergovernmental organizations and nonstate actors in the international legal system. Equally important, she connects the content of laws to current issues and problems, using case studies to bring the subject to life. The result is a rare text that effectively explains the role that international law plays in the changing arena of world politics.

Shirley V. Scott is associate professor of international relations at the University of New South Wales.